Lovin' the Skin You're In

The JUICY WOMAN'S GUIDE to MAKING PEACE with FOOD and FRIENDS with YOUR BODY

Andrea Amador, CEC, M.NLP

ISBN: 978-1-4751553-0-3

http://www.thejuicywoman.com/

Contents

FOREWORD

by Beverly Nadler, CHT

When I first met Andrea at a class I was teaching in New York City, I knew she stood out though I didn't know exactly why at the time. Some years later, when I received an email from her, I realized what I had earlier perceived in this dynamic young woman that set her apart—she had a very curious mind and an exceptional ability to express herself.

When we began to work together, I discovered that Andrea takes in information like a sponge, that she immediately uses what she learns, and that she loves to share what she knows with others. She is a natural student *and* teacher. A rare combination!

If you're interested in improving your body image, self-image, self-esteem and/or your self-confidence, you're reading the right book. This book is as practical as it is fascinating and interesting. You will learn *what* to do and *how* to do it, in order to accomplish *your* goals.

Andrea is one of the few people who truly understands what "The Energy Model" (as described in my book, *Vibrational Harmony*) is about. She knows that everything, *everything,* on the physical, mental, emotional, and spiritual plane is energy. She also knows that the laws of energy are *also* the Universal Laws that govern every aspect of our lives. Andrea *applies* this knowledge and understanding to her life. And she will show you how to apply it to *yours.*

If you're familiar with *The Secret*, you've heard of The Law of Attraction. This is only one of the laws of energy, and it is really the Law of Vibration in operation. However, *The Secret*—as valuable as it has been in introducing the public to the concept that "everything is energy"—does not describe *how* the

1

Law of Vibration really works, nor does it explain the other Universal laws, which include the Laws of Polarity, Rhythm, Cause and Effect, and Relativity. That's why so many people are not getting the results they expected from reading the book or watching the DVD.

The Energy Model explains that energy can never be created or destroyed, it can only be changed. And *that* is the key to transforming your life! You, like everything else in the Universe, are energy—your body is energy, your mind is energy, your beliefs, thoughts, and feelings are all energy. You will learn how the energy of your mind and the energy of your body impact each other.

When Andrea first learned the energy-psychology techniques she has included in this fascinating book, she was startled to discover how well the techniques worked. She soon became masterful in her application—not only to her body image, but to her entire life. She will show you how to use the powerful energy of your mind so that you too will be able to affect the energy in many areas of your life.

Did you know that your subconscious mind is like a computer, filled with "programs?" Did you know these programs are the instructions for your life, just as the programs in your PC are the instructions for your computer? Did you know that by using energy-psychology techniques you can literally "tap out" negative thoughts, feelings, and subconscious programs that stop you from getting what you want? Did you know that there are other effective tools that can help you reprogram your subconscious mind? Most people don't.

Further, the sad truth about many people who know some of the techniques is that they don't use them! Stay with Andrea, for she will motivate and inspire you to use what she shares.

This exceptional book is the result of major changes in her life—changes she has made by using exactly what she is sharing with you.

Everything in this book comes from Andrea's heart and personal experience.

Enjoy the journey she will take you on!

Love,

Beverly Nadler

Speaker, trainer, author of *Vibrational Harmony* and *Loving the Game of Life*.

www.beverlynadler.com

Introduction

"Life doesn't begin 20 pounds from now."
— Jessica Weiner, best-selling author and speaker

Every woman I have ever known who struggles with being overweight wishes deep down in her heart that she could love and accept her body and stop talking the language of fat. No matter what her age or size, she hopes that one day she will be able to stop arguing with her thighs, stomach, breasts, or whatever particular wobbly bits on her she despises most.

Your Thoughts Are Making You Fat!

First and foremost, this is not a diet book. It is intended to give you tools to help heal your broken relationship with food, and to understand the root of this dysfunction: your thoughts. If you're an emotional eater struggling with excess weight, food has had the upper hand for a long time. No diet will ever fix that. If you're uncomfortable with who you are and how you look, it's not the fat on your body that needs to be addressed—it's the fat in your head. Your thoughts are making you fat!

Hi. I'm Andrea Amador, professional coach, body image/self-esteem expert, and former dieter-turned-Juicy Woman. As a curvy, plus-size gal myself, I've learned that people are not limited by their bodies, only their minds. Author Jack Canfield says it best: "It doesn't matter what you say to me, what's important is what I tell myself after you finish speaking."

Like so many women, I used to swear on a stack of bibles that one day my life would be different when I lost weight. I spent years waiting and hoping to become perfect, always believing that a diet was the solution to all my problems. But even after I achieved my goal weight I was still miserable; always obsessing and never happy with myself or my body. As much as I tried I just couldn't stop thinking about food. Within five years I had regained all the weight back again.

Deeply ashamed, disgusted with my body, and hating myself, I attributed my failure in weight loss to weakness and lack of self-control. I searched desperately for a solution. My mind set at that time was that I was miserable because I had fat thighs. Then one day during my coach training, I came to the sober realization that it was actually the hateful and toxic thoughts I had about myself and my body that kept me in patterns of overeating and self-abuse.

It was then that I finally realized that my overweight thighs were my body's way of screaming out for help, begging to be loved and accepted. Until I began to love myself, thighs and all, I didn't have a hope in hell of ever being able to get my emotional eating under control.

After thirty-three years of procrastinating and living a life bound by my food fear, I decided to stop dieting. My whole world changed. I wrote this book to encourage you to live and love your body now because as long as you continue to hate yourself, food will forever enslave you.

My lifelong battle with food began in 1970. I was eight years old and lived with my parents, Frank and Doris, and my three year old brother, David. We lived in New York City, in the Washington Heights section of Manhattan. As far as I knew, I had it all. I lived in a beautiful big apartment building in a place called Castle Village. We had a doorman and a garden right downstairs. I had plenty of toys, tons of friends, and my Nana and Grandpa were just an elevator ride away, living on the top floor in the penthouse. Life was good. Then my parents divorced.

Mom took my brother and I and we went to live in a cramped little apartment not too far away. I was heartbroken missing my Dad so much. I still got to see him, but it wasn't the same. Soon thereafter, my mother remarried a man named Jorge who after a few short months of acting like Prince Charming, quickly turned into a toad. He was an abusive, rageful, alcoholic, with a jealous and mean streak a mile wide, but my mother was completely under his spell. To appease Jorge, we ended up moving to Florida where his family lived. Living in Miami seemed as distant from my dad as I could ever be.

And as happens to far too many innocent children, I was sexually abused. No gruesome details, I promise. Suffice it to say that those years were probably the most miserable time of my life. Because I didn't have any other way of dealing with my pain, I used food to protect me. It was my way of trying to build a wall around me in an attempt to keep myself safe.

When I was eleven years old, I finally came back to New York to live with my father and his fiancée, Rosie. Dad was shocked when he first saw me. I had gained thirty pounds in less than a year and nobody but I knew why. He rushed me to the doctor to see if everything was okay. That was when I was put on my first diet.

To my immature way of thinking, it seemed that all of a sudden I was cursed by the fat fairy and given this enormous set of thighs which became the object of everyone's concern. For the next several years, Dad and Rosie did everything they could to help me get control over food, but the more I was told I couldn't or shouldn't be eating something, the more I wanted it. My Dad used to say, "Andrea, you're too damned fat, and you have no self-control around food." That was when I really started hating my body.

People kept saying that if I wanted to lose weight and be pretty, I had to learn to control my appetite. But the more people tried to stop me from eating certain foods, the more I wanted them and the more desperate I became to get them.

Let me ask you a question: When you were a kid did you ever sneak eat? I did, lots of times. I remember so many nights when I would wait patiently in bed, listening for sounds telling me that everybody was sleeping and the coast was clear. As soon as I could hear Dad's snores, I knew it was safe to make my move. Like a thief in the night, I'd peel back the covers, rise up out of bed, and tiptoe toward the kitchen being so careful, trying not to make a sound. Damn those squeaky floor boards!

If I heard a noise, I'd freeze dead in my tracks and wait, holding my breath and listening until it was safe to continue. Once I got to the kitchen,

I'd crack open the refrigerator door enough so I could see what I was doing, but nobody would be woken by the light. Then just like a little squirrel gathering nuts, I stuffed as much food as I could in my pajamas and filled both pockets of my fuzzy pink bathrobe.

Quickly and quietly I retraced the steps back to my room. I crawled into bed and, with a flashlight under my covers, emptied my pockets and quietly started the process of peeling, opening, pulling, sucking, chewing, and consuming all my goodies. They were all mine, the cookies, pieces of cheese and meat, canned pudding, frozen donuts, cold Chinese takeout, and all sorts of foods I wasn't allowed to have on my diet.

From that experience and many others like it, I believed for the next thirty-five years that I was out of control around food. This belief caused me to be deeply ashamed of myself.

In an effort to tame what I thought was the voracious feast beast lurking inside of me, I kept on riding the diet roller coaster, pinning all my hopes on the dream that one day I would lose weight and become thin and beautiful. Now that I look back on those years spent dieting, I realize that diets confirmed my belief that I couldn't trust myself around food.

Diets gave me the message, time and time again, that I was fighting an addiction and had no self-control. I believed that foods I loved were off-limits—food like fatty steak, potato chips, bacon, sausages, bagels, french fries, chocolate cupcakes, Ring Dings® and Yodels®, cookies, cakes, pies and soda, buttered popcorn, and even my Nana's famous pasta.

These foods came to be considered the "fattening" or "bad" foods, and for me to eat them, or even want them, meant I was undisciplined and out of control. But despite feeling shameful for craving those yummy goodies, my desire for them led me around by the nose.

Cheating on my diet made me feel like a criminal, although my only crime was one of passionately wanting food I was told I couldn't have. I lived in constant shame, torn by guilt and self-loathing. The ripple effect of how that shaped my life still continues to amaze me today and is the reason why I am writing this book and sharing my wisdom with you.

For years, I cursed myself and my weakness, blaming all my problems on the size of my thighs. Now I know my thighs and my eating were never the real problem. They were only a cover-up—a big fat lie that everyone wanted me to believe to keep me on a diet. It worked for a long time, because for most of my adult life, I was completely fooled into thinking I was miserable because I had fat thighs. I never considered the possibility that I had fat thighs because I was miserable.

Up until several years ago, when I decided to stop dieting, I swore I couldn't feel safe around an open bag of potato chips, a plate of freshly made brownies, or a steaming bowl of pasta. But now I know I can, and you can too! I'll just bet you don't believe it. Maybe like me, you've been raised to believe the problem is you, that there's something wrong with you. Nothing could be further from the truth.

What stories are you telling yourself? What things have you been saying to your body? What feelings do you get every time you look in the mirror?

The nasty things you say to yourself don't just stay in your head. Your thoughts are energy—an integral part of the universe—and each thought has its own ability to affect the world, and, most importantly, you and your body. As we go on, I'll explain to you how your thoughts, specifically your negative self-talk, can make you fat![1]

Can you relate to my story? Do you feel tortured, twisted, and desperately worn out by your relationship with food? Are you sick and tired of hating your body? If you are overweight, unhappy, struggling with a low self-image, and suffering from feelings of shame and guilt, you may often find yourself using food to comfort you. Don't blame yourself.

You're not alone in your struggles, and your challenges definitely do not make you a bad person. You're only doing what your body has done before to make you feel safe; eating. It's been your way of taking care of yourself and there's no shame in that. However, if you're no longer willing to allow food to enslave you, it's not time for a new diet; it's time for a change.

Diets by their very nature support a negative self-image, pushing you to believe that something is wrong with you. They guide you toward disconnecting and distrusting your body's internal wisdom.

---

1   If you want to find out more about the connection between energy, your thoughts and how the energy of your thoughts affects your body and the world around you, I recommend watching the movie, "What the Bleep Do We Know" (2004 Captured Light & Lord of the Wind Films)

As a child you took in information like a sponge and believed everything you heard. This became your story. Now, as an adult, you have the opportunity to doubt the lies you've been told, to question limiting beliefs and create a new foundation upon which to live. You can return to trusting yourself and that's what you need to do to restore harmony and balance in your relationship with food and your body. To tune into that wisdom, you must go within.

Your journey begins with a spoonful of self-acceptance. By learning to welcome and fully accept the good, bad, and the ugly, flab, wrinkles, bumps and all, everything becomes possible. Resistance melts away.

The challenge is that you can only love yourself, make friends with food, and accept your body if you're willing to stop playing the role of victim. Are you?

If you are, then I'm ready to teach you everything I know. Come follow me and I'll show you how to bust loose from the poor little me, ain't I helpless game, reclaim your life and love the skin you're in now, today. Turn the page and let's get started.

Chapter 1
Getting Reacquainted with Your Body

*"Every extra pound you carry on your body equals a
pound of emotional pain you're carrying in your heart."
– Doreen Virtue, PhD, "Losing Your Pounds of Pain:
Breaking the Link Between Abuse, Stress and Overeating"*

We've all seen those diet commercials where a beautiful, happy, slender woman is talking about her weight loss success as she stands beside a life-sized photo of herself "before" she started her diet. In the photo, she looks sad and miserable. She looks at her before photo with disgust and disdain and pushes it away, out of sight, showing that she has no feeling or connection to that picture. Despite having felt that way in the past about myself, now seeing those commercials just makes me want to cry.

C'mon 'fess up. Are you waiting to become thin for your life to begin? Think about it. Haven't you believed dieting was temporary, something you just had to grin and bear until the day came when you were finally thinner and then the real you could come out and play?

Juicy Woman Note:

I used to think the time I spent "losing weight" was like living in a vacuum. It didn't really count, I reasoned, because I was waiting until I reached my goal weight. Now I understand that I was living my life in a holding pattern.

I wouldn't buy new clothes because I didn't want to waste my money. I wouldn't go dancing because I didn't want people to see me shaking my fat. I wouldn't want to make love with my husband because I wanted to have that beautiful thin stomach and strong tight, toned legs ... so I waited. I was in a perpetual state of waiting (weighting). How about you? What have you been weighting for?

In our pluck and tuck, thin is in, beauty in a bottle culture, we've come to devalue the person in favor of the packaging. The photos of models and celebrities you see plastered all over magazines have been retouched; their "flaws" have been taken out. Yet in our endless pursuit of perfection, we still yearn to look like them. The truth is none of us are perfect; we all have our flaws, and to accept them means we have the power to rise above them.

The Importance of Accepting the "Before" You to Make Way for the "After" You

If you've been a dieter and lost weight, or even if you've just tried to watch what you eat and develop healthier habits, you know how it really works in those silly commercials.

It was that "before" woman who got the smiling, thin woman to the place where she could actually enjoy her "after" life. It was the "before" woman who dragged her butt out of bed every day to go to the gym or go walking when she didn't want to. It was the "before" woman who had to say NO to the cookies and the ice cream and any other food she wanted. It was the "before" woman who did all the work and then the "after" woman has the nerve to shun her and dismiss her like she's a piece of dirt.

You would never treat someone else like dirt. Would you? Yet if you've been shunning yourself, waiting for that "after" you to make her appearance, that's just what you've been doing—to yourself.

I used to do the same thing. It made losing weight and keeping it off seem like the impossible dream. No matter how hard I tried, it never seemed like enough, and I always pushed myself to achieve more. In order to mold myself into what I considered the "perfect" body, I was meaner to myself than anyone else ever could be. My desire to lose weight became a compulsion that eventually took over my life, made me miserable, and eclipsed my soul—the best part of me.

No More Dieting For Me!

Several years ago my life took a radical turn when I decided to stop dieting. Besides wanting to do it for my own reasons, it had become apparent that I had to make the change for the health and well-being of my daughter.

At the time Cara was ten years old. She was steadily gaining weight and showing signs of being an emotional eater. Oblivious and not really knowing what to do to help her, I was beginning to repeat the same desperately ignorant parenting mistakes my father had made. I, too, had become a hypocritical role model, espousing healthy eating one moment and binging whenever anyone's back was turned. As a woman with my own disordered relationship with food, I realized I was the worst role model for Cara.

Desperate to get her eating under control, I watched her like a hawk, made backhanded comments about her weight, criticized her food choices, obsessed over everything she ate, and in general began to lose sight of my precious girl. It was killing our relationship and she was starting to hate me.

After seeing how the legacy of my tortured, twisted thinking and dysfunctional eating was affecting her, I knew that if I didn't stop this runaway train, Cara would end up like me; fat, perpetually unhappy with herself, and hating her body. I couldn't live with the idea of doing that to my daughter.

That was when I realized that diets were a big part of the problem. Sarcasm, criticism, and meanness were the only ways I knew how to talk to myself. I used these same desperate attempts at communication with my daughter which was toxic to our relationship. Our closeness was being destroyed. In order to help her regain her sense of balance and comfort around food, I had to first help myself.

Deep down in my heart I knew that as much as I wanted to help Cara find her way to peace in her relationship with food, I couldn't, because I was cluelessly lost myself. I vowed to find the answers for both of us and prayed for help so we could begin our healing. Soon afterward, the universe sent me a gift—Dr. Harold Frost.

I met and befriended Doc Frost in an online networking group. Doc was in the process of retiring from a successful twenty-five year career as a therapist and co-founder of an eating disorder clinic in the Midwest. He wanted to share his experiences by writing a book and I offered to help by giving him feedback on his writing. He eagerly accepted and explained to me his work with women who had eating disorders.

Hearing him speak of his patients and their struggles with such tenderness and care, I instinctively knew I could trust Doc. I confided in him and shared my story, asking for his help and guidance. He explained to me that in order to change the way my daughter related to food and to her body, I had to challenge many of the limiting beliefs and assumptions *I* had about food and *my* body.

Doc said that as a dieter, I had learned to fear food and think of my hunger and my body as "the enemies." This had set up an unnatural relationship with food and kept me hating my body. As long as I lived with the dieters' all or nothing mentality, I would always end up craving foods that I thought I shouldn't eat.

When I reached the point where I couldn't stand denying myself a moment longer, I would give in and binge. My associations with guilt, fear, and shame around food, combined with bad feelings about my body, kept me in an endless cycle of binging and dieting. Doc offered to teach me an alternative to dieting: a non-diet weight control method called *intuitive eating*.

Making the decision to stop dieting terrified me. I saw it as the ultimate form of giving up. As much as I hated dieting, it was the only way I knew to control my voracious appetite. I figured if I ever began eating without being restricted by a diet, I'd never stop. Doc assured me this wasn't true.

At that time, in July of 2006, American Idol contestant Katherine MacPhee shared her eating addiction story with People® magazine. She talked about her amazing recovery using a process called Intuitive Eating. In reading the article I discovered she had lost thirty pounds eating all the foods she loved. That got my attention.

Doc then sent me an audio tape of his entitled, *Loving the Child Within*™. He said I should learn about intuitive eating by listening to the stories of his former patients.

One such story was of a woman named Megan. On the tape Megan spoke of the abusive and chaotic atmosphere in which she was raised as a child. When I listened to her I knew I had found someone to whom I could relate. Like me, she had spent most of her life trying to disconnect from her painful past by using food to numb her emotions.

Megan described how her work with Doc had changed the way she dealt with food. He had helped her heal much of her rage and she had developed a new appreciation for her body. I realized that if she could heal her broken relationship with food and with her body, then I could too.

From that moment on, I decided to have faith. Faith, that just like Megan and Katherine MacPhee, my body's inner wisdom would effortlessly and naturally guide me back to my natural size.

Along the road I've learned that along with using the non-diet process of intuitive eating, you have to love and accept yourself in order to finally make peace with food. If you can't find compassion for the vulnerable parts of you, you'll continue to unconsciously abuse yourself by overeating.

> ## Juicy Woman Note:
>
> Can't stop eating? Think of it as valuable information telling you something is wrong. Just like a tiger with a thorn in its paw, something is causing you pain. Overeating is a symptom. It's not the problem. As long as you continue to do the same things, you'll get the same results. To change how you feel, you have to be willing to do things differently.
>
> I've learned that when you remove anxiety in your life by coping with your stress, you will stop hating yourself. Unless you handle what's bugging you, your stress will only keep you running 'round in circles, making you feel hopeless and helpless. You're not, but unless you deal with the buggin' you's in your life, you won't ever believe it.

The point is you can't combine liver and onions and expect to get an apple pie. The body you have today is the result of the thoughts you've been feeding it. Your body is a snapshot reflecting what you have believed to be true. It's the result of the combination of years of beliefs and actions and inactions that have brought you to this place; hating your body.

If, like me, you've grown a healthy pair of thighs or a big butt, it's probably evidence of believing what you've been told. The good news is these beliefs aren't permanent and you can change them. Your thoughts are powerful ingredients that mold your life and ultimately determine your success. By changing them, you change your results.

The truth is we do many things in life without consciously thinking about them. Whether you know it or not, your subconscious mind is always at work behind the scenes. Hard wired to your survival instinct, its intention is to keep you safe and in your comfort zone. Although what your subconscious mind is telling you may not be the least bit comfortable, it's what you know. Fear of the unknown is what prevents most of us from changing our lives.

The thing to keep in mind is that there are perfectly good reasons for why your body is overweight. And until you begin to go within and find out what emotional needs your excess weight is fulfilling, you will stay within your comfort zone and continue in patterns that will keep you fat.

Think of your beliefs as the foundation upon which you base all your life choices. Your beliefs develop from years of other people dumping their rules, assumptions, and interpretations about how the world works on your mental doorstep. This colors your world and becomes the filter through which you see your life. The stilted view then becomes your comfort zone. As a child you were expected to take everything you learned at face value. At that age you didn't have a voice or a choice—but now you do.

You've probably heard the saying, "Too many cooks spoil the broth." It's true. Think about your beliefs as being contributions from different cooks in your life, people who wanted to make an impression on you; parents, teachers, society, the media, etc. Other people's beliefs had a direct effect on you and your relationship with food.

If those unwanted, limiting beliefs you've been carrying around are not giving you the results you want, then it's time to change the recipe. Just because things have been done the same way forever, doesn't mean you can't switch them around now. You can, and I'll help you do it.

Food: What Does it Really Mean to You?

Like me, you probably also picked up the belief along the way that you couldn't trust yourself. You had to rely on the wisdom of others to get by. Maybe you also believed that the world wasn't a safe place, but you could always rely on food to make you feel good.

No matter what route you took to reach a place of disordered eating, it affected you and your relationship with your body. The outcome was that food became more important to you than it really is.

Food became a source of comfort, a means of expressing your identity; it gave you a sense of having control in an uncontrollable situation. It became a way of saying, "It's mine and you can't take it away from me."

Realistically speaking, food doesn't have this kind of super power… because after all, it's only food. Logically, food is only a means of filling a hungry tummy, but if you've been struggling with emotional eating, you've attached more meaning to it than it deserves. If that's the case, then it's not really the food you're after, but the feelings you get from eating it.

In other words, in your pursuit of trying to recreate that one-time experience of some kind of wonderful, you've been eating a bunch of blah or a ton of just plain terrible.

If you've watched your weight for any length of time, you've learned to think like a dieter. The dieter's fear-of-food thinking comes from years of being told you must do whatever you can to control your hunger and avoid eating what you want, so that you can one day be happy, thin, and beautiful.

The problem is it's been found that diets don't work for up to 98 percent of all people because they don't help you deal with the emotions that push you to eat when you're not hungry.

But I will.

First, you must bear this important truth in mind:

LOSING WEIGHT DOES NOT GUARANTEE HAPPINESS!!!

It's Not What You're Eating; It's What's Eating You

I began dieting when I was eleven years old. For nearly thirty-three of my 49 years, I was an on again/off again member of Weight Watchers®.

In September 2001, I finally achieved what I considered my goal weight. I felt strong and healthy. At 5'2', I was a size eight, had a perfect hour glass figure, and when I wasn't obsessed with hating my thighs, I grew to love my heart shaped butt. I weighed 162 pounds. Working out all the time, my body was tight and toned.

The gals at Weight Watchers® suggested I continue to slim down until I reached a lower, more appropriate weight, 110-125 pounds. Despite their recommendations, I decided that I was finally okay with my body and chose to stop losing weight. With a note from my doctor, I began to work on weight maintenance.

I thought life would settle into a picture of perfection once I got down to my ideal size. But it didn't happen that way.

I still had big trust issues that prevented me from feeling safe, receiving love, expressing myself, setting boundaries, asking for what I needed, feeling worthy, being independent, feeling confident, speaking out, and so many other things that I thought would magically resolve themselves once I lost weight. Life didn't settle into the image of peace and ease that I expected.

Instead, after I lost the weight it became a daily struggle to keep it off. I lived in constant fear of gaining the weight back and not fitting into the clothes that I loved. I couldn't relax around food without a pile of guilt and shame heaped on top of every extra morsel I ate over my allotted food that day.

If you've been among those who were lucky enough to have lost weight on a diet, you probably recognize the struggle I describe. Maybe you even traded one obsession for another. I sure did.

I went from being obsessed about losing weight to being obsessed about maintaining my new weight. In truth, nothing really changed. I was still obsessed. I found myself thinking about food all the time, calculating calories, Weight Watchers® points, or fat grams. In my head I was running a constant tally of every mouthful I ate.

Every single step I took I did so with the goal of either wanting to lose weight or as a desperate attempt to offset the food I intended to eat later. Food was my master and I was its slave.

Now, looking back, I realize all that time spent living under the burden of my food and weight obsession prevented me from living my life. I was waiting for my life to begin and looking outside myself for the answers.

One day while working out at the gym, my trainer, Rob, said to me, "Andrea, it's all in you." He said those words with the intention of motivating me to believe in myself.

Now I'm going to turn around and tell you the same. It's all in you! I want to remind you that you have all the answers you need right inside of you. You just have to be able to quiet your thoughts long enough so that you can find them.

I've learned that crazy thinking comes from being stressed and that leads to crazed eating. Stress is the enemy that will always distort your relationship with food. It will keep you in patterns of resistance and fear that will continually push you to want to eat when you're not hungry.

The Importance of a 'Piece of Quiet'

In the book: *Naomi's Breakthrough Guide: 20 Choices to Transform Your Life*, author and singer, Naomi Judd shares her path to living through and recovering from her own life-threatening health crisis with Hepatitis C. She credits her healing to the many insights she sought while learning and applying everything she could about the mind/body connection. One of the key elements she includes in her daily health regimen is to sit in silence each day. She says, "Select a spot that is quiet and comfortable for you, as my kitchen table is for me. Designate that space your own sacred "growth place."

When you learn to make space in your day for a piece of quiet, you'll calm that inner turmoil. When you make your inner peace a priority, you'll be able to focus better and listen to the wisdom within. When you actually follow up and take action on this wisdom, you'll feel more at ease.

This new sense of peaceful ease will increase your awareness of gratitude. Along with gratitude comes appreciation and self-respect with a bonus of becoming more compassionate with yourself. When you have developed a new habit of compassion and being gentler with yourself, you'll find that you won't be so quick to beat up on yourself with all the old negative-Nancy chatter.

Juicy Woman Note:

As I continue along this road toward making peace with food and becoming friends with my body, I know that my success and happiness rests on choosing to set aside time for me.

Now, whenever I fall back on my old habit of emotional eating, I recognize the patterns and understand that I've forgotten to take time for myself each morning. Once I notice this, it's easy for me to just forgive myself and start over, renewing my commitment to make time for myself to enjoy a much needed piece of quiet in my life.

This new found sense of inner calm keeps the relationship between food and my life in balance. I have to take time out to go within and listen to my body. Having the commitment to build that inner trust has enabled me to release the resistance I had around losing weight.

Try it yourself. Create a new wonderful routine of self-care and make time in your day to enjoy a piece of quiet. See what miraculous changes occur.

Why You Must Release Your Resistance

Let's look at this issue of resistance and how it affects your body. Two aspects of resistance are probably working in you right now, preventing you from having the body you want.

You've most likely heard the saying, "What you resist, persists." In our context, this means as long as you refuse to accept the body you have today, it will never change.

Here's what I mean. Do you call yourself names, endlessly criticize your weight, and pick yourself apart?

These thoughts send a stream of negative commands to your brain which reinforce a fat and ugly self-image. When you think you're fat, you feel fat, and when you feel that way, nothing but food can make you feel better. Right?

This is because your frustration with your weight leads you to seek out comfort in the way that is most familiar to you. If you eat when you're upset, you'll continue to gain weight. The first aspect of resistance is your hurtful and negative self-talk.

The second type of resistance you may be dealing with is fear of the unknown. For too many women being thinner means being more sexual, having more success, being more confident, and in general, having a perfect life. This is a tremendous burden.

I want you to know that as you change your relationship with food, you will feel so much more in control of your life. The place to begin is where you are now; accepting the body you have today. This is going to require compassion and forgiveness on your part and I'll teach you how to get there.

To release any resistance you may feel toward getting thinner, you have to take a leap of faith and make it okay to be the size you are today— just like I did. I like to say that I found my perfection in the folds of my imperfection. This choice to be okay with myself now, as I am, no matter what, was what I needed to end the ravenous hunger that drove me.

To break free of those desperate cries of wanting and longing, I had to lower the bar and change my goal. I realized that as long as I hated my body, I would never really be able to stand by myself, loving me, exactly as I am, warts and all. After spending so many years being my own worst critic, I realized it was time to stop.

I changed my goal from losing weight to finding ways to be happy and accept my body as it was right then. This meant I couldn't wait until later to be nice to myself. I had to start being kind and gentle and appreciative of my "before" body, so that I could pave a path of love for my "after" body.

How 'bout you? Be honest. If you lost weight in the past did it really calm your inner turmoil and solve all your problems, or did you just switch obsessions like me? What will it take for you to be okay with yourself now?

Take Back Your Power

The one thing I've learned through this whole experience is that you always have a choice. It may not seem like it, but you do.

By sharing my seven step *RECLAIM*™ system, I'm going to teach you that food is not the enemy. Stress is. If you're not looking at what's bugging you and taking responsibility for making yourself happy in life, you'll continue to abuse food.

Wouldn't you agree it's time to take back your power? Have you heard the saying, "It's impossible to love someone while you are judging them?" This applies to you as well. As long as you hate yourself and put yourself down with nasty self-talk, you can't become your own best friend. Resentment and blame you harbor toward yourself or others will always back up on you.

Repeat after me: Resentment strips you of your power, and therefore makes you absolutely powerless.

Being nice to yourself through choosing self-acceptance is the first step toward creating change. Isn't it time to end the war you've been waging on your body through endless dieting, deprivation, and self-hatred? After all, how has being mean to yourself been working out for you?

Where have all the years of playing the body-hating game gotten you? Have they made you thinner, encouraged you to feel better, bucked you up when you were feeling down? I doubt it.

My mother used to say, "You catch more flies with honey than with vinegar." The same is true for being nice to yourself. Change the way you communicate with your body by learning to speak to yourself with love and gentleness.

After all, if you plant a seed and do nothing but stand around and yell impatiently waiting for it to grow, it will seem like it's taking forever. Your yelling is not going to get you any closer to reaping the harvest.

However, if you tend lovingly to the seeds, water them often, fertilize them when necessary, and give them plenty of sunlight and care, you will have an abundant garden.

The changes you'll be making by using this book are internal and, just like with seeds, you may not be able to see the results of your work immediately. However, once they take root and become habits, not only will you notice the difference in your body, but all throughout your life.

The Mind/Body Connection

Let's get down to the nitty gritty. Your body is made up of a network of communities of cells, constantly in communication with each other and the world around you. If you're overweight and struggle with negative thoughts about your body, not only are you probably eating to soothe the pain, but your body is releasing stress chemicals. It's simply operating under the primordial "fight or flight" mechanism.

Overeating is a warning sign that your body is out of alignment with its natural ability to balance and heal itself. Signals are when you feel bad, angry, sad, resentful, and generally unsettled. If you're suppressing your needs and pretending that everything is hunky dory when it's clearly not, the pain will only get stronger.

You've probably heard your body's messages urging you to pay attention, yet you were unaware of what they really meant. Perhaps you've been ignoring them for years, hoping they'll just go away. But they don't. As one of my mentors, John Felitto, says, "Emotional discomfort first comes in a whisper, then a scream, then a shove on the shoulder, and ultimately a frying pan."

Something is hurting you, causing you to eat compulsively and think about food when your body is not actually physically hungry. This same thing is causing you to resent the body you have and wish you could change it. Your feelings of unhappiness are telling you that something is wrong and off balance.

So how do you turn it around? How do you see past the subconscious programming that's been poisoning you and find the source of your pain? It's not enough to think positively, that's akin to putting perfume on a pile of poop. Eventually it begins to smell and you fall back on your old stinking thinking.

You have to change the underlying emotions. If you don't, the emotional and physical discomfort will remain, and eventually get worse.

Try It! – Exercises to Dig Your Teeth Into!

Years in the trenches of the business world have taught me that if you want to remember something, write it down. Similarly, my training in *NLP* (*Neuro Linguistic Programming*) emphasized that if you want to make an indelible impression on your brain, create an experience.[2]

As your coach, I'm going to help you challenge the ratty and fatty beliefs that have been keeping you overweight. I've learned that if you want to get control over what you're eating, you start by changing what you're thinking. In this book you'll have a ton of opportunities to put what I say to the test.

Since we learn best by experiencing, I encourage you to try your new tools out as you read along. I'll provide *Try It!* exercises which are exercises for you to practice right then and there.

---

2   A quick definition of NLP: It's a set of mental tools that give you the ability to change the way that you think and feel about yourself, your life and the world around you. All change starts in your mind.

From time to time, I'll also share more of the *Juicy Woman Notes* you've already seen. These are tidbits I learned on my way to making peace with food and becoming friends with my body. I want to share them with you to make your journey easier. It is my hope that my goofs can be your gain!

The first step toward creating change in your life is to become aware. I want you to become cognizant of what is stuck in your mental programming that causes you to act out in ways that don't support you. Following my *Try It!* exercises will give you that awareness.

I recommend you use a notebook or create a new folder on your computer that you will dedicate specifically to completing the exercises throughout this book. Each time you do a *Try It!* (a wink and a nod to my beloved days as a Brownie Girl Scout® leader) record it in your notebook or folder. Be sure to write down the name and description of each, then *Try It!*

Juicy Woman Note:

Consider that, just like a good mutual fund, in order to get something out of this process you must first put something in. By deciding to read this book you are making an investment in your happiness. By actually doing the Try It! exercises you are doubling your rate of return.

Try It! – Who's In Control Here?

Make a list of every single part of your body you don't like, feel critical of, and are embarrassed by. Then, next to each body part, write what you would like to say to it.

For example, you may write, "Butt." Next to "Butt" write something like "I hate you, you disgusting, fat, flabby butt. I wish that I could take a butcher's knife and slice you up. I'd cut off a few chops and roasts and still be able to feed a family of four with plenty left over to fill my jeans."

Write what you really feel!

Why You Need to Start Feeling Your Feelings

Weird, huh? Well, I want you to start connecting with how you honestly feel about your body. Angry? I bet. Despite what you've been told, anger is good. Heck, feeling your feelings is good. But for now, let's deal with anger because it's pretty easily accessible to most people. When something pushes our buttons we can get pretty hot under the collar, can't we?

If you're like me, you may have a tendency to sit on your feelings and push down your anger until you feel like you're apt to explode. Hiding your feelings by playing games of trying to look in control when you're not and doing things like clenching your teeth and saying, "I'm fiiiiiiiiiiiiiiine," when you're really not, isn't healthy for so many reasons. The least of which is because the stress of whatever you are feeling will most likely cause you to overeat.

To give you an outlet to relieve your stress so that you'll be able to enjoy the clarity of listening to your inner wisdom, I want you to get in touch with your anger and any other negative or overwhelming emotions you may have. Doing so will flush away all the crud that's dammed up in your system. This crud is fermenting in your body and causing a disconnection between you and your body's inner guidance.

In the section on *"Coping with Your Stress,"* I'm going to teach you how to make those feelings work for you. It's this pent-up energy held in your body and keeping you stuck that makes you feel afraid and perpetually believing you are less than the wonderful person you really are.

Juicy Woman Note:

The most important takeaway I want you to get from this book is that we teach people how to treat us and it's never too late to change. Throughout the chapters, I'll share different aspects of my story demonstrating the truth of this statement.

If, like me, life has taught you that you're just a pretty face and your value rests on the size of your thighs, your golden locks, or your flat stomach, you will learn to judge yourself harshly, discounting nearly every true asset you have.

It's those painful run-ins with nasty critics, fat phobics, and abusive people that have most likely hurt you and kept you feeling uncomfortable in your body.

I know for a fact that when people put you down enough times, telling you that you're not good enough, pretty enough, thin enough, or any other enough you can be, you start to believe it. Their mean lies become your stories. And those stories attract more of the same nasty, ugly reality. Because, face it, deep down you don't believe you're worthy of anything else. Do you? In my opinion, that's the real fat that's been keeping you fat!

If you're putting yourself down and hating your body, there's a good chance you learned to do it from someone who first did it to you. You've been walking around with their voice in your head. Haven't you?

Why Are You Overweight?

My experience has taught me that if you're a chronic emotional eater, the problem is not food. It's easy to say, "Well I just love food, and I have no self-control." But as true as that may feel to you, it's not the real truth.

Liking food may account for being an extra twenty pounds or so overweight, but if you're dealing with a larger amount, or find yourself struggling much, much too hard to keep it off, you're eating for a reason other than just enjoying the taste.

Geneen Roth is an international teacher, speaker, and writer of best-selling books on emotional eating. Her belief is that we eat the way we live, and all of us have exquisitely good reasons for overeating.

Perhaps you've heard the saying, "The way you do one thing is the way you do everything." To quote Geneen, "Our relationship to food, money, love, is an exact reflection of our deepest-held beliefs about who we are and what we believe we deserve."

In order to break the cycle of compulsive eating and find out what we truly hunger for, we need to be curious and kind with ourselves. Geneen calls this exploration process feeding your hungry heart. Here's why it's important for you to be more compassionate and kind with yourself and your body:

Your Body Under Stress

Einstein proved that everything in the universe is made up of energy, even our thoughts. These invisible particles of energy are called atoms and are constantly moving and vibrating. Scientific research has proven that our body is a low level electro-magnetically charged system. Every thought we think generates a flow of chemicals from the brain that either makes us feel better or worse.

When the energy in your body is balanced you feel good. This is your body's natural state. Anything other than this indicates your energy is out of balance.

Stressful thoughts overload the body, creating a sort of short circuit response, throwing your energy out of alignment. According to the ancient science of acupuncture, electricity is constantly circulating throughout our body in paths called meridians. When you experience stress, your body responds by shutting down and blocking the free flow of energy through these meridians.

It's because of these energy blockages that you get hit with sudden cravings for food and eat to cover up feeling hurt or vulnerable or any other overwhelming emotion. The pain that triggers your urge to eat and obsess about food when you're not hungry, comes from a time when you felt emotionally overwhelmed in some way and you used food for comfort to make you feel better.

It's a conditioned response; similar to what the Russian scientist Pavlov proved when his dogs learned to salivate in response to hearing a dinner bell. In other words, it's a knee jerk reaction, something done automatically without conscious thought.

As an emotional eater, at some point your brain received the message: food = comfort. This is why you've been struggling with compulsive eating. As long as your energy remains blocked, your brain will continue to associate food with comfort.

This energetic distortion in your body is keeping you caught up in a loop, making it nearly impossible for you to will your way out of the undesirable behavior of binging. Just like a broken record, stressful situations and thoughts will continue to trigger your eating habits each time you experience similar emotions.

You may have a sense of when, specifically, you turned to food in order to feel safe, validated, or loved, or maybe you have no idea. The important thing to know is that your body remembers.

In order to break free of the old, negative pattern of eating when you're not hungry, you must use alternate methods besides eating to deal with your stress. If you don't, your internal operating system will continuously default to its old programming; eating to soothe your soul. For you, as an emotional eater, food equals comfort. Without new programming your stressed-out body will misguidedly push you to eat when you're not hungry.

By using the stress relief techniques that I'm going to teach you, you can release the negative charge on the memories and emotions that are keeping your energy blocked. By opening up these blocked channels, your energy will flow freely again, creating a sense of wellbeing. When you feel good again, your resistance will melt like hot butter, leaving you free to move forward.

Deep down inside, your body knows what is right for you. At any given moment, if you stop and listen to your body, it will tell you what you need. The secret is in being willing to listen to your feelings.

To clear the self-abusive patterns of overeating and talking unkindly to yourself, you must be honest about what's on your mind. This means being willing to look at how you feel about what's going on in your life.

No sugar coating and no Pollyanna stuff. If you want to curse and swear in your *Try It!* exercise book, then that's what you must do. Express your real feelings. I know those are often pretty ugly, but you certainly don't want to walk around trying to fool yourself into thinking stuff that's not true.

Try It! – Who's Watching Over Your Body?

Write down several examples of times when you recently pushed your body beyond its limits, burnt the candle at both ends, and just plain overdid it.

Here are two examples:

1) You have a deadline to finish a project. It's getting late, your body's tired. You ignore the warning of feeling sleepy. You grab another cup of coffee in an effort to deny your exhaustion, demanding your body to work harder until the project is done.

2) You eat to the point of feeling overstuffed and uncomfortable. Ignoring the signs of the pain in your stomach and the sensations of nausea, you continue to eat because you like the taste of the food.

Now write examples of your own when you overloaded your body.

I think it's time you start giving yourself a little more respect and credit. Don't you? Although you've probably sworn you'll never accept yourself as you are, I encourage you to question the value of that decision. Can you imagine how much resistance gets broken down when you just learn to accept how you look and where you are? It makes being happy and living joyfully possible right now.

Let me help you get reacquainted with the wonderful woman who may have gotten buried under a ton of lies, fears, and false assumptions: You. You've probably been buying into a lot of limiting beliefs that have been making you miserable. This is most likely why you are feeling bad about yourself and pressured to lose weight.

You are you. You can only be the very best you, you can be, nobody else. It doesn't serve you to wish that you looked like someone else. When you start eating real food and begin to live and eat as a naturally slender woman, you'll notice that you will eat less and your body will begin to reshape. This is your body's way of readjusting to its former natural shape.

Just like in the children's game of tug of war, when you finally let go of the rope and stop trying so hard, you release all the tension. When you feel more relaxed, you're more at peace. If you let yourself continue to be pressured by society's standards of fleeting beauty, you only guarantee yourself misery.

Diets are not the answer. I'm encouraging you to let go and stop resisting, but don't listen to me. Start to pay attention to your own inner wisdom.

Juicy Woman Note:

I know it's no fun. Probably lots of foods you love are technically "not good for you." Here's my take on that. I know for a fact that whenever I eat chocolate or anything with sugar in it, my body will be affected and make me tired. I've learned that the affect differs depending on how much I eat.

Since I'm aware of this and have become in tune with my body, I don't want to eat these foods as much because for the most part they don't make me feel good. Usually, if sugary foods are around and I'm hungry for them, I'll have a few bites and call it a day. But more often than not, I typically have them in my house for weeks on end and I won't even be interested or give them a second glance until I actually want them.

On those days when I'm actually craving something sweet, instead of using tricks to boot the craving, I assume that I want to be nurtured. I recognize that they will hit my energy and make me tired, but I like taking naps, so I use that knowledge and I eat them and then I fall asleep, which is probably what I was after to begin with.

My suggestion to you is to be gentle with yourself and avoid judging the times when you do overeat. Good reasons are always behind every binge. It's up to you to find out what's triggering your urges to eat these foods when you're not hungry.

29

Your Body Gives You All The Answers You Need

The heart, as part of your body, is electromagnetically charged and carries impulses to your brain and throughout your body. It communicates and offers vast stores of information that often go unnoticed or disregarded.

Whenever something feels right or is true for you, you feel it first in your heart. Some people call this intuition or inner guidance. To my way of thinking, it's all a way of accessing your soul's higher intelligence. God, Buddha, Higher Power—no matter what you call it, you can tap into that internal communication and wisdom on a consistent basis.

Try It! – Finding Your Truth

Place a hand over your heart and slowly read aloud the following quote by Doreen Virtue, Ph.D. Repeat it several times.

"Every extra pound I carry on my body equals a pound of emotional pain I'm carrying in my heart."

Keeping your hand on your heart, take some time to think about the words and what they mean to you. Notice what images or memories come to mind. What words or thoughts do you hear when you think about it? What feelings arise when you read those words? Now, with that new information, keep your hand over your heart and ask yourself, "Does this feel true to me?"

Where Do You Carry Your Armor?

Think about where your fat is on your body. Is it on your face, neck, across your arms, back, chest, legs, or evenly distributed making you seem like a large woman? Is it concentrated in one area, maybe on your thighs making you a pear shape? Or does it manifest in your stomach and abdomen area where the rolls of fat cover your genitals? Where is your excess weight?

Where do you carry your armor? Yes. Let's think for a moment of your extra fat as being like a suit of armor. In her bestselling book, *You Can Heal Your Life*™, author and speaker Louise Hay explains there are really just two mental patterns that create disease in our body; anger and fear.

The armor of extra weight you've been building up in your body has been an unconscious effort of yours to deal with your anger and your fears.

According to Hay, where you carry your weight speaks volumes about the type of emotional pain you're holding in your heart. She goes on to describe a variety of correlations between body parts and illnesses that in turn correspond to various emotional blocks within the body. She calls these probable causes, and offers new thought patterns to release the blocks.

Now think about it. What has your body armor been protecting you from? If Dr. Virtue's statement felt true for you, what would the emotional pain be that you carry on your body and in your heart?

If your body could talk, what would it say? If your thighs could ask for something, what would it be? What would your arms want to tell you? What message does your stomach have to share? Sounds stupid, I know, but your body has been trying to tell you something every time you stuffed food into your mouth when you knew you weren't hungry. Isn't it time that you listened?

Let me get you started having a conversation with your new friend, your body.

Try It! – Join BlogHer's, "Letter to My Body" Campaign

BlogHer, a fast growing blogging community for women on the internet, has a new initiative. Suzanne Reisman started a campaign called, "Letter to My Body," encouraging women to write letters to their bodies and begin a much needed, long awaited conversation.

As a woman who has spent much of my life avoiding, running away from, and hating my body, this has been a powerful experience for me to participate in.

Over the past few years I've been learning how to love my body and trying to spread the message of self-acceptance to empower other women to be more accepting of their bodies. Writing a letter to your body is a groundbreaking opportunity for you to get to know yourself intimately. Please sit down today and open up that line of communication with your body. There is such healing and beauty that awaits you.

Don't be surprised if your letter is filled with anger and hatred. As I said, there's no judgment. It's just a way for you to begin a conversation with a part of you that you may have long ago unknowingly disowned or discounted. I invite you to go online and read the letters of countless women who have also participated in this process: http://www.blogher.com/lettertomybody

What's Your Story?

Remember, your body has a memory and every one of your cells is alive with all your experiences. Each of us has our own story in life which we tell ourselves over and over again.

In my case, it was my encounter with sexual abuse that became my story. It laid the groundwork that made me believe I wasn't safe in my own body and couldn't take care of myself. My story reinforced my belief that I had to rely on others and search outside myself to feel secure and happy. This in turn activated a long cycle of people pleasing madness that kept me stressed out, feeling helpless, angry, burnt out, and resentful. I ran to food because I felt so desperately out of control in my life.

For years, as long as I identified myself by my story, I was able to tell myself I was a victim. Now I know that by doing so, I gave energy to the belief that this *poor me, ain't I helpless?* way of thinking I had adopted was the only possibility that existed for me.

By constantly thinking of myself as a poor, helpless victim, and therefore that misery was my only lot in life, I attracted situations and people that continually reinforced my victim identity. I blamed all my miserable circumstances on the fact that I had encountered abuse throughout my life. Despite having been through eighteen years of therapy to reconcile my past, I was not able to get over the hump and move on with it. I was stuck.

Juicy Woman Note:

Please note that when I refer to being a victim it is not intended to place blame or find fault, it is merely bringing to light the possibility that our actions are not always guided by our best intentions. Rather than being in charge of our life, we often mindlessly sleepwalk through our day by day existence experiencing one knee jerk reaction after another. This is because when a person has experienced abuse, they often shut down and move into survival mode, trying not to feel anything at all.

As a survivor of abuse, I've learned that living under the cloud of painful memories is almost like being suspended in time—a part of you gets stuck in the past and is not able to move forward. Despite the fact that I am a grown woman, for many years I responded to various circumstances in my life like a young child.

Because your memories may be so vivid and negatively charged, it may seem like a younger, more frightened part of you is holding all the cards. That's not true, but you won't know that until you understand the experience from a different perspective.

Living in fear of being hurt or reminded of being "that vulnerable again" is why many women with abuse issues use food for comfort. It's easy and it feels safe. There's nothing wrong with that, but it will never give you the sense of being in charge of your life that you truly seek. Food can only provide a temporary source of comfort. To truly heal your relationship with food and your body, it's up to you to acquire the coping skills you need to deal with all the upsets in your life.

Like me, you may have experienced abuse in your past, but until you recognize that you are now a grown woman capable of making

33

choices, you won't be able to get out of your victim thinking. As long as you perceive yourself as a victim, you will be a victim.

Nobody other than you can make you happy or make you feel safe. You're in charge of what you choose to believe and that will affect the way you feel. You alone must provide the comfort and love you seek.

If you're hanging your hopes on others and expecting them to validate your existence, then you'll never be able to stand tall and proud. To reclaim your power, you have to change the way you tell your story. That will change the way you feel. When you are able to change the way you feel about something, you can do anything.

Juicy Woman Note:

Throughout this book I'll share with you many of the stress relief techniques I use often and always. In many cases, I credit them with keeping me sane during a pretty insane time in my life. They are the bees' knees as far as I'm concerned. But as wonderful and effective as they are, they will never be capable of replacing the care and attention of a skilled professional.

If you've encountered abuse in your life and have not yet sought out the guidance of a trained therapist, please do so. Then use these techniques as a supplement to deal with your stress with the advice and consent of your therapist. Remember to always take full responsibility for yourself and your emotional and physical well-being.

"Lies told long enough or often enough & shouted
loud enough, become the truth."
– Minister Eugene R. Palmore

Wrapping Up
Chapter 1: Getting Reacquainted with Your Body

Here are the juiciest morsels covered in this section. Savor them mindfully.

- Can't stop eating? That's valuable information telling you something is wrong. Overeating is a symptom. It's not the problem. It's not what you're eating. It's what's eating you!

- There are perfectly good reasons why your body is overweight. Until you go within and find out what emotional needs your excess weight is fulfilling, you will stay within your comfort zone and continue in patterns that will keep you fat.

- Losing Weight Does Not Guarantee Happiness!

- Crazy thinking comes from being stressed and that leads to crazed eating. Stress is the enemy that will always distort your relationship with food.

- No matter how miserable you are, you can choose to be happy by learning to tell yourself a different story. That will change the way you feel. When you are able to change the way you feel about something, you can do anything.

- It's all in you. Deep down inside, your body knows what is right for you. At any given moment, if you stop and listen to your body it will tell you what you need. The secret to ending your overeating is in being willing to feel your feelings so you won't continue stuffing them.

- Think of the excess fat on your body as a suit of armor. What has it been protecting you from? What emotional pain are you carrying on your body and in your heart?

- To break free of your body's natural resistance to getting thinner, you have to be kind, gentle, and appreciative of your "before" body, so that you can pave a path of love for your "after" body. Think about what it will take for you to make it okay to be the size you are.

35

🍓 To truly heal your relationship with food and your body, it's up to you to acquire the coping skills you need to deal with all the upsets in your life. I'll show you how.

🍓 It's all energy. You will attract what you spend the most time thinking about. Want a thin body? Stop thinking of yourself as a fat person.

In the next chapter, you'll discover why diets have kept you thinking, feeling, and being fat.

Chapter 2
Diets Don't Work: Food Fallacies That Have Been Making You Fat!

You've probably been fed the "my way or the highway" approach to weight loss. You might have swallowed whole the belief that someone else knows better than you what you should and shouldn't eat. Maybe like me, you also received the subtle or not so subtle message, "You can't be trusted."

As a result, you were encouraged to ignore your own impulses and suppress your needs, because in the end people told you that "you don't really know what's good for you." The result has probably led you to resent the tremendous amount of restrictions you've endured, and made you turn on yourself for not having more self-control.

In our weight-obsessed society having self-control means being able to stick to a diet and to eat less food. Or else you are told to consume gruesome grub that grosses you out, having to choose food for its nutritional content while spurning the goodies you crave. To me, that's not self-control. That's self-torture.

In order to lose weight, you have to diet, right? Wrong! Diets are the kiss of death. They only focus on what you can see: weighing, measuring, and buying certain foods. Diets ignore the invisible stuff, the emotions that drive you to eat too much in the first place.

There are other ways to control your food intake without restricting yourself from eating the foods you love. Given the chance, wouldn't you love to say goodbye to dieting once and for all? I'm sure you'll agree there's nothing enticing about a diet other than the flimsy promise of quick weight loss and how has that worked out for you so far? Probably not too well.

If you've "failed" at diets, it's not because there's something wrong with you. We've never been taught how to relate to food in a healthy way. We've been caught in a web of shame and doubt spun by the diet industry, implying that if we haven't lost weight by now, something must be wrong with us.

Get real! Even though you may have been successful during a period of dieting, and feel that if you could just get that same motivation back you could do it again, wouldn't it be fair to say that diets haven't worked for you over the long haul? Do you want to know why?

Myths & Fallacies Keeping You Fat!

Myth #1 – Eat on schedule. – As a kid, I used to love spending time with my Mom's parents; my Grammie and Grandpa. When I went out shopping with them and it got to be around lunchtime, Grandpa would take a look at his watch and say, "Oh boy, it's twelve o'clock. We should be eating now."

Does that sound familiar to you? Have you been eating by the clock? Don't worry. You're not alone. This is one of the biggest reasons why diets don't work.

In order to truly become free of food's psychological hold on you, you need to tune back into your body's feelings and sensations of hunger. I know you probably don't understand what that is and how it feels, especially if you've been dieting for a long time.

The problem is diets encourage people to stay far away from hunger; to avoid it at all costs. The implied message is that you can't be trusted around food because you have a feast beast lurking inside of you, just waiting to pounce and eat everything in sight. That's a lot of hooey!

Your body has its own clock and way of telling you when it wants to eat. Most likely, through years of dieting that sensitivity has been dulled down and anesthetized. I'm sure you're familiar with the old saying, "Never allow yourself to get too hungry."

I can't tell you how many times I've heard my Weight Watchers® leaders say that to our group. Hearing it so often led me to believe I should always protect myself from getting too hungry. This meant I always ate something before I went out so I wouldn't arrive ravenous. I actually ate a meal before I went to eat a meal. Ridiculous!

I was actually afraid of getting hungry even though I was more than sixty pounds overweight. Consequently, I carried food with me all the time. I seized on every opportunity to eat even if I didn't like the food; all because I had this pervasive fear that I never knew when I was going to eat next.

The truth is, by obsessing over a rigid eating schedule you are messing around with your body's delicate metabolic balance. Eating by the clock will throw off your ability to know when you are physically hungry because you'll be walking around semi-stuffed.

Think about it. If you've eaten your lunch and throughout the afternoon you've been snacking to ward off the dreaded hunger, by the time dinner rolls around you won't know when to stop eating, because you began eating the meal when you were already full. In order for your internal satisfaction switch to trigger, it has to first recognize the sensation of hunger.

Your hunger is a natural and physiological phenomenon. It is entirely dependent upon when, how much, and what you ate last—not on the clock. If you're eating all fat free and low fat foods you might feel like there's a hole in your stomach as you're constantly hungry and perpetually unsatisfied. As a result, you're probably eating too often, because you're eating food that tastes like cardboard which doesn't satisfy.

When is the last time you asked yourself, "What do I want to eat?" Usually we eat what we think we should eat, and do our best to avoid the foods we really want. But oftentimes those cravings are so strong we end up giving in anyway and overeating.

Try It! – Hi Body, It's Me

Most of the time we're unaware of the many sensations we have throughout our body. We only become attuned to them when we are reminded to pay attention. You may not be aware of the feeling in your knee until I ask you to focus and pay attention to it.

Here's a simple awareness activity you can use anytime you like to maintain a friendly connection between you and your body. Similar to placing your hand over your heart in the previous chapter, this is another way of accessing your intuition and building self-trust.

Find a quiet spot where you can sit silently for a few moments. Place your hand over your stomach and close your eyes, tilting them down toward your stomach. Your stomach is located in the upper portion of your belly beneath your rib cage. Notice how your stomach feels.

Have you eaten recently? Is your last meal sloshing around in there? Does your tummy feel peaceful or are you in pain? If your body could talk, what would it say?

On a piece of paper write down the following question with your right hand, "What am I feeling?" Now, switch the pen/pencil to your left hand and write the answer to that question. Without censoring yourself, write down whatever comes up for you.

This is a method of connecting with your inner guidance and intuition. It will give you valuable information. Your intuition resides in the right hemisphere of your brain and it gets activated when you use the left side of your body.

In order to eat in response to your body's natural signals of hunger, you have to learn to become aware of how your body feels. In dieting you are taught to eat at certain times, ignoring how you feel.

I'm going to teach you how to communicate with your intuition. I'll guide you toward becoming aware of new ways of thinking about yourself. Think of it as if your intuition is a caring, nurturing friend, just waiting to be asked for help. It wants you to be happy and healthy and steer you clear of pain and misery.

Myth #2 – Eat a good breakfast, it's the most important meal of the day. – Most of us were taught that we need a good, rib-sticking breakfast in order to give us the energy we need for the day. I've come to believe that if you're not hungry at breakfast, or any other meal, you shouldn't be eating. Your body is still working on digesting the previous meal, especially if you indulged in a late-night snack.

Spending weekends with my Grammie and Grandpa always meant getting a break from the weekly diet crazed, calorie-counting routine my father and Rosie pushed me to follow. At home I was used to eating a measured portion of Special K® cereal and a splash of Carnation® instant milk. Yuck! But at Grammie's house all bets were off and I could eat whatever I wanted. She always cooked a huge breakfast for Grandpa and me and we all sat down to eat together.

First came a glass of juice while Grandpa had his cup of coffee. We each had a donut or some other pastry and washed that down with juice. Cereal and a banana came next, and, naturally, since I was a growing girl, I had an extra glass of milk. After we got down to the bottom of our cereal bowls, Grammie made us a big plate of eggs and bacon which we topped off with buttered toast and jelly. Good grief! It was a miracle I could get up from the table.

But Gram never ate much. I remember she was perfectly content drinking a cup of coffee and eating lightly buttered toast.

The truth is, unless you're a farm worker like my dear friend, Sandy, who used to own a dairy farm in upstate New York, you don't have to have a big breakfast in the morning. Your body doesn't normally require those heavy-duty energy reserves.

When your body settles down to slumber, all its processes slow down. Very little energy is expended and you get a nice peaceful rest. So you don't have to eat a lumberjack's breakfast before you head out the door for the day. But by all means, if you're hungry, then you must eat.

Remember: You are in control, no one else. I promise you that you will be surprised many times over by your body's responses to this new level of freedom. It's truly amazing what happens when you strip off the blanket of restriction.

Juicy Woman Note:

Believe me, I was shocked when I realized that like my Grammie and my Nana, I, too, usually prefer eating a small breakfast. On a typical day, I'll get hungry around 7:00 or 8:00 a.m. and have a piece of fruit. Then I get hungry again around 11 or 12 and I'll sit down and have something more substantial to eat, which might even satisfy me until dinner.

Adhering to the Naturally Slender Eating Strategy, which you'll learn about later in the book, I choose what I want to eat based on a couple of factors.

Taste is very important to me, so I want something that tastes great. The next consideration is what food will give me the energy I need? If I'm planning to write for several hours, I want something that will keep me feeling great and wide awake. For me, that would usually be protein.

When I first started to experiment with food and let myself eat what I really wanted, I ate a tremendous amount of what I now consider junk. These are the foods that although they may taste good, end up making me feel terrible. I'm talking about eating cakes and pies in the morning and chocolate all day long.

After a while, the sweet taste became boring and the overabundance of sugar made me want to sleep all the time. Now I always consider how a food is going to make me feel, and not only in the present moment but several hours ahead.

For me, I've learned that the best combination is eating a protein with a carbohydrate. I don't want to get nuts about this, but for the most part that's what gives me the most energy in the late morning and throughout the day.

After that initial piece of fruit disappears and my hunger resurfaces later that morning, I might whip up a couple of scrambled eggs or enjoy a piece or two of thickly sliced challah French toast with maple syrup. I might even fix a peanut butter and jelly sandwich, or pick at some leftovers.

Since I usually work out of my home, I'm free to eat anytime I get hungry. And I do looooooooove to wait until I get hungry. It gives me such a tremendous sense of personal pride, knowing that I do indeed have the control that I never felt I did. Now I enjoy eating just enough to fill a corner, rather than a cavern.

I'm curious to know what you'll discover.

Myth #3 – Eat only low-fat or diet foods. – I wonder if you never went on a diet, would you actually choose to consume those foods?

I used to swear up and down that I loved the taste of Diet Coke®, fat free salad dressing, light ice cream, and every other diet or low-fat mass produced food on the market. Who was I kidding? When I started to eat real food I became aware of how artificial tasting, bitter, chemically, and just plain nasty those foods are!

For the most part, all mass-produced diet foods are filled with additives and chemicals to make them taste good or to fool us into believing that they taste good. These companies have spent billions trying to mimic the taste of their higher-fat original versions, the good stuff. Have you ever compared a slice of real cheesecake to a diet version? There's no comparison. The diet cheesecake is plugged full of artificial sweeteners and fat substitutes.

Of course, taste is subjective. Some people like the reduced-fat, artificially sweetened, chemically processed foods. It's up to you. Maybe you do, maybe you don't. Maybe like me, you've fooled yourself into thinking that you like them. Only time will tell.

Juicy Woman Note:

Over the past several years, I've taken to making my own sweet tea like my Nana always used to have on hand. She would brew a big teapot and add several Celestial Seasonings® tea bags. My favorite was peppermint. Then she would add lemon and honey to taste.

Lately, I've been enjoying the tradition of making Nana's homemade sweet teas again, combining the different flavors and adding honey and freshly cut fruit slices to the tea. It's a real treat for me to sit down and enjoy a nice cool glass of homemade Nana-infused goodness.

Recently I went to Chili's® and ordered an unsweetened ice tea. Since sugar does not dissolve in cold liquids, I never use sugar to sweeten iced tea. For years it was my habit to pour several envelopes of quick dissolving Equal® artificial sweetener into the tea.

Without thinking I grabbed a few envelopes of the packaged sweetener and poured it mindlessly into my tea. After tasting it I nearly gagged, immediately recognizing the artificial flavor.

My point is that for years I had a habit of thinking I loved the taste of Equal®. But after I began enjoying tea with real sugar or honey instead of artificial sweetener, I realized I don't like the substitute at all.

As dieters, we're encouraged to eat chemically produced sugar and fat substitutes. Lots of 'em. What often happens is we then overeat. I'm sure that, like me, you've figured if you can eat a substitute of something that has significantly fewer calories and fat than the original, then you can naturally eat more of it. Would that be a fair assumption?

Without even knowing it, you've been practicing nonfat gluttony. The diet food industries encourage you to pig out and lose your mind because then you'll buy more of their product. That's why most diet plans have gotten hip to selling food under their own label, such as South Beach®, The Zone™, Atkins™ and who could forget my favorite, Weight Watchers®?

Myth #4 – Don't eat beyond a certain hour. – Now, honestly, do you really think your body blows the whistle and shuts down all the works after, let's say, 6:00 p.m.? No way. Again, it's all according to your own personal schedule and what you've eaten throughout the day.

Right now for me it's 12:10 a.m., I haven't eaten since six this evening. I'm hungry and since I took a nap earlier, I anticipate writing for several more hours. So I'm heading downstairs to have a glass of apple juice with some toast, mustard, and a slice of cheese and tomato. Even though my daughter made chocolate chip cookies this evening, they don't capture my attention now. I'm waiting to eat them when I really want to and know that I'll truly enjoy the experience.

According to the process of intuitive eating and the *Naturally Slender Eating Strategy* which I'm going to teach you, what and when you eat is up to you and what you feel is appropriate. Provided you've learned to tune into your body's needs.

When I began this process a couple of years ago, if I got hungry at midnight I would have devoured the cookies my daughter made, or at least something that would have seemed forbidden, like ice cream or cake. Now, although it's often here in the house, this type of food doesn't turn me on the way it used to and I don't eat it the same way because I'm keenly aware of how it makes me feel.

For the most part, the allure is gone. Now I gravitate toward foods that satisfy me, instead of just wanting to eat the foods I shouldn't be eating. You'll also get to this point. For now, just keep in mind that your body is working on your behalf and if you are feeling hungry—your body's signal that it wants food—then you should eat.

Myth #5 — When you overeat, you have failed. – As emotional eaters, we get comfort from food. This means that whenever you feel the need for security or safety, you run for the Fritos® or grab a slice of pizza, shovel down M&Ms®, or whatever is your chosen poison.

If food has become your best friend and failsafe then to rip it out of your hands, as dieting attempts to do, is to throw you into a state of shock.

This only triggers you to binge and want more food. You eat more because you're afraid you won't get to eat again. There's nothing worse than the feeling of being deprived. You always want what you think you can't have.

When you overeat, it is an indication that you are overwhelmed and unable to handle whatever stress is affecting you. Your body is doing its best to tune out that upset and anesthetize you from the pain. When your body's in this state, it's trying to alert you to trouble. There's a yellow alert going on in your brain, telling you that you are under stress. In the absence of having other coping strategies besides food, you will eat.

Years of dieting have conditioned you to think of these events as mistakes and you've probably been led to feel guilty for your poor judgment. You likely decide to make up for this by doing penance which may include not eating, doing strenuous exercise, or eating low calorie food that tastes like cardboard.

Like a baby learning to walk, as you learn to eat like a normal eater it's important to expect to fall and make mistakes. Respect the needs and desires of your body. In fact, all progress involves setbacks.

In one of Dana Carvey's comedy specials, he referred to failure as "deferred success." That's a pretty cool reframe. Isn't it?

Myth #6 - Weigh yourself often. – You have to weigh yourself to check your progress. What a load of malarkey! I want you to toss out your scales.

A client of mine, Shoshana, moved to Montana. One day soon afterwards she took her scale outdoors to where she had targets for shooting and she shot the dickens out of that piece of scrap metal. She said it was a beautiful thing to watch it flying through the air and then crash and fall to the ground.

Now I don't suggest you go out and practice shooting your scale, but I recommend that you toss it out. If you are in a family where it is important to others to have it around, negotiate a place where it won't bother you.

For years, I had my scale inside a large walk-in closet in the bathroom. Each morning before I dressed I would jump on the scale and weigh myself. I would then get dressed and weigh myself again. I'd weigh myself with my shoes on and then take them off. You get the idea. It was nuts. Step away from the scale.

46

Here's why. One day among many others when I was living in my guilty little world of scale obsession, I was presented with a great opportunity to speak at a networking event and introduce myself to other businesswomen in my local community.

I was pretty excited to get to know the other movers and shakers in my area. This also meant coming out from behind the safety of doing teleclasses and phone coaching, and presenting myself in the flesh as **The Juicy Woman**. This fantastic exposure had all sorts of benefits connected with it.

But I knew I wasn't at the top of my game. The night before I'd eaten more than I wanted to and my body felt bloated and fat. Normally I would have been a lot more confident, but because it had been awhile since I had spoken live I was nervous and upset, afraid the women there would judge me as a big fat fraud.

After all, most people would reason that a plus size woman has no right in the world calling herself a body image and self-esteem expert. It just doesn't compute for many people and that morning it didn't add up for me either.

I was just about to pull my clothes from the closet and get dressed for the day when I made this incredibly stupid bargain, goading myself to get on the scale. Here's how it went.

> *"Andrea, you don't have anything to worry about, sweetie. We're just checking here. What's the harm in knowing? Knowledge is power. Right? You know that those tortilla chips will probably show up as a gain so as long as you expect it. What's the big deal? No matter what the scale says it won't matter, because you're stronger than that. After all, you live and breathe this stuff. You teach it all the time. You already know how your thoughts affect your body, so you won't let that happen. Right?"*

I swore up and down to myself that I knew what I was doing as I stepped on the scale expecting to see a weight gain and promising myself it would be okay. No matter what the scale said, I promised myself I could handle it.

Yet for some reason I was unprepared for the level of disgust, disdain, and disappointment that rushed in when I saw the number. Hello! It doesn't take a rocket scientist to figure out that overeating the night before would show up on the scale the next morning. I weighed myself anyway and even expected a gain, but the results still twisted me up inside like a pretzel.

I hung my head in shame, glanced at the mirror, and watched the big, salty tears running down my cheeks. I knew there was no way I could go to that meeting. I had lost the magic. **The Juicy Woman** had left the room.

I hated myself for the weakling I was as I dialed the phone and called Marcia, the organizer. I told her I "was under the weather and can't come tonight." Immediately afterwards I hung up the receiver and ran for the safety of my covers, hiding under mounds of pillows and blankets. I cried hysterically, feeling sorry for myself like the old victim.

It was just Andrea there, feeling shaky and scared and it was all brought on by my stupid addiction to seeking validation from that damned piece of scrap metal. Please, by all means learn from my mistake. Protect yourself from the heat, and step away from the scale. I promise you won't be sorry.

Myth #7 – Avoid fattening foods. – Aw man, those are the best foods, aren't they? They are the ones you want the most. By avoiding those yummy goodies you are denying and depriving yourself to the nth degree. If you believe that certain foods are off limits then you will want them more. You'll feel deprived not having them and crave them like mad. Then when you get a chance to eat them, you'll go out of your mind and lose all control.

When I first met my husband, Angel, and we began dating, he brought me a big box of my favorite Godiva® chocolates and my favorite flowers, daisies. At the time I was on a diet, so the flowers were tremendously appreciated, but I felt enormous pressure having all that chocolate in my house.

I remember a time soon after we got married; Valentine's Day, 1992. We picked up his twelve-year-old daughter, Janelle, so that she could spend the weekend with us. Angel had given us each a box of chocolates and left us to hang out and relax while he took care of our newborn son, PT.

Janelle and I sat all snuggled up and watched Melrose Place together. We decided to eat some chocolates. She opened her box and I opened mine. As we sat hypnotized by the events on the screen, watching the latest Heather Locklear scheme unfold, we lost track of time. In my happy TV trance I moved like a robot, stuffing one chocolate in after another.

I glanced over at Janelle and she had only eaten about three of her chocolates. She'd bitten into them and left the rest. I, on the other hand, had almost systematically demolished the entire one-pound box. I reasoned to myself, "After all, if I still have these around tomorrow, how can I get back on my diet?"

Does that thinking sound familiar to you? I felt pressured to eat them all because I had to get rid of the evidence before midnight. I'm so glad that hysteria is behind me and now I can finally feel safe around chocolate.

Now I do what Janelle did. I'll look at something, pick it up, smell it, taste it, and then take a small bite. If I don't love it, it won't make the cut and I won't end up eating it. Or if by some chance I do decide to swallow it, you can bet I won't want any more of it.

However, once in a while there are still days when I'm not quite as picky and I'll end up eating more than I intended. Those are the times when I recognize that something is bothering me. But now, rather than give into the old temptation to get hung up on what I ate and feel bad about myself, I make an extra effort to be more gentle and compassionate. I take the time I need to lovingly explore what pushed my buttons.

By filling your pantries and stocking your cabinets and refrigerators with the foods you love, you are sending your brain the message that you are not depriving yourself any longer. You are telling your body that the drought is over and it can relax. Before you know it you'll look at those foods with new eyes.

It may seem odd to you now, but as you move forward in this program you'll see how actually having these foods around will give you a tremendous sense of comfort. Believe it or not, there will come a time when you'll want these foods in your home but you won't want to eat them.

In some instances, your preferences will change because you'll finally get an opportunity to really taste the foods you've been eating. You will find new ways to satisfy your emotional needs other than through food. And knowing that you can eat anything you want, food will find its new, rightful place in your order of priorities.

Like a food critic, you'll pass up the mediocre to enjoy the fabulous. Always seeking the best, you'll keep on discovering foods you adore. You just get pickier.

Myth #8 – You Can't Be Trusted with Food. – As a dieter, you've probably been brainwashed to believe that you don't have control over what you eat. You know the old saying, one is too many and a million is never enough. Whenever we want something that we can't have, the desire to get it becomes overwhelming.

You only think you can't be trusted around food because you've never really given yourself permission to enjoy it. When you eat the foods you love, you consider them bad and think of yourself as breaking your diet and falling off the wagon. That's a heck of a lot of pressure. How can you really enjoy food under those circumstances?

I remember times when I tried to shove a Ring Ding® or cookie in my mouth before someone came back in the room. How incredibly mortifying it was to have my husband, son, or daughter walk in and find me with my mouth filled with chocolate, trying desperately to hide my guilt and change the subject. I felt so shameful and embarrassed, like a criminal, only instead of committing grand larceny, I was caught with my hand in the cookie jar.

When you open yourself up to the idea of legalizing all foods and eating what you want, then you won't want them with the same degree of desperation. Those chips that you used to crave may sit on the counter or in the cabinet uneaten for hours or days, weeks or in my case even months.

Those brownies that you swore you couldn't live without are starting to taste different to you. When you have the ability to stand back and relax instead of being in the middle of your own food war, you notice distinctions that you hadn't been aware of before. "Mmmm, did that rice pudding have nutmeg in it? Yuck! I don't like that. Was that coriander? It's not for me."

Besides becoming picky, you will also see your habits in a very different light, allowing for much greater understanding and compassion.

The simple truth is that you can trust yourself around food. You don't have to give up your power and sacrifice your satisfaction. In fact, you'll become even more sensitive to what tastes you enjoy. It's up to you, but you may find that you won't want to eat the prepackaged diet meals that are low in calories and short on taste. You'll want to eat the good stuff.

Maybe you'll want to cook for yourself more often or bake or upgrade the quality of the foods you're eating. Your body will slowly learn self-mastery around food and naturally regulate itself when you start eating what you want.

Myth #9 – Eating fat will make you fat! – That's a lot of hooey, completely untrue. I'm sure you're familiar with the fact that the French eat a much richer diet than we Americans. They will typically eat real butter, heavy creams, rich sauces, and cheeses. Yet they don't gain weight like we do. They also have a lower incidence of heart problems.

I've personally done a lot of experimentation here. I used to be a non-fat everything kind of gal. Then once the blanket of restriction was pulled off, I experimented with all sorts of former forbidden yummies; fat laden foods I craved yet would never eat because they were so "fattening."

I started buying Hebrew National® salami and all kinds of wursts; bratwurst, liverwurst, knockwurst, burgers and hotdogs, butter and cheese, salads with mayonnaise, potatoes and sour cream, macaroni and cheese, lasagna, and all sorts of goodies that I love and good grief, let's not forget rare steak with fat—lots of it!

But as the novelty wore off I discovered things about each that I had never noticed before. First, when I ate them slowly and mindfully, these fatty foods filled me up so much that it surprised me. Now when I eat them, I only want a small bit in order to get the pleasure. I'm aware that if I over-eat those foods, I'll feel really sick.

Fat by its very nature satisfies the body longer. It takes a longer time to metabolize and it stays with you. Therefore, as the edge of your desperation wears off, you'll want to eat much less fat. But you'll discover this on your own in a very natural, intuitive way. Don't censor yourself. Eat what you want.

One of the toughest transitions for me was using real salad dressing with oil or mayonnaise. I had become so used to eating salads with diet dressing that it was unthinkable for me to consider wasting valuable calories on such a frivolous food. Are you kidding? It wasn't even a food.

But once I began to eat more for pleasure, I noticed that when I had a salad for lunch with olive oil or caesar dressing on it I would be satisfied for hours. It still amazes me how much more satisfying food is when I prepare it with olive oil, butter, or margarine. I highly encourage you to experiment and see what works for you as far as breaking the mold of fearful thinking around eating fats.

Eating fat won't make you any fatter than eating anything else, including nonfat foods. In fact, as I just mentioned, when your body begins to regulate itself you'll only need a small amount of fat to be satisfied for a long time. You could eat a peanut butter and jelly sandwich at noon and not want to eat again until dinner. It's happened to me.

Wrapping Up
Chapter 2: Diets Don't Work: Food Fallacies
That Have Been Making You Fat!

Here are the juiciest bits covered in this section. Savor them mindfully.

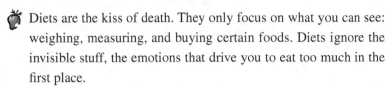

Diets are the kiss of death. They only focus on what you can see: weighing, measuring, and buying certain foods. Diets ignore the invisible stuff, the emotions that drive you to eat too much in the first place.

Eating by the clock will throw off your ability to know when you are actually physically hungry because you'll be walking around semi-stuffed. Your hunger is nothing to fear. In order for your internal satisfaction switch to trigger, your body has to first recognize the sensation of hunger.

If you're not hungry at breakfast time or any other meal, you shouldn't be eating. Your body is still working on digesting the last thing you ate.

Diet foods - Without even knowing it, you've been practicing non-fat gluttony.

No food past 6:00 p.m. - Nonsense. Eat when your body says you're hungry.

As you take steps to legalize and decriminalize all foods, your craving for the old forbidden fruits will fizzle out. You'll notice there will come a time when you'll actually choose a baked potato over french fries, or a salad over a Snickers®.

When you overeat it is an indicator that you are overwhelmed and unable to handle whatever stress is affecting you. In the absence of having other coping strategies besides food, you will eat. No guilt, no judgment, no shame. By eating more than you wanted, you haven't done anything wrong. Do yourself a favor and find out what is making you feel so awful.

Like a baby learning how to walk, as you learn to eat like a normal eater it's important to expect that you'll fall and make mistakes. Respect the needs and desires of your body.

- Don't treat your scale like a horoscope. That nasty piece of sheet metal doesn't have the right to tell you what kind of day you're going to have. Step away.

- You only think that you can't be trusted around food because you've never really given yourself permission to enjoy food.

- Want to break your addiction to chocolate, pasta, pizza, etc? Pack your fridge and cupboard with those goodies. When you surround yourself with the foods you love it will squelch your urge to over-eat them. Result? Incredible self-respect and killer confidence.

- When you have the ability to stand back and relax instead of being in the middle of your own food war, you notice distinctions that you hadn't been aware of before. You little, picky eater, you.

- Eating fat won't necessarily make you fat! Eat what you want, not what you think you should have. Fat by its very nature satisfies the body longer. It takes a longer time to metabolize and it stays with you. As the edge of your desperation begins to wear off, you'll want to eat much less fat.

In the next chapter, we'll discuss the key that really makes this all work: self-acceptance.

Chapter 3
Self Acceptance Starts with Making Peace with Food

"It's almost like I don't want to waste my hunger on something unless it's absolutely wonderful! It is surprising how much food is either bland, oversweet, or artificial once you taste it properly."
– *Jomay, UK, Losing Weight Without Dieting Participant*

Toss the scale! Stock the cupboards! Kiss the tape measure goodbye! But what comes next?

The challenge to you is to take the information I'm going to share with you about intuitive eating and resist turning it into just another diet. That's what I did. I got all loopy and wound up, tangling myself in my old diet-y way of thinking. Miss perfectionism.

As great as intuitive eating is, it doesn't teach you how to change your limiting beliefs and cope with the emotions that push you to eat anything that's not nailed down, but I will. I want to give you the benefit of being able to learn from my goofs!

> ## Juicy Woman Note:
>
> Since I'm a bit of a Type A personality, I understand completely if you're chomping at the bit, eager to skip ahead and get right to the goods. But take it from me, a hard headed gal who had to first gain a lot of weight before I learned my lesson: It's not what you're eating, it's what's eating you.
>
> To be successful in making peace with food and eating intuitively, you've got to change the way you think and stop focusing on what you're eating. I urge you to read through and understand all the information that precedes the instruction on intuitive eating.
>
> Without having the appropriate mental framework, you are likely to have similar consequences if you make the same hasty assumptions that I did and turn something that is so natural and gentle into something very complicated and rigid.

The universal law of "Cause and Effect" says for every action you take, there's a reaction (also called a consequence). In my case, I barreled through and took the intuitive eating guidelines literally. I made them the most important thing in the world to me and therefore lost sight of everything else.

As a result of not knowing what in the world to make of these rules and over-analyzing their simplicity, I became so obsessed with food and my body that my insecurities resurfaced. The renewed feelings of being unsafe and uncertain led me into a lot of fights with my family, especially with my husband. We always fought over my father because, like many women, having my father's love and approval meant everything to me.

The Roots of My Resentment

Understanding the roots of your emotional stress is crucial to finding peace with them. You may never figure it all out, and that's okay, but the more you can, the better. The more you understand what causes your emotional stress, the more easily you'll be able to stop using food to deal with it.

I have come a long way in dealing with the roots of my resentment. The following is a piece of my story. Maybe you'll find something within it that will help you along your journey.

From the time I was a little girl I adored my father. He and my step mother, Rosie, gave me a wonderful home and sense of security that I'll always hold dear to my heart. I'm forever grateful to my dad for inspiring me to begin my study of personal development in my early teens.

Despite the fact that we're now estranged from one another, I have many wonderful things by which to remember him. He endowed me with a passion for learning and a love for helping others that fills my soul. I'll always think of my relationship with him as my greatest gift. In many ways, if it weren't for his nurturing support and love this book would probably never have been written.

In 1985, soon after my stepmother, Rosie, passed away from lung cancer, my father faced a personal crisis that changed all of our lives forever. Unable to continue running his real estate business, I felt obligated to leave college prematurely to help out my family. With mixed emotions I left school before my second year at NYU and, as they say, jumped from the frying pan into the fire.

The long and short of it is that once I stepped in to run his business, I seemed to have lost my place in my father's heart. Somewhere down the line I just became his employee. Managing three residential buildings in Manhattan with 110 tenant families and a 40 coin-machine operated Laundromat with my Nana was no piece of cake. I learned my lessons and have since emerged a powerful businesswoman by those years of trial by fire.

Having grown up with a silver spoon in my mouth, I was painfully naïve and unaware of anything to do with finance. I never considered that my work or contribution had any value.

My father, ever the savvy businessman, had me on a short leash. For years I was on call 24/7, actually running a multi-million dollar empire. Despite having full power of signature and the ability to write myself or anyone else a check for any sum, I continued to draw a salary of $150 each week for nearly fifteen years.

For all that time, I was a woman in power who allowed herself to feel powerless. Because I had deluded myself into believing I had no value, I allowed my father and so many others to convince me I was right.

At one point I grew a backbone and confronted him. I threatened to quit unless he agreed to sell the business and share 49 percent of the proceeds with me. When push came to shove it was me who negotiated the sale of the properties for $10.5 million, along with a life lease for him to live in comfort for less than $250 a month.

Unfortunately, I trusted my father implicitly and continually ignored the pleadings of my husband and friends who urged me to demand a signed contractual agreement gifting me 49 percent of the proceeds. My father ended up with everything and quickly took legal steps to disown me and my family.

The personal and financial losses have been devastating, but through it all I can now say I've become a stronger person for having gone through the experience—I may have lost my father, but I gained myself.

Juicy Woman Note:

Today I realize that the sexual abuse I endured at the hands of so many men in my past, was like a walk in the park in comparison to facing the insidiously damaging influence my father's emotional and verbal abuse has had on my life.

It was, and often still is, his criticism that is the hardest to overcome, not the sexual abuse of the others. The devastation he caused with his sharp tongue and mean words seeped into my soul, pounding my heart to bits. For years it led me to question my own worth.

The doubt he created in my mind about myself and my capabilities crept into my life in so many horribly unexpected ways. For years I felt unentitled and worthless. These feelings undermined my marriage, my relationship with my husband, our sex life, my health, my ability to parent, my relationship with my kids, my finances, my willingness to trust and build friendships, and so much more.

Now I have a handle on understanding it was my father who had the problem of not being able to appropriately demonstrate his love and caring. It's so much easier to be more compassionate with myself and to recognize that he wasn't the perfect dad I set him up to be.

Most people understand that sexual abuse is harmful, and this type of gross invasion of a person's physical boundaries is capable of scarring them for life. But I've never heard of anyone tell the story of how damaging and far reaching the effects of verbal and emotional abuse are.

I want to demonstrate the link between abuse, emotional eating, and a low self-image. I want my story to help you understand that it is possible to overcome a negative self-image.

Like me, many women have been hurt and damaged by people in their life who actually care for them but lack the social and communication skills to convey their feelings. The women trust them and don't question enough what they say or consider that perhaps they don't deserve to be treated poorly.

I'm here to say that it's up to you to tell others how you want to be treated. This lesson has cost me an emotional and financial fortune. I don't want you to pay the price and make the same mistakes I did.

Remember, we teach others how to treat us. If you don't like the way someone is treating you, take a stand and tell them right now !!

Self Sabotage: Facing My Own Resistance

Being raised by my father, I picked up many of his bad habits. I was a perfectionistic, workaholic, martyr, always looking for blame and venting my anger on those I loved. For many years I was angry and resentful, feeling burdened and stuck having to run the family business.

The stress of working all the time and juggling all my other problems gave me a short fuse, with each of my blowups widening the gap between me and my family. It also kept me eating out of control. I watched helplessly as the pounds crept up. I had to know what was causing my resistance. Why couldn't I stop eating?

Now I realize the problem was not what I was eating, but what was eating me! It was easier to distract myself with thoughts about my body and food so that I wouldn't have to face the pain of what was going on in my life.

Just like dad, it was my habit to always push past my limits. I refused to be gentle with myself. I never even considered using alternative ways to deal with my stress. Despite knowing that EFT (Emotional Freedom Techniques®), which you'll learn about in Chapter 7, worked to dissolve cravings in minutes, I was being a martyr and refused to rely on anything that I knew would make things easier. "No crutches," I promised myself. So in the absence of having any other way of dealing with my stress, I ate.

However, since I had stopped dieting at that time, I reasoned that I was eating intuitively. Now I know that I was just plain eating and totally ignoring my body. Because I needed to numb myself from the pain, I wasn't open to receiving any messages from my body other than "Eat, Andrea. You'll feel better." So I kept eating until one day when I looked in the mirror I faced the fact that I had allowed myself to regain thirty-five pounds.

Obstacles Are What You See, When You Take Your Eyes Off the Goal

In June of 2007, as I was sitting at my son's elementary school graduation, my inner critic was having a field day:

> *"Andrea, what the hell is the matter with you? Why can't*
> *you figure out why you can't stop eating? You're a friggin'*

fraud telling your clients what to do and not doing it yourself. Whatever happened to walk your talk?"

The distant voice of the presenter onstage jolted me back to the present when he said, "Obstacles are what you see, when you take your eyes off the goal." Suddenly a river of truth tears came flooding down my cheeks. I finally got it. All this time, all these years, I had the wrong goal—to lose weight. I wanted to get thinner because I thought that would make me happy.

To get past my resistance, I knew I had to change the goal from losing weight to learning how to love and accept myself as I was—with the extra thirty-five pounds on me, my new round, fat belly, and my ever-present big fat thighs.

In that moment of clarity, I realized the nasty way I had learned to speak to myself was the same critical, intimidating way my father had spoken to me for years. I realized that in many ways, I had become him. As I heard the speaker repeat the line, I knew I was ready to accept this new, larger—and to my way of thinking, less attractive—version of Andrea.

My transformation didn't require a change of eating habits. It required a change of thinking habits. To break the cycle of my self-abusive ways, I had to stop criticizing and judging me as my father did, and instead discover wells of compassion for myself that I didn't yet feel.

I had to step out of seeing myself from his perspective and start looking at the real me—excess weight and all—through new, gentle, loving eyes; perhaps for the very first time. I resolved to look for what had long been missing: Me.

Losing Weight vs. Making Peace with Food

There is so much more to life than obsessing over food and weight. When you discover this on a deep, heartfelt level, you'll be in awe of the power you have over your choices.

It's one thing to understand something with your head, but it's quite another to really get the message in your heart. That's when big changes take place and your life moves forward again.

I've come to think of my past obsession with food as a sort of ice age period. During that time much of my life was static, unmoving, and dead.

Even though I was able to achieve certain successes or squeeze out some joy, I was surrounded by my need to feed my obsession: food. My every thought revolved around how I looked at any given time, how I would next feed the hunger beast inside of me, and how to keep myself under control at all times. It was exhausting.

That obsession superseded everything else in my life. When I was living under the tyranny of dieting, and later when I first experimented with eating intuitively, high stress inevitably led me straight for the next binge. During those times nothing was more important than food, not my husband, my kids, or my commitments. Nothing mattered more to me than getting my next fix. Food was my drug of choice.

I don't know about you, but one of the most degrading things for me as an emotional eater was feeling like I could never control my runaway appetite. I used to think I was a bottomless pit, a "volume eater," dare I say it, "a garbage can."

It didn't much matter if I ate a whole bag of potato chips, a pint of ice cream, and a pound of chocolates during a binge, or an entire bag of steamed vegetables and a head of lettuce when I was "in the zone." I thought of myself as a big eater and accepted that as being who I was. That was me: Andrea, the animal.

I was wrong. Now I know my desperate sense of hunger was not rooted in my body, it came from unfulfilled emotional needs that I had become expert at suppressing. As a result, my cravings and my voracious appetite led me around by the nose.

Over the years I'd heard my father say, "Andrea, for God's sake, you have no self-control. You have no friggin' discipline. If you could just push yourself away from the table, and stop eating…"

But no matter how badly I wanted to lose weight, I wanted and needed the food more. I swore I was a slave to my cravings. I swore it was the taste of the food and my lack of control that kept me going back for more.

I've engaged in just about every illicit, undignified, and demoralizing behavior that you can think of having to do with food: lying to myself and others, eating stale or moldy leftovers, raiding people's kitchens and pantries, retrieving tossed food from the garbage, offering to clear the table as a way of getting to the scraps, smuggling food on my body, concealing snacks, sitting on the cold, hard tile of the bathroom while stuffing my face, keeping a food stash, stealing bites from my kids' plates, manipulating my husband to order dishes that I wanted and eventually commandeering his plate, and any other sad and desperate act associated with feeling hopelessly and helplessly deprived.

Doing these types of things made me think of myself as a pig with no sense of discrimination or propriety around food. My self-image of being out of control, disgusting, and disgraceful only added fuel to the fire, increasing my hatred and disgust toward my hopelessly distorted view of my body.

That's why I'm sharing what I've learned about overcoming emotional eating with you, so you won't have to live a moment longer with fears and feelings of hatred toward yourself like I did.

There is hope and no matter how out of control with food you may be, you can change. As I learned, you have to call a truce on the war with your poor body and make friends with it instead. I'm talking about all those parts of yourself that you curse every time you look in the mirror. For me the battle always waged around the size of my thighs and until recently the three of us have never been friends.

How about you? You've probably been despising your 'wobbly bits,' haven't you? The truth is, you may or may not be overeating, but somehow, somewhere along the way you adopted distorted beliefs about food and your curvy body. If you want to ever reach the point of accepting yourself as you are right now, then you need to find balance in your relationship with food, because we just can't run away from ourselves.

If you're ready to live comfortably with what you think of now as temptation, find out what makes you want to eat when you're not hungry. Deal with those issues head on and say goodbye to dieting. Are you willing?

I can assure you that by giving up dieting, you are most certainly not giving up! In fact, it's probably the kindest thing you'll ever do for yourself. By learning how to listen to the wisdom of your body, you will eventually gravitate toward foods that make you feel good inside and out.

The side benefit is that you will get thinner because you will eat differently. Even if you still choose to dine on cake and ice cream, you won't require the same large amounts to satisfy you. You'll enjoy food more and get satisfied more quickly.

Most important of all, saying goodbye to dieting means you are actually demonstrating a great deal of compassion, love, and self-respect by being willing to rattle the illusion that your body is the source of all your problems. Don't you wonder when all the food frenzy began?

The Roots of Your Food Obsession

When did the foods you love become forbidden? Maybe as a kid you were told you couldn't be trusted around food. Maybe, like me, people stood over your shoulder and counted your M&Ms®, rationed your chips or cookies, and eventually put you on your first diet.

What you need to understand is that somewhere along the way you got your wires crossed and started thinking about food as more than just a means of filling a hungry tummy.

All those messages your brain received that made food seem alluring yet forbidden monkeyed around with the energetic balance in your body, causing you tons of stress. Food bore so many unnecessary burdens because it was no longer just associated with pleasure, it was also getting linked up with pain.

In order to overturn that rotten apple cart of defiant and disordered eating, you have to neutralize the charge on the conflicted emotions that instigate the need to eat those chips beyond the point of satisfying your hunger.

I'd venture to say that years of wanting what you've been told you can't have through dieting has led you to feel helpless and overwhelmed by your cravings. You may have found yourself living to eat, instead of eating to live.

Perhaps, like me, your life has been revolving around food and your addiction to it. Maybe you decided you are a lost cause and somewhere down deep have even quietly surrendered and reconciled yourself to being fat forever.

It doesn't have to be that way, but in order to climb out of the hole you have to be willing to commit to yourself and stand by you, no matter what. You see, you've been led to think of yourself as your own worst enemy. Because fat is so deeply despised in our society and the media has us believing that only toothpick thin models are beautiful, you have been conditioned to look at your body and think of yourself as a fat person.

The way to get past all that media, body-hating static, is to tune into yourself and rediscover your self-compassion.

To help you rediscover self-compassion, I want you to reconnect with an old memory of yours. I'll bet you remember a time when you learned to think of yourself as worthless, fat, stupid, ugly, or hopelessly incompetent because you were overweight. I sure do and before I launch into the guidelines of intuitive eating, I'd like to share my story and maybe that will spark a memory to help you with yours.

My Big Fat Thighs: So Many Sighs Over Size

Who would ever think there would be so much fuss over how we look? My obsession with my body kicked into high gear pretty early on. I remember one particular event that cemented itself in my brain as an iconic symbol for how I would think of myself for years to come.

As I mentioned earlier, my parents divorced when I was eight years old and I went to live with my mother. When I was nine, Mom remarried and took my baby brother, David, and I to live in Florida. I hated it there and wanted to go back and be with my father.

When I was eleven, after a horrific couple of years in Florida, my dream came true and I had the opportunity to return to New York and live with my Dad and his fiancée, Rosie. At the time, I didn't know her very well so I wasn't sure if I liked her or not.

To my way of thinking, she was as beautiful as a model. She reminded me of Cher with her bold confidence and striking features, her long, naturally curly auburn hair, big brown eyes, and petite figure. I knew Dad was crazy about her because they were always happy together and he showered her with gifts of furs and jewelry.

One day that first year back with my dad, I went shopping for school clothes with Rosie and him at the Bergen Mall in New Jersey. We had been shopping for days and now were going through department stores in the mall trying to find pants that fit me.

After having been through the entire length of the mall once, we were making our way back to the very beginning. I was exhausted when we ended up in Lerner Stores (now known as New York & Company). Dad sat outside waiting while Rosie and I combed through the racks and grabbed armloads of pants ranging between sizes twelve and fourteen.

Before we went into the fitting room, I said a quick, silent prayer that this time something would fit. "Please God help me." We'd been through so many stores trying on clothes, and I was sweaty, tired, and hungry. I felt awful, wishing I could fall through the floor. No matter where we went nothing fit me. It seemed that every pair of pants I tried on wouldn't budge past my fat dimply thighs. I was so ashamed of my chunky little body.

As I got close to the bottom of the pile I picked up speed and breathed heavily as I wrestled desperately with the buttons, buckles, and belts on each pair of pants. A couple times I even remember grabbing them defiantly from Rosie. I was so furious with myself and I kept wondering, "Why am I so fat? Why are my thighs so big? Why can't I find pants that fit me? What's wrong with me?"

The big sizes that managed to go up over my fat thighs were way too big on my waist. I couldn't stand the pressure or the heat any longer. The dam burst. I started wailing and crying hysterically. I stood there in the middle of Lerner's fitting room, feeling helpless and ugly and fat, in those damn pants that wouldn't go up past my thighs.

I wanted to die. I'd lost all control and was completely overwhelmed. After an embarrassingly tearful display of what I considered a real lack of self-control, we walked out of the store. Silent and empty handed, we headed down the mall to have lunch at Wolfie's, my favorite deli. Eating usually helped me feel better no matter what or where.

At Wolfie's I loved to pick up the dill pickle slices in the barrel with the pickle tongs that the waitresses placed on our table. It was usually such fun. It reminded me of going fishing. But this time I didn't touch the pickles and I choked down my food, probably because my stomach was upset from being too hungry and crying so much.

The silence was so thick you could cut it with a knife. After lunch Dad said I needed to get shoes, so we headed to Baker's Shoe store in the mall. I still felt pretty raw from the meltdown that I had earlier and just wanted to go home, but I had to get shoes for school. Like my thighs, I also hated my wide feet.

As the salesman tried on shoe after shoe with nothing fitting, I looked over and saw Dad's expression. He looked utterly disgusted. I watched him make his way over to a display called Earth® shoes. They looked like orthopedics, old lady shoes—so hideously ugly I wanted to die. Tears welled up inside me again. Could he really expect me to wear those?

He picked one up and said, "I'd like to see this in an eight in whatever colors you have." I was stunned, shocked, stupefied. As the salesman returned with his arms full of boxes, a part of me zoned out. I could feel him putting the shoes on my feet and lacing them up, but I was lost in my thoughts. "These have to be the ugliest shoes in the world and nobody in school would wear them. Everyone will make fun of me." I was shaken out of my reverie when Dad said, "Okay, They fit. Time to go home."

The ride back to Manhattan was silent. Soon after we settled for the evening, I was told that since we couldn't find any pants that fit me and we'd already been looking for days with absolutely no luck, Rosie's sister, Aida, was going to make my clothes. I was mortified. I figured I must have been so fat that no store would carry my size. I cried myself to sleep that night.

Several weeks later, Aida came over to the house and proudly unwrapped her creations; twelve pairs of pants with elastic waist bands and big muumuu tops with ties that looked like maternity wear. That's when it hit me: This was who I was. I was a fat girl!

Try It! – Getting Reacquainted with Your Little Girl

Find a picture of yourself from a time when you were extremely vulnerable. It can be when you were a little girl or as an adult, but the picture should epitomize the essence of who you were at a certain painfully memorable time.

Look for the picture that demonstrates the phase in your life where you learned it was unsafe to feel whatever you were feeling and that in order to be acceptable you had to stuff down your emotions.

If that time in your life occurred when you were a little girl and you are unable to find a picture, draw one or think of a loaded word or image that best represents the characteristics you remember from your childhood that make up your inner little girl.

I remember just once my father said, "Andrea, you'll get so f***** fat, one day I'll be able to roll you down the hill like a f**** meatball." Hence, at one time the image of a meatball rolling down a hill would have reduced me to tears. Not anymore, I can assure you, thanks to a tool called EFT I'll teach you later.

Get creative and go fishing inside yourself. Find that shadow side of you and tell her she's about to get some love.

Your picture may show a toothy ten year old with mussed up hair teetering on the monkey bars, or a chunky, pimply faced thirteen year old with sad eyes trying to smile for school pictures. Maybe it'll be of a young teen trying hard to be perky but whose eyes are filled with uncertainty because she was always told she was "Too fat and boys don't like chubby girls."

No matter what age you choose, that picture will best represent the little girl or hurting woman inside of you who wants to eat when you're not physically hungry. Put the picture in a place where you can see it every day. Doing this will remind you to be compassionate and to love and accept yourself no matter where you are in this process.

Making Friends with Your Body

Every time I think of myself in those damned ugly Earth® shoes and muumuu tops, I want to hug that sad and insecure little Andrea part of me and tell her, "Sweetie, it will be alright." Now, having that picture in my head gives me a much greater awareness of my humanness and vulnerability at a time when I was only just beginning to shape my ideas about life.

You may have been slender as a child, but you might have experienced something so painful that you lost your equilibrium. No matter if it was a death, a loss of some type, a violation, neglect or abuse, this is the part of you that triggers your desperate craving for food.

By giving voice to this part of your personality and opening up your heart to those memories and emotions, you'll gain new power over food.

For me, it's really helped having a bead on that little Andrea because it's much easier for me to understand why I do the things I do. It makes it easy to be compassionate towards that desperately needy little girl in me.

This in turn paves the path to forgiveness and helps me to be open to new ways of doing things in a much kinder and gentler way. I rarely talk to myself in the same nasty way I used to. This is one of the greatest benefits you'll ever get from learning this process of intuitive eating; learning how to do things in a loving, respectful, and gentle way.

The thing to keep in mind is that whatever internal picture of yourself you have as an emotional eater, that's the part of you that needs more love and compassion. Despite every conscious attempt you make to lose weight and get thinner, if that part of you doesn't feel safe, nothing you do will work.

That's why I want you to have a clear reminder of that scared and uncertain part of you that probably believed dieting was the only way to achieve happiness.

Speaking of happiness, let me introduce you to the ultimate in food freedom, a process called intuitive eating.

What is Intuitive Eating?

Have you ever watched a baby being nursed or bottle fed? Perhaps you've noticed that infant turn her head away at some point during the feeding. That's because the baby is paying attention to the feeling of fullness in her tummy. She is responding to her body's reduced hunger signals. By turning her head away from the bottle or breast, she is honoring her hunger, indicating that she doesn't want any more food.

Eating problems often begin with mom. In her belief that she knows best what her baby needs, she will try to cram that bottle or breast back in the baby's mouth to make sure she's not hungry. According to what mom learned from watching her mom and other women with children, she knows a full baby is a happy baby that will go right to sleep without a fuss.

Don't blame her. Poor thing, she was probably suffering from sleep deprivation and had to do whatever she could to ensure she would get a few solid hours of rest. Overfeeding is the quickest solution.

Just like the baby, we all have that same ability to listen to our bodies, eat when we are hungry, and stop when we are satisfied. However after years of dieting or trying to "watch your weight," you may have learned to mistrust your body and ignore its messages. You may have been told to fill up on low Cal foods and drinks in an effort to control the hunger monster lurking inside of you.

Despite that negative programming, it's simple to get back on track and pay attention to your body so that you can eat what you want and lose weight naturally without dieting, pills, gadgets, or gizmos.

All you have to do is learn how to trust your body again. As I've mentioned before, your body is already doing a great job for you in other areas. It tells you when you need to relieve your bladder, regulates your heart beat, blood circulation, and sleep rhythms, and so much more. Face it. Your body is a miracle. This means you can also trust it to regulate your weight.

Juicy Woman Note:

The term "intuitive eating" was first coined in the early 1990's by two prominent nutritionists and registered dieticians, Elyse Resch, M.S.R.D., F.A.D.A and Evelyn Tribole, M.S.R.D., in their book, Intuitive Eating: A Revolutionary Program That Works.

As far as I'm concerned, there is no other book available that can explain the entire process of how to become an intuitive eater as precisely as this one. It rocks! In the following section I'll share some of their main ideas. Although they cite ten principles, I have condensed these down to six basic steps. Since I can't possibly do these authors enough justice to explain the process as well as they do, I highly recommend you read their book.

Six Steps to Becoming an Intuitive Eater

Step #1 - Say goodbye to dieting. Yippee! Now you get to toss out all your old diet books, stop counting calories, points, carbs, or fat grams, and for goodness sakes, stop thinking of food as either good or bad. To your body, it's all equal. I know it sounds crazy to think that a chocolate sundae and a piece of cheese can be considered by your body as equal, but I'll explain how within these guidelines.

In terms of nutritional content, naturally there are foods that are healthier for you and more beneficial, but for the sake of making peace with all food, you have to level the playing field. The goal is to learn to rely on your body to gauge what is right for you.

No more diets.

As I mentioned earlier, ditch your scale. It only serves to light up your internal fat circuit board by consistently telling you in no uncertain terms, "I'm still fat."

Juicy Woman Note:

Can you relate to this? You wake up feeling good because you've been a bit more active and eating less food lately. You have somewhere important to go today. You jump on the scale to get a quick bit of positive reinforcement and to your shock and dismay, you see that you have gained two pounds.

You instantly feel depressed and upset. You glance in the mirror and suddenly it seems like you are heavier than you were just a minute ago. "Oh Sh...!" you scream, as you run downstairs desperately seeking ice cream.

Okay, 'Nuf said. Step away from the scale.

Step #2: Pack your pantry and stock your fridge. The battle is over. Give yourself unconditional permission to eat what you want, REALLY! In a restaurant order what you want to eat, not what you think you should. By doing this, you will quickly develop new abilities to be discriminating. You will soon learn that you truly can trust yourself with all foods. I'll take my steak rare with the fat left on it please!

Step #3: As often as you can, eat only when you are physically hungry. Doing this makes it easier to say "no" when you're not feeling that physical urge to eat.

Here's what you need to know to understand a bit more about how to eat in accordance with your body's natural hunger. Generally speaking it takes between five and nine hours to fully empty your body's energy reserves. If you've eaten a full meal, your body will not be hungry for quite a length of time.

When this concept of eating in response to your hunger clicks into place for you and you are truly able to eat in accordance with your body's biological hunger, then by waiting to eat until you are hungry, you will be able to tune in and discover how satisfying your food can really be.

This is when food tastes the most delicious, when you wait until you are good and hungry. It also reinforces the message to your brain that you are in control of your food. As this message gets repeated it creates a new subconscious habit. You will soon develop a strong preference for eating only when you are hungry and it will become easier and easier to refuse food when you don't feel hungry.

Step #4: Eat intentionally and mindfully without guilt. Take back your sense of self by setting a new precedent. Eat what you want in full view of anyone and everyone. No more fear, no more guilt, no more feeling as though you are cheating. You're not. It's time to take back control of what you eat, and let the critics know that they have no right to comment on your body or what you eat, ever again.

Step #5: Feel Your Fullness. Listen to your body and become sensitive to the new sensation of satisfaction and fullness. You might like to pause in the middle of a meal and ask yourself how satisfying the food tastes and gauge your level of comfort. My grandfather used to say, "Just walk away from the table." Remember, if you're hungry you can always eat more.

Juicy Woman Note:

In Japan, on the island of Okinawa, the people are reputed to have extremely long life spans, often living well past the age of 100. One explanation for their longevity, besides their preference for more activity and a low fat, mostly plant based diet rich in fish and vegetables, is their cultural habit of taking in fewer calories than the average person. They do this naturally without effort by practicing what they call, "hara hachi bu" which means eating until you are only 80 percent full.

I've made mention of my preference to eat to fill a corner, rather than a cavern. This is my way of thinking about what the Japanese call, "hara hachi bu." If you make a habit of eating this way you'll notice that about twenty minutes after you eat, your body will register a greater sense of satisfaction and fullness than you felt before you decided to stop eating.

This is because your stomach's stretch receptors take about twenty minutes to tell the body how full it really is. This is the reason why all diets have routinely encouraged people to eat slowly.

I have found that you don't have to slow your pace to a crawl or get crazy chewing your food to the point of mush, just aim your goal to eat only enough to satisfy your hunger and a tiny bit more. Remember, there's plenty of food available and the drought of deprivation is over. You can always eat more when you get hungry again.

I encourage you to experiment with your portion sizes and see what works for you.

Step #6: Rediscover the satisfaction factor in your food. When you eat what you want in a pleasing environment, your satisfaction will be enhanced. As you gain more pleasure in food, you will naturally find that you eat smaller portions. Feast all your senses. Smell, taste, touch, and fully enjoy your meals.

Try It! – The Hunger Scale

The Hunger Scale is a fabulous tool for becoming aware of how your body feels. Oftentimes we overeat because we don't listen to our bodies and instead adhere to a schedule. This tool will help put the control back in your hands and on your stomach, by giving you a way of keying in and noticing how your body feels. I recommend you use it as a guideline so that you can know what sensations to look for as you begin and finish eating.

The Hunger Scale

1. Physically faint – weak, woozy, and lightheaded
2. Ravenous – extremely uncomfortable, irritable, cranky, and unable to think clearly
3. Uncomfortably hungry – your stomach is growling, you may feel a burning in your stomach
4. Slightly uncomfortably hungry – beginning to feel the signs of physical hunger
5. Neutral or Comfortable – you feel pretty satisfied, but you could still eat more
6. Pleasantly satisfied – perfectly comfortable and feeling satisfied, not wanting more
7. Full – a little uncomfortable, not wanting to eat any more
8. Uncomfortably full – you feel pretty bloated
9. Extremely uncomfortably full – you need to loosen your clothes
10. Stuffed – you feel nauseated

> Take a few moments and explore how your body feels. Tune into the sensations in your stomach, and ask yourself, "How hungry am I?" Although everyone feels and experiences hunger a little differently, as a general rule you will want to eat whenever you notice your hunger between a level #3 or #4 on the scale. That is when you are uncomfortably or slightly uncomfortably hungry but before you become ravenous (#2).
>
> If you wait until you get down to #1 or #2, your body will go into starvation mode and you'll wind up eating more than your body needs and storing the excess as fat.
>
> Ideally you'll want to stop eating when your body begins to notice a sensation of being neutral or comfortable (#5) to pleasantly satisfied (#6). This is what is known as "hara hachi bu."

It's natural that if you have a history of emotional eating or dieting, you will have difficulty paying attention to how your body feels. This is because you've become accustomed to overriding your body's natural hunger signals.

Don't worry. Your body is already aware of how to eat when you're hungry and stop eating well before you get too full. I'll teach you how to use stress relief techniques and energy tools to help release fears and doubts about being able to tune into your body. It's a matter of uncovering the naturally slender, wise woman in you, by lifting off and removing all the old limiting beliefs that have been keeping you in patterns of overeating, shame, and self-abuse.

Practice tuning into your body and paying attention to how you feel frequently during the day. When you feel compelled to overeat but know you're not physically hungry, you'll soon recognize these are times when the stress in your life is knocking on your door, pushing all your hungry buttons.

Painful and overwhelming emotions like sadness, loneliness, and anger can feel like deep pits of emptiness and are easily confused with hunger. To avoid the situation I faced, eating to calm my troubles with my Dad, I had to make a habit of dealing with stress when it popped up.

My Experience with Intuitive Eating:
Freedom from Diet Prison

Many people learn the process of intuitive eating easily and quickly without as much as a wing or a hitch. They seamlessly make the transition into normal eating without ever having a serious problem with food again.

Fortunately for both of us, I wasn't one of the lucky ones. I say that with all sincerity because although intuitive eating gave me the ability to get impossibly picky with food, I wasn't able to stop eating once I started.

Earlier I mentioned how runaway appetites are a sign of unfulfilled needs. That was my case. In hindsight, I realize that I was filled with anger, and the anger was covering up extreme sadness. Rather than being comfortable dealing with those unpleasant emotions, I ate and tried my best to sit on my feelings.

I had been conditioned by years of dieting to think of myself as a person with a huge appetite and so I feared my hunger way too much. Being hungry made me feel vulnerable and that was frightening, so I kept eating to fill up the emptiness. Consequently, I ate my way clear up to a thirty-five pound gain after nearly six years of successful maintenance on dieting. It was devastating to me to regain that weight and I searched desperately for answers to what was happening to me.

One of the people from whom I learned so much about myself and the roots of my eating obsession is the bestselling author and speaker, Geneen Roth. She is a woman with over forty years of experience in learning how to make peace with food. In her book, *Feeding the Hungry Heart: The Experience of Compulsive Eating*, she really hit the mark in explaining why so many of us struggle with a subconscious resistance to losing weight. She says,

> *"Fat becomes your protection from anything you need protection from; men, women, sexuality (blossoming or developed), frightening feelings of any sort; it becomes your rebellion, your way of telling your parents, your lovers, the society around you that you don't have to be who they want you to be. Fat becomes your way of talking. It says: I need help, go away, come closer, I can't, I won't, I'm*

angry, I'm sad. It becomes your vehicle for dealing with every problem you have. If you take away the fat without uncovering the needs it is expressing, you are left without a way to say what you do, don't want to, or don't know how to, or feel you can't say directly. Fat speaks for you."

Juicy Woman Note:

In the midst of my pain, I just couldn't stop eating. Because I was so dead set on not wanting to rely on what I considered tricks or coaching games to derail my appetite, I created my own misery. I never realized until after I gained those extra thirty-five pounds that it was my martyrdom that was keeping me fat.

Since I wasn't walking my talk and using the stress relief tools I was teaching my clients, I didn't have any other outlet for my stress or way to express my needs. As long as I kept eating like a train wreck, my relationship with food and my body was a mess.

I was pretty screwed up because although I was going through the motions of earnestly trying to learn how to listen to my body, I sabotaged myself at every turn by never allowing myself to feel hungry. I kept eating and the pounds piled on.

Boy was the cocky dieter in me eating crow. But in hindsight, I recognize that I needed to regain the weight I did in order to get back something that I had lost, my humility, my compassion for myself and other women struggling with emotional eating. I could never have served you if I would have been the way I was. I thought I had it all figured out and anyone who was overweight just wasn't trying hard enough. Boy did this experience give me a reality check.

> I guess you could say that I chose to take the long road or as my Nana would say, "the slow boat to China." Like many of my clients, your changes may be much faster, and you may breeze along, but remember to go at your own pace and stay true to yourself. That's why this is not a diet; it's a new way of living and thinking.

By teaching you methods of dealing with stress, I'm extending a helping hand and showing you that you can choose things besides eating to soothe yourself. But in all honesty, I don't always follow my own advice and I sometimes just choose to feel sorry for myself. At times I lapse and eat half a bag of Swedish® Fish or too much pasta. Eating may win out over dealing with my problems in the short term, but not long term anymore.

I've made a decision that I'm in no rush to get thinner. I'm taking this at my own pace and I hope you will too. It's thrilling to me beyond belief that the daily obsession that food used to occupy in my everyday life is gone and I can feel safe knowing there's chocolate in the house or freshly baked pie on the counter. Knowing that I can toss out bits of leftovers and perfectly good food that I don't want, without feeling a sense of being deprived or feeling compelled to do something to make it inedible is a huge step for me.

I still have my share of lapses and goofs, but now I use those opportunities to go deeper and explore what I'm really after, because now I truly know it's not about the food.

I refuse to use exercise for weight loss ever again and will only do it when the mood strikes me. That defiant little Earth® Shoe girl in me, says, "No. I don't want to." Exercise is no longer that same burning priority that it used to be in my life. I may get back there again one day, but just like eating, I have to find my own way and do it in my own time.

Step by step, little by little, I like the changes I've made and nobody has pushed them on me. I like to think of my way of getting thinner as the least invasive possible. I've been through all the insanity and now I just want to take it easy.

For now I'm happy with myself as I am because it's deeply important to me to let my outsides catch up to my insides. I have a lot of stuff to still sort through, especially in the area of feeling safe with sex and trusting men. I've decided that I'm willing to accept my curvy body as it is right now. It's so much nicer being able to actually like myself at a size sixteen as opposed to hating myself at a size eight. This new sense of self-acceptance has done wonders for my relationship with my husband.

So please take my experience for what it's worth. It's just a benchmark, but it will give you an idea of how this all works. You've been living for a long time under the tyranny of dieting, and eating and thinking in this new gentle way is going to be a big change.

I've decided to share my experience so you won't be inclined to beat up on yourself if you notice that you're knee deep in wanting to eat ice cream for every meal for weeks or months on end. It's natural, just like a toddler goes on food jags and will only want to eat hot dogs or broccoli for a week. Just when Mom's about to pull the hair out of her head and give up, the little one suddenly switches to crustless peanut butter sandwiches or boiled carrots.

The changes you'll be making are yours, nobody else's. Unless you allow them to, nobody will tell you what to eat by saying things like "I think it's time to stop eating those french fries, don't you?" But one day you'll notice, "Mmm, I think I'll have a baked potato instead of fries. After all, they weren't so great, too greasy." Your body will regulate itself once it knows that all is safe and there is no famine in your future.

Keep in mind that the goal in adapting this new way of eating is to create harmony and develop a new relationship with food. Eating less becomes a natural consequence of having a healthy relationship with food. You are healing the hurts in your history with food and your body.

The Later Lady

I'll just bet you're thinking that without the structure and clearly defined boundaries of dieting, it will be impossible to listen to your body, eat in accordance with your hunger, and slowly reshape your body. You probably also believe that within you lies a wretched feast beast, a bottomless pit of hunger and desire, making it impossible for you to control yourself around food.

Trapped by your own weakness, you become a victim of the voices. Maybe the *Later Lady* inside of you says "we'll listen to our body tomorrow."

Follow along with me and I'll teach you the importance of decoding your cravings, how to identify what's bothering you, and how to look beyond the obvious to understand what's driving your desire to eat.

When is Being Hungry Not Really Being Hungry?

If you're an emotional eater, you have a little voice in your brain that's pushing you to eat food when you're not hungry. The *Later Lady* is a character that Elaine, one of my clients, used to walk around with inside of her head. *The Later Lady* pushed Elaine to eat when she wasn't hungry. *The Later Lady* kept her picking or grazing on food all day long, eating pasta until she felt sick, or running to the safety of red velvet cake when things got tough.

I had another name for this *Later Lady*. I used to call it "my bottomless pit." By whatever name you choose to recognize your desperate urge to overeat, the effects are the same. It leaves you feeling weak and helpless.

See if you can recognize some of these *Later Lady*/bottomless pit statements.

 "Don't worry, honey, you go ahead and have that piece of cake today and we'll start dieting tomorrow."

 "Let's stop at the drive thru and get a burger, it smells so good."
"I think a donut would be the perfect reward for that great job you did."

 "Just one more piece of cake."
"You know you can't be trusted around an open bag of potato chips. Have one."

The primary difference between emotional eaters and naturally slender women who are able to eat in response to their body's biological hunger, is that emotional eaters are unfulfilled in their lives and have been conditioned to use food to fulfill the needs they are lacking.

I learned from Connirae Andreas, the creator of the *Naturally Slender Eating Strategy*, that naturally slender women are able to pinpoint what is lacking in their life and fill that need without resorting to overeating. They focus on paying attention to how they feel so they can express these feelings.

Decoding Your Cravings

Cravings can have both physical and emotional causes, and both are equally valid.

When you crave a food and you satisfy that craving, it is a healing experience. A chemical reaction is triggered in your body that produces a sense of wellbeing. The rush of feel-good chemicals flooding your brain sends signals down to the body to relax and feel good. This sensation fulfills a deep urge that sources back to a need to feel safe and satisfied. It's part of your basic survival instinct.

One of the foods you may recognize as making you feel good is chocolate. Many people have cravings for chocolate. Eating chocolate satisfies both emotional and physical needs. In my opinion, chocolate has gotten a bad reputation.

If you believe dessert and sweets can only be eaten after you've finished your main meal, you're setting yourself up to overeat. Dessert as a reward is probably responsible for more kids and adults getting fat than any other eating rule. Having an abundance of sweets on an already full stomach prevents you from fully enjoying the food you really want, which will keep you in a cycle of obsessing about it and overeating it every time you get the chance.

You may not want to eat a full meal, and may instead choose to just eat chocolate or some other dessert-like food. By doing this, you will reclaim your power over that food.

You will know when you want to choose a piece of fruit over a cookie, and I've learned it's best for this to become a natural and very organic transition. However, for now, in order for you to arrive at that place of safety, you'll want to explore the foods that have long been considered forbidden. As you progress and discover you can trust your body, you will eventually start craving foods that are considered good for you.

I encourage you to have an intense experience with the flavor of the food you crave. If that food is chocolate, then I would ask you to make it the main event for at least one meal. It will be an experience like no other. You may want to do this when you have some privacy, because it will require really focusing on the pleasure of eating chocolate in the moment. I've learned that savoring chocolate mindfully is a very different experience than grabbing it out of the kitchen cabinet and stuffing it into your mouth when someone's back is turned.

My recommendation is to treat chocolate and any other sweet craving as a regular food. I suggest doing this so your body can get the message that nothing is off limits and it's okay to eat anything you want. By extending that permission, your desire for chocolate will neutralize. That's when you'll notice that you can truly just eat one and be as happy as a clam.

Please know that I don't encourage you to eat chocolate all the time. Although it has some nutritional value, it doesn't make up a full day's eating requirement necessary for good nutrition. Although I don't advocate making a steady diet of chocolate or other sweets, I do want you to reclaim your power over those foods. I want you to truly realize that it is you who is in control and not the candy, cake, pies, or any other goodies that may now be calling your name.

Try It! – Giving Yourself Permission

In this activity, I encourage you to write a sentence or two responding to the following questions:

How entitled do you feel about having chocolate when you want it?

Does that idea make you feel safe or bring up fears?

What are those fears?

Next, take a tip from Geneen Roth and consider carrying around a bar of chocolate in your bag to have close to you. It's so nice to know that it's there when you want it.

Juicy Woman Note:

It's best to move at your own pace. If your forbidden desire is full fat yogurt and you only eat the nonfat variety, eke it up a bit and buy the low fat variety, rather than the higher fat type. Do what feels right to you. Pace yourself.

Nine Bags of Chips: A Cry for Independence

I've struggled with my own disordered eating for over thirty-four years. As of today, I've been doing intuitive eating for six years. Through this process, I've discovered my freedom.

I have moved way beyond knowing I can trust myself around an open bag of M&Ms® or a bag of chips, or even a fresh baked batch of chocolate chip cookies, brownies, or cake. I now know my favorite ice cream can actually develop freezer fuzz while standing for weeks uneaten in the freezer in my home.

In the early part of this process, I ate chips compulsively. At one time, I had nine bags of chips in my cabinet: Doritos®, Fritos®, Lays® potato chips, taco chips, Baked Cheetos®, Fried Cheetos®, cheese twists, Garden of Eatin'® blue corn chips, and pita chips. I ate all of them constantly. Each time I passed the kitchen, I grabbed another handful, completely disregarding my hunger. As time passed, I began to just eat them occasionally with a sandwich.

Eventually, I discriminated even more. A single taste would tell me it was too salty, or too cheesy, stale, the wrong size or shape, too thin or too thick, too twisted or too flat, too greasy, too, too, too. For months afterwards I would know I no longer liked them. I kept them in the cabinet and did a quick mental count each time I opened the door. Nine. I had nine bags of chips in the house that I could eat anytime I wanted to. I looked at them all arranged like soldiers on my bottom shelf. Nine. Andrea had nine bags of chips.

Those nine bags of chips helped me thumb my nose at the well-meaning but ignorant things my dad and stepmother, Rosie, had me do. They told me they counted all the potato chips in the house. They made me eat broccoli with lemon for lunch and cut the fat off my steak because they wanted to help me lose weight. Those nine bags of chips were a shout out against them. They were my cry for independence.

In 1973, when I moved in with Dad and Rosie, it was only about three months after my mother and stepfather, Jorge, had gotten married and moved to Florida. Over those three months I had gained thirty pounds. Nobody knew that I was trying to build a wall of fat to protect myself.

Once I started dieting, chips were among the first things to go, yet because Rosie was slim and Dad loved junk food, the foods I loved were always in the house, but I couldn't have them. Ah…so close and yet so far. Boy did I want them, so I did whatever I could to get them.

Being the resourceful gal I am, I wangled my way around every obstacle and planned my food attacks. Whenever Rosie would go downstairs to do laundry and leave me in the house alone, I raided the cabinets and refrigerator and shoved handfuls of tempting goodies, M&Ms®, cookies, donuts, bagels, cold leftovers in my mouth, just waiting to hear the outside elevator door close and listening for the key in the lock.

One day, Rosie came back from the basement after folding the clothes and called me into the kitchen. She had a strange look on her face. It was the serious one that intimidated me.

I searched Rosie's eyes for clues as to what she was thinking. Her big brown, warm loveable cow eyes told me something was brewing but I couldn't tell what it was. I knew I was in some kind of trouble.

Breaking the tense silence, she said, "Andrea, did you eat any of the potato chips?"

"No, I said. I would never."

Then she asked me again with her voice a little firmer this time. "Andrea, did you eat any of the potato chips?"

"No," I said, my voice cracking a bit.

Then she asked again, "Andrea, tell me the truth. Did you eat any of the potato chips?"

I swore up and down that I hadn't.

Then she said, "Andrea, I counted them."

I broke into sobs and confessed my guilty sin. At which point, she laughed and told me, "Silly — how am I going to count potato chips?"

Stung by my own innocence, and heaped on top of buckets of shame, I now felt stupid. This is the reason those nine bags stayed in my house even after I knew I didn't like them anymore. Now, knowing that I'm not a human garbage can indiscriminately devouring everything in my path, I am finally finding out for the first time who this Andrea really is.

What's Your Weakness?

For me, it was chips, for you it may be cookies, Grandma's blueberry pie, Mom's Sunday lasagna or some other food you feel you'll never get enough of. If you're depriving yourself and trying to avoid that food, it's holding your happiness hostage. As long as you feel you have to keep your distance, you'll never know who's really in control. As a result, you'll fall back into believing what other people have told you about yourself in relation to food.

As an emotional eater, you've developed preferences for which foods give you the ability to cope with your stress. A client of mine, Ayla, said that when she was in need of comfort, bread was her go-to, when she wanted excitement in life, she would have ice cream, and cake was for celebrating. Each type of food represented her way of engaging in life.

Like me and so many other women, Ayla was also sexually abused, so food became her safe way of expressing her emotions. Food gave her safety and refuge from the fear she faced in living day to day, feeling so empty and haunted by her memories of the past. When she joined my Losing Weight without Dieting program, she had no idea how much food had controlled her life. She went on to lose over sixty pounds by becoming more mindful of her choices. She credits the *EFT* work that I did with her as being the tipping point to understanding she thought she had nothing to live for but food. (I'll teach you the *EFT* process soon.)

When I led her through the *EFT* exercises, I remember saying, "Even though I have nothing else in my life but food to love and care for me, I deeply and completely love and accept myself. Even though I can't trust anyone else in my life besides food—it will never let me down—I love and accept myself anyway. Even though up until now, food has been so meaningful in my life, it's filled up all the emptiness and made the sadness go away, I can choose to take care of myself, I can eat what I want, when I want, and not worry about dieting. I can choose to eat or not. It's always my choice.

Throughout the *EFT* process she sobbed quietly. I knew a lot of energy was moving in her body.

Immediately after that session, she looked at her life and realized the beliefs that kept her running to food were the result of old thinking and feeling so unsafe. She realized she had an adoring, faithful husband, friends who supported and loved her, and a career that made her heart sing. From that point of understanding, she said it was easy to make choices that honored her. She is still amazed to this day how she was able to go on an anniversary cruise with her husband, eat everything she wanted, and return from vacation weighing two pounds less.

Before she had the realization of how wonderful her life really was, eating had been her way of filling her emptiness. It was as if a gaping hole lived inside of her, aching to be filled. Yet one of the constants for her was that she rarely gave herself time to enjoy whatever she was eating. As much as Ayla professed to love food, she rarely got a chance to really taste it.

The Message in My Applesauce:
The Value of Slowing Down and Tasting Your Food

One day I woke up early, around 5:00 a.m., actually feeling hungry, or so I thought. For the past several months I had gotten into a comfortable pattern where I didn't feel hungry or want to eat breakfast until about 11:30. Back in the days when I was dieting, that was absolutely unheard of; I was always starving as soon as I woke up. Now, especially if I'm busy, I can go for hours without the first glimmer of hunger.

After deciding that I wanted something light, I chose applesauce and spooned a few spoonfuls into a dish. Feeling a bit pressured to get my day started and finally finish the editing on my book, I ate the first bite quickly with a kind of desperation. I didn't even taste the applesauce. Then I realized that I was stressed about the book and this was showing up in a resurfacing of my old habit of eating fast.

Separating myself from my feelings of urgency for a moment, I wondered what would happen if I ate the next bite more slowly. I noticed that my thoughts instantly changed and began to slow down. As I took another even more conscious spoonful, I noticed that the applesauce was much more tart than I would have liked. Curiosity rose up in me and I found myself thinking, "Why do I want this now? It's not even that good. It's been so long since I've had an early breakfast, why now and what does this applesauce remind me of?"

Then it hit me as I looked down at the dish. It was as though I had been transported back in time to my Nana's kitchen long ago. In my memory, I was sitting at her sparkling white kitchen table contentedly surveying the apples we had picked together. They were strewn all over her counter top, and I imagined I smelled the wafting scent of the cinnamon soaked apples gently simmering on the stove top waiting to be made into fresh pies and apple sauce for the upcoming church bazaar.

As I continued to sit and stare into the dish of apple sauce, I went a bit deeper into the memory and could see the patterned wallpaper adorning the kitchen walls and feel the cool, hard flooring under my feet. In this lovely memory, I was sitting in my favorite chair looking across the small kitchen out the window at the magnificent view of the Hudson River and the New York City skyline. I watched cars cruising along the George Washington Bridge. I could even see my Nana, all smiles, as she stood at the stove in her frilly hand-sewn apron peeling and dicing the apples with her deft fingers moving so quickly. I could even make out the details of her wedding ring.

Caught up in my reverie, I had one more spoonful of applesauce and realized that I no longer wanted it. I took the rest and put it away for later. I knew that the applesauce had already done its job. It brought me back to a place where I remembered feeling such love and warmth and happiness.

Here's the takeaway from this story. Different foods have different associations in your brain. This is why emotional eaters get cravings for certain foods. You are actually craving the emotion that the food holds from the memories that are connected to the food. If you are an emotional eater, food has more meanings and connections for you than people who don't feel so attached to eating.

When you take an extra moment and linger over your food and ask yourself what it reminds you of, you are putting yourself in the position of being an observer. It's like being able to unzip your skin and step out of your body and watch yourself from a distance. When you can do that, you are able to notice more because your vision is not clouded by emotion. You are no longer unconscious of what you are doing.

It is when we are unaware of what we are eating that we eat more, because we don't experience the satisfaction that comes from the enjoyment of food.

So let's be clear, from this point onward when I talk about getting satisfaction from food, I'm talking way beyond what you can taste. I'm interested in you getting to the core of what you feel. When you do this, many times you'll be able to recognize foods that are actually quite mediocre tasting that you craved before.

You may choose to eat those foods that don't taste as delicious as you may want them to, but one bite, one cookie or a muffin, or a single taste of whatever it is, will satisfy you in the same way that it used to take a dozen bites or more. When you extract the feeling from the food, the food just becomes food again. In some ways that's really great, and in some ways it's also very sad, but true.

Don't get me wrong, you can still completely override this awareness and go back to unconscious eating again. You can choose to overeat those foods, but the difference is it is now a choice, rather than a must. You will learn that you can indeed control yourself, but you may not always want to and that's fine, because it's essential that you always go at your own pace.

What do you think of slowing down and noticing what you are reminded of when you eat your food? Who knows? Like me, it may change the flavor completely. You may need to just sit in silence for a few minutes and really let those memories seep into your soul, and enjoy knowing they will live in your heart forever.

Remember, it's not the food you're seeking, it's the feeling. Go for the feelings. Notice them. Amazing things will come of it.

Now, without further ado, let me share with you a process that I created in the first few weeks of trying to figure this all out for myself. It's called Mindful and Gentle Eating.

Interrupt the Pattern Of Emotional Eating:
The Mindful and Gentle Eating Exercise

Mindful and Gentle Eating allows you to reawaken your sense of how to eat mindfully and in full conscious awareness of your thoughts and feelings.

If you're inclined to be a fast eater, like me, I know how hard it is for you to eat more slowly. Eating fast is a sign of compulsion that stems from fear of lack. Many non-diet weight loss programs advocate eating slowly as a means of breaking the compulsion that drives speed eating. I don't agree with that.

As a gal who has always eaten very fast, I resented it when anyone told me to eat slowly. The resistance you feel is that little survival part of you that refuses to be made to feel unsafe ever again. I promise I won't ever take anything away from you. My only desire is to add to what you already have.

I encourage you to learn by giving you the opportunity to enjoy contrast. I believe that choices are essential to being happy. In order to create new habits effortlessly, you have to feel really good about what you choose. You'll notice in this exercise, I'll ask you to eat slowly and then I'll encourage you to eat at your normal pace, whatever that may be, and then alternate between the two speeds. This is done so your brain can reorganize itself and find an intermediate speed that will become a new comfort level for you.

Now, if you're ready, let's begin:

Try It! – Mindful and Gentle Eating

Choose to eat anything you want, it's up to you. This exercise is done to consciously slow you down. You may find it a challenge at first, later it will become a joy.

A. Find five emotional food connections in your life that have in the past compelled you to eat when you were not hungry.

B. What has that food meant to you?

C. What memories rise to the surface when you think about the food?

D. Go out and get that food and bring it home or prepare it.

Before you are ready to sit down and eat your chosen food, set your place with the appropriate silverware and a napkin (even if you are eating a pint of ice cream or a sandwich, make sure that you at least have a napkin). You don't have to serve your food in a bowl or a plate unless you choose to do so.

1. Bring your journal to the table.

2. Have your silverware and optional plate or bowl ready along with your napkin.

---

3. Place the food on the table.
4. Sit down facing it.
5. Look at it.
6. Smell it.
7. Be present with your feelings as they surface.
8. Notice those feelings.
9. Sit for a few moments and write down your observations of the food and your feelings connected to it.
10. Close your journal.
11. Pause and think for a moment, offering thanks for this food.
12. Pick up your utensil.
13. Take a small bite or spoonful.
14. Place the food in your mouth and allow it to rest on the tip of your tongue.
15. Swirl it around in your mouth for 3 to 7 seconds.
16. Notice the sensations that come up for you.
17. Slowly chew it or allow it to gently glide down your throat.
18. Put down your fork or spoon and resist picking it up for a moment. If you have to sit on your hands, then do it.
19. Just sit with those feelings for 10 -15 seconds.
20. Repeat the process from stage 12-19 until you are satisfied. Notice the degree of that satisfaction. Do this at least three times during the week. The rest of the times eat at your normal pace. See what you discover.

Now that you have a sense of a new way of being and acting around food, and have a better understanding of the essential importance of treating yourself with more kindness, you're ready to start learning why you must commit to being your own best friend.

Wrapping Up
Chapter 3: Intuitive Eating: Self-Acceptance
Starts with Making Peace with Food

Here are the juiciest bits covered in this section. Savor them mindfully.

- We're always teaching others how to treat us. And it's never too late to pull in the reigns, take back control, and demand respect.

- There is so much more to life than obsessing about food and weight. When you understand this, you'll be in awe of the power you have over your choices.

- By giving up dieting, you are not giving up! In fact it's probably the kindest thing you'll ever do for yourself.

- Cravings got you by the nose? That's because you always end up wanting what you don't believe you can have. To break the cycle of deprivation, stop dieting.

- By eating what you really want, you will quickly develop the ability to be discriminating and discover that you truly can trust yourself around temptation.

- When you make a habit of eating when you are physically hungry, it becomes effortless to say "no" when you're not feeling that physical urge to eat.

- To reclaim your power over food and increase your sense of self respect, eat what you want in full view of others. Tell people that comments about your eating and your body are no longer acceptable.

- Painful and overwhelming emotions like sadness, loneliness, and anger can feel like deep pits of emptiness that can easily be confused with hunger.

- If you're depriving yourself of foods you love, food is holding your happiness hostage.

Chapter 4
Committing to Being
Your Own Best Friend

"Friendship with oneself is all-important because without
it one cannot be friends with anyone else in the world."
– Eleanor Roosevelt

If your friend calls you on the phone in tears asking for help, feeling crushed and devastated by life, you probably wouldn't hesitate to comfort her. When your precious kitty gets into a scrap with the neighbor's crabby calico, you're always there to protect your baby. But when it's you who's in trouble, needing help, feeling weak, unloved and unwanted, we tend to beat up on ourselves and find fault with every single thing we do.

Despite being brilliant at taking care of others, if you've never had an advocate stand up for you, it's not easy to take on that role to actually stop, get off the blame train, and know how to lovingly support yourself. It doesn't come naturally. We learn how to care for ourselves based on what we see and what we've been taught by our parents, caregivers, and their role models.

Since children learn what they live, there's a good chance you picked up the habit of overeating and trash talking your body as a kid. Maybe you spent hours, days, weeks, or years listening to Mom or Dad, Aunt Emma, or Grandma obsess over everything you ate. Perhaps, like me, you came to the conclusion that you were fat and ugly and if only you were thinner, you'd be okay.

However, your body hating habits may have come from a much less obvious source. You may have had them passed down to you, second hand like Grae Drake, who nominated herself to appear on the show, "*How to Look Good Naked.*" You'll read her story later in this chapter. Grae spent years listening to her parents obsess about her sister's weight, swearing that no matter how she looked, she'd never be good enough.

Warts and All...

The next step in the process of gaining more self-acceptance and in making peace with food and friends with your body, is for you to hold the little girl inside of you. Cradle her in the palm of your hand, committing to nurture her—yourself—warts and all, and become your own best friend. This is the only way you can break out of the rut of endlessly beating yourself up and hating your body, which threatens to keep you in perpetual poor-me mode.

It's those painfully negative "I hate my fat thighs" thoughts that have you twisting in the wind, buying into the illusion that it's your body that's the problem. It's not. It's your thoughts. It's the mistaken belief that this is all there is, you can't do any better, and that you are hopelessly dead-locked, unable to change the part of your life that isn't working. It's the feeling that you're cursed and can't do anything about it.

As you begin to move beyond feeling helpless around food and obsessed with your weight, you'll notice that the way you feel about yourself will change. Your life will become more fulfilling in the areas where it is currently lacking because it will feel like you've been given permission to come out of hiding.

Imagine what it would be like to have the power to recognize that you are a worthwhile person no matter what! How would that change your life? What would you do differently? The possibilities are endless. How kickin' cool is that?

My Fat Thighs: More Sighs over Size

I recall one time soon after the Lerner's incident, near my twelfth birthday and after taking the Silva Mind Control® seminar with my dad, he said to me, "Andrea, I could give you the gift of thinner thighs by focusing on it, but you have to do it yourself. You're responsible for your own thoughts and your own thighs."

I knew what he meant. I knew that I just had to think of myself as skinny and see my thighs as thin. But I kept asking myself, "Why can't I do that?" After all, I wanted those thin thighs so badly I could almost taste them.

I berated myself constantly for my lack of faith and my weak-willed thinking, feeling deep down inside that I would never be equal to the challenge my fat little body had presented. In order to get thinner, I had to be constantly on guard, waiting to arm wrestle down my negative thoughts about my fat thighs in order to make room for a vision of seeing them as thinner. It seemed impossible. A part of me knew I was just lying to myself.

Day after day I couldn't help but notice that my fat thighs were as big as ever. But I kept telling myself, "I love my legs, they're strong and beautiful." Despite what I was saying, it seemed like I kept getting fatter.

Every day I walked into the bathroom, stared at my reflection in the full-sized wall mirror and stood in judgment of my big butt and fat thighs. With a desperate prayer in my heart, I turned my pear shaped body every which way to see if my wishing and hoping by some miracle had made them smaller. But it hadn't, nothing changed, they were as fat and ugly as ever. It seemed like they were there to stay ... forever.

After a while, I became convinced that no amount of dieting, no amount of exercising, and no amount of positive thinking was ever going to change my fat, ugly body. But despite how I really felt, I still tried desperately to convince myself that I could change the way I saw my thighs.

And so the struggle ensued. I was consumed with how long it was taking, I worried about each negative thought I encountered. Having learned a basic understanding of the law of attraction, I was certain that my negative thinking was delaying my progress. But I couldn't stop obsessing over how much I hated those fat thighs, why other girls had skinnier thighs, and why I looked so disproportionate in my clothes. I was so clear about what I didn't want—fat, husky, chunky, pudgy thighs and my big, fat, ugly butt. I kept thinking about how angry I felt and how mortifying it was to have these huge, fat, ugly thighs.

Sadly, it was no surprise that I didn't get a pair of thin thighs for my twelfth birthday, or any other for that matter. But until last year I wasn't willing to be okay with the ones that I have. I didn't understand that by wanting thinner thighs so much I was creating a huge amount of tension and resistance in my life. By doing this, I would always be on the outside looking in, wondering why I hated my body so much.

Now I know it was my constant, never-ending obsession with my thighs that prevented me from being able to actually manifest what I wanted. Even during the times in my life when I was thin, I failed to recognize that my thighs were not as horrible as I thought. The point is, no matter what the size of my thighs, I wasn't able to see them realistically. This was my curse.

Unlike me, you may not have any issues with your thighs, but you may hate your butt, flat chest, flabby arms, muffin top, or saggy breasts. None of us are perfect, but we are still lovable and worthy anyway. That is because we are so much more than just a collection of body parts. Yet we don't see it, and we blindly walk through life disregarding, disrespecting, and disowning our bodies.

I want you to embrace that little girl in you who represents your imperfect self, the one who you have been trying to push away and ignore. You know what I'm talking about. It's that often neglected part of you that holds your self-esteem hostage.

I'm encouraging you to pull out that picture of yourself and have it on hand because by seeing yourself as already lovable, precious, and worthy, you'll be giving that neglected part of you the love and respect, attention and compassion it needs. That's the real nourishment you crave; self-acceptance. No amount of food will ever fill those gaps. Only you can.

Are you willing? Are you open to accepting that less than perfect, droopy, saggy, baggy, wrinkly, dimply, fat, and wobbly older version of you? Are you willing to dig deep, look beyond the surface, stop judging your overeating, and find some compassion so you can finally become your own best friend? Here's what I learned when I decided to stop judging my binges and beating up on myself long enough to be curious as to why I just couldn't stop eating.

My Turning Point: 35 Pounds Later

One day, after months of eating out of control, I stood naked in front of my mirror, horrified by what I saw. There she stood, the old Andrea, that sad and pathetic little girl, the one I'd' tried so hard to forget. I hated her with those damned Earth® Shoes and fat girl clothes. This pathetic doormat of a woman was how I saw myself in private. It was the reason I hid from confrontation, allowed family and "friends," employees, business associates, and anyone else to walk all over me. It was why I feared men, settled for scraps, refused to demand what I deserved, avoided social interaction, and struggled with so many trust issues.

Glaring at my reflection, I watched the tears roll down my cheeks. With disgust, I noticed the roundness of my stomach, the heavy arms of a linebacker, and those damned ever present thighs. I knew it would be so easy to keep on hating myself, but that moment I realized I had a choice. I could either choose to love me exactly as I was, or continue fighting against myself, living forever in fear of food, restricted by a diet.

That moment I knew that the way that I felt about my thighs was just a metaphor for the way I felt about myself—disgusted and ashamed. Because I was so used to giving away my time and talents, I had no sense of personal value. I had created my own misery, allowing people to take advantage of me because I didn't think I deserved anything better than I had. I thought that because I was blessed I always had to be the giver. With my nest egg and financial security now gone, I was facing a mountain of debt. Despite knowing that I had to start charging for my services, a part of me just couldn't do it.

A woman on my forum named Anna sent me an email, begging me to help her. She was desperately unhappy with her body and felt completely out of control around food. She offered to pay me an astronomical sum to go to her home in Manhattan and coach her. Feeling undeserving and lacking confidence in myself, I ignored her email, attempting to push her and her money away. Not being one to give up, she continued to send me emails requesting my coaching. I kept making excuses. Although I knew I was being foolish rejecting her, I kept up the charade for months because I just couldn't place a value on my services. Then one day I met a woman named Linda Storey and everything changed.

Juicy Woman Note:

Now, as I look back on the occurrences of the past years, I realize that my experience with sexual abuse opened the door for me to believe that I was unworthy. Once the door was open, other people with less than honorable intentions came in and reinforced my already negative and limiting belief.

The takeaway for you is that if you've ever had an experience in your past that created a similar belief, and if there's still a negative charge when you think about it, it's still triggering that memory that keeps you stuck, feeling less than and not good enough. Unless you do something to neutralize the charge on that emotion, food will always beckon to you, promising a quick feel-good fix.

Your body is only one frontier. There is much more to your life than your flesh and bones. However, if you start to notice like I did, that the limiting beliefs and self-talk used for talking about your body are also now leaching into other areas, you must run, don't walk to get help and support. I urge you to accept my story as the cautionary tale it is. Know that left to run rampant, these sick and twisted beliefs of unworthiness, unlovableness, and incapability will ruin your life, right down to your purse strings.

A Soul Plan for Prosperity

Linda Storey is a dear friend and colleague who invited me to join her *Soul Plan for Prosperity* program. After more than a decade of experience in banking, Linda decided to share with women the secrets she had learned in creating a successful, soul-centered business, using a balance of heart, intuition, and head. Going through that experience was a real head turner for me. It was exactly what I needed to release my old victim story and get a new, healthy understanding of my value.

Unlike my father's tough and cold-hearted knock 'em down spit 'em out criteria for success, Linda's seven elements of financial freedom blew my mind because I realized I had all of them in spades. The following seven qualities are what Linda names as the foundation of being a great businessperson:

"faith, vision, playfulness, compassion,

contribution, awareness, resourcefulness."

Now I had something I could sink my teeth into. I could relate to each of these characteristics because they were me. Yet these were the same qualities my father had recognized in me and saw fit to constantly belittle. Now it was time to marry my intelligence with my deeper, more spiritual, and extremely well developed intuitive wisdom. But in order to do that successfully, I had many years of negative programming I needed to release. I sought help from someone who could understand me.

I found help in the form of a dear friend who agreed to be my buddy coach. Every Saturday we would get together and coach each other using *EFT*. She's chosen to remain anonymous, so I'll refer to her as my tapping angel.

Between doing Linda's program and working with my tapping angel, it took a lot of tapping and a ton of tears to move from where I was to where I am today. I had to get serious about venting my hurt and angry emotions before I recognized that I was more than ready to coach others.

One day I shared with the Soul Plan group the story of Anna, the client who was pursuing me to coach her. They challenged me to get back in touch with her and make arrangements to coach her immediately. When we reconnected, Anna was so thrilled to hear from me. We made arrangements to meet at my office the following week for a private coaching session. That day we spent several hours together for which she gladly paid me $200/hr.

With my Soul Sister support team's help, I finally realized it was my own experience and journey overcoming emotional eating that made me such a valuable commodity to my clients. Because I was able to relate to them, speak their language, and offer them solid solutions to their problems, they felt safe trusting me. Imagine my surprise when Anna told me exactly the same thing.

Gradually, as I began focusing on doing what I loved and finally charging my value, I came to the realization that the old voice inside my head telling me for years that I was stupid, incompetent, naïve, and a miserable business person, was my father's, not mine.

I started to live by an understanding of the concept of "Universal Good," where each person involved in a transaction benefits equally. After doing much soul searching and personal growth work around this concept, I finally decided to recognize my value in every aspect of my life, not only in terms of money.

Overall, this process of committing to stand by myself through thick and thin has been a real growth experience for me. Recently I made the decision to stop stewing in my victim mentality and quietly resenting my father for his greed.

The biggest lesson I learned during this time that I want to pass on to you, was that making peace with food was the much easier part of my challenge. My real issue was making peace with my body and thinking of myself as worthy. I needed to learn to clearly state my value to everyone, most especially family members.

As an intensely private person, I've had to struggle with a big part of me that wanted nothing to do with this whole idea of being **"The Juicy Woman."** I resisted putting myself in the position of being an example and teaching others the benefit of what I had learned. After all, it makes me pretty vulnerable.

Yet I am driven to help other women and am fueled by my desire to pay my many blessings forward by supporting others to overcome their pain. I am committed to doing whatever I have to do to leap over my own fears and insecurities in order to share my wisdom so that others will be able to avoid similar circumstances.

To get to that place of willingness, I had to become a role model for self-love and compassion. Now, as I think back on it, I realize it's no wonder that I've struggled with so many body issues for so long. Like so many emotional eaters, my biggest mistake was looking for love in all the wrong places. I was seeking validation outside myself and hoping I could find the secret to happiness in dieting.

To combat that, I had to step out of seeing myself through my father's eyes and see myself instead through the eyes of love. I knew I could never stop hating my body as long as I continued to see me through his fat-phobic eyes. I had to free myself of the last vestiges of his control over me. It was time to fire my inner critic and transform it from the nasty body-bashing boogeyman it had become to a gentle and kind loving coach. It was high time for a change.

I had to switch my focus, and that meant finding role models, real women who were stepping out and living life, fearlessly, fully aware of their talents and following their passion, unencumbered by the size of their thighs. That's just about the time when I found the show, *How to Look Good Naked*.

How to Look Good Naked: Lifetimes' Reality TV Comes to the Rescue for Body Haters

I'm a huge fan of reality TV because I'm fascinated by what drives people to do the things they do. In January of 2008, a new type of make-over show made its debut: *How to Look Good Naked*, or *HTLGN*. Unlike the many other makeover shows that have become so popular, *HTLGN's* emphasis is on striking a balance between inner and outer transformation as opposed to just creating external change via a new hairstyle, makeup, and better clothes. As a coach, I can tell you this is the best medicine I know to combat the body hatin' blues.

As I sat watching the two pilot shows back to back, I was mesmerized by how gentle and caring Carson Kressley was in his position as host of the show. He is warm, funny, and endearing, and a true supporter of women who struggle with emotional issues that undermine their self-esteem.

From the first day, standing beside them at the mirror while they wear only their bra and panties, Carson leads each of the women on his show through a personal transformation spanning five days ending in a big reveal on a live billboard after a professional photo shoot is done tastefully in the nude.

The next day they are led to expand their image of themselves by doing something they have always wanted to do but have been afraid to attempt. The premise behind this is that since they already went through the fire of doing a nude photo shoot, they can now easily glide back into their lives taking new risks moving forward.

In my quest to explore and share these women's thoughts and feelings with you, I realize it's not realistic to expect you to run out and nominate yourself for the show. That's crazy. I just want to encourage you to take some of the nuggets they have to share and learn how you, too, can love your body right now. To sweeten the pot, they've also added bits of their experiences working with Carson and being on the show, so you also get to enjoy a peek behind the scenes of one of Lifetime TV's most famous reality shows. Here are a couple of their stories:

Shannon Flores:

Shannon Flores is 29 years old. She's a beautiful, curvaceous, plus-size woman who lives in sunny California with her husband, Jeremy, and four children, Ryan, Samantha, Kaitlyn, and Kyra. Although she has a pool in her back yard, prior to being on *HTLGN*, she never used to enjoy it because she was embarrassed to be seen by her husband or the neighbors in her bathing suit. After having four children back to back, she said, "My chest just drooped. My hips got bigger. My thighs got larger. My butt got bigger. It seemed like every part of my body just fell apart. It's not fun what babies do to your body."

Shannon was used to taking care of everybody and that meant she always came up last on her list. Hoping to one day get thinner, she refused to buy new clothes and hid behind her old dull and drab mommy duds. Avoiding mirrors, bathing suits, and anything revealing her curvy body, Shannon felt uncomfortable with her plus-size figure and was at the constant mercy of her nagging and nasty inner critic.

She admits to not being as physical with her husband as she'd like to have been, saying, "It definitely put a damper on our relationship. And with the lights off, I still felt uncomfortable." Keeping herself tightly closed in a box, she knew she wasn't really living. She admitted to being ashamed and disgusted with her body, not wanting even her husband to see her naked.

Shannon's motivation for change, and the deciding factor that pushed her to participate in the show, was her love for her children. Her body hating ways had begun to creep into their language. That's when she realized how her own issues with her body were affecting her kids.

During the time she was on the show, Carson Kressley helped her to see her body in a new way. One of the things she experienced was hearing what other people had to say about her body. That was when Shannon got a chance to see herself from someone else's perspective.

In my interview with Shannon, she candidly shared with me, "When they stuck that picture of my body on that truck and they asked everybody, 'What do you see? What do you see?' Not one of them said, 'You know she's perfect. She's got a model's body.' Because I don't. But they pointed out the good things. Look at her eyes. Look at her skin color. Look at this. Look at that. And I started realizing, I'm not half bad. My body is more than my thighs. That's not the area everyone is looking at. So I started realizing that I need to look at life that way too. I need to start looking at all the positive things, even if they're little. I just need to point out those and start focusing more on them."

In another perception correction exercise that Carson led her through, she was asked if she could visually determine if a woman's hips were bigger or smaller than hers. In every instance she was wrong. After realizing that her perception of her hips was so completely off track, Shannon marveled at the beauty of all the women who stood before her. She realized if they can feel good about their body and have confidence in their beauty knowing their hips are even wider than mine, then what's stopping me from feeling good about my body now?

On the day after she did her nude photo shoot, Shannon knew that she could do anything. Carson gave her a challenge to participate in a swim suit fashion show, and she knew that she could do it. Feeling fabulous, she flaunted her curvy confidence for over 500 people and her family in a swimsuit fashion show. As Shannon unwrapped her pareo, baring her thighs, with that reveal she shed years of old body hatred.

Now Shannon enjoys her pool at least twice a week, either to swim or sunbathe, saying, "I don't care. I walk around in my front yard with my bathing suit. Life is way too short to be concerned about what other people think about me." After gaining back thirty of the sixty pounds she lost on Weight Watchers® following the birth of her last child, she said, "I'm pretty good. I feel great. I look good and I'm not going to put any more effort into trying to lose weight." When I asked her to share some special advice with women who are in that spot now where she was then, she said, "Just feel good with who you are in the moment, right now."

Shannon's struggles with her heavy thighs are easy to relate to for many women, including me. Because she has an hourglass figure it's easy to notice that she has a set of thighs. Yet women come in a variety of sizes and shapes. Although they may not be perceived by others as being overweight, they still feel fat and hate their bodies. The sad thing is that they are automatically discounted and many times rejected by other heavier women because we do tend to play body comparison games.

Grae Drake: Health Minded Reality TV Show Producer Seeks End to Body Loathing

Back in October, I sent a broadcast to the women on my **Juicy Woman** email/newsletter subscriber list letting them know that I planned to interview Grae Drake. In the broadcast, I included Grae's after photo showing her to be a stunning woman in a beautiful red dress. In response to the email I sent, one of my clients wrote back saying,

"I know firsthand how as women our minds can run riot when it comes to body image and how when we look in the mirror we can really distort our own image....but I'm looking at this woman below and I don't know what the problem is. I'm looking at her arms thinking I would love to have arms that looked that toned."

I wrote back to her saying, "Grae's story is an excellent example of the mania that we live with every day. My book is intended to address size acceptance, and that includes women of all shapes and sizes."

As I learned firsthand, you don't have to be fat or ugly to believe you are. When I interviewed the women for this book and the rest of the Lovin' series to follow, I chose a variety of body types so that you could see that body bashing is not only done by women who are overweight. Our thinner sisters like Grae Drake are also really struggling with lovin' the skin they're in.

Grae is a twenty-eight year old film editor who lives in Los Angeles. Being healthy has always been important to her. At 6 feet tall and 170 pounds, despite all her efforts at being fit, nothing Grae did was good enough for her.

Whenever Grae would talk about her body, she would always concentrate on what she considered to be her flaws. Comparing herself to other women, Grae always seemed to come up short.

She never once considered that she had issues with a low self-esteem because she reasoned that she didn't have an eating disorder that required treatment. She knew she was smart and there were many things about herself that she liked, but her body wasn't one of them.

Grae never heard her mom say anything nice about her. She said "Ever since I was young, my sister has had a weight problem and I heard my parents give her a hard time, and I always heard my sister say mean things about her body. So, for me, whenever anyone would offer me a compliment, I would just shrug it away. I was so tired of hearing anyone talk about weight, I just ignored it."

When I asked Grae what inspired her to nominate herself for the show, she said, "I was obsessing about what I had been eating lately. I was thinking about it, and turning it over and over in my head, like when your mind just won't stop. After several hours, I remember hearing a voice coming into my head that said, 'What if your commitment to health and fitness is really just a veiled way of not being okay with yourself?'"

Grae was stunned by the question and wondered if she was wasting her time worrying so much about what she looked like and what she ate. She said, "I kept thinking that the saddest thing I could think of would be turning eighty and thinking, 'Man, when I was twenty-seven, I was a total hottie and I didn't appreciate it.'

"And I fell asleep with that peaceful thought, 'Wow! I kind of get it.'"

The next morning she was looking on Craig's List and saw an ad that said, "Do you feel like your body image is holding you back from doing something important?" That was exactly what she needed to get unstuck.

When Carson first met Grae, he asked her, "Grae, why am I here? You're so gorgeous." She was dumbfounded and realized that she didn't know why she felt the need to be on the show.

When we discussed her view on what Carson had told her about taking risks, she shared, her insights saying, "I think about it almost daily, because I don't do things when I don't know how they are going to turn out. I see that operating in my daily life. I will shy away from going out on a limb because

I don't know what's going to happen when I get there. And now since going on the show, every time I notice that I try to counteract it as much as I can. So, if I'm having a moment like, 'I don't know how this is going to turn out. I'm not going to do it.' I say, 'No. You're going to do it and it's going to be great.'"

In an attempt to correct her flawed perceptions about her body, Carson showed her three poster images of three headless women's bodies with different color and complexions and asked her which one she liked best. She was automatically drawn to the second image because, "It was a woman with a really athletic frame."

After he unpeeled the paper from the poster, Grae saw that it was actually her body that she was admiring. She was stunned. In a private moment, the executive producer, Riaz Patel, took Grae aside and said to her, "Do you see how mean we are to ourselves when we know it's us?"

Grae said, "It really hit me hard to know that I make such a huge effort to be nice to people all the time, and to treat people with respect, and to do the right thing, and to make people feel good. And I had not ever done that for myself."

She was shocked because like so many of us, we pride ourselves on being self-aware. Yet we fail to consider that we hold others in a much higher regard than we think of ourselves.

From her time with Carson, crying standing at the mirror, her magical experience posing nude on top of a famous Hollywood landmark, to the moment when she danced the tango in front of an audience of friends, family, and supporters, numbering in the hundreds, Grae transformed from an extra sleepwalking through each day to the star of her own life.

As you can see, both Grae and Shannon experienced a perceptual shift. Despite not actually losing weight, undergoing surgery, or changing their appearance in any radical way, other than hair, makeup, and clothes, they learned to accept and love their bodies exactly as they were. During their time with Carson, Shannon and Grae were both able to have compassion for themselves and develop a new appreciation and awareness of their natural gifts. Their experience of being on the show was equivalent to getting a self-image makeover.

What would it take for you to get a perception correction? What would it take for you to find compassion for yourself and start to accept your body?

Finding Your Way Toward Compassion for Your Inner Penelope

The movie *Penelope* is a sweet, modern fairytale with a unique twist on the classic happily ever after romance. In this film, a la Cinderella meets The Ugly Duckling, Penelope is an heiress born under an unusual curse.

Born with a pig snout in place of a nose, Penelope's curse could only be broken when a high society blue blood accepted her as she was. Her family was so ashamed of her deformity that at one point they felt the need to fake her death.

In an effort to break the horrible curse, Penelope's mother and father tried to find her a suitable husband. All the blue blooded prospects swore they would love and accept Penelope, yet couldn't after they actually came face to face with her disfigurement. One day a fellow named Max came to meet Penelope. Everyone wondered, "Would he be the one to break the curse?"

The Curse

The truth is we all have what we would consider our curse.

 Mine has been my thighs and my history of abuse.

 My mom, Doris, has always been hung up on her nose and embarrassed by the fact that she stutters. When she was a young girl her nose was broken when she got in the middle of a football pass. Soon after, she started stuttering.

 My step mother, Rosie, as stunning as I and everyone else thought she was, always said she hated her breasts. She complained that they were too small. Also the fact that she couldn't have her own children was devastating to her.

 My Nana, Helen's, curse was her knees and her hands. She always complained and called herself knock-kneed. She never felt comfortable wearing shorts and despite the fact that she was so talented in all forms of handiwork, she struggled bitterly with painful arthritis in all the joints of her hands.

Curses. All of them.

Heather Magee, Grae Drake, Shannon Flores, Layla Morrell, and Kelly Park are five beautiful women who nominated themselves for the show, "How to Look Good Naked." Like myself and so many other women, they also struggled with their own curses which caused them to hate and resent their bodies. Each had a different reason:

 Heather's curse was all the scars covering her body following her many heart surgeries. She thought her scars made her look like a monster. Heather was so deathly ashamed of them she hid in clothes that covered her nearly head to toe and did everything she could to avoid going out in public.

 Kelly felt the need to hide her post pregnancy tummy in maternity clothes years after her daughter, Sidney was born. Ashamed of her new curvy, mommy-shaped body, she avoided having sex with her loving hubby, John, for nearly five years.

 Grae hated her hips. Her obsession with her imperfections and her tendency to compare her body shape and size to other women, caused her to avoid taking risks in her life and doing many of the things she loved like dancing and singing.

 Shannon despised her thighs. Despite having a wonderful pool in her backyard, she avoided wearing a bathing suit and swimming for fear that her neighbors would see her and judge her thighs as fat.

 No matter how many diets Layla attempted and how much exercise she did, she just couldn't come to grips with her shapely and curvy hips.

After each of these women went on the show their "curses" were lifted. Although nothing actually was done to change them physically, they transformed nonetheless.

Heather's scars didn't fade. Kelly's tummy stayed the same. Grae's hips didn't budge. Shannon's thighs remained the same, and Layla still had her very curvy hourglass shape. None of these women did anything to change the way they looked on the outside. They all came to the show with their curses intact.

Some were visible to the audience and others were not, but nonetheless their perception of their curse was still there. Yet after having the experience of being on the show, they each left with their curses lifted, feeling like new, beautiful women. They didn't go on any diet or endure plastic surgery. Their bodies remained the same, but their perception of them was altered.

Believed to have been transformed from ugly ducklings to beautiful swans, the only thing that changed was how they saw themselves. During the course of their time with Carson, they were each reminded of a twinkling, bright, and beautiful version of themselves that they had once known. As a result of now seeing themselves as beautiful and lovable women, they have since gone on to change their lives because they have stepped into their new positive self-images and these have become their new reality.

How about you? What curse has had you under its spell? Better yet, are you ready for what I like to call a self-image makeover? I'm not talking about a regular quick fix change that begins and ends with a new hairstyle or some great clothes. I'm suggesting that you go much deeper than that. Let me tell you why.

The Snapback Effect

Many women who get makeovers often revert back to their old ways. This is because without actually following up and keeping the flow of change coursing through your life by creating new habits to support your new beliefs, things will fall back into the default position. This is called the snapback effect. Similar to a rubber band that's been stretched beyond its limits, it will eventually snap back on you. If you want to stretch beyond your comfort zones and keep the change, you have to do it slowly and condition yourself to get comfortable with the new you.

That's what happens when someone makes a change through dieting, exercise, plastic surgery, or some other external means that only alters their outsides. It's like redecorating a house by buying new furniture and replacing all the fixtures and things you can see with your eyes, but leaving the rotting floor boards and damaged electrical system alone.

If you don't deal with the sagging foundation and the bad wiring, all the work you put into restyling the house will be for nothing because it will either catch on fire or cave in beneath you. You've got to take care of both the insides and the outsides if you want to make a permanent change.

Breaking Free from My Curse

I gained thirty-five pounds when I couldn't face the fact that my father and I had reached an impasse in our relationship. It was so much easier to blame my frustration and hurt feelings on being fat and avoid facing the truth. For years I had given up my power to my father and let him tell me who I was and what I was capable of achieving.

As a young girl, he believed in me and was a tremendous source of empowerment and support. However, when I got older and began to handle his business, a part of him felt threatened and that caused the rift in our relationship. The resentment that he felt towards his own situation came out in the form of anger towards me. He felt victimized, so he felt the need to victimize others. I was always there and available so I had made myself an easy target.

In order for me to halt the self-perpetuating poor me cycle of victimization that had become so much a part of my identity, I had to make a break with that old scared-of-her-shadow Andrea. That meant saying goodbye to thinking of myself as a victim, loving and accepting all my imperfections and taking full responsibility for my life.

I had to stop giving other people permission to usurp my power. I had to start believing that only I could make myself feel good or bad about anything in particular. Nobody could actually make me feel happy or sad. That meant I had to reassess the relationships in my life where I noticed I always felt bad and remove myself from them.

Sadly, this meant that I had to cut the apron strings with my father and set new boundaries, asserting my newfound independence. When I finally set those new limits he was not agreeable to them, and eventually he just disappeared from my life. As much as it hurts, it's okay because now I know that my feeling okay with who I am doesn't rest on anyone else's shoulders but mine.

When Things Go Wrong As They Sometimes Will...

Here's the story of my client, Ayla, who had an enormously successful experience with changing her eating habits and getting thinner without dieting until a tragedy happened in her life, and much of her success started to unravel. Here's what happened:

After Ayla had successfully lost over sixty pounds and gotten all the way down to a size 2, people started to tell her she was getting too thin. One day a woman approached her and said."Ayla, you have to stop. Your face is starting to look gaunt." Ayla said, "I beamed. Gaunt. She thought I looked gaunt. My name and gaunt had never been in the same sentence, could this even be possible that she was talking about me I thought. I couldn't help myself from smiling, inside and out! Her concern totally fell on deaf ears as all I could feel was a sense of accomplishment…to lose enough weight that someone could even notice me was huge."

Still unconvinced that she had lost enough weight, Ayla was committed to continuing to eat in a way that would guarantee her getting thinner. During the months that she was focusing on building her business, she had completely given up cooking. Instead, she chose to fall back on Lean Cuisine® meals because she sought out the element of portion control, feeling certain that she couldn't keep a cap on her appetite.

She said, "I'm not binge eating. What I have been doing is eating what I considered were regular, non-diet portions. It seems the only way I can lose weight and keep it off is if I do constantly watch what I eat and deprive myself of the foods that I really like. I wish I could say I'm happy in my skin but I'm not. I feel tired, my nice 'skinny' clothes no longer fit, and I feel like I look ten years older. It seems when I relax from my 'police-woman' food mode that the pounds pile on.

"Everyone noticed my weight loss except one person, my husband. I dropped seventy-six pounds in total and he didn't blink an eye. At one point, he said he couldn't really tell if I lost weight or not as I was around him all the time.

"By the same token, I have gained much of it back and he doesn't say anything negative either. I feel invisible and the pain cuts me to the bone at times. I was invisible as a child, and now as an adult I often feel the same way when it comes to me—the personal Ayla. Sometimes when I eat I just want to cram the food down my throat whether I want it or not. I try not to focus on 'it' or what I do with regards to my food addiction but I know it's there. I feel like the roots of a tree. Above the ground I can stand tall and straight with my branches wide. Yet beneath the soil my roots are somehow tangled and matted when it comes to my self-esteem and body image. So much so that I feel a part of me is dying."

Ayla said she lost all track of how much of her life she was sacrificing by choosing to focus on her career. One day her computer was not working and her husband offered to lend her his. When she opened the email program, she noticed that an old girlfriend of his had just sent an email and it was sitting in his inbox.

Fearing the worst, being reminded of all the pain and betrayal of her years of being sexually and physically abused first by her father and then her first husband, she felt compelled to read the email. It basically stated that the woman was looking forward to seeing him again.

After her husband returned home, she confronted him with the information and he denied anything happened. Then very calmly she said, "We won't ever have this discussion again and I expect that you will never see this woman again. If I ever hear that you have gone to see her, that's the end of our marriage."

True to her promise, Ayla spent the next several months keeping her word. They didn't rehash the argument; however, what happened for her was that all of a sudden her weight, which had been moving on a steady downward spiral, had now begun to pick itself back up. Now she was beginning to regain the weight that through years of struggling with anorexia and bulimia she had fought so hard to lose.

She shared, "By July my weight had started to creep back. I stopped weighing myself but my clothes size started to increase. I went to a size 6, then 8, and now today, a full twelve months later, I'm back at a size 12. I'm too afraid to step on the scales as I know that in order for me to have gone up this much in my clothes (and I can see it on my hips) I must have gained at least forty-five to fifty pounds."

Ayla's story has a powerful lesson for all women. Stress is the enemy. Food is not. Backsliding is a painful reality that you may have to face.

Ayla had what I would consider a one-minute wonder experience with *EFT* in my class. In retrospect, I believe it was stirring enough to have moved her to change her subconscious thinking, especially recognizing that her husband was a great and loving supporter of hers. But since her experience of finding that email, all that belief that she deeply held in her heart about his goodness and loyalty was thrown into question. This illustrates the importance of dealing with all aspects of a situation in order to completely neutralize the painful emotions around it that set off our self-abusive impulses.

I understand from speaking with her that she had not ever pursued using *EFT* to deal with her hurts. As a fellow abuse survivor, I am daunted by her strength. But as a woman who has also dealt with having to constantly handle the pain of triggers that pop up and remind me of feeling unsafe and insecure, I would urge women to use the tools that I share. They work. It is amazing to me that Ayla could come so far having had such insurmountable odds against her.

The painful lesson to be learned from her story is that although you may experience a whirlwind change and see yourself dropping pounds like melting butter, if you have something that broadsides your life, and like Ayla you don't have any way to deal with your stress other than with food, you will gain weight. I would urge you to take care and always make dealing with your stress your number one priority.

Breaking the Curse

Back in the movie, *Penelope*, she got rejected by Max, a guy she really grew to like. She was distraught, automatically assuming that he was repulsed by the curse of her pig snout.

For poor Penelope, living under the threat of her mother's constant meddling, this was the last straw. Bound and determined, she decided to run away from home, hoping to find her own identity, seeking to gain her freedom.

As she began to come out of her shell, she learned that she could have fun, make friends, and see the world in a different light. She started to believe that there were people who could actually accept and appreciate her, snout and all.

But her mother's disarming influence catches up with her and she manages to convince Penelope that in order to be happy she must settle down and marry.

While standing at the altar, Penelope faces the biggest decision of her life. Should she marry a man she doesn't love, and who doesn't love her, only for the sake of breaking the curse, or should she risk the unknown? After a moment of thought, she calls the wedding off, storms away, and locks herself in her room. Her mother follows quickly behind reminding Penelope that she is just one "Yes" away from having a whole new life and a whole new self.

Then in that moment, Penelope realizes that she doesn't want or need that. She shouts back at her mother saying, "I like myself the way I am."

Bam! Penelope got it! Once she accepted herself the way she was, pig snout and all, her curse was lifted. Putting it all together, Penelope said, "The curse was so simple. Me. One of my own kind. I had the power all along."

At the end of the movie, in a touching scene, Penelope is gathered together with a group of children discussing her experience. When she asks them, "What do you think the story means?" One little boy stands up and says, "It's not the power of the curse; it's the power you give it!"

The Courage to Change: "It's Not the Power of the Curse, It's the Power You Give It!"

How much power have you been giving your imperfections and your story? After reading about these women, are you willing to see yourself in a different light? Are you more likely to find greater wells of compassion toward yourself?

Before I share the next process with you, I'd like to give you another spoonful of my perspective.

Juicy Woman Note:

Maybe you're not relating to these stories because you have a great relationship with your father or have a wonderful husband or just don't seem to have the same type of situation as the person mentioned in the story. That really doesn't matter. If your goal is to love and accept yourself more, then here's what I want you to keep in mind.

Some relationships are meant to stand the test of time and others just aren't. Remember—a reason, a season, or a lifetime. Some people come into our lives for a specific reason, others remain with us and stay for a period of time, a season in our lives. Then there are those blessed relationships that when nurtured and cherished will last a lifetime. Since we can't make others feel something they don't, it's not always up to us to determine the length and duration of our relationships. We must be willing to make changes and know when to compromise and when to take a stand.

The most important relationship you can ever have is with yourself. Since it is by default one of those lifetime commitments, it's up to you to make it good. If, like me, you got caught up allowing people to treat you with less respect and appreciation than you deserve, your relationship with your "self" will surely suffer. No matter what, in order to have maximum peace of mind, you must always be okay with who you are. This is a non-negotiable deal breaker. If you're not feeling okay with yourself then start to notice when, with whom, and under what circumstance(s) that occurs.

If you notice that you have people in your life who seem to be invested in making you feel less-than, intimidated, uncomfortable, unworthy, incapable, stupid, or any combination of this caustic cocktail of condemnation and criticism, you do yourself a special kindness by first becoming aware of that pattern.

They may not even realize what they are doing, but once you become conscious of it yourself, you have two options, either tell them or not. If you choose to remain tight lipped and refuse to acknowledge your unhappiness, your body will soak up your malcontent like a sponge and you're in for a mixed bag of misery. I swear that I will never again take that gamble on my health and sanity. I've already gone that route and wasted nearly thirty-five years blaming others for my unhappiness.

Letting time slip through your fingers and realizing that you can't get it back doesn't feel good. If you're not happy with your body, yourself or your life, you have to muster up the courage to change. I'm going to encourage you to take hold of the reigns and recognize that you are in charge of your life right now, nobody and nothing else has power over you but You!

To get a fresh perspective, I want you to be willing to open up and seek out the nuggets of wisdom in the stories of the people that I've shared in this book. If you've been feeling the burden of your "curse," you don't have to continue to believe that you are powerless. The first thing you can do is commit to filling your life with more love. Ask yourself what would that look like? It may mean some of your relationships are about to get a good overhaul.

To do that, you have to take a brave step and voice your feelings, and risk sharing your thoughts and needs with others. If they love and support you and want to continue to be in your life, they will honor your requests to be treated differently and in many cases your relationship will be better than ever.

Always bear in mind that it's not entirely the fault of the other person that your relationship is in a state of disrepair. If you have allowed friends, co-workers, associates, clients, your spouse, family members, kids, or anyone else to treat you off handedly and disrespectfully in the past, they automatically take it as permission to continue to treat you in the same way in the future. As an engrained habit, this is often done without thinking. Consider that while you are re-educating your own mind and learning how to treat yourself with more respect, you must also teach them as well. The burden falls upon you to redirect others to understand and know how you want to be treated.

If they are unable to manage the change, or feel threatened by your transformation and unwilling to treat you in a way that you ask, then you may have to let them go. It's not fun, and sometimes it hurts like hell, but to my way of thinking it is a lesser pain than allowing them to continue to walk all over you. It's better than allowing them to take advantage of your goodness and kind nature and put you in a position of being dishonest with yourself, lying and pretending that everything is just fiiiiiiiiiiiiiiine when it's really not.

It's time to step up and demand what you want/need. But that's not easy if you're stuck with someone else's voice in your head. To love yourself more, you have to be love. Love is a verb. If you want others to love and respect you, you must first love and respect yourself. That comes from changing the way you talk to yourself.

As a student of *NLP*, I learned that we change the way we think of ourselves by being able to shift perspective. Doing this changes the way you feel, and it's called a state change. The way you feel, your emotions, the state of mind you're in at any given time, all are distilled down to chemical storms going on inside your brain.

During my *NLP* training, I learned a way of seeing things differently that has really stayed with me and become a source of great strength. It was taught to me by my *NLP* instructor, Kevin Creedon, and it is the most profound tool I know to create an instant shift in thinking. Now, instead of talking to myself with my father's nasty voice and attitude, I enjoy the love and unconditional acceptance and support that comes from seeing myself through my Nana's eyes.

Whether or not you have an actual person with whom you can identify in this exercise, does not matter. What really counts is that you think about a person with positive and loving qualities. The idea is for you to imagine yourself being coached by several people, one of whom is you, another is an observer, and the third is someone who loves and respects you. This truly is one of my favorite strategies. If you want to walk through the entire *NLP* Self Coaching Strategy exercise, you can find it on my **Juicy Woman** website. Just go to http://www.thejuicywoman.com and click on the link that says "Free Articles." Enjoy!

> ## Juicy Woman Note:
>
> The power to change the way you think about yourself is now yours. I think of this process as a real gift because it enables you to first become aware of whose voice you're carrying around inside of you, and then it gives you the power to choose another. This has been such a wonderful process for me; I can't wait for you to try it so that you can let me know how it's working for you. Please share your stories with me at andrea@thejuicywoman.com or fill out the Contact form on my website. Touch base with me and let me know how you're doing.

The Two Wolves Battling Inside of Each of Us

At any given moment we are faced with a choice. There's an old Cherokee legend that beautifully illustrates this idea. In a conversation between a grandfather and his beloved grandson, the old and wise man explains to the boy that within every person there is a battle being fought between two wolves fighting for dominion.

One wolf is Unhappiness. It feeds on fear, worry, anger, jealousy, sorrow, self-pity, resentment, and inferiority. The other is Happiness. It's strength comes from joy, love, hope, serenity, kindness, generosity, truth, and compassion.

After the grandson considered this thought for a moment, he asked his grandfather, "Which wolf wins?" The wise man simply replied. "The one you feed."

It's so important to keep in mind that you can always choose your next thought. It only takes 17 seconds to flip switch your thinking and up your vibration. By making that quick change of thought, you will attract different things into your life.

As the Cherokee tale demonstrates, you can either be miserable or you can be happy. It's up to you, depending upon which thoughts you choose to feed. I've shared my stories and examples with you to make it crystal clear that no matter what, you don't have to be a victim of your circumstances. So the question is, what do you want — to be happy, or miserable?

If it's happy you want, then you have to find things that make you feel good. I'm going to encourage you to take stock of all your old successes and create a new image for yourself of who you want to be. This will be your new north star.

Here's one of my favorite self-image makeover memories that I often pull out of the closet and dust off when I need a reminder of my true essence.

The Power of a Pyramid

As a child, I had many experiences that most would consider extraordinary; one incident springs to mind, which always makes me chuckle.

One thing's certain about my childhood years with my father and Rosie. Life with them was never boring. I was always learning something new and exciting. They were fascinated by the personal growth movement and always thinking outside the box, which was so exciting to me.

Early on I developed a love and passion for learning. We went to seminars and workshops to learn about developing our minds' potential. My experience with Silva Mind Control® was my first introduction to The Law of Attraction.

There I was taught the concept that we create our own reality by the power of our thoughts. And in order to become master of my own destiny, I had to get comfortable using a bigger part of my brain.

To do that, I learned how to meditate and focus my mind using positive mental imagery. As a passionate learner, I had seen evidence of psychometry, clairvoyance, past lives therapy, and "hands" healing. By the time I was in fifth grade, I was clear on my belief about reincarnation.

As a young teen I was close with my father, and had absolute soaring self confidence in my abilities. Although I wasn't too happy with the state of my thighs, my father helped me to recognize that I had many wonderful and special talents. In many ways, dad convinced me that there was nothing I couldn't do. I had learned that I had a very powerful intuition and I was able to "see" and know things that other people couldn't.

By the time I was fourteen, among other things, the family developed a fascination with the power of pyramids. This came about because my dad and I loved to watch the TV show, "National Geographic." We learned about a noted physicist who studied the effect of the geometry of pyramids on various forms of matter.

We had pyramids all over the house. There was a whole collection of them; they were everywhere, in all sizes. Dad and Rosie even had a huge one suspended over their bed. Hmmm. There were groupings of them facing North, South, East, and West. Pyramid mania even extended to the bathroom. Dad was told they could sharpen razor blades.

I figured that if they could sharpen razor blades they could also sharpen my tool, my brain. Since that early age, I understood on a basic level that everything was made up of energy and that it was entirely possible to tap into the power of the universe

At the time, I was in the throes of preparing for a big biology test in school. It was my sophomore year at Mother Cabrini High School. I got the idea that I could use the power of the pyramids to ace this test in school.

That morning as I put on my school uniform, I visualized Einstein on my right shoulder while Isaac Newton perched on my left. Then to top everything off, I placed one of the pyramids on my head and walked proudly out of the house.

As soon as I stepped out of the building, I noticed stunned expressions and stares but that didn't bother me. I knew I must have looked like a nutcase, but I was a gal on a mission.

I remember that day. I even stopped to chat with my friend, the parking garage attendant, old man Bill. As I stood tall and proud talking with him, I felt a little smug and certain that I was going to ace my bio exam.

Once I got to school I was met with more incredulous responses along with laughter and whispers. What seemed like negative attention had no impact on me whatsoever, but just in case, I decided to remove my pyramid at least until I got to the biology lab.

Once I reached my seat. I felt beads of sweat roll down my brow. Taking a big risk, I carefully reached into my bag and clasped my beautiful copper pyramid. Then in the blink of an eye, I placed it on my head. We were ready; Einstein, Newton, and I began the test.

Suddenly I heard a shrill pitched voice. I turned to see Sister Arlene coming up behind me. Her eyes were like saucers. She sputtered my name, "Andrea Perrella, what do you think you're doing with that thing on your head?" That's all I remember.

Looking back, I know her intent was to burst my bubble and lead me into uncertainty and insecurity about what I was doing and who I was becoming, but she failed. What followed is a total blank. But I'm sure I got an A+ on that test, because I was, after all, an excellent student. I loved learning, still do.

The most valuable lesson I learned that day was that this crazy blonde pyramid girl was fearless in the face of adversity. Courageously she broke new ground and was unconcerned with being different. She was truly a pioneer. Even today, I still refer back to that image of myself to help inspire doing what is necessary to reach my goals.

Paging Your Pyramid Girl

All of us have stories and memories of times when we succeeded at something that went against the grain, defied the odds, and boggled the mind. We're all capable of amazing things, but if you've been living with resentment toward your body, thinking of yourself as just a pair of thick thighs or flabby breasts, then you've probably gotten side tracked and discounted all the many wonderful things you've achieved that make you who you are today.

Just like my pyramid girl, you also have experiences you can draw upon to reinforce a more positive, confident self-image. By summoning those memories to the forefront, you put yourself into a state of being where you are much more resourceful and able to do lots of things you normally wouldn't feel comfortable doing.

Embrace Your Right to Bare Arms, Legs, or Whatever, Girl

Over the years I'm sad to say I lost track of my Pyramid girl and let other people's opinions of me guide my actions. Because it had become second nature for me to feel so self-conscious about my arms and legs, I used to avoid wearing sleeveless tops and shorts out in public. Every summer I hid beneath baggy black capris, sweating bullets, resenting every woman who wasn't in my sad and miserable predicament.

In 2008, I made a pinkie promise and swore to myself that I was going to commit myself to thinking and acting just like a naturally slender woman. It was high time for me to release my old fatitudes and that meant changing the way I thought about my body and doing things differently.

I prepared for an upcoming summer vacation to visit my step daughter, Janelle, in hot as Hades North Carolina. I knew this would give me a great opportunity to break out of my comfort zone and wear tops and shorts in public.

The previous year I had already broken some ground when I decided to wear shorts, bathing suits, and sleeveless tops during the family vacation in Puerto Rico. But I just couldn't imagine wearing them in my home town of New York City.

So I resorted to my cure-all, break-through method, and I tapped, tapped, tapped on feeling fat and hating my thighs, and any other negative screaming meanie that was hanging around in my brain that day. Within a few minutes I had brazenly decided to wear my shorts to go buy more shorts in the mall.

As I stepped off the escalator in the Palisades Mall, with my sights set on two of my favorite stores, New York & Company and Lane Bryant, I listened to my heels click, click, clacking and felt wonderful and triumphant wearing my shorts, sleeveless top, and cutsie shoes. Bonnie Raitt's song "Let's Give Them Something to Talk About" was playing on the loudspeaker.

For what seemed like the first time, I really listened to the song and the lyrics came to life for me. I felt completely relaxed after my tapping session that morning, because I had cleared away the cobwebs.

Juicy Woman Note:

Let me digress a moment and explain that the title of this book, *"Lovin' the Skin You're In"* was chosen by me for a very specific reason. It represents an ideal outcome to which you and I can aspire and direct our intention and target our goal to reach that place. It certainly doesn't mean that I always love the skin I'm in or that you will either. It's a matter of recognizing that you will develop a new preset or default switch in your mind.

What this means is that once you have this new vision of yourself, the old image you have of your body that you're holding inside of you will be as dissonant as nails dragging across a blackboard. It will feel like sand paper on your soul. More often than not, it's the new belief and acceptance that will prevent you from tolerating the old hate games and put downs you used to accept as truth.

Now this is no panacea. You'll still have your dark or insecure moments when you and your body just are not seeing eye to eye, however with the tools I offer you, these times will be significantly diminished. You'll notice that the duration, intensity, and frequency of your upsets will significantly change and be reduced. This is a process and it will increase in effectiveness as you practice it more often and make it a part of your life.

As I walked through the mall, I noticed a spring in my step and a bit of sass in my trot. Before I knew it, I was shaking my generous fanny and swinging my hips in tune to the beat. That day I learned that no matter how badly I may feel about my body in the moment, if I spend just a few minutes tapping on those negative thoughts and thinking about what's really bugging me, I can flip my thinking instantly. I can brush away any old fears and self-doubts that keep me thinking and feeling fat. I know that I can go from seeing myself as fat and ugly one minute to feeling gorgeous and sexy the next.

I like to think of *EFT* as my courage in a bottle. Thanks to *EFT*, that summer marked the beginning of my newfound independence. I was beginning to appreciate my body as it was, without feeling the old desperate urges to get thinner. With that new sense of freedom and budding self-confidence, I went on to buy a ton of great new clothes, embraced my right to bare my arms and legs, and began a new love affair—with myself.

Now I want to share a story of a woman who must have left the house that day without doing the tapping necessary to tame her screaming meanies.

Stop Weighting for Perfect

Since I had been celebrating my new relationship with my curvy body, I was feeling more confident and comfortable buying clothes that actually fit me. I had been to Lane Bryant (a plus size women's retail store) a few weeks earlier and purchased some lovely blouses, one of which I was actually wearing. I returned to the store that day and buzzed through, making my choices from the racks and plucking out an armload of clothes ranging in sizes from 14-18.

As I was making a beeline for the fitting room to try my clothes on, a lovely woman stopped to compliment me on the blouse I was wearing. It was a blue and green mosaic design short sleeved peasant blouse.

When I got dressed that morning, I had deliberately pulled down the elasticized neckline of the blouse to expose my neck and shoulders because I enjoy wearing clothes in a way that highlight my best features. I like my "creamy white shoulders" as someone once called them.

As I looked at the woman who complimented me on my blouse, I noticed her eyes had a wistful, almost mournful expression. I wondered why. Then I smiled at her and said, you know this same blouse would look incredible on you. I pointed to the rack and told her, I bought it here. It's still available. What do you think of getting it? I watched as her lovely smile faded and the corners of her mouth turned downward into a sullen frown.

She said, "Oh no, my arms are too fat. That type of blouse is not for me."

I told her that her thought was probably coming from the screaming meanie critics that are perched on her shoulder, holding her back from wearing these types of blouses and doing other things she really wanted to do in life. I explained a little further about the internal voice we all have and how it pushes us to be afraid and believe we're not good enough, pretty enough, or just not able to measure up.

Then, in a private moment to myself, I remembered how for years I would never have had the confidence to bear my arms in public even when, by society's standards, I was an average weight. It took me having to go through the experience of regaining weight after I had successfully but painfully maintained my weight loss for nearly six years, to finally get it. All those years lost. So much time wasted on thinking about what? My body? Obsessing about the size of my thighs? How insane!

I was tired of hating myself and feeling ashamed of my appearance. I couldn't stand it anymore, putting off my life, waiting until I lost weight. I knew that with all the insights I was having, I was finally ready to make the decision to accept my body as I was, with all my imperfections intact. No more sitting around and waiting for perfect. Not me.

Later as I stood at the counter paying for my purchases, I noticed the woman was also there. I asked if she bought the blouse. She shook her head and said, "No, I didn't but I got a very similar one. You inspired me. I feel better about myself now."

I count that as a triumph over the meanies. My guess is that this lovely woman finally got a glimpse of herself from someone else's eyes, in this case, mine. Just for a moment she stepped outside of the box that her negative self-talk, evidently fat and ugly self-image, had built around her and she saw that she could be, do, and have more.

How about you? Do you feel burdened by the weight of that critic that sits on your shoulder and pushes you to feel constantly ashamed of yourself, to judge yourself harshly, and compare yourself to other women? Are you tired of freaking out about wearing shorts in the summer, terrified of exposing those precious chunky dimpled thighs? Are you ready to make a change, take responsibility, step up, and stand in your power?

Turn the page and let me show you how to get started taking 100% responsibility so you can *RECLAIM*™ your life.

Wrapping Up
Chapter 4: Committing to Being Your Own Best Friend

Here are the juiciest bits covered in this section. Savor them mindfully.

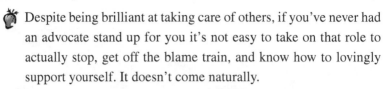

- Despite being brilliant at taking care of others, if you've never had an advocate stand up for you it's not easy to take on that role to actually stop, get off the blame train, and know how to lovingly support yourself. It doesn't come naturally.

- The way to gain more self-acceptance, make peace with food, and become friends with your body is for you to hold the little girl inside of you. Cradle her in the palm of your hand, committing to nurture yourself, warts and all.

- It's those painfully negative "I hate my fat thighs" thoughts that have you twisting in the wind, buying into the illusion that it's your body that's the problem. It's not. It's your thoughts.

- None of us are perfect, but we are still lovable and worthy anyway. That is because we are so much more than just a collection of body parts.

- By hating your body as it is, you send your brain a message that you're not worthy or good enough and you don't deserve to be happy. By holding onto this stressful thinking, you will keep yourself in a state of resistance, making it nearly impossible to lose weight. Start by accepting yourself as you are, now.

- The real nourishment you crave is self-acceptance. No amount of food will ever fill those gaps. Only you can.

- Stop judging your binges and beating up on yourself for overeating. Be curious to find out why.

- We often fail to consider that we hold others in a much higher regard than we think of ourselves.

- The truth is we all have what we would consider our curse. How about you? What 'curse' has had you under its spell? Remember, it's not the power of the curse; it's the power you give it!

If you've been feeling the burden of your "curse," you don't have to continue to believe that you are powerless. The first thing you can do is commit to filling your life with more love. Ask yourself what would that look like?

If you're not happy with your body, yourself, or your life, you have to muster up the courage to change.

The burden falls upon you to redirect others to understand and know how you want to be treated. The most important relationship you can ever have is with yourself. To love yourself more, you have to be love. Love is a verb. If you want others to love and respect you, you must first love and respect yourself. That comes from changing the way you talk to yourself.

Chapter 5
Responsibility: Take Charge of Your Life

"We cannot go back and make a new start,
but we can start to make a new beginning."
– *Maria Robinson*

How many times have you looked in the mirror and really seen your body? I'm not talking about what you'd consider your best features, your assets, your beautiful dark curly hair, or your lovely hazel eyes. I'm talking about the bulges of fat and dimpled skin and all those overflowing and flabby parts that you'd rather die than put out on public display.

Often, when we walk past a mirror and catch a glimpse of some part of our reflection that is remotely displeasing or even downright disturbing, we quickly glance away, gazing down at the floor, feeling shameful and fat.

As overweight women, we've been taught and trained, cajoled, pushed and prodded to sort and scan for flaws; to view our bodies in the mirror with a mixture of regret and apology, making empty promises that we'll pass up that cheesecake, get to those crunches, and return back to our exercise program soon. We spend as little time in front of the mirror as possible. Some women don't even own a full length mirror. As far as they are concerned, they are merely a walking, talking head.

Are you ready to move closer towards being okay with your body as it is now?

You may wonder, why should you? I'll tell you. I want to move you forward to another essential aspect of making peace with your body: deciding to take 100% responsibility for yourself and your life. No more blaming. No more waiting. No more putting your life and your happiness in the hands of others. It's going to require some bold thinking to step out of your old uncomfortable comfort zone thinking that you can't do anything about whatever situation you're facing.

Are you willing to let go of your weight obsession and change your focus to the bigger things that have been getting covered up by your weight distraction?

Being overweight is not the problem. It's only a symptom of the problem.

Have you ever considered the bold possibility of just looking at your body, noticing your large self, and arriving at the point of being okay with you at this size? Why does your body only become acceptable when you're thinner? More often than not, the prospect of seeing yourself overweight will make you feel like a failure. It may push you to tears, triggering you to arm wrestle racing thoughts as you look at all your many imperfections. You might wish, "If only I were thinner, had smaller thighs, could lose this weight, didn't have such a big stomach, big fat butt, or these flabby arms, my life would be different???"

Would it really?

What if you never lose the weight? What if you're always like this? What if you get even fatter? Will the world end? Will you lose someone's love? What's the answer? Run back to dieting? How well did that work? How willing are you to consign yourself to living that depressing dieting life of misery and restriction until the day you die? How many years have you already wasted letting your size determine your right to happiness?

I wouldn't be surprised if by now you felt a burning urge to fling this book across the room and then run scared as hell back to the nearest weight loss center. But if you're still with me, this is the chapter that you must read because without taking the step named here you will never go anywhere. You'll always be doomed to hate your body, foolishly putting your fate and happiness in the hands of others, swearing that you've been cursed by the fat fairies or any other evildoer lurking nearby.

The Funhouse Mirror...

Have you ever walked into a funhouse and looked at yourself in those mirrors that distort your perception of your body? If you're tall and slim and you look at a mirror that makes you short and fat, you would have a hard time believing that you don't actually look that way. That's what goes on in your mind's eye when you hold an image of yourself as a fat woman. It prevents you from being able to see your body as it actually is. You know the old saying, "Everybody's got a nose, but you just can't see yours." The reflection you're looking at in the mirror is getting distorted by the image that you have of yourself in your mind.

Here's another example of what I mean. I'm sure you've had the experience of looking through your old photo albums and finding pictures of yourself during a time when you were thinner but still very unhappy with your body. I have. About a year ago I found a bunch of photos of me that were taken during my late teen years up until the point when I had my son, PT. I was shocked when I remembered that during those years I used to shop and buy clothes that were a size 6. But because I always had thighs that were not in proportion to my waist, I always believed that I was huge.

Psst. I want you to know that your mirror is playing tricks with you. Right now at this moment you're probably not really seeing yourself as you are. This is why it is so hard for many women to look in mirrors. It's because when you see yourself, you're looking at what you expect to see. A fat woman.

The Grass Is Always Greener on the Other Side

We generally assume that people who are thinner are happier and have all the good stuff connected with being thin and happy. But it's not necessarily true. No matter how much weight you have to lose, whether it's a large amount or small, it's still the same. Painful. To you, as well as to the gal with only five pounds to lose, your excess weight represents the burden of your life, a huge emotional pain bearing down on your soul.

Perhaps, like me, you have also fallen into the habit of comparing yourself to every woman you meet. This is a consequence of the diet mentality pushing you to believe there is only one ideal body type: thin. But that's not true. Beauty can be found everywhere. Now it's time to expand your definition of beauty; to see yourself from a different perspective.

If you're struggling with obsessive thoughts of food, it's no wonder you've been eating out of control. You've been hurting. Society has been pushing you to think of your body as the root of your pain and pressuring you to believe that you should work hard to fix the unacceptable parts of yourself. But more often than not, change doesn't occur in a hostile environment. Maybe you've given up and become used to disowning, disrespecting, and disregarding your body. I want you to look beneath the surface and really see yourself and who you are beneath the struggle.

The piece you are missing is compassion... for you, for your body.

It's going to take some time to get thinner and release the excess weight that you have on your body. The way I look at it is that you have two options. You can keep on doing what you've been doing and getting the same results, or you can do something different. I am going to encourage you to look past what you see reflected in the mirror and to focus on dealing with the real problem; changing the way you see yourself.

This chapter represents a turning point in the book. It's focus is to get you to see that you've been looking in funhouse mirrors, and it's distracted you from seeing what you need to change your life. The problem is not what you're eating. It's what's eating you!

At the very core, this chapter on taking responsibility is intended to get you to shift your attitude and see that you have so much more power over your life and your choices than you think you do. But because you've been thinking that you'll never be okay until you're thinner, you haven't felt as though you've had the right or ability to exercise your power.

The first step to reclaiming your power is to see yourself for the woman you've become. Think about what life situation or event has brought you here. Like me, you may have grown up as a chubby girl and that's when your obsession with your body began. But weight issues can happen anytime in life.

Do any of these situations seem familiar?

Shoshana was always a high achiever. Straight A's and awards were the norm. But when it came time to deviating from her parents' plan for her future, she just couldn't say "No" and risk her dad's disappointment. So potato chips became her new best friend.

 Like Maria, you may have suffered horrible experiences of abuse as a child and been raped and molested in your teens. You may have found comfort in food and discovered that gaining weight could help you to build a wall of protection around yourself so that nobody would ever be able to get in again.

 Beverly was a latch key kid. Nobody was ever there when she came home from school. Feeling so lonely, sad, and unloved, she ate cookies and drank cokes until late in the evening when her parents came home.

 As a nurse, Pamela works double shifts all the time. She's always there with a smile, no matter how bad she feels inside. She's the gal you can count on. But as much as she loves her work, she's tired and needs a break. Not wanting to rock the boat, she decides to eat another Twinkie to get that extra burst of energy.

 From the time that she had her first child, Gemma just hasn't felt like herself. She's always tired, cranky, and feels overburdened. Now with five children and another on the way, she doesn't see an end in sight. Feeling totally overwhelmed and disgustingly fat, she keeps on trying to diet but can't get control of her cravings.

 Working desperately to get her business off the ground, Malia feels like she's never doing enough. No matter what she does or how much money she spends, she can't seem to find the success she's after. Working from home, she finds herself always eating.

 Finding out that her husband was unfaithful and had an affair with his secretary was the last straw for Barbara. After years of trying to be beautiful and thin for him, she went into a full scale binge and gained fifty pounds.

 After her miscarriage, Jennifer felt so empty. The precious baby that she and her husband had wanted for so long was gone. Now, with nothing but time on her hands and a whole day alone waiting for her husband to come home, she doesn't want to do anything but sleep and eat.

 After her mother died, Jan wanted to disappear off the face of the earth. She felt as though she had lost her best friend. All she could do to feel close to her mom was to eat all the foods she used to love as a girl.

 When her husband lost his battle with stomach cancer, Elaine's life crumbled into a million pieces. Now in her late fifties, she was a woman alone and lonely. Nothing could offer her comfort like the cakes and pies of her childhood.

 After nineteen years of dedicated service to the school where she worked, Geena was handed a pink slip. For the next year all she wanted to do was stay home, watch TV, and eat all day long.

Did you recognize yourself in any of these scenarios? If so, you can certainly see how each of these situations represents a woman or girl who is hurting and in desperate need of love. But if the way you look is your first concern, how will you ever be able to see past what is causing you to reach for food when you're not hungry?

If your best friend told you she was struggling with overeating and she shared her pain with you, you'd probably have the greatest compassion for her. Wouldn't you? Now how 'bout you? If it's you, can't you see that you also deserve love? After all, you really are so much more than just a collection of body parts. But you may not yet believe this so I'm going to share another perspective with you to help you find the compassion for yourself that you need.

As you start to feel greater compassion toward yourself and your situation, you'll have "Aha" moments that will help chip away your body's armor. For me, when I began to accept those rolls of fat and the extra roundness on my stomach and arms, I started to truly understand, forgive, and appreciate that little girl in me. The girl who yearned for love and attention, desperately trying to get me to accept her by craving love in the form of chips and Ben & Jerry's® Mint Chocolate Cookie ice cream, donuts and hamburgers, and steak with extra fat on it. I was begging for love in the form of food and I had no clue that it meant I never really wanted the food, only the love—the love that only I could give myself.

All those years wasted of being a beautiful woman and never really recognizing it, never letting that perception of beauty permeate my being. It took years of banging my head trying to fit my square peg into diets' round hole to understand that I was living in limbo, waiting for perfect and perfect never came. I put off life and joy and playing because I couldn't imagine that I would be worthy of these things if I weren't a size 6 again. So I kept blaming myself for my shortcomings, swearing that if only I could stop eating and lose weight, that's when my life would be perfect. Each of us has a list of reasons why our lives suck, and being fat is probably in the majority's top two.

In this chapter, you'll learn how to break free of the shame of blame and move closer toward a greater degree of self-acceptance, so that you can stop playing the victim game. You will learn to end the perpetual waiting for life to begin and start to live the life you have.

You'll learn the value of asking some different questions which will lead you to different answers. Come with me and discover the how's and why's you must take 100% responsibility for your life, become willing to forgive, make your goofs your gains, and keep your eye on the bigger picture.

In the juicy bits and personal stories that I'll share, I hope to inspire you to tilt the axis on your all-or-nothing stinking thinking so that you too can progress along the road of self-acceptance and one day end your weight and food obsession.

Now that you're starting to get a glimpse behind the size-wise wool that's been pulled over your eyes, you can start to look beyond the myth and find out what is really pushing you to eat, what stops you from loving your body, and find how to reclaim your power and take back your control at any size.

Re-Evaluate and Reclaim Your Life

It's very likely that your decision to accept your body will not come in a flash. It will probably come to you in a whisper. As you learn to listen to your body, you'll develop a new respect for yourself as a person. You'll learn to appreciate yourself in new ways and discover things about you that you never knew had been covered up by years of body hating and food and weight obsession. Now that you're in the process of clearing out the clutter in your life, you'll have a chance to get to know yourself better than ever.

As you begin to feel safer eating the foods you love, and as you become conscious of how your associations with those foods are shifting, your relationship with your body will follow the spiral of change as well. In the same way that you'll now become more sensitive to the popcorn being too salty, or the donuts being too sweet, you'll also notice that same mindful selectivity will expand to other areas in your life.

Gradually you'll notice that many of the old unconscious habits you had as a dieter, like people pleasing, stuffing your emotions, and avoiding confrontation, will begin to feel uncomfortable for you. You'll become more aware of the times that you fall into those old habits. Awareness is the first step to change.

Since you will be changing the way you relate to food, you'll notice that you're more aware of how you feel. This won't happen overnight, but with the tools that I give you in this book you'll be able to make these changes and they will feel very natural for you. This is because you'll be working on releasing the old limiting beliefs that have been keeping you stuck. At the same time you'll learn new ways of coping with your stress without using food.

You'll also probably become more vocal and clear about your preferences beyond food. You may find that you're starting to call people on the little things that used to bug you that you've long kept to yourself. If you've been inclined to pretend to ignore things, you may not feel so comfortable being passive anymore. This is because as you clear away your stresses, you'll regain a sense of your powerful self, remembering how good it feels to be in charge. As the kinks and distortions in your body's energy field get ironed out, it will become second nature to want to feel good.

Taking care of yourself doesn't always mean eating—and feeling good doesn't necessarily come with a double scoop of Baskin Robbins® Rocky Road ice cream smothered in hot fudge sauce with mounds of whipped cream and nuts.

When you're in the zone, feeling good means being productive and having plenty of energy to keep on doing what you love to do. You'll start to notice that as you take risks expressing your feelings and saying what's on your mind, the payoffs are often so much sweeter than any edible goodie.

You may discover that along with your new ability to make more distinctions and take bigger risks, your friendships may also undergo shifts. Some relationships that used to fit you like a glove may no longer feel right. You'll want to re-evaluate how you spend your time. This is because you're becoming aware of and clear about what you like and what you don't. It's likely that you'll no longer want to do the same things you used to.

If you've been relying on food to numb your feelings, it's likely that you may have been unconsciously putting up with a lot of things in your life that have made you feel unhappy or uncomfortable. As you clean up your relationship with food, you will feel as though you are coming out of a trance, seeing those things more clearly perhaps for the first time.

It may start with nixing some types of movies and TV shows in favor of reading, or choosing to be silent when everyone else is talking. Perhaps, like me, you may become more outspoken and decisive, finding yourself becoming more comfortable joining in the party rather than being the consummate wall flower. No matter how you slice it, change is in the air.

Juicy Woman Note:

Remember, if you are struggling with a painful challenge that is pushing you to eat indiscriminately and more often than your physical hunger dictates, your body is telling you that it needs to release its stress.

Always moving at your own pace and in your own time, you'll gradually want to reorganize, remodel, and reshape many things in your life that no longer work for you. If something feels really good to you now, it will probably feel even better. If something doesn't feel good, and you become newly aware of it, it will probably get to the point of feeling worse, especially if it's been ignored for a while.

The choice is up to you. By setting down new limits, stating your preferences, and telling people what you like and what you don't, what you need and what you want, you will find yourself shaping and shifting your life in a way that really suits you. You're in charge. You don't necessarily need food anymore to hide or stuff down your emotions. There is a choice.

I like to say that as I started to feel safer around food, and as I built up my confidence by learning I wasn't a walking, talking garbage can, I began to realize all the places in my life where I was settling. I noticed spaces in and around my home that I wasn't using and enjoying, and I paid more mind to all the little messes and situations in my life that I let pile up and accumulate.

I'd been tolerating uncomfortable situations and avoiding confrontations because I didn't have the skills to deal with those sticky situations and tight spots. I didn't know what to say or feared being the one to rock the boat because I didn't feel good enough about myself to express what I needed. So I started to address all the little things that I had turned a blind eye and deaf ear toward which kept me living tightly closed in a box labeled, "Resentment."

Little by little, bit by bit, moment by moment and day by day, I came crawling out of my box, and you will too! *RECLAIM*™ your life.

The Road to Self Acceptance: Fat Is a Feminist Issue

In the mid 70's, during the middle of the second wave of the women's lib movement, two women came together who would later become pioneers of their time, leading the way for all women to explore the question of how our lives would be different if we just liked our bodies.

When Susie Orbach first joined Dr. Carol Munter's women's only discussion group on compulsive eating and self-image, neither of them had any idea of the impact their meeting would have on their lives and the ripple effect it would have on society's views towards women, weight loss, and body image.

In their discussion group, they gave women a place to let their hair down, a space to feel safe talking about their bodies and their fears.

Being in the presence of other women, they felt safe and that enabled them to talk about whatever was bothering them. Each member had the opportunity to mourn her losses, share her story, tell her tale of past diet disasters, talk about crazed diet pill pusher doctors, insane binges, psychiatrists, health farms, and fasting. After realizing they all shared a common thread, they all wondered the same thing: Why was it so important to have the perfect body and why couldn't they stick to a diet?

In an effort to share an alternative to the pain of dieting and self-hatred, Susie and Carol discussed their own experiences of non-dieting. They talked about self-acceptance and learning to trust and feel safe in their bodies as being the key to weight loss. They explained that we could only do that by making friends with our fat.

The most common scenario was for women to gain a bit of weight in the beginning as they gradually made their way through to feeling safe around food, but it was most important to make peace with their bodies at every size.

In her book, *Fat is a Feminist Issue,* Susie Orbach explains her philosophy in this way, "This new approach has another function. If you can experience yourself as existing throughout the fat, then when you lose weight you will not feel you have lost a protective covering: you will feel you have become compressed. This is because if you feel yourself all through the fat then what is all of you is part of you. In giving up the size you are making an exchange – you swap the fat for your own body, and that is power."

They taught the women how to make friends with their fat. They did this by walking them through a series of exercises designed specifically to help them accept their larger size and guiding them to recognize that the excess weight on their body was actually a part of them as much as their hands, knees, ears, or toes.

They encouraged the women to see themselves first from a standpoint of artistic beauty, noticing dimensions and texture, lumps, bumps, and ridges. Next they led the women to notice how their miraculous bodies functioned through breathing and blinking and moving and simply being. By seeing their bodies from this new perspective of self-appreciation, the women were gradually able to welcome and become more accepting of their bodies.

In Carol and Susie's early groups, they flipped the participant's firmly held beliefs about dieting and thinness, causing them to completely change the way they felt about their bodies. Slowly the women took the risk and decided to stop dieting. To quote Susie, "Nothing terrible happened. Then with that new understanding of how to make friends with food and end their obsession, they were able to focus all that wasted diet-thinking energy on much more important pursuits. That led them to become more open to exploring their lives, footloose and fancy free, eager to discover what made them tick."

These exercises led the women to understand that by accepting their bodies exactly as they were, they would be able to move past their obsession with their imperfections and gain a new appreciation of themselves as people and get on with the task of living. If you want more information about these exercises, you can visit my **Juicy Woman** website. Just go to http://www.thejuicywoman.com and click on the link that says "Free Articles." Enjoy!

As you can see, these women experienced a huge mental shift in their thinking that made it possible for them to be able to appreciate their bodies and accept their imperfections. You're probably wondering what you need to be able to do the same for yourself?

"You can't be thin if you're thinking fat."
– *Dr. Nancy Bonios*

I'll tell you how it's worked for me. My experience was similar to theirs. For me, dieting became the ultimate pain and I couldn't imagine living the rest of my life under that kind of limitation. That's why I was prepared to gamble my entire weight loss history in order to find out if I truly could trust myself around all food. What I learned was astonishing. I discovered that despite becoming a very picky eater, I was unable to control my voracious appetite until I took an important step I had been avoiding.

I had to take responsibility and stop defining myself as a victim.

Learned Helplessness

I haven't been to see the circus in a couple of years but whenever I go with my family, I marvel as I watch the elephants balancing on one leg, sitting up, or twirling around. I've often wondered how such enormous animals could ever be trained. One day in an *NLP* class, I was told the story that explained how it is done.

When circus elephants are trained as young calves, they are taught to obey their trainer's every command. This is done by placing a thin chain around one of their ankles which is attached to a stake driven deep into the ground. Being just a tiny baby, their little pulls and tugs are not strong enough to break the chain or uplift the stake so they eventually give up trying to escape. This is an example of what is called learned helplessness.

Naturally, I know that you're very different from an elephant and you don't have a chain around your ankle preventing you from moving, but can you relate to these situations?

 Have you ever made the decision to avoid doing something or going somewhere because you didn't feel good enough?

 Have you been feeling awful about your body?

Have you been thinking of yourself as someone who is out of control?

 Have you ever spent more than a second analyzing your flaws?

Have you spent too much time consumed with thinking about food and being fat?

 Have you ever believed something about yourself that wasn't true?

 Have you been limiting yourself to only doing what you know you can do?

 Have you ever sworn that you can't do something now, because you couldn't do it before?

 Have you given up on yourself?

These are all examples of the shackles that have been keeping you stuck.

Just like the little elephant, you've been boxed in by people who have trained you to believe that you weren't strong enough to break free of your own self-imposed limits.

Maybe you have no idea why for most of your life you've struggled with a nagging feeling that you just weren't good enough, smart enough, or pretty enough. Feeling like a loser, you find yourself mimicking the critics of your past, asking yourself dead end questions like, "What kind of idiot am I? Why can't I do anything right? Why am I so fat, Why am I so ugly? Why can't I stop eating?"

Just like the little elephant, perhaps you've tried to buck up against all the judgments and critical statements and the people who said them when you were smaller, weaker, younger, more naïve. Eventually you gave up and stopped trying to assert yourself because it was too difficult to swim against the current. It became easier to just give in and not make waves.

Eventually, the more insecure part of you allowed these statements to become a part of who you are. They slowly seeped into your soul. It didn't happen immediately. It evolved over time without you even realizing it. It was a slow erosion. You accepted these limitations as part of your identity. These are the buggers that have to be dealt with in order for you to feel safe enough at any size and make peace with foods like the much beloved, french fries and pies.

In previous years, I hung my hat on the hope that other people would make me happy, keep me feeling safe, take care of me, and give me the assurance I needed to know without question that I was lovable. Those years were fraught with tension and turmoil, and filled with chaos and confusion. It seemed that every time I was disappointed by something someone said or did, I could always blame it on the size of my thighs or the fact that I was a victim of abuse. Today I know that blaming my thighs or anything else for that matter is a waste of my precious time and energy because it buys into the illusion that I am powerless. I'm not a victim anymore. I'm a survivor. And so are you!

My thighs are not my problem and your excess weight is not yours. It's only been distracting you from seeing the real problem, things that you can do something about.

The fact is, until you break those chains and free yourself from your mental, emotional, and spiritual bondage, you'll never be able to look in the mirror and accept your body in any state—fat, thin, or in between. Because, like me, it is not your body that you hate but the chains that bind you.

The Different Ways People Influence Us

Now let's talk turkey. There will always be people in your life who are going to test your limits. They'll try to rain on your parade, push your buttons, and just in general give you a hard time. They may be doing it intentionally or without an ounce of malice.

Tethers and chains are often put in place by people who truly love us and care deeply about our wellbeing. However without setting proper boundaries and taking care of our own needs and expressing our unique individuality, we can easily fall into the trap of thinking that we're helpless when we're not. The first step to change is becoming aware of what's going on.

How to Deal with the Nasties – Get Your Words Off Of Me!

Try It! – Who's Got You in a Twist?

Make a list of the people in your life who try to influence you and make you do what they want or what they say is best for you. This may be an overbearing and lovable mother, or a critical father, or a friend who doesn't support you, and often wants to drag you down so that she can have a partner to join her pity party. Who are the enablers in your life? Next to each person, put a smiley face if they are trying to be nice about it and a frowning face if they are just plain mean, nasty buggers.

Many people are misinformed and think that abuse only falls into the context of inappropriate touching or hitting. Many of us have family members who are abusive, or at the very least insensitive and intrusive. They put people down and bandy about using nasty language and intimidations designed to get you to knuckle under and do or say what they want. Others are really good at subtle manipulation. No matter how you slice it, people will always try to pull your strings.

Whether it's from a father, mother, brother, sister, husband, or friend, no abuse is ever okay and it's up to you to teach people that you will not stand for it. In the worst case scenario, at the point at which you know that nothing you can do will ever change them, you just have to stop playing the game and let the chips fall where they may. It's not an act of hate to let them go, it's an act of love to choose to stand by yourself.

Juicy Woman Note:

Disclaimer: If you are being physically abused or are in danger make sure you get help to change the situation. Always think of your safety first.

Since I have been learning how to step up, speak my mind, grab the reigns, and take more responsibility in my life, I have noticed that as I assert my newfound independence, doing so creates a delicious ripple effect that floods every aspect of my being. I like and respect myself now more than ever before. It's affected all of my relationships, the way I handle money, how I think about sex, my business has taken on new meaning, my faith has increased, my confidence has soared, my ability to speak, teach, and write has improved, I've become fearless in so many ways.

Despite not always being able to apply what I've learned, I now know the secret to being happy is just being me. That is what has brought me the most success in being able to be comfortable with my body and change my relationship with food.

As part and parcel of being committed to being my own best friend and taking 100% responsibility in my life, I can't do what I used to do which was beg out and pretend I didn't care about things. To change the parts of your life that aren't working, you have to care. That means you have to pay attention to what's going on around you. Now, I am increasingly sensitive to how people speak to others and to me in particular. I make no bones about the fact that I grew up around a great deal of dysfunction and that is the norm for many people in my past.

I've chosen to take a stand and make clear to certain members of my family that no abuse will ever be tolerated. To truly embrace yourself, love your body, and feel safe around food and any other temptations, you must do the same. You must take responsibility, and be willing to open your eyes and see what's in front of you. Then if you don't like what you see, gather the courage to do something about it.

I'm sure you'd agree that acting like an ostrich with its head buried in the sand and avoiding what you don't want to see hasn't worked so far. It's only fed your weight and food obsessions and kept your focus on the wrong thing. This has made you want to eat more and kept you hating your body. If you're acting like an ostrich, pick your head up and get it out of the sand. Remember it's never too late to make changes in your life. You deserve to be happy.

Love/Hate Relationships

Do you have a love/hate relationship going on in your life? Do you sometimes love the person to bits and then wonder how you could ever stand them the next? What if they're members of your family?

When you find yourself in a head-to-head battle of wills with the person who challenges you, don't assume anything. Take the time you need to gather your thoughts and know what you want to say. Rather than giving into the passive tendency to just avoid them, give the relationship the benefit of the doubt and speak to them honestly. Share how you feel.

When you show a person that you recognize and respect their values, you will gain rapport with them. That doesn't mean that you are knuckling under, giving in, or letting them walk all over you. It just puts you on an even footing, helping you to understand them better. Now you can agree to disagree and nobody has to get hurt.

In all your relationships, if you want to be happy and not live like a hermit, you have to know how to set boundaries. Boundaries are limits or rules, decisions that you make to protect yourself from people taking advantage of you. For lots of specifics and how-to's on setting boundaries, read the chapter called *Boundaries and Beliefs: When You Care Enough to Set the Very Best*. By creating new agreements and setting boundaries in your life this will empower you every step of the way to love and accept your body.

I've given you many tools here, but please consider that if boundaries are an issue for you, then they are a real concrete goal to work on achieving—learning how to set better boundaries. It might be worth it to pick up a couple of books on being more assertive and knowing specifically what to say in various situations. I've done that and it has been incredibly valuable to me in all my relationships.

As a result of setting limits with many of the people in my family, the dynamics of our relationships have changed. Some of them have just sort of fallen away and disappeared out of my life. I no longer see them anymore or speak with them. It saddens me deeply but I concentrate on spending time with the family I adore, forgiving and releasing the others to the universe.

To explain this in terms of energy, by setting my boundaries and enforcing them I put myself on a different vibration which means that we are no longer in resonance with one another. I no longer feel angry about it.

It's not up to me to make decisions for anyone but myself. I can only be responsible for my own actions and thoughts, so letting go with love and detachment is the best path for me. That's sometimes the cost of loving and respecting yourself. I feel it's so worth it. What about you? Do you have any family members, colleagues, acquaintances, or friends who are toxic influences?

You Can Choose to Be Happy

By blaming other people and events for our misery, we are inadvertently giving away our power. Happiness is a choice. If you believe that your happiness is tied up and contingent upon certain circumstances or people, then you'll always be trying to catch the elusive butterfly.

Try It! – What are you waiting for?

See how many of these happiness crushers you can recognize in your own life. Check those that apply and then get creative and dig into exploring your own bubble bustin' joy suckers. Just fill in the blanks for the following phrases, "I'll be happy when.... Or, If only...

I'll be happy when I can fit into my skinny jeans

I'll go on vacation when I can wear a bathing suit

If only I didn't have these fat thighs

I'll be happy after I make more money

I'll be happy after I find the right diet

If only I didn't have these fat arms

I'll be happy when my husband stops drinking
I'll be happy when I write my first book
I'll be happy when I'm in a relationship
I'll be happy when I'm a size 6
I'll be happy when I have a house
I'll be happy when I retire
I'll be happy when I'm successful
I'll be happy when I start my own business
If only I weren't so short
If only I had finished college
If only I would have invested the money

When we're quick to blame our situations on things outside of our control and foist off responsibility for our life, we cut ourselves off from being able to experience happiness. The screaming meanies that have you in their grip, keeping you all tied up, have had control over how you felt about yourself for a long time. Are you ready to take back your power and give them their walking papers? If you are, it's going to require cultivating a new awareness, and then questioning some of those beliefs that keep you chained up doing the same twisty things over and over again.

For those beliefs that work and give you what you want—No sweat. Keep on doing what you're doing. But those buggers that leave you feeling helpless, frustrated, angry, guilty, and all that messy stuff, those are the ones that prevail upon you to put on your detective cap and go exploring.

Most people think their happiness is out of reach, in other people's hands, or in a perpetual state of being put on hold. Are you waiting for that moment when things are just perfect? Is that when you think you can be happy?

Try It! – Unveiling Your Saboteurs

In a previous Try It, I asked you to categorize the people who influenced you by putting either a happy face or a frown next to their name, indicating if they were positive or negative influences. I wanted you to do this because in the final chapter of this book we'll talk about the importance of creating a support network for yourself.

If you already have people in your life who prop you up, rally around you, inspire and appreciate you, you're well ahead of the game. I want you to become more aware of who they are, because it will serve you well to spend more time with them. After all, you can't fly like an eagle if you're surrounded by turkeys.

As for the other people, make a list of the saboteurs and pro-vocateurs who try to get a rise out of you. You'll know them by how gleeful they are when you get upset. It can be completely transparent or not quite so obvious. Contenders for this spot may be that friend who thinks she's your personal diet cop, or your uncle Don who makes mean comments about your body, or the ex-husband who talks about you to the kids.

Next, after you've listed who they are, beside their name write down what they really want from you. One of the NLP Presuppositions states that "People are always doing the best they can under the circumstances."

It's all that they can do. Your friend may be trying to get you to feel bad about yourself so that she can feel needed or thinner by comparison. Your uncle could feel powerless in his own life, so he's giving you guff and trying to making you feel bad so that he can feel good. Feeling empowered by disempowering you may be a cheesy way to feel good about himself, but that may be all he knows. Your ex-husband could still be hurting that you left him, and he wants to stick it to you because you broke his heart and deep down he feels emasculated by you.

Don't Buy Into What Saboteurs Say About You!

If you accept the role that your saboteurs are offering you as they desperately try to stomp all over your feelings, use you for a doormat, guinea pig, sugar mama, or just a plain old garden variety sucker, you will play the part of their victim, eventually losing your identity.

In my case, I accepted the belief that I was stupid and had no common sense. Consequently, I avoided making decisions and speaking what was on my mind. I overspent, overate, acted inappropriately, became passive aggressive, avoided social situations, didn't feel confident asserting myself as the boss, and feared most every type of confrontation.

Are you buying into what they're saying about you? It's time to *RECLAIM*™ your power and take back your life. Once you do that consistently and make it a priority, you'll see the changes in your body. You'll notice your hunger will be satisfied by eating less. You'll gradually begin to reshape and get thinner without ever dieting or depriving yourself again. The key is taking responsibility.

Take it from me as your coach, you can have the best of the best techniques and tools at your disposal, but if you don't take responsibility for your own happiness, you'll be miserable.

Take 100% Responsibility for Your Life

The concept of taking full responsibility for your life is a basic principle that is taught within many schools of thought. In creating my *RECLAIM*™ system, which you'll read in these next seven chapters, I've learned that taking this step is the key to your success in making peace with food and friends with your body.

Your success hinges upon committing to this one principle and acting on it every day. If you're not willing to take full responsibility for your life and instead choose to keep on blaming others for your misery, you'll never stop hating your body and food will always have the upper hand.

Thinking of yourself as a victim is the wedge that exists in your life. It keeps you living in the past with regrets, isolating you, and preventing you from being more self-compassionate. As long as you're caught in this cycle of negative thinking, you will never be able to love and accept yourself.

Under the siege of stress, you'll find yourself doing things that give you a false sense of security. These are the fallback methods we use when we don't feel good about ourselves inside. It's different for everyone. You may have stashes of food hidden throughout the house, grab a drink, pop a pill, catch a smoke, give into a midnight binge and eat too much, or just blow your top and lose your cool. These are just some of the things that people do when they're overwhelmed.

How Can I Take Full Responsibility for My Life?

It's completely understandable that we find ourselves getting overwhelmed. Let's face it, life can often be overwhelming. So who in their right mind would ever be willing to take full responsibility for everything in their life? After all, taking responsibility is hard, and you can't do it for other people's actions. There's so much out of your control.

What you can control, though, are your own actions and responses. The next time that you find yourself falling into the old pattern of wanting to hide, notice that you're doing it. Give yourself credit for being able to step back and see the behavior that isn't serving you. That's big because when you can recognize that you're doing something, it's no longer unconscious.

Once you see what you're doing, you can recognize that it's your way of saying that you're scared or overwhelmed. It's your body's way of crying out for help. Making yourself feel more shameful about it won't help you at all. You have to love your way through it.

Nobody said this was going to be easy. Because it's not.

No one would arm wrestle you or challenge the fact that life isn't a bed of roses, but it's not going to help you one iota to continue to focus on all the pricklies. Life isn't a fairy tale and anyone who tells you it is, is either living in a dream world or lying. But somehow we've all been misguided and led to believe that life is supposed to give us everything we want, make us happy, and keep us safe. Unfortunately, it doesn't work that way. If you're ever going to make peace with food and love your body, you're going to have to let go of some of the old illusions that have been keeping you living at odds with your body.

First things first. Complaining and blaming is a total and complete waste of your precious time. Believe me, I know that it's easier to point a finger and blame others for what's wrong in our life. But it doesn't work. Does it?

Perhaps you've already been blaming your spouse, your boss, your diet, your thighs, your saggy breasts, your abusive past, your kids, your parents, your lack of money and piss poor finances, President Obama, your job, your loss, your lack of schooling, your teachers, lovers, friends, etc. The sad truth is if we waste our time twisting in the wind blaming others for our misery, it's like taking poison and expecting someone else to die.

Playing the Blame Game: The Kiss of Death

Despite the fact that it may feel better to foist off the blame for your misery on other people and situations, it doesn't serve you one bit because it keeps you helpless. It strips you of your power to change your circumstances. Here's why, as long as you truly believe that you can't do anything to change your situation, you are stuck. Your decision to play the blame game keeps you caught up in patterns that sabotage your success.

An example from my life is when I was involved in a family business for nearly twenty years. Because I trusted the integrity of my father who was my partner, there was no written agreement. When he decided that my partnership threatened his security I was cut off and left without a safety net. All the financial security I had been promised all my life and taken for granted dissolved into thin air, leaving me with a mountain of debt, unanswered questions, and regrets.

More than that, it was the fallout from the betrayal by him, as my dad, one of my most beloved family members. It twisted me all up inside and left me reeling and feeling absolutely helpless for well over a year until I finally embraced the meaning of taking 100% responsibility for my life.

When I finally realized how I had contributed to my own misery, I could see how my behavior was reinforcing the message that it was okay to take advantage of me. That's when I started to really get an extra helping of understanding that we teach people how to treat us.

I made choices that put me in some very weak positions. I ignored all the signs, refused any help, and dug my own hole. When I realized that I had made those choices and they represented the best decisions I was capable of making at that time, that's when I was able to forgive myself.

As I began to realize that I deserved to be forgiven, I started to act much more lovingly toward myself. I realized that the thorn in my heart that was causing me so much pain was the fierce resentment that I continued to hold towards my father.

I began to stop acting like a victim, feeling sorry for myself, and being so damned hard on myself. As I gained a new compassion for myself, I no longer felt compelled to eat everything in my path. It became more enjoyable for me to wait until I was hungry. I started appreciating the much stronger, albeit heavier, Andrea that had come from the whole experience, joyfully recognizing that I was so much more than just a number on the scale.

I realized that my father's image of me was totally inaccurate. Yet for far too long I bought into it, hook, line, and sinker. I realized that I was not tapping into my potential, and that I had convinced myself that I was helpless, when in fact I wasn't. That's when my bottomless hunger started to disappear. Like the circus elephant, I needed to break free from the chains that bound me. How about you? Do you have a situation that twists you all up inside, making you feel powerless?

Now let me explain what this principle really means to you and how it will change your life. Taking 100% responsibility means acknowledging that you create everything that you have in life. It means that you understand that you are the cause of everything that happens to you. All of your experiences rest with you.

It means that you have to stop waiting for your life to begin, shaking your fists at God and blaming situations and people who are out of your realm of control. The only way that you can come to make peace with yourself and see your body for what it is—perfection—is to release your hold on the past, realize that you create all of your current conditions and only you can uncreate and/or recreate them. In short, you are the one who holds all the cards. Only you.

Now you have to ask yourself, are you ready to take full responsibility for what's going on in your life now?

No More Excuses

If you're going to invest in this precious stock called "responsibility" then you've got to give up all your stories about being a victim. You have to detach yourself from the blame game and stop making so many excuses about why your life is not working. It's nobody's fault but your own. Believe me. I know that's a tough pill to swallow, but stay with me and I'll explain how you can reclaim your life, bust loose from your excuses and justifications, and hitch a ride on the happiness train.

Do you remember the lesson that Dorothy learned in *The Wizard of Oz?* By the end of the movie, she understood that she had the power to change all along. Just like Dorothy, I want you to recognize that it's been inside of you all along. I know that you've been thinking that you could find it by going to the next Weight Watchers meeting, or getting the killer dress, buying that diamond ring, stepping on the scale and seeing x number, having your breasts done, face lifted, legs waxed or haircut, but, in fact, you've already got what you've been searching so hard to find.

All Situations Lead Us To Love

As I was going through the process of becoming certified as a coach, I learned many new concepts that reinforced this principle of taking full responsibility. My coaching instructor, Dr. Bruce Schneider, taught us that it doesn't serve us to judge things as good or bad, because that only keeps us caught in a loop of being a victim and that will never get you anywhere.

The simple fact is bad things happen to good people and nobody has a written guarantee of happiness. But if you are able to move past your anger, and not only forgive others but also forgive yourself, you will lighten your load, literally and figuratively.

I've learned that if you've experienced abuse or hardship, or any pain or suffering, by making the choice to let go of the past you can move beyond it. By doing that, it can actually make you stronger. If you're still stuck playing the blame game, you may have fallen into the pothole of allowing the experience to harden you and make you become less of who you are. That doesn't serve you and it will most definitely result in keeping you hating your body.

Rather than growing stronger and becoming more resilient, able to roll with the punches and sway with the breeze, your brittleness will eventually cause you to bend too far and break. In the next chapter called Embrace Your Emotions, I'll give you a fail-safe method for understanding the needs that are really driving your emotions.

You Are Always in Control of How You Respond to Situations

Just like pressing out cookies with a cookie cutter, we're used to doing things the same way every time. When you get yourself into a pattern this becomes your habit. If you don't like the situations in your life that you've been cooking up, by changing the recipe you'll get a different result.

Which option will you choose?

Blame...

1. You can blame the event and make it responsible for why you are broke, frustrated, angry, hurt, sad, in pain, out of work, about to lose your house, stuck in a bad relationship, hating your body, an emotional eater, etc. There's no end to who or what you could blame. But let me ask you, how is that really working out for you? There's always an endless supply of blame to spread around, but what does that really change? My guess is nothing. Isn't all that learned helplessness making you want to run screaming to the freezer so that you can rip open a container of ice cream, start digging in and not resurface until you hit bottom?

Or

Taking Responsibility...

2. You can take responsibility for whatever is going on and realize what you did or didn't do to create the situation in the first place. You can recognize the power of your thoughts and make the decision to change your focus. You can learn how you can spend your energy more wisely, in a way that will truly benefit you. By doing this, you can take back the power you've been giving away to others being angry and resentful, wishing things could be different.

When Things Go Wrong...

For whatever reason, there will always be times when it feels like life's getting you down. You feel like a failure, life's victim. It could be a low sex drive, traffic on the freeway, a lack of clients, a husband/boyfriend who's been unfaithful, a demanding editor, a teenager exploring drugs, a couple of bratty kids who keep you up all night, an overbearing mother, a critical father, a demanding friend, a dying grandmother, live-in parents, 100 pounds extra, low income, no income, a failing business, abuse in your past, a spouse who hits you, a lying lover, a fat day, a problem with drinking, feeling self-conscious at a party, a tight skirt, a chronic illness, a plane that's late, 9/11, a daughter or son in the armed forces, being raped, hair loss, wrinkles, boobs gone south, an outie belly button, small breasts, being late, getting pregnant, an old car, a president you didn't elect, an administration you resent, a boss with an attitude problem. These are all examples of events over which you have no direct control. No one's saying they don't exist. They do.

But by tossing up your hands and giving in, you are doing nothing and feeling helpless. You become captive to your circumstances just like that little elephant who eventually grows into a mammoth creature internally bound and chained, prevented from escaping because years ago his body learned that he was too weak to pull the stake out of the ground. That cute little pachyderm matures into the huge elephant you see at the circus today; never realizing that just one baby tug on his chain would break the stake like a toothpick, freeing him instantly. What are some of the events in your life that you'd like to free yourself from?

Try It! – What's Eating You?

Make a list of several events that eat at you and cause you to feel helpless, ticked off, pissed, peeved, defeated, deflated, intimidated, angry, sad, and any other mixture of overwhelming and upsetting emotions. Just for kicks and giggles, place a check next to those that make you want to eat when you're not hungry. Is it all of them? Be curious about that and willing to explore it going forward.

Believing In Yourself

When people believe in themselves and have confidence that they have what it takes to overcome any obstacle, they are given the tools to overcome those obstacles. Henry Ford once said, "Whether you believe you can or can't, you're right."

Two people can go through the exact same circumstances and one will be inspired to grow and overcome the challenge, and the other will be paralyzed and stuck. You are not your problems and they do not define you. If you over identify with them, you will lack the observer's perspective needed to pull yourself out of the mess.

For every reason that one person will say it's not possible, another person wanting it more will say that it is. How much do you want it?

You are the only person who can ever really stand in your own way. We are so often our own worst enemy. By doing things that sabotage your goals, you prevent yourself from achieving them. Limiting beliefs, giving in and giving up, bad influences, and hanging out with people who make us feel miserable, are all examples of things that sabotage our happiness.

We ignore so many things that can help us like valuable assistance and feedback. We hide, keep ourselves out of touch, overmedicate, judge people, give in to gossip, avoid situations that challenge us, dodge opportunities, avoid confrontations, people please, overspend, fail to invest, lie, fear asking for what we want, avoid exercising, and all along we wonder why we're so miserable and life sucks, while continuing to place the blame outside of ourselves! But what's that really getting you?

Try It! – Excuses, Excuses, Excuses

Make a list of the ways you try to get yourself out of tight corners, life's uncomfortable situations. When you've got a hot head and cold feet, what's your chosen method of escape? Consider how you've been standing in your own way. What are some of the actions you do to sabotage your happiness and peace of mind?

As you review your list, please bear in mind that there is no room for judgment here. Remember that NLP presupposition we discussed earlier, "People are always doing the best they possibly can given the circumstances they have." You've been doing the best you can. No beating up on yourself, promise. If you've been eating every time your brain goes into freak out mode, that only means it's been your body's way of protecting you and making you feel safe.

As your coach, here, I'll teach you many other ways to get that feeling so you won't have to resort to overeating. Always remember that safety is an important thing to every one of us and all of our behavior centers around how safe or unsafe we feel.

Staying Safe: The Real Reason We Make Excuses

Believe it or not, being fat has its benefits. In *Neuro Linguistic Programming (NLP)* there is another presupposition that states:

"There is a positive intention behind every behavior even if it is not easily recognized or understood." In other words, there are perfectly good reasons why we do the things we do.

The challenge I offer you is to figure out what you are getting out of choosing to remain overweight. Consider the following list and ask yourself: What's the upside of being fat? Are any of the following statements true for you?

1. I get to eat more, I love eating.
2. I get to stay out of the public eye since I want to hide and keep my light hidden, not expressing myself.
3. No honey, not tonight. I have a great game that I play to put my partner through their paces to demonstrate the degree of their loyalty, love, desire, need for me. By keeping them wanting me and refusing their advances, I can still feel desirable and in control and most of all safe from their rejection.
4. I get the validation of understanding that I can be loved for myself despite how I look and feel about my body.
5. I get to spend more time zoning out, watching TV, in solitude, relaxing, reading, feeling sorry for myself, and remaining in a safe cocoon.

6. I get lots of sympathy from people when I share my story of my ongoing battle with my weight, my abuse, or my broken marriage.

7. I get to sing my sad song... Why poor me?

If any of these benefits are resonating with you, it means you are recognizing that you are not being the amazing person you know you truly are! For some reason, you are hiding your light and remaining hidden.

Take Action Now

If you're mad as hell and not going to take it anymore, good, it's time to do something different. You already know the definition of insanity is doing something the same way over and over again and expecting a different result.

Now that you've gotten the excuses out of the way, you can look at another possibility that will actually create change in your life. Are you ready to take action? That means pulling yourself up, dusting yourself off, and getting back in the game.

Instead of sitting idly by and cursing your circumstances, letting your inner-child subconscious mind run the show, or giving up like the little elephant, you can change the way you respond to the things that make you crazy, those chains that bind you. You can change the way you respond to the events in your life until you get the outcomes you want.

Easier said than done, but this is how you do it. You can change your thinking, you can change the pictures you hold in your head, you can change what you tell yourself, you can change your behavior, which changes the things you do. These are really the only things over which you have direct control.

In an upcoming story in the chapter on Visualization, I share an interview I did with author, speaker, and radio talk show host, Lisa Bonnice. Lisa explains how she overcame years of weight obsession and hating her body after she finally stopped worrying about dieting and made peace with food.

She visualized herself thinner by telling herself she was thin before she was. Because she convinced herself she was thinner, she was able to do things a thinner person would do. She breathed differently, smiled more, began to walk with a spring in her step, spent more time outdoors, she climbed stairs with more energy, and so many other things. When her body actually caught up to her thoughts she slimmed down over fifty pounds.

To make peace with food and love your body, you must do what Lisa did:

1. Change your thoughts
2. Change your internal pictures
3. Change your behavior

Do, Be, Have

Carol Tuttle is a Master Energy Therapist, spiritual teacher, creator of the Dressing Your Truth program, and author of many books explaining how to leverage the law of attraction and create more abundance, health, and joy in your life. She says that we live in a have, do, be world, which means that we are raised to believe that we have to do to be. This is not in the flow with attracting what you want, because it creates a lot of resistance.

According to Carol, as a vibrational being, you have a God given blueprint that is best reflected as **Be, Do, Have**. This is the law of attraction expressed in its simplest form. Anything other than this will keep us painfully aware of what we are lacking.

For example: Carol says if you believe you **Have** to **Do** a lot to earn money in order to **Be** financially free, you will create a lot of stuff to do with very little income and a whole lot of stress.

We've spoken about the importance of vibrating in resonance with what you want. You'll recall my thigh story and remember the lesson I learned was that because I was so focused on everything I did not want, and how miserable I was with my thighs, I kept myself in a state of continually vibrating that sense of lack. Since I have changed my thoughts about my thighs and feel much more neutral about them, I notice that they are finally slimming down. Best of all, I haven't done any exercise or radically changed my eating to make that happen.

Consider that your sense of "I am" is the be. This comes from what you believe. When you change your beliefs, you change your vibration. When you change your vibration, you change what you attract.

In Lisa's case, she changed her thoughts about her body first. This created a new belief of how she saw herself. This in turn triggered a domino effect that led to her making effortless changes in her choices and actions. Without even thinking about it, she found herself attracted to an activity that made her feel really good. She found a doctor who understood her needs. She began getting turned off to certain foods and turned on to others. Her body started to do things after she changed her beliefs.

Lisa changed the recipe and that affected the results. Rather than continuing to give into her frustration about gaining weight, feeling old and ugly, and not being able to do anything about it, she put her faith in knowing that the law of attraction could work for her. Having an understanding of the importance of being in resonance with what she wanted and recognizing that she was constantly co-creating with the universe, she knew that she had to start putting herself into a mental and emotional space of already having what she wanted. If you, too, are unhappy with your body, then this is what you must do.

It all starts with adopting different beliefs. When you change your thoughts, which are the core elements of your beliefs, your brain creates internal pictures that go along with your new thoughts and beliefs. When you have compelling internal pictures, driven by feeling strong emotions, it's like footsteps in the sand. It makes it so much easier to just get up and walk that new path. Action to support your new beliefs becomes a no brainer and you create new habits effortlessly.

But this is a process and it takes time to make it a habit. You'll have your share of goofs and frustrations, but the most important thing to remember is a line in one of my favorite poems, "Don't Quit." Remember this:

Rest if you must, but don't you quit.

Consider my favorite Andreaism that comes from my beloved *NLP* training. Mistakes are good. They teach you what to do better next time. I like to think of times when I goof and make a mistake or overeat as part of the plan. I figure what's done is done. In *NLP* speak, "It's feedback, not failure." No use crying over spilled milk and there's certainly no cause for blame.

It's Time for a Change

In *NLP* there's a presupposition that states that the part of something that has the most flexibility is the strongest. That only means that if what you're doing isn't working, try something else. The more flexible and resilient you are in life, the more successful you will be. When you can't change a situation, roll with the punches. Go with the flow.

This speaks specifically to the importance of changing the recipe. Okay, so you can't do anything about the event you're dealing with, but you can change the response you have toward it. When you do that, you will create a new outcome. Be flexible.

Although you don't have control over certain aspects of the situation, you do have control over how you respond to it. To change your response to things, you have to create a new meaning for yourself of the situation.

If you've been abused, rather than using that as an excuse to avoid living, recognize that whatever doesn't kill you can only make you stronger. If you've been fired from a job, realize that you now have an opportunity to find something better. You are always making meaning out of every situation in your life.

Surviving Cancer

I have a dear friend who is a two time cancer survivor. Dee is a brilliant therapist who was struggling financially because she couldn't find it in her heart to charge what she deserved to be paid for her services. She worked with indigents and homeless mothers and anyone else who couldn't pay for therapy. If she charged them at all, she would ask for $5.00. As big as her heart was, she lived in a world where money was important. She had to pay her rent and buy food. She was barely scraping by.

She was diagnosed with breast cancer several years ago. After facing her fears and being told that she would die, she decided that she was not going to allow cancer to strip her of her right to live. She was going to fight.

And that meant that she wasn't going to take it lying down. She was going to change the recipe and adapt her response to the painful news. Rather than feeling sorry for herself and giving up, she made many changes. She changed her diet, she lost weight, she started caring for herself in ways that she never did before. She started to release her resentments from the past, forgiving a father who sexually abused her, a mother who beat her, a system that ignored her talents and skills.

She started letting go of all of her emotional and physical clutter, and began treating herself with love and respect, recognizing when she was overdoing it and pushing herself too hard. She put her finances in the hands of a manager who encouraged her to charge fairly for her services. It meant releasing some of her old clients, but she was able to refer them out to social organizations and other volunteer helpers. Her confidence grew as her caseload increased. Now people paid her happily without complaining, thanking her for her outstanding service.

She sought out alternative healing, got a coach, became a Shaman, spent time and energy being more active, visualized herself healed, and one day she went to the doctor and was told she was in remission.

Several years after things were going smoothly, her life took another turn for the worse. She stopped going to her weekly massages and she gained weight. Her parents were dying, she had accumulated more paper clutter, and had several years of unpaid taxes. Unresolved guilt and sexual issues from her past began to resurface, coinciding with a recent break up. Her life started to hit the skids again.

At the five year point, a critical time for cancer survivors, she was told by her doctor that she had a tumor in her ovary. She regrouped and realized that her life was again causing her to become ill. She pulled back on all her unnecessary commitments and reassessed how she was spending her time. Once again she began paying more attention to her thoughts and went back to meditating. After struggling with her inner demons and fearing a negative outcome, she decided to take the reins of control and beat the odds. Today she is in remission.

In order for Dee to fight her illness, she had to want to live. She had to want to live so much that it pushed aside and eclipsed her fears of dying. She focused exclusively on visualizing what she wanted. One of the most important things she had to do to heal herself was learn how to say the word, "No." Her example taught me to have real appreciation for the word and to recognize that "No" is a complete sentence and anyone who doesn't respect it, is stepping on your boundaries and trying to push your buttons. In the section on Boundaries and Beliefs, I share many ways to say "No" that will get the point across to the thickest of heads.

Cancer was the life situation or event that was out of Dee's control. Setting boundaries in her life and learning to say "No" to others and "Yes" to herself was a change that she was able and willing to make. Instead of blaming and digging herself more deeply into despair, she chose to take a more proactive path and ultimately reclaimed her life. By doing everything within her power to support the work of her medical team, she was participating in her own healing. As a result of changing her response to her diagnosis, her outcome changed. She went into remission, not once but twice.

Try It! – Building New Resources

You know how you can really get stuck in the muck and mire of a problem? You lose your way and aren't able to see the signs or feel your way out of the darkness.

Next time you're feeling stuck, take a moment and allow yourself to step back and glimpse the situation from a different angle. Turn it around and shake it up a bit. Then I'd like you to imagine that you have a magic bag of tricks that will give you the ability to do something different.

One of the resources you can pull out of that bag is to imagine that you are someone who has already handled the problem, feeling confident in your success and achievement. Now stand as you would be standing, breathe as you would be breathing if you were that person with those abilities. In that way, you can step back and see the situation from a different perspective.

This is one of the fun little processes you can do to get yourself unstuck in any situation.

No More Whining or Complaining

I'll be honest and tell you that I spent a lot of time being a capital B Blamer, especially when I was struggling with blaming my father for pulling the business out from under me. It was all that pent up anger that kept me eating out of control. But it took a long time for me to see it because I was completely stuck in my victim groove and so preoccupied with my own drama that I couldn't see past all the smoke.

Complaining, eating, blaming, complaining, eating, blaming, complaining, eating, blaming. I was caught in a never-ending cycle.

Here's the thing about complaining. You only complain about things if you believe they can change. Deep down, you're complaining because you know there's something better waiting for you. That's why you're stuck in your broken record of complaining. You want something to change, and you believe it's possible but don't have the first clue how to do it.

Try It! – What Are You Putting Off?

The credit for this simple exercise goes entirely to Tony Robbins. It was the first exercise on his series of Personal Power II® tapes and it left the biggest imprint on me. It's so simple. I encourage you to do it and watch how effective it is.

What are four things you've been avoiding? Take one small action toward doing each one of them. Tony says, "Never leave the site of a goal without taking action. Do it." You won't believe how good you'll feel after it's done.

What is that action you need to take? Go ahead. Write it down. If it's a phone call you need to make, grab your cell and start dialing. If it's a pile of clutter, start to clear a small corner, keep it small and chunk it down reasonably so that you don't overwhelm yourself. By keeping it manageable you stack the odds of success in your favor.

Who Are You Complaining To?

If you have a problem with your spouse, you may complain to your mother or your girlfriends, but you wouldn't tell your spouse, would you? The thing is that your spouse is the only one who can work with you to actually change what's bugging you. Talk to your spouse and you can compromise. That's a situation you can help to change, so it's on your mind. Things that you can't change you don't think about, or they don't bug you because you just let it go.

You'd never get your knickers in a twist over gravity. Right? It's just something you accept. It's part of life and you've learned to live with it. The cool thing is because we accept it as something that can't be changed, we've learned to play with it and use it to our advantage. If it weren't for gravity, there would be no skydiving, gymnastics, dancing, golf, or any of our favorite sports.

The Courage to Change the Things You Can

Since you're not walking down the street moaning and groaning about gravity you have more clarity in your head so you can actually think about what's bugging you. What are the circumstances in your life that you know could be different? I bet your body is way up there on the list. Isn't it?

Here's the deal. I'll just bet that the situations you're complaining about are things that you can change. You may not know exactly how, but deep down you know that you've got more control over what's bugging you than you think you do.

Here are some actions you can take to help you to change your situation:

- You could say "No"
- You could say what's on your mind
- You could make your happiness a priority
- You could de-clutter your life
- You could start wearing more attractive clothes
- You could avoid hanging out with negative people
- You could pay more attention and be more mindful
- You could listen to your intuition
- You could ask a question
- You could re-evaluate your relationships
- You could ask for help
- You could hire a coach
- You could change doctors
- You could start your own business

But doing these things is scary. It means stepping out of your comfort zone and taking a risk. It may or may not work out to your advantage. It means possible rejection, failure, frustration, insecurity, loss, sadness, pain. You could end up unemployed, divorced, ridiculed, judged, criticized, or laughed at.

Who knows what could happen! You run the risk of being disapproved of by anybody and everybody. But as long as you stand in fear, you're paralyzed, unable to do anything. That makes you a victim of your circumstances. How's that make you feel? Pretty icky I'm sure, and I bet that makes you more willing to take that risk. It sort of smoothes the edge off stepping off that cliff.

To get out of the rat trap here's what you need to do:

Begin making requests of people who can do something about the situation. If you're upset with your daughter and her friend for making noise and keeping everyone awake, don't waste time complaining to your husband, tell the girls.

If your husband is going to be late for dinner, make a request that he call you before you start to cook so you can choose what you want to do, cook, don't cook, eat in, or take out. If your friend always runs late, make a request of her to let you know that she's going to be late as soon as she can.

If you're feeling like you need a break from housework, chores, or cooking, make a request to get some help. Consider hiring a housekeeper or ask your husband to lend a hand. If your kids are old enough, get them involved by having them do age appropriate tasks.

If you're in an uncomfortable situation, decide what you can do and make changes to either get out of it or make it more peaceful. Learn to make requests and take action to get what you need instead of complaining to the wrong person who can't do anything about it.

Make an appointment to see a therapist or speak to a coach. Decide to leave the marriage or commit to stay. Don't just sit there and complain. Do something. Set the intention to walk more often. Prepare dinner earlier. Put your sneakers by the door or leave your gym bag in the car. Tell your well-meaning food cops that they're fired and you're taking over now. It's all in you. You make the decisions. You take the actions. You decide how much happiness you want and go for it.

As both Dee and I learned, in order to make peace with food, love your body, and respect yourself, you've got to exercise your "No" muscles and do things differently.

Take Charge of Your Life

All too often we fall into patterns of tolerating things in our life that displease, bug, and annoy us. Whether they are a leaky faucet, a disorganized mess, a broken bathroom tile, a dirty kitchen, a closet full of clothes that don't fit, piles of clutter, an inbox filled with junk mail, or a jacket in need of mending, the effect on your psyche is the same. If you consent to live with these irritations, knowing full well that you do so at the risk of your comfort and peace of mind, then they have control over you. You are at their mercy.

When you find yourself trying to ignore the upset and would rather live with these little buggers, it sends a message to your brain that you are not worthy of a better life. Ignoring these frustrations can feed into a negative self-image.

That's when you may become complacent and cajole yourself into believing that you are being too picky or difficult to focus on such small things. It's when you consent to wearing a polka dot dress that you hate just because your mom expects or wants you to.

You reason that you don't want to rock the boat and be a pain to make something an issue if it's not. "Let's let sleeping dogs lie," you may say. But if it's bugging you and isn't contributing to your happiness, then it's just making you miserable.

Try It! – Clearing Your Emotional and Physical Clutter

Look at your life and reassess it. Notice what irritates you and causes you frustration. Go through every room of your home and office and make a list of what bugs you. Keep an inventory of what holds an emotional charge for you and take steps to change it or get rid of it. If you're holding onto a polka dot dress that you hate, it's time to let it go.

Get four boxes and label each one accordingly. Donations, keepers, mend, toss. Be vicious and ruthless and let nothing that bugs you remain. You're doing this to reclaim your space.

Is it an overflowing closet that you avoid opening or perhaps a crooked picture that doesn't hang straight on your wall? Start to take note of the things in your life that you have been saying, "Oh, it's okay, I can live with it."

Try It! – Make a Bug List

Make a list of 100 things that put your knickers in a twist, tie you in knots, and just plain make you mad. Each day commit to taking three little steps to eradicate those bullying buggers.

Now, since you've eased your mind by writing those things down, they don't have to haunt you anymore. You'll feel motivated to handle them because their absence from the list just makes you feel so darned good. You can get right back down to the business of taking it easy and food may never even enter the equation, right? Who knows what fun things will happen!

You owe it to yourself to handle the little irritations and bug'ems that annoy you, because if you don't they will eat at you until you do. Before you know it, you'll eat more than you want or will nervously pick at the frosting of a donut that you realize you don't even like. To avoid falling into that rut, here are a couple of ideas that I have to help you deal with that mental and emotional clutter:

You're Always in the Process of Creation

By allowing circumstances to continue or actively choosing them, you are always creating your life. Things are exactly as you created them to be. If you're unhappy with your job, it's the result of choices you've made that put you where you are.

If your sex life is in the toilet, you contributed and participated enough, or, as the case may be, perhaps you didn't participate and just tried to avoid having sex. Maybe, like me, you made up lies or overate knowing it would make you sick in order to give you the excuse you needed to get out of feeling so damned guilty for rejecting your mate yet again.

If your house is a mess, you chose to avoid taking care of it and clearing the clutter before it got overwhelming. You let the kids color on the walls in the living room, you didn't replace the vacuum bags, and you left the dirty dishes in the sink. You chose to pretend it wasn't all that bad. You said, "Not today. I'm too tired. I want to take it easy. I never get any help."

If you're disconnecting from your family or husband, then you contributed by ignoring their requests to spend time with you, avoiding their disappointed glances, and trying to convince yourself that it wasn't that big a deal.

If you're overweight, you made a consistent habit of eating when you weren't hungry. You eat every time you think of food. You keep telling yourself the same old fat stories, playing the role of victim. You decided to sit on the sofa when the family suggested taking a walk together, you decided to eat a mountain of popcorn with extra butter and tell yourself you're still hungry. You let the scale, the diet organization, the group, your husband, kids, or parents, determine how you feel about yourself.

The things we do have consequences and the things we don't do also have consequences. Action and inaction both yield outcomes. This is the law of cause and effect.

Warning Bells

You know that things don't just happen out of nowhere. We have a hand in their creation. Our thoughts bring them to fruition and that makes up our reality. Most women have what's called women's intuition. It's your internal radar system that tells you when something doesn't quite feel right. Guys have it too, but for the most part, we have a much more highly developed system since we use our brains differently. We process information faster and more effectively than men. We notice things like telltale signs, twinges, feelings, the way someone sounds, snide comments, rude remarks, and other things that give us advance warning of things to come.

Different kinds of warnings exist, both internal and external.

Internal

There's a whole language that describes these "can't quite put your finger on it" internal warnings:

 Clues, feelings, suspicions, inklings

 Handwriting's on the wall

 I had a feeling

 My intuition told me

 My stomach says

169

- Something's telling me
- I could see it coming for a mile
- I could just feel it
- My gut's telling me

This is how you can recognize these internal signals:
- The queasy feeling in the pit your stomach
- That inkling you had
- That sense that something feels fishy
- The shiver down your spine
- The sudden fear you felt
- The fleeting thought that just maybe…
- The dream that woke you in the middle of the night

External

External signs exist too. You can recognize them by paying attention to and relying on your senses. These warning bells are the ones that you can see, hear, feel, taste, or touch:
- Your friends warned you
- That funny smell
- That odd look he gave you
- His edgy tone when he spoke
- His quick temper
- His falling grades

Changing Your Responses

It's your wonderful internal guidance system of your emotions that gives you the ability to change the way you respond to life's circumstances. When you're feeling good, you're in the flow and that's when things will click into high gear for you. When you're not feeling good, your body will tell you what you need in order to guide you back to that sense of feeling good.

All this information is waiting for you, but you have to be willing to trust and have faith in yourself, believe in what's important to you, and take the risk. So that means following up on those internal feelings that tell you to do things that often fly in the face of logic. It means being willing to do scary things like asking about the charges on the Amex bill, requesting others to lend a helping hand, telling someone you don't trust them, speaking up when you're afraid of being judged, and stepping out of your box.

It's the avoidance of unpleasant things in your life that have kept you in patterns of overeating and feeling frustrated with your body. Believe it or not, by slowly and gently taking steps to face them squarely, one by one, in your own way, on your own terms, life becomes easier and the wrinkles in your day will start to smooth out. By allowing yourself to take a risk and become comfortable being a bit uncomfortable, the payoff will be enormous.

You'll take action to create what you want, increase your self-confidence, take bigger steps, assume greater risks, and you'll notice yourself making giant leaps because you'll think about yourself differently. You'll value yourself differently. You'll know that you're not just a fat pair of thighs or a flabby tummy, droopy breasts or a big bottom. You're a woman, making things happen in your life, getting more and more excited with each new step you take, getting more and more of what you want.

As you take steps to prove to yourself that you can defy your old self imposed limits, you'll notice that your self-talk will make some radical changes. The old opera that's been playing in your head, "You're not good enough, you're too stupid, you'll always be fat, ugly, broke, and dumb..." will lose its sizzle. You'll get pretty impatient hearing that, and it will become easier to speak to yourself in different and more loving ways that I'll teach you.

Ask a Better Question

The most powerful way to change the meaning you give to something is to shift your focus. Since focus is controlled by the quality of questions you ask, doing this one thing will change your life.

The most powerful way to control your focus is through the use of questions.
– *Anthony Robbins*

You will change your life by changing the questions you ask yourself.

The first thing I learned when I started my coaching certification was how to ask proper questions. You may say that's ridiculous. Anyone knows how to ask a question. That's true. Asking run of the mill questions is very easy, but in order to activate your creative imagination and spur your intuition, you need to ask questions in a certain way. In coach speak, this is called asking empowering questions and the result of doing so creates a powerful impact.

Unlike a closed question, where a one word response will suffice, open ended questions or empowering questions will get you to dig beneath the surface. By learning how to use these types of questions, you will be able to evoke discovery, elicit insights, motivate commitment, and inspire taking action.

Questions that are open ended such as those beginning with the words **how** or **what**, fire up your creative brain, temporarily pushing aside your analytical left brain. This is the logical, methodical, gatekeeper that is your inner critic. By shoving aside your inner critic, you get to connect with your wise self, your intuition. This is your right brain.

Kurt Wright, author of the book, *Breaking the Rules: Removing the Obstacles to Effortless High Performance*, says that there are several questions we can use at any time to change our situation. These are five levels of what Wright calls "What's Right Questions." Using these questions will get you out of a rut, give you boundless energy, and some honest to goodness working direction to create a strategy. Up until now they have been the domain of visionary thinkers and little kids.

According to Kurt Wright, the following is the five level structure of asking Right questions:

Level 1: "What do I know about this situation that's already working? This question gives you a place to start to become aware of your situation. It puts your focus on what you're doing that is already benefiting you. By being aware of this, it's easier to continue doing more of what works.

Level 2: "What is it about what you're doing that is making it work? This question is a hotline to your subconscious mind giving you the awareness of what is already working and what makes it work.

Level 3: In a perfect world, what situation would be your ideal? What would that look like to you?

This question gets you to envision what an ideal outcome would look like for you.

Level 4: What's missing?

This enables you to step back and look at the big picture and to see what part of the plan is still not fitting in with your vision. Ask yourself, "How is this working for me so far?"

Level 5: What situations, people or knowledge can you leverage that will help you to get to where you want to go?

This question pushes you to work out the details and get to the nitty and the gritty.

By using questions in this way, you'll focus on what changes you need to make to get more of what you want. As author, Kurt Wright mentions in the book, when he described this method to Fred Smith, Federal Express founder, and Chairman, Smith remarked, "This is the first time in my life I have ever had anyone describe to me the exact same process I used to build this company."

Now you know. It's good stuff. Give it a go.

Ask For Feedback

Most people can't stand being criticized by others. But if you ask qualified people who you trust to give you constructive feedback, you'll learn faster what you need to do differently.

Think in terms of using open ended questions. Here are a few ideas:

How am I doing? What do I need to do to improve? What's the best way to do that? What can I be doing better? What else could I be doing? What's missing? What's not working? How much is enough? How will I know I'm doing this right? How do you see me limiting myself?

Asking questions of people tells them that you respect their opinion and consider them an expert. It also shows them that you're a go getter who appreciates their time and wants to put their wisdom to work so you can succeed. Always check in with your heart and see what's right for you. Then weigh your heart's guidance against what you are asking for and you'll know which path is right.

Weighing Your Results: Pay Attention to Feedback

This means using all your senses to evaluate and pay close attention to what results you're getting. As I said, you have to care. This process requires that you become more aware, disciplined, focused, dedicated, and willing to experiment and take risks. If nothing is panning out the way you want it to, then do something different. If you're focused on your goal, feeling good and seeing results, keep going.

As my mentor, Jana Stanfield, recommends, make it a point of taking at least three small baby step actions toward a goal and noticing what results you are getting before you decide to shift gears and change directions.

Keep taking action and asking for feedback all the way through. If you don't ask for feedback from someone else, check in with yourself.

There's absolutely no shame in asking for help. It's dysfunctional thinking to believe that you can do it alone. I made that mistake for too long.

Here are some questions inspired by Jack Canfield's book, *The Success Principles*™. You'll notice that most of these questions begin with the words "How" or "What." That's done to get you thinking using your speedy processing intuitive right brain.

Ask yourself:

What am I doing that is making things worse? What am I doing that is causing this situation to occur? What are my actions or inactions saying about me? What do I need to do more often? Should I be more assertive, ask more questions, think before I speak, take time to meditate, plan better, be more organized, be more present, a better listener, be more affectionate, speak from the heart, etc).

What do I need to change? (Am I too demanding, being a bully, wasting time, eating out of control, being overly critical of myself and others, spending too much time on the computer)

Juicy Woman Note:

I highly recommend reading *The Success Principles*™ by Jack Canfield. It is filled with proven techniques you can immediately put into practice in your life. As I said before, don't believe me. Try it yourself and see what you think. He really is the master of self-esteem building.

What things could I try to see if they will make me feel better? (Can I get more sleep, do more tapping, carve out more time for myself, get together with a supportive friend, go for a walk, give belly dancing a try, ask a friend for help, hire a coach, go to the doctor, take a yoga class)

All you have to do is try things out and if they don't work, try something else. Keep on noticing what results you are getting and move forward. In the next chapter, called Embrace Your Emotions, you'll find out how you can actually make those cruddy bubble bustin', joy sucking' feelings actually work for you.

Wrapping Up
Chapter 5: Responsibility: Take Charge of Your Life

Here are the juiciest bits covered in this section. Savor them mindfully.

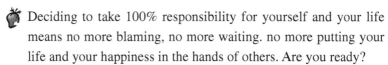 Deciding to take 100% responsibility for yourself and your life means no more blaming, no more waiting. no more putting your life and your happiness in the hands of others. Are you ready?

It's going to require some bold thinking to step out of your old uncomfortable comfort zone thinking that you can't do anything about whatever situation you're facing.

Are you willing to let go of your weight obsession and change your focus to the bigger things that have been getting covered up by your weight distraction?

Being overweight is not the problem. It's only a symptom of the problem.

Psst. I want you to know that your mirror is playing tricks with you. Right now at this moment you're probably not really seeing yourself as you are. This is why it is so hard for many women to look in mirrors. It's because when you see yourself, you're looking at what you expect to see. A fat woman.

It's very likely that your decision to accept your body will not come in a flash. It will probably come to you in a whisper.

As you clear away your stresses, you'll regain a sense of your powerful self, remembering how good it feels to be in charge. As the kinks and distortions in your body's energy field get ironed out, it will become second nature to want to feel good.

You must take responsibility, and be willing to open your eyes and see what's in front of you. Then if you don't like what you see, gather the courage to do something about it.

Happiness is a choice. If you believe that your happiness is tied up and contingent upon certain circumstances or people, then you'll always be trying to catch the elusive butterfly.

You are the only person who can ever really stand in your own way. We are so often our own worst enemy. By doing things that sabotage your goals, you prevent yourself from achieving them.

 All too often we fall into patterns of tolerating things in our life that displease, bug, and annoy us. Whether they are a leaky faucet, a disorganized mess, a broken bathroom tile, a dirty kitchen, a closet full of clothes that don't fit, piles of clutter, an inbox filled with junk mail, or a jacket in need of mending, the effect on your psyche is the same. If you consent to live with these irritations, knowing full well that you do so at the risk of your comfort and peace of mind, then they have control over you. You are at their mercy.

 When you find yourself trying to ignore the upset and would rather live with these little buggers, it sends a message to your brain that you are not worthy of a better life. Ignoring these frustrations can feed into a negative self-image.

 Believe it or not, by slowly and gently taking steps to face them squarely, one by one, in your own way, on your own terms, life becomes easier and the wrinkles in your day will start to smooth out. By allowing yourself to take a risk and become comfortable being a bit uncomfortable, the payoff will be enormous.

 As my mentor, Jana Stanfield, recommends, make it a point of taking at least three small baby step actions toward a goal and noticing what results you are getting before you decide to shift gears and change directions.

Chapter 6
Embrace Your Emotions: Creating Feelings of Safety Within

"Your overweight self doesn't stand before you craving food. She's craving love. Falling off the wagon isn't a weight issue; it's a love issue."
– *Marianne Williamson*

No matter how many muffins, cakes, pies, steaks, or goodies you consume, you will never be able to eat enough to fill that part of you that aches for true fulfillment and substance: love. As a flesh and blood human being, your biggest craving is for love and comfort. We all want and need that.

You may have deluded yourself into believing that you'll only be worthy of love, security, and happiness when you get to a certain weight, stop procrastinating, make X amount of money, marry the perfect mate, win his/her love, close the deal, buy the car, get the degree, ace the test, get the client, etc. But these aren't really the things or the actions you're after. They're not what you really want. What you really want can't be bought, purchased, sold, or bartered.

"The controlling force that directs your life is
what you link pain and pleasure to."
– Anthony Robbins

Every single thing we do is merely an attempt to change the way we feel. To some degree, each of us holds a core belief that we are not enough just the way we are. Within each of us we hold an image of our potential. From that image, we create our life. You only want the things you say you want because you think they will make you feel good and feeling good will bring you closer to feeling lovable and worthy.

Chapter Preview of Coming Attractions

In this chapter, I'll explain how your emotions are actually living vibrations that function like an internal guidance system. Best of all, I'm going to teach you how to create those ooey gooey feelings of goodness, happiness, pleasure, safety, and comfort that you used to only get from food. Using the cookies in milk strategies and yummy delicious tools you will learn in this section and throughout the book, you'll be able to deal with the barking emotions and chaos causing circumstances that are triggering pain in your life. You will learn to take back the power that food has stolen from you as you build a stronger, more positive self-image.

As you begin to tease apart fiction from reality and notice that you can choose the way you feel as opposed to being in constant reaction mode, a curvy and more confident self will become second nature. You will notice that as you learn how to use your body differently, and draw upon more experiences that add to making you feel better about yourself, you won't want to use food for comfort quite as often as you have in the past. You'll rely less and less upon food to do it for you.

By the time you've completed this section, you'll know how you can go from feeling gloomy to glorious, wrinkled to relaxed, and sour to sweet. It's all about changing state and managing your mood. And that is what's on the menu today.

Eating in the Light of the Moon

In her book, *Eating in the Light of the Moon: How Women Can Transform Their Relationships with Food through Myths, Metaphors and Storytelling,* author Anita Johnston, Ph.D., describes the importance of finding the real meaning behind the need to eat compulsively. She explains the philosophy behind her statement that "Food is not the real issue." It is a smoke screen. Your struggles with food have been distracting you from taking a closer look at what situations in your life have been the core issues bugging you.

As long as you focus all of your attention and energy on what you're eating, how much, when, the size of your thighs, how much you weigh, and all that other body hating fluff and food obsession, it doesn't leave much energy left over for living. As a result, you'll find yourself chasing your tail, running in circles always trying to pinpoint and blame your misery on the size of your body and your eating habits.

During a vacation in Puerto Rico I read, *Eating in the Light of the Moon.* It was then that I had my first real Aha moment and understood that being fat kept me feeling safe. It meant I didn't have to venture into the world to take risks or be rejected.

As I delved deeper into that insight, I realized that by learning to talk to myself and think of myself in the way that my father had been doing, I had been practicing rejecting myself for the majority of my life.

I knew that if I was ever going to break through this harmful dynamic, I had to start thinking differently and see myself from the eyes of one who could love me unconditionally.

That's when many other things began to tumble into place for me. I knew that I had to end my obsession and desire to lose weight and stop looking at my body from the mental eyes of my far too critical father. I had to start looking at other areas of my life where I had allowed his toxic opinions of me to form the basis of my relationship with myself. I had to dig deep and be willing to find out how deep the damage ran. That was when I knew that my problem was never really the size of my thighs.

I had deluded myself for years thinking my thighs were the source of my misery. Without ever realizing it, I had allowed that single belief to take over my entire life. In March 2009, when I created the So Many Sighs Over

181

My Big Fat Thighs video, I was shocked to realize I had actually let nearly thirty-four years of my life slip away because I had become my own worst enemy. I had come to hate a body which was perfectly lovely, although I wasn't able to recognize it at the time.

I made the mistake of letting someone else tell me how I should feel about myself. I was completely blinded by my bad habits. I only saw myself as a reflection of my father. Because he couldn't love me, I had judged myself as unlovable.

When I began the work of acknowledging the deep hurt and anguish over the loss of my ideal father-daughter fantasy, and I realized that my father only did the best he could, it became crystal clear that I didn't want to be like him anymore. In his perpetually disconnected state from his emotions, I could see that they were running his life. His anger was eating him up. Suddenly, that realization made it possible for me to want to learn how to master my emotions so that my fate wouldn't be the same as his.

That's when I began to allow myself the gift of accepting more of me. I knew that I liked myself when he wasn't around, and I was willing to get to know this woman who I had spent years trying to run away from. Me!

Since I had been used to living for far too long in a closed environment where problems were not spoken about, discontent was rarely voiced, and emotions were neither given respect nor treated with dignity, it was a real challenge for me to feel safe expressing my emotions.

I realized that in my years of over-identifying with my father's ways, I had attracted a man who had a similar disposition toward expressing his emotions as my father. My husband, Angel, although a wonderful man, was basically very uncomfortable sharing his feelings or having me express mine. I had my work cut out for me.

I knew that if I were going to preserve my marriage, I had to appeal to him from my heart and recognize that my new way of dealing with my emotions was going to mean a lot of change in the family. It wasn't going to be easy, and I had to understand that.

What am I asking this food to do for me?

One of my clients, Sarah, had been struggling with a resurgence of her sugar craving that wouldn't go away after attending a friend's wedding.

When she joined my Losing Weight without Dieting program, she was eager to learn what was really behind her sugar urges.

After I gave her the first assignment, the Mindful and Gentle Eating Process, she came back and shared her insights with the group. She said, "I gave myself permission to eat sugar this week, whenever I felt like it I ate sugar. And then when I ate it, I tried to understand what it made me feel like. Better yet, what was I asking it to do? And usually I was asking it to either comfort me, soothe me, make me feel happier or better, less anxious—all of the emotions that fuel people to eat."

Jen was another client who came to me to lose weight. She had been struggling with chocolate cravings that were driving her crazy. When she discovered what was actually behind her desire for chocolate, she was amazed that the cravings disappeared almost instantly.

Jen had lost her mother to breast cancer a few years prior, and since that time she had gained about eighty extra pounds. That coincided with her decision to give up smoking. Feeling the urgency to fill the emptiness that her smoking addiction used to satisfy, she began to crave chocolate.

As we tapped together, it became clear that her cravings for chocolate were a desire to feel reconnected to her mother. She had never gotten a chance to properly mourn her loss. Once she began to grieve for her mother, her chocolate craving disappeared.

Identify Your Triggers

Begin to notice when you're reaching for that second helping or panting at the thought of grabbing a snack right after you've already eaten. Looking back now, I realize that if I would have paid attention to the times when I was overeating and taken a position of being curious, wanting to know why I wanted to eat rather than being judgmental and hang myself up by my thumbs for having no will power, I likely would not have gained the thirty-five extra pounds that I did.

To get off the diet mentality, the make-or-break, all-or-nothing merry go round, you have to become aware of what triggers your thoughts. You'll go a long way toward legalizing food when you're able to identify the internal and external cues that push you to eat when you're not hungry.

In the same category as these cues, keep an eye out for any and all black and white thinking that leads you flailing headfirst into the perfection pit.

Rethinking Your Ideas About Pain and Pleasure

There are two major forces that shape our lives: pain and pleasure. What meanings you link to each of them determine how you live.

As a child, you learned how to think about pain and pleasure from your parents and other people who had a hand in raising you. Their beliefs about the world have become what Gary Craig, inventor of the *Emotional Freedom Techniques® (EFT)*, calls "the writing on your walls."

Emotional eaters link extreme pleasure to food. This is the underlying reason why diets don't work for most people, because they move you away from gaining pleasure and toward creating pain. That only increases your desire to eat more which still keeps your relationship with food off balance.

If you want to balance out the scales and enjoy more harmony with food and your body, it's going to require you to change the way you think about pain and pleasure. On a recent vacation I had the opportunity to spend some time with my mother and that experience taught me a lot about the importance of creating new meanings for old situations.

When Crisis Hits...

Like many women, I often have a very tense relationship with my mother. With a few exceptions, I've spent most of my life estranged from her. The truth is I hardly know her. Despite the fact that she is probably one of the sweetest, most loving and generous people in the world, I often find myself harboring so much resentment and anger toward her because she is a constant reminder to me of a disempowered woman. Sadly, much of the time I find myself thinking of my mom as a lost soul, because she's not really living or enjoying her life. She's just existing.

Many years ago when I was a child, she made a choice that affected her life. She chose to remain with her sexually abusive husband over me. Because she never dealt with the stress that decision created in her life, about eighteen years ago she developed bipolar disorder. She basically "checked out."

After many years of avoiding her, staying away, and holding a grudge, I learned about the power of forgiveness when I first experienced *EFT*. That was when I tried to "rescue" her and do whatever I could to help her control her illness. For the sake of reconnecting with my mother and finding my own inner peace, I even forgave her husband, my abuser.

But due to mom's illness, I always came full circle knowing that I didn't have the right or the power to choose wellness and health for her. As I've been continually reminded over the years, the control is in her hands, and her husband's, not mine. And I've had to realize and accept the fact that I can't do much to help her without her cooperation. So I've had to let go with love, but it's not easy.

Because we've been closer lately, speaking on the phone often, I hoped her latest visit would be different. I wrongly assumed that the old mom would come back and we could get to know one another again. But after a day of being able to enjoy bits and pieces of the old mom, her illness returned and she ended up spending the rest of the six days avoiding eye contact, looking frightened and sad, staring into space, and being mostly unresponsive—a shell of her former self. At one point she told me that she just wanted to be back home with her husband because she felt comfortable there. It breaks my heart to see her this way, but I know that I've got to let her go.

How about you? Do you have a parent, family member, spouse, friend, or other person in your life who seems to be gradually pulling away? Is your heart telling you "it's time to let go?" How have you been dealing with those feelings of loss? Have you been using food to comfort you?

The first couple of days when mom was here, I noticed myself eating more than I normally would. Then after realizing that I was falling back into my old pattern of overeating in reaction to feeling helpless, I remembered that I had a choice. I could either volunteer to be miserable or choose to find whatever happiness I could and enjoy the small bits of time when she was coherent and more like her old self. As I told her, "I can love you between the spaces."

First, I had to start with forgiving myself for all the lost time I wasted staying away. Then I had to assuage my fears that I wouldn't end up like her, because I've made the choice to love myself and care deeply about my health. I'll do whatever I can to overcome my fears and limiting beliefs and not live imprisoned by them.

Recognizing how angry, hurt, and sad I was to see that she was slipping away yet again, I chose to take care and comfort myself by investing more of my time meditating and tapping. That gave me the peace of mind I needed to know that every moment counts. It enabled me to connect with my heart and love her without being overwhelmed by a cascade of mixed emotions.

Holding on and Letting Go

Eating to calm your stress only feels good in the moment. But because it doesn't actually eliminate the source of your stress, eventually you'll find yourself overeating again.

When I was going through my *NLP* Practitioner training, I learned a phrase that is often used in Hypnosis, "Holding on and letting go." This comes from the word artistry that world renowned hypnotherapist, Milton Erickson, became known for. "Holding on and letting go" is a bit of tongue twister for your brain, because it would seem that it is impossible to hold on and let go at the same time. At least that's what we know from playing the children's game tug-of-war. But life is not a rope. And it's this black and white thinking that often creates so much stress in our lives because it limits your options to only two, holding on or letting go.

But what if you knew that you could do both, hold on and let go, at the same time? For example, in my life I know I can hold on to the love that I have for both of my parents and let go of the hurt and anger I feel toward them. I know I can hold onto the happy memories and let go of the painful ones. I know I can hold onto hope and let go of fear. I know I can hold onto my connection to my body and the universe and let go of seeking validation outside of myself. I know I can hold onto my ability to say "No" and let go of my need to say "Yes."

Overall I've learned that knowing when to hold on and let go is one of the biggest keys to overcoming the tendency to consistently overeat. The old Andrea, the consummate control freak, would always confuse the two because I used to equate holding on with being secure and happy. Letting go always meant losing something. Now I realize that happiness is a choice and the worst thing you can do is expect others to make you happy. To do that, you leave yourself open to losing ground every time change happens. And let's be honest, that's when the cries of hunger are the loudest. Aren't they?

So how do you think you can apply this in your life? What do you need to hold onto and let go of in order to be happier, less stressed, and satisfy your emotional hunger?

Emotions: Your Vibrational Indicators

In the New York Times Bestselling book, *Ask and It is Given*, by Esther and Jerry Hicks, Esther channels the guidance of a spirit called "Abraham." In the book it is explained that your emotions are similar to the GPS in your car, because they function as indicators letting you know where you are and where you're going. They show what vibrational frequency you're sending and this will determine what you are manifesting or attracting.

Your emotions measure how close or far away you are from your natural source, God, the universe, etc. Depending upon how connected you feel to that divine essence of creation, you'll either be more happy and joyful or less.

Consider that the law of attraction is like a huge flowing river filled with rapids. As you move downstream there is no resistance and your raft will go very quickly. However, if you are attempting to paddle your way upstream you will be moving against the natural current and it will take enormous effort to get wherever you want to go.

If you've been trying to control your weight by doing things like going on a diet, buying exercise equipment that you haven't enjoyed using, taking diet pills, fasting, eating foods you hate, dragging yourself to the gym, and depriving yourself of the foods you love, these are all examples of going against the natural flow of abundance. This is suffering and that's no fun.

You may say that the problem is your metabolism, perhaps you're getting older and your body is slowing down. Although this may be true, it is also the result of being in resonance with that vibration of sluggishness and lethargy. When you begin to resonate and "Be" that person who you want to be, your attitude toward food and your relationship with it will change completely. Your energy will balance and you will feel more at ease. As a result, your resistance will drop and you'll be in the flow enjoying your life more. That's when you'll notice your body shifting and reshaping, getting thinner without the struggle.

The Vibrational Scale of Emotions

In order to be successful at breaking through the barrier of resistance that your subconscious mind has in place, you must be able to raise your vibration. That comes with changing the way you feel about yourself, food, and your body.

Your goal is to reach the highest vibration possible at any given moment. Sometimes this will be contentment, other times passion, boredom, anger, happiness, or optimism. As emotional eaters, we've learned how to use food to cut ourselves off from feelings and how to tune out our emotions

In order to rebalance your relationship with food so that your body can reshape and feel good again, you need to start paying attention to what you are feeling.

In the book, Abraham names twenty-two different levels of emotions and arranges them on a scale from the lowest to the highest. The ones at the bottom are the least desirable and make you feel worse. The ones above them are more desirable and make you feel better.

Just like the GPS on a car, you can only get to where you want to be if you know your starting point. Using the scale will tell you where you are now. No judgment. It's all good. Wherever you start is fine.

For the most part, it's difficult to take a leap and move from being severely depressed to overjoyed. This is why it's best to take a step by step approach to reaching for the next best, lighter emotion. Your only goal is to feel a little bit better and keep on improving.

Your body is your best indicator telling you if you feel more relieved and better, or less relieved and worse.

Here is a copy of that emotional scale:
1. Joy/Knowledge/Empowerment/Freedom/Love/Appreciation
2. Passion
3. Enthusiasm/Eagerness/Happiness
4. Positive Expectation/Belief

5. Optimism
6. Hopefulness
7. Contentment
8. Boredom
9. Pessimism
10. Frustration/Irritation/Impatience
11. "Overwhelmed"
12. Disappointment
13. Doubt
14. Worry
15. Blame
16. Discouragement
17. Anger
18. Revenge
19. Hatred/Rage
20. Jealousy
21. Insecurity/Guilt/Unworthiness
22. Fear/Grief/Depression/Despair/Powerlessness

The above list represents Abraham's emotional scale that reflects the twenty-two levels of emotions. Now that you have this information, you can use this scale to judge if the way you are feeling is better or worse.

Consider where you spend most of your time. This would be your default setting. No matter where you are on the scale, you can either go up or down, depending upon what you think about, what pictures you make in your mind, and what you do.

Here's an extra bit of deliciousness that comes from one of my wonderful editors, Karenna. She came up with the following great idea for this next *Try It!*

Try It! – "Exploring Your Hunger"

Make a copy of the Abraham emotional scale and put it on your fridge. You may want to take the names of the emotions and create your own visual images or photos to match each one. If you

---

would like to play and be creative, take out a camera and have someone take a picture of you acting out each of the twenty-two different emotions. As long as you can identify them and label them, they will work for you.

Then after putting your emotional scale poster up on the fridge, consult it often, especially during times you feel the need to eat when you know your body is not hungry.

With one quick glance, you can either read the emotion or see the image; you'll be able to pinpoint how you are feeling.

Then ask yourself the question, "What am I really hungry for?" This will support you in seeking the truth behind your craving and dealing with your emotions.

Creating Your Own Sense of Safety

If food has been your safe haven, your refuge from hurt and disappointment, it's likely you've been using it to protect yourself for quite a while. If that's the case, you're probably doing it because you don't have a strong sense of what it's like to be safe in your body.

I don't know about you, but now I realize that on some subconscious level I have relied on my excess weight to give me a sense of substance and strength that I didn't feel I had without it. In business, I've relied on my ability to "throw my weight around" to give me a sense of being capable and qualified to do the job at hand. I wanted people to listen to me and respect me. I didn't want a cute and sexy body to interfere with my ability to be taken seriously.

In my personal life, I know my remaining weight continues to dissolve as I deal with my issues of feeling safe being a woman. Being sexually abused left me with many negative thoughts and fears around my right to feel safe and enjoy being sexual.

> ## Juicy Woman Note:
>
> The above Try It! is a fabulous tool to use to prepare you for the Emotional Freedom Technique. By knowing what emotion you are feeling, you'll be able to choose what you want to feel instead.

Many times I remember eating a pint of Ben and Jerry's® Mint Chocolate Cookie ice cream late in the evening, knowing full well that it would cause me discomfort and make me sick. I did that in an attempt to avoid having sex with my husband because I was insecure about my body and feared he was repulsed by me. I thought the first chance he got, he would leave me for a thinner, more beautiful woman. How about you? Have you been feeling insecure or unsafe in some part of your life?

Try It! – The Circle of Life

For each of the following sections of your life, give it a number between 1-10 indicating how safe or secure you feel in that area. 1 indicates the lowest level of safety and 10 is the highest.

After you've determined the degree of safety you feel in each of these areas, use the Emotional Scale to determine what emotional set point is your default setting for each of these aspects of your life.

Family/Parenting

Personal Development

Spirituality

Fun & Enjoyment

Intimate and Social Relationships

Health/Aging

Personal Finance

Career/Profession

Clues You May Be Feeling Unsafe

There are so many ways we demonstrate feeling unsafe in our lives.

1. If you're usually a gal who eats on the run, you're conveying a message to your body that danger is around the corner. If you're an emotional eater, you'll recognize that you probably wolf down food rather than savoring every bite.

2. If you're a worrier, then you've learned to be constantly on guard, cautious and fearful, suspicious of everyone and everything.

3. If you're a person who is considered clumsy, or always gets into accidents, you're probably feeling pretty unsafe always having to be on guard to protect yourself.

4. You may notice you go for long periods of time when you're working intensely, and then go for long periods of time when you completely stop working. You then go back to working really hard and then stop, continuing the same cycle.

If you're not feeling safe, then you're in a position of being constantly afraid of people rejecting you. This gives them power over your happiness. This may show up in terms of not being willing to take risks, undercharging for your services, and not asking for what you want.

Try It! – How Is Your Excess Weight Protecting You?

Make a list of the situations in which you tend to eat when you're not hungry. Do you get a case of the willies if someone invites you to a buffet? Do you feel compelled to get the double buttered popcorn at the movies? Is cake a necessary evil whenever there's a birthday? When visiting your food-pushing friends and family, how easy is it for you to say, "No thanks. I don't want any more now. Let's just wrap it to go." Notice which areas of your life are affected most by your food and weight obsessions.

Making the Expression of Anger Feel Safe

I'm not usually a person who gets angry easily. However, now I have a much healthier respect for anger than I ever did before. Where I used to think that only people who were out of control expressed their anger, I now know that a healthy expression of anger will help you get back in control much faster than if you just choose to feed the feelings.

Stuffing my emotions has always been my way of dealing with my anger because I have had a fear of being out of control. This comes from my habit of bottling up my anger and letting it fester by pushing it down with food. I don't know about you, but I was taught that ladies don't express anger. What a lot of hooey! You'll notice as you look at the list on page 188-189, that anger is #17 on the scale, which is considerably higher than fear/grief/depression/powerlessness at #22.

By reading the book *Ask and It is Given,* and others like it, and by using *EFT* to vent my anger more often, I've opened up new insights about different parts of my life. This has led to a lot of anger and resentment popping up.

When I first began this journey, I automatically judged and discounted my anger, reasoning that "I shouldn't be angry and that it was so long ago and there is nothing that I can do to change history." Accepting the belief that I, "had no right to be angry" and I should let it go and be the bigger person, I fell into a deep depression and began to grieve parts of my past and my disempowered actions.

After learning that valuable lesson and having plenty of time to stew in my own juices, my depression lifted and I got angry again. Anger is five spaces above depression which makes it a more favorable emotion. With that second wind of anger pulsating in me, I decided it was okay and I would deal with it through tapping. Not surprisingly, it worked like magic and put me back on the road to personal power in the one-to-five range once again.

Here's my question. Are you having the same experience I did? Do you automatically discount your anger and try to forget about it, ignore it, or stuff it down with food?

If you do, recognize that the biggest problem with anger is that we often fail to give it adequate space to breathe. Anger often contracts and internalizes making you think you have no right to feel this way. When you think your feelings don't count and you have no right to them, you will naturally slip down into deeper depths of despair.

Try It! – Eecking Up the Ladder

At your next opportunity, consider where you are in the moment with your emotions. Then think about just getting up to the next level. Notice how a small effort is enough to make you move from one point on the scale to the next. Ask yourself, what would I need to believe, think, or have in order to feel the tiniest bit better? What will it take to move up to the next level? Just think about moving one space at a time. According to the law of attraction, it's not sufficient to make the leap from Depression to Joy without having a bridge of feelings in between. By baby-stepping your way up the ladder, you create a slow and steady momentum, moving you up the scale of emotions in a way that feels true to you.

It's Feedback, Not Failure: From Yippee Yahooie to Yikes

Just like a plane in flight, you are also on a journey. It's expected that you're going to zig and zag, rise and fall. That's the difference between a process way of thinking vs. formula or linear thinking.

At this point, since you're playing some new games with food, everything is bright and shiny again. You're in what I call the Yahoo phase, where you may find yourself overeating and perhaps gaining weight. Please don't panic. That's pretty natural. You've been deprived of eating real food for a long time, fearing the wrath of diets.

If you have already given yourself total, unbridled freedom to eat, in many ways you're probably feeling like a kid on Christmas Day finally able to open up all your presents at once. All the Mars® bars, milk shakes, cheesy pizza, chocolate ice cream, and boat loads of pasta are yours for the taking. Nobody's stopping you from eating what you want, when you want it. It's completely natural and understandable that you would tend to go a bit haywire at first.

To protect you from falling into the same pothole I landed in, when I found myself unable to stop gaining back much of my old weight, I'm going to tell you one thing. Pay close attention to how you feel and what you're thinking when you eat. If your eating is triggered by stress, your thoughts and internal pictures will reflect that. Here's an example from one of my clients of what that looks like.

Laura participated in my Losing Weight without Dieting Program. One day fairly early on, after experimenting with the process of Mindful and Gentle Eating, she came to class and shared her findings. One night she was eating supper and noticed that the food was nearly gone from her plate. After thinking about it, she realized that she had completely tuned out the whole experience of enjoying her dinner. She didn't really even taste what she was eating because she was caught up having a mental argument with her brother who had passed away many years before.

In reality, Laura's brother had no place on her dinner plate. And your problems have no place on yours. When you notice that your eating is out of control, there's some valuable information there worth exploring. Beware because it's the overwhelming, unsettled emotions rolling around in your head that will cause your appetite to go on automatic pilot whenever food is around. They may come dressed as actual thoughts or they may show up as just negative, disturbed, upset, angry feelings that you have in your body. Check in with your body often or consult the emotional scale. Then once you pinpoint what you're feeling, ask yourself, "What do I really want?"

Keep in mind that eating in response to pressure is a well-worn habit that is probably second nature to you. Like Laura, you may also be starting to become aware when you're eating under pressure. Awareness is the first step to change.

Try It! – Keeping a Feelings Journal

In the old days of watching your weight, you were taught to write down everything you ate, right down to every little B, L, T, bites, licks, and tastes. I don't know about you, but that screams Weight Watchers® to me and for me, it's a big turn off. Nonetheless, you decide what's best for you.

I think it's much more important to become aware of how you feel when you eat. If you'd like, rather than mentioning amounts, you can just write down the food you eat and how you feel. For example: ice cream – feeling angry, remembering argument with my brother.

In your journal, take a moment before you eat and pay attention to how you feel internally. What emotion is driving that forkful of pasta to your lips? How does that feel in your body? Remember the goal in using the Mindful and Gentle Eating Process is to increase your awareness over time, and to become more mindful of what you are eating and how you feel. Then you can take an action step toward feeling just a little bit better.

If you want to stop overeating and feeling worn out from using food as a temporary measure to cope with overwhelming feelings like boredom and loneliness, sadness and grief, you must choose to change your focus. There's so much more for you beyond food. However, it's up to you to make the decision to choose to change. You have to give yourself permission to do things differently. Are you willing to do that?

Developing new habits isn't easy. It takes time and effort. You'll have to learn to be compassionate with yourself, give yourself a break, and be willing to fall or fail a lot in pursuit of learning how to fly. It means being open to forgive yourself and others, and making it okay to start over again and again until you get the results you want and the new habit feels so natural it becomes effortless.

My Experience of Re-experiencing My Emotions in Recovery

Nothing quite prepares you for the level of onslaught that comes with making the choice to face your emotions head on without using food as a buffer. When you arrive at the point where you truly recognize that food no longer is the answer, it's a bittersweet moment in your life.

Today I can't imagine why I wasted so much time using food for comfort when all I had to do was just listen to my emotions and act on them. But I realize that everything happens in its own time, and I probably wasn't ready to take this leap before this point. You will know when it's right for you to start allowing yourself to really notice your feelings.

Here's a good example of a recent time when I dealt with my emotions without resorting to food.

As I sat down to breakfast that morning, I could feel the swelling up of emotions. Unconcerned with trying to pinpoint what I wanted to eat, I scanned the counter and found two chocolate chip cookies from the batch that my son, PT, had made the other night. I remembered seeing him come into my office that evening and standing so proudly with the warm cookie in his hand, aiming it toward my mouth. I knew I didn't want it, but to please him I took a bite and smiled, complimenting his baking. I noticed that although it was good, the chocolate was too sweet and cloying.

The next morning I wondered if I would feel the same way about the cookie, so I lifted the lid off the cake plate where they were stored on the counter. Taking a bite from one corner, I immediately noticed that the freshness and crispiness that I had come to appreciate was already gone. The cookies were now a day old. As I gently placed the lid back down, I realized that today they were definitely not good enough for my liking.

I knew that my step daughter, Janelle, was expected to drop in for a quick visit. I had been feeling emotional and sad about the decision to sue my father, and was afraid that my reticence would cause a rift between my husband and I. It felt like my back was up against the wall, but more than anything, I was feeling the pangs of jealousy of having to watch Janelle and her dad, my husband, be themselves and be the loving daughter and father I knew them to be. My insecurities were eating at me, and I swore that I wouldn't be able to handle it.

That morning I had done a lot of tapping and just paying close attention to what I was feeling, allowing anything I felt to be okay. From being a tapper, I knew that as long as I was willing to accept my emotions, it would lower some of my resistance and take the edge off my pain.

But that day I had places to go and people to see. With the intention of going to get our taxes done, late again, I climbed into the passenger seat of my Jeep® and let Angel drive. I thought for a moment how nice it was to not feel pressured to have to be "on" all the time and to just coast in neutral, letting myself feel whatever I wanted to, not having to put on a face or pretend that I was fine when I wasn't. As I sat limp as a wet noodle in my seat, I heard so many songs that reminded me of the old days when I was such a happy kid living with Dad and Rosie. As I recognized my new reality as distant from him, it made me want to cry and smile at the same time. My emotions were in a mix master.

As we pulled into the driveway back home and I prepared to exit the car, I knew Janelle was already there with the kids. If I was going to hide my emotions, I had to get my game face on and do some quick tapping. I told my husband, "I have to pull myself together because now I don't have the luxury of being able to feel my feelings. I don't want to be a burden to Janelle."

As soon as I walked into the house, Janelle opened her arms to give me a big hug, but it was too much for me. I could feel and almost taste my sadness. I returned her hug and gave her a quick peck on the cheek and ran right into the bathroom to do some tapping in private. I closed my tapping session with the statement, "I choose to feel my feelings and be okay with that."

When I walked into the kitchen Janelle's face was the first one I saw. Then I noticed everyone else gathered 'round; Angel, my husband, Aiden, Janelle's son, Angelica, her step sister, and our two kids, PT and Cara. Janelle looked at me with such love and understanding in her eyes and said, "How are you doing, Andrea?" Suddenly it seemed like time stood still and I could feel the emotions rising up in my throat.

I took a risk and meekly smiled as I asked her, "Do you want the truth or the pat response?" And she said, "You know you can always tell me the truth. I'm here for you." Suddenly with that permission, the tears came pouring down my cheeks. I could see Cara and Angelica from behind Janelle, watching me wondering what was wrong, but I was too caught up in giving way to my emotions to comfort them. Janelle moved next to me and pulled me closer to her, cradling my head and holding me while my body released its pent up pain.

Between the sobs, I unburdened my heart and told her what was bothering me. I shared that I felt so sad because although my father wasn't dead, I knew that I had to release him and close that chapter of my life. He didn't want me anymore. I told her how I had been trying so hard to be so strong for the whole family, and that I hadn't yet really gotten to the point of feeling angry because I was still feeling so hurt. And that I didn't feel safe sharing that with her dad, my husband, because he had so much anger toward my dad and didn't understand why I was sad. I felt so misunderstood and judged by him.

I had tried to cry and release those hurt feelings around him before, but several times he had told me to "Be strong." To me that meant it wasn't safe to express my weaknesses or share my true feelings of emotionally losing the connection with my dad. I cried and cried, and she held me all the while, cradling my head. Then, after my tears were long dried and my mascara was smeared all over my face, I was able to laugh again. I felt as though someone had lifted an elephant off my chest. I thanked her profusely and felt so guilty for being petty and jealous of her relationship with her dad. I realized that I was truly blessed to know that she was someone who I could really talk to about this hurting.

During the next week or so after that time with Janelle, I noticed I wanted to eat more than I had in the past several months, and many of the things I craved were very different from the foods that I would normally have chosen to eat when on an even keel.

In the past, it would have been tempting to think of this as backsliding and judge myself for being weak. But now I know that chocolate, cookies, chips, and the tuna melts all have a purpose and they've helped me reach this new understanding about myself.

As much as I used to crave food when I thought I couldn't have it, I now realize that what I truly yearn for is to have more opportunities to let go as I did with Janelle.

I used to cry a lot, but when the chips fell and it became clear that my father had left my life, my tears suddenly dried up. On the few occasions when I did cry, Angel would walk in and I'd feel the pressure to stop, be strong, and move on. Now I realize that as long as I allow his values to determine my actions, I am not being true to myself.

Since I know that crying has always helped me, I'm going to cry a little bit every day until I don't want to cry anymore. I don't know how or why or where I seemed to have adapted Angel's machismo attitude toward tears, but it certainly isn't right for me. And now I know that if I find myself doing that again, I'll most likely end up craving all the old foods that used to make me feel safe. When I start craving them again, especially when I'm not hungry, it's a sign to me that I need to release more tears. It's nice to know that I can choose to eat them when I get hungry, but don't have to feel compelled to consume them when I'm not. My craving is to release my tears and let go of my pain. What's yours?

Have you ever just paused whatever you were doing and taken a moment to ask yourself how you felt? I'll invite you to do that. Are you feeling anxious? Tired? Frustrated? Happy? Disappointed? Fat? Ha, ha, gotcha. Fat is not a feeling.

Yet we can all relate to feeling fat at one time or another. This is because when we say we feel fat, it is a cover up for emotions that are lying beneath the surface. In the next chapter titled, *Cope with Your Stress*, you'll learn more about what to do with your emotions once you pinpoint them.

Wrapping Up
Chapter 6: Embrace Your Emotions:
Creating Feelings of Safety Within

Here are the juiciest morsels covered in this section. Savor them mindfully.

- As a flesh and blood human being, your biggest craving is for love and comfort. We all want and need that.

- Every single thing we do is merely an attempt to change the way we feel.

- You only want the things you say you do because you think they will make you feel good, and feeling good will bring you closer to feeling lovable and worthy.

- Your struggles with food have been distracting you from taking a closer look at what situations in your life have been the core issues bugging you.

- Eating to calm your stress only feels good in the moment. But because it doesn't actually eliminate the source of your stress, eventually you'll find yourself overeating again.

- Take a break often throughout the day and just ask yourself, "How do I feel now?"

- Fat is not a feeling. When we say we feel fat, it is a cover up for emotions that are lying beneath the surface.

- You have to give yourself permission to do things differently. Are you willing to do that?

Chapter 7
Coping with Stress: Your Anxiety Relief Tool Kit

Don't Give Up - *Anonymous*

When things go wrong, as they sometimes will,
When the road you're trudging seems all uphill,
When the funds are low and the debts are high,
And you want to smile, but you have to sigh,
When care is pressing you down a bit-
Rest if you must, but don't you quit.
Life is queer with its twists and turns,
As every one of us sometimes learns,
And many a fellow turns about
When he might have won had he stuck it out.
Don't give up though the pace seems slow -
You may succeed with another blow.
Often the goal is nearer than
It seems to a faint and faltering man;
Often the struggler has given up
When he might have captured the victor's cup;
And he learned too late when the night came down,
How close he was to the golden crown.

Success is failure turned inside out -
The silver tint in the clouds of doubt,
And you never can tell how close you are,
It might be near when it seems afar;
So stick to the fight when you're hardest hit -
It's when things seem worst that you must not quit.

Your Stress Relief Toolkit

"The cause of all negative emotions is a
disruption in the body's energy system."
– Gary Craig, creator of Emotional Freedom Techniques®

If you're not where you want to be in your life and your cravings for food are leading you around by the nose, it's not evidence of a lack of will power, a personality defect, a chemical imbalance, a slow metabolism, rotten genes, or a bad habit. It's none of those things.

The real cause of your overeating is an imbalance in your body's energy system. Without getting you all twisted up in knots by going into the whole science of how this works, let's just suffice it to say that your wayward emotions are what keep you in patterns of feeling miserable and that leads to overeating. When you smooth out those hurt, angry, sad, and overwhelmed feelings, the distortions in your body's energy system will disappear, taking with it your desire to eat when you're not hungry.

"Overeating temporarily masks the food addict's anxiety, which is
really caused by an imbalance in the body's electrical system."
–Dr. Roger Callahan, Ph.D, creator of Thought Field Therapy

The Energy Field Outside Your Body

You may not be able to see it with the naked eye, but modern science has proven that there is an energy field outside as well as inside of our bodies. By using the techniques shown here, you'll be able to erase the negativity of the past, remove emotional blocks, limiting beliefs, and pain, and basically have a lot more Ahhhhhhhhhhhhh in your life.

Acupuncture is the great big granddaddy of many of the stress relief techniques discussed in this chapter. It is a 5,000 year old healing science developed by the Chinese which uses needles on specific areas of the body called energy meridians. These are invisible lines of energy that run up and down the body and are named for the organs they pass through.

The Chinese understand that our bodies have incredible natural healing powers. When these comfort spots or meridian points are activated or stimulated by an acupuncturist's needle, they have the immediate effect of relaxing specific muscles and trigger points, giving you a wonderful feeling of Ahhhhhhhhhhhhhhhhhhh. This is because they stimulate the brain to produce natural pain killers (endorphins, dopamine, etc.). The result is you feel relaxed and relieved.

Today, acupuncture is commonly used in Asia and is now gaining popularity in western medicine, sometimes even being used as anesthesia in hospital settings.

Juicy Woman Note:

Unfortunately, since I'm not an acupuncturist, I won't be teaching you the how-to's of it here, but having personally experienced acupuncture, I can highly recommend this healing technique. Acupuncturists say there are circuits in our body through which electricity is passing. Acupuncture is just one of the methods you can use to reawaken your body's own natural healing abilities and release the blocks caused by this dormant energy stuck in your system. Performed by a trained and licensed acupuncturist, it can be a wonderful toe curlingly fabulously luscious experience. I have enjoyed it immensely and found the process to be so delightfully relaxing that I've fallen asleep during the treatment. To my way of thinking, its only drawback is that it can only be done by a trained practitioner.

As an energy coach, in this chapter I'm going to show you several tools you can use to coach yourself back into curvy confidence, radiant health, and supreme sanity. First, let's talk a bit more about energy.

There are four ways to move energy in the body:

1. Tapping — Gently tapping or stimulating the endpoints of these acupoints or channels of energy, as is done in *Emotional Freedom Techniques® (EFT)*, or *Thought Field Therapy*.

2. Warming – Placing the hands over the body, as in Reiki. (This method will not be covered here in this book, and I don't have any personal experience with Reiki, but I've heard many wonderful things about it.)

3. Holding – Placing the hands directly on the body as in Tapas Acupressure Technique. For those people uncomfortable with the sensation of touch, it is also possible to do TAT by simply holding your hands over your body. This is the warming method as described above.

4. Intention — Simply thinking about moving the energy in your body as in the Z Point Process™, Affirmations, Afformations, *NLP*, and Hypnosis. When you redirect your thoughts, you affect your body. These are all examples which employ the use of cue words and/or a series of steps to change whatever issue you're working on.

A Brief History of Meridian Tapping

Since very few people can run around with a package of acupuncture needles, it made sense to find an alternative with all the benefits and none of the fuss. In the 1960's, a chiropractor from the US named Dr. George Goodheart read a book about acupuncture written by the president of the Acupuncture Society in Britain. He became fascinated with the idea of combining acupuncture with his own work and went on to discover a method called *Applied Kinesiology*.

Dr. Goodheart realized he could substitute physical pressure or light tapping in place of the needles typically used in acupuncture. This new no-needle approach was a huge advance because it made this acupuncture derived method more accessible to the mainstream.

Standing on the shoulders of Dr. Goodheart's discoveries, in the 1970's an Australian psychiatrist, John Diamond, M.D., found he could treat emotional problems using affirmations (positive statements of thoughts) in combination with stimulating the acupoints. He called this Behavioral Kinesiology. However, his emotional version of acupuncture required more structure in order to be taught to the mainstream.

In the 1980's, Dr. Roger Callahan, an American psychologist with over fifty years' experience, specializing in anxiety disorders, also wanted to find a way to help his patients. Seeking to discover a method more effective than traditional talk therapy to treat anxiety and phobias, he learned *Applied Kinesiology* and studied the meridian system of acupuncture.

As he began to experiment, he discovered that fears and anxiety could be removed, often permanently, by tapping on various acupoints of the body.

Dr. Callahan first tested this out with a patient named Mary. He had been working with her for almost two years in an attempt to rid her of the most crippling case of water phobia he had ever seen.

Water terrified Mary. She couldn't take baths in a tubful of water. She couldn't bathe her children. She was afraid of rain, and despite living in California, she refused to drive along the Pacific Coast Highway because the mere sight of the ocean paralyzed her with fear.

At wit's end, and doubting his ability to help her, Dr. Callahan sat with Mary in his backyard within sight of his swimming pool. Fidgeting in her chair, Mary became agitated and eventually very upset saying, "I feel it in the pit of my stomach. Every time I look at or think of water I feel it right here in my stomach."

Dr. Callahan knew that a spot under the eye was the location of an endpoint to the stomach meridian. On a whim, in a moment of desperation and hope, he asked Mary to tap with her index and middle finger on her face just under her eye, and at the same time to think about her fear of water as she continued tapping under her eye. Mary tapped. After just two minutes of tapping, she stopped and glanced at Dr. Callahan with a look of amazement in her eyes. "It's gone!" She jumped from her chair and ran toward the pool.

From this discovery, Dr. Callahan went on to create the technique that is known today as *Thought Field Therapy* or *TFT*. It works on the basis of using a variety of different tapping codes or sequences called algorithms on various acupoints on the body. His method relied heavily on using muscle testing to accurately diagnose the problem and determine the correct sequence to tap based on the individual's need. Using this process, Callahan achieved considerable success over the years and began teaching his technique to others.

Despite the fact that *Thought Field Therapy* worked well, it had drawbacks which prevented it from being more user friendly. It was time consuming and cumbersome. Several of Dr. Callahan's students knew that it could be improved.

Simultaneously and without knowing each other, psychologist Dr. Patricia Carrington and Stanford trained engineer and peak performance coach, Gary Craig, both arrived at the same conclusion: a single-algorithm method could be just as effective as the more complicated procedures of *TFT*.

Both worked independently to achieve their individual goals of simplifying Callahan's method and create a single, universal tapping sequence that could be used to address all issues.

By 1987, Dr. Carrington had developed a single algorithm tapping method called *Acutap*. She shared this Callahan-inspired process with patients and workshop participants. To eliminate the need for muscle testing, she simply asked people to tap on all of the acupuncture end-points each time they did a round of tapping. Using this method, she was able to help her clients in ways that had never been possible before.

Similarly in the early 90's, Gary Craig created his own single algorithm approach to tapping which he called *Emotional Freedom Techniques® or EFT*. EFT became the method of choice and the most widely used process in the field of energy psychology.

Dr. Carrington realized that the benefits and features of *EFT* outweighed her *Acutap* process and eventually chose to adapt *EFT* as her preferred method of treatment. In 2000, Carrington developed her *EFT* choices method, a variation endorsed by Gary Craig which exponentially expanded the scope of Craig's method, making it more user friendly than ever.

Building upon the foundations created by *TFT* and *Emotional Freedom Techniques®*, meridian Tapping Techniques are continuing to grow and evolve. Highly skilled experts in various fields are consistently innovating new methods of tapping. Let's just say that by whatever name you call it, tapping works. Here's why:

It's so accessible. Anyone can do it. Best of all, no needles!

 You can choose to tap alone—a very DIY, user friendly technique.

 Most people already feel comfortable touching, holding, patting, and rubbing themselves for relief from stress.

 You can customize how you want to feel. Go from feeling gloomy to glorious at the speed of thought.

 You can either choose to tap quickly on an issue in the moment and get a quick hit of relief, or you can spend a longer period of time tapping on a more complicated emotionally charged issue.

Because it's made such a powerful impact on my life, EFT is my favorite go-to stress-relief method which works like crazy and I simply love it. That's why I want to share it with you.

Emotional Freedom Technique: Freedom at Your Fingertips

Lots of people appreciate *EFT* because it is a powerful, safe, easy to use, stress relief/healing technique with no reported negative side effects. It has won many praises and been enthusiastically endorsed by such well known and highly respected people as Dr. Bruce Lipton, coach, Cheryl Richardson, self-esteem guru, Jack Canfield, bestselling author, and noted physicians, Dr. Norm Shealy and Deepak Chopra.

My first experience with EFT made me an instant believer in the power of its ability to transform. Those few minutes of being tapped on by my colleague were like having a huge boulder lifted off of me. For the first time ever I stopped seeing myself as a victim and I realized how my unwillingness to forgive those who had abused me was keeping me stuck.

The next steps I took were to learn as much as I could about EFT. But rather than giving me more clarity, it actually confused me more because I tend to be a very rule-based person and it's very important to me to do things right.

Because I was so hung up worrying about doing EFT correctly, how it looked and wanting to know everything about the way it worked, I ended up missing out on EFT's benefits because I just didn't use it. I urge you not to make the same mistake I did. EFT is a most forgiving process and you really can't do it wrong as long as you just do it.

Although it's not perfect, it is pretty darn fabulous. The basic premise behind *EFT* is that the cause of all negative emotions is a disruption in the body's energy system. To correct the imbalance, all you have to do is tap on your body's natural comfort spots (acupoints) as you focus on the problem.

Juicy Woman Note:

In my opinion, from big to small, EFT can be used to address it all. Although nobody has had 100% success clearing all problems using EFT, it still has an incredible success rate.

You Can Change Your Response

Let's consider that the source of the irritation in your life causing you to eat when you're not hungry isn't going to go away anytime soon. For the sake of argument, let's say it's part of you or a situation in your life that you are having trouble accepting.

You can recognize these irritations by thinking about all of the "If only..." statements that you say to yourself when you're feeling down. For example, if only I weren't so fat. If only I didn't have these flabby arms. If only my stomach weren't so big. If only I would have finished college. All these statements imply that everything would be great if only you didn't have this problem.

There will probably be many times when you catch yourself looking in the mirror and falling into the trap of saying mean things about your body, calling yourself fat and ugly and just in general feeling sorry for yourself because you're overweight. You may even feel tempted to run back to calorie counting or feel a sudden urge to start restricting your food.

The fear and anxiety that you may be feeling at this time is a perfect example of your energy being out of alignment. It's a mistake to think that the real issue lies in the fact that you are overweight.

That's just a symptom of what's buggin' you. It's not the real problem. But by handling the big and small things that eat away at you, it will give you new insights into seeing yourself with greater love and self-compassion.

If you want to change the way you relate to food, you have to first deal with the problem of whatever issue is bugging you. EFT is the quickest way I know of to change how you respond to any stressful situation

As an EFT Practitioner, I will share that EFT's success rate is conservatively estimated at 20% – 60%. However my experience and the experience of other practitioners who use EFT on a regular basis is much closer to 95%.

Disclaimer: EFT provides impressive results for most people but there is no guarantee it will achieve your goals or be as painless as it is for others. Please consult your physician and/or therapist regarding your use of EFT.

Why I love EFT

In this section, among other stress busting goodies, you'll get my twist on what Gary Craig calls his Basic recipe which would normally include other tapping points and steps that I've chosen to omit for the sake of keeping things simple.

I've been living with and loving *EFT* since 2004, but it's only been the past couple of years that I've come to think of this humble, silly look-ing little tapping process as my survival kit for sanity. As my favored go-to stress relief method, it's become a big part of me. I've found that it is so versatile, effective, and easy that I use it every day.

Whenever anything creeps into my space that causes me tension, up-set, frustration, or any other emotion that isn't what I would consider an Ahhhhhhhhhh kind of feeling, I'll use *EFT* to bring me as close as possible to that Ahhhhhhhhhhh feeling. Since making a habit of clearing my body of stress, I've learned how to manage my emotions and my thoughts using *EFT*. And this is what you will learn too.

After I had my first wonderful experience with *EFT*, I learned how to apply it to eliminate cravings. It was fabulous and worked like magic. After doing several successful seminars with women teaching them how to do the same, I realized that I wasn't using *EFT* in a way that truly suited me. After all, I didn't really have a desire to zap my cravings altogether, I wanted to learn how to feel safe around what I considered temptation. I yearned to break free of the obsession behind wanting and needing food all the time. I had to know in my heart of hearts that I had the power to choose what was right for me.

Years later, when I made the decision to stop dieting, I realized that rather than using *EFT* to eliminate the cravings, I could use the process to explore why I wanted to eat the food. That would give me a new level of understanding and, from that, a greater degree of choice. I could either choose to eat the food or not. There was no judgment, just a desire to understand what drove the craving. I call this questioning your phantom hunger.

A Common Example of a Typical Problem – An Overwhelming Emotion

EFT works on everything from problems to pains, emotional to physical. When you're working with limiting beliefs, you will be determining how true something feels to you. *EFT* is the best method I know of to enable you to question your limiting beliefs and bring doubt to your negative thoughts. But I'll demonstrate how that works later. First, let's look at how *EFT* can be used to deal with an overwhelming emotion that you can't quite articulate what it is.

Many times people become accustomed to hiding their emotions as a means of self-protection. This makes it difficult to pinpoint what you are feeling. But your body is still reacting to the emotional turmoil and it's times like these when you may find yourself eating for comfort. No judgment here.

Here's a quick description of an emotionally charged situation I'm sure you've faced before. I know I have. Let's use this as our example to demonstrate how you can handle overwhelming emotions:

You wake up one morning and you feel terrible. You overate the night before so now you're bloated and uncomfortable. You drag yourself out of bed, look in the mirror and you can't stand the sight of yourself. You know you've got to get out of the house, put on your game face, and get things done today, but you feel disgusting and all you want to do is go back to sleep. Basically, you feel horrible.

This is a perfect time to use *EFT*.

But consider that the way you feel is made up of many different conflicting emotions that are triggering a surge of hormones and chemicals coursing through your body. To get back your sense of equilibrium, you have to get clearer on what's bugging you. There are probably many different conversations going on in your head at the same time, tipping you off to let you know what's upsetting you. You may be feeling angry, disappointed, sad, defeated, or disgusted. In order to untangle this mix of emotions, you have to tease them apart a little bit at a time.

I suggest starting with the most obvious emotion you may be feeling.

When I'm feeling crazed out of my mind, upset with how I look, caught in a loop of judging myself for overeating, and just, in general, feeling down on myself, I know that I have to first deal with my anger. When I do this I can uncover whatever emotion is hiding behind the mask of that anger.

This is because for many people anger is a pretty accessible emotion. Remember that in order to release any emotion you have to first allow yourself to feel it. If by chance you feel another emotion besides anger, then work on that one.

To get in touch with your anger, you have to tune into what is going on in your head and amplify it as much as you can. You can increase the intensity of your emotion by raising your voice, or even screaming. Since I was raised to be a prim and proper lady, I get a charge out of cursing when I'm angry. It feels like a great release. I also find that I can diffuse my anger by overstating my problem exaggerating it to the point of ridiculousness.

EFT in an Andrea Nutshell

I like things that are simple. Here's my way of easy-peasying this whole section on EFT. If it works for you, great. If not, you have the whole rest of the chapter to understand it further.

My preference for using EFT as a quick fix band aide in any live situation that is happening in the moment is an intuitive, chatter boxy method that I use all the time. If you can babble on and complain, you're good to go. No matter which method you use, I want you to keep in mind that, like any tapping method, EFT works when you work it.

Tap and Gripe

Basically when something is bothering you in the moment, I'm just going to tell you to tap, rub, or hold the side of either hand where a martial artist would break a block of wood. Then, while you're doing that, with all the feeling you can muster just let' 'er rip. Say what's on your mind. Complain, moan and groan, kvetch and rant on. We can all do it. Now I'm giving you permission.

This was taught to me by one of my dear friends and colleagues, CJ Puotinin. She learned it from Rick Wilkes, EFT coach extraordinaire and creator of the Thriving Now site at http://www. thrivingnow.com. Rick calls this method Tap and Gripe.

A quick note to keep in mind is that this tap and gripe method will not work for painful memories that are emotionally associated with specific events. For that, you must be willing to take time and tap on each individual piece or aspect of those memories to neutralize them once and for all.

EFT: Basic Recipe

EFT is basically a process for relieving stress. Like any recipe, you can keep it simple, or make it complicated. It's up to you. Here, I'll give you the fundamentals and teach you how to follow the steps.

It may seem a little daunting at first, but once you memorize what to say and how and where to tap, you can do a round of tapping in under a minute. Once you get the basics under your belt, you can easily learn shortcuts and variations on your own.

There are six simple steps to learning my version of Gary Craig's *EFT*. They are the following:

Step 1 – Name the problem

Step 2 – Measure the intensity

Step 3 – Choose a Set Up Phrase (repeat 3 x while tapping on
        karate chop point)

Step 4 – Choose the Reminder Phrase

Step 5 – Perform *EFT* Tapping Sequence

Step 6 – Re-evaluate the problem (measure of intensity)

Step 1: Name the problem

By verbalizing what is bothering you, your mind and body can pre-pare for the energetic shifts about to occur. It's like switching on a light in a darkened room. Once you state the problem, it loses a certain amount of power over you.

Have you ever desperately wanted to change something in your life and found that you just couldn't follow through? Ever wondered why you just couldn't stick to a diet or an exercise program? This is because some part of you was holding onto the status quo and getting a benefit from staying exactly as you were. You may not know it, but if you can't seem to gain traction doing or achieving what you want, this is why. You are unknowingly sabotaging yourself. This is the phenomenon that I described earlier. It is called the psychological reversal. It is the result of an energetic imbalance.

No worries. Most people face this resistance at one time or another. You're just a few taps away from letting it go and breaking through the resistance. The first thing you have to do is focus on the problem.

To get your feet wet with *EFT*, begin by thinking of a situation that you want to change in your life. Don't reach for a huge honker of a challenge, but something that is bothering you, right now, in the moment.

It can be anything that is tangling you up in knots. Is it a headache, do you have soreness in your neck, a pain in your knee, or maybe a toothache? Maybe it's not a physical problem, but it's mental or emotional like worrying about something that hasn't happened yet. Maybe you're feeling all twisted up inside like a pretzel worrying about an upcoming presentation. Or have you been struck by an attack of the 'lazies' when you've got work to do? Maybe it's that time of month, or you're feeling lonely and the ice cream in the freezer is calling your name.

Maybe you want to give someone a piece of your mind, but because you feel intimidated by them you've come down with a case of cold feet. Give it some thought. What do you want to work on? Describe the problem on a piece of paper or in your *Try It!* journal.

Step 2: Measure the Intensity

To get in touch with whatever challenge you're experiencing, you have to tune into what is going on in your head. Now you're going to rate the intensity of how much you are disturbed by what's bothering you on a scale of 0-10. The stronger or more intense a feeling or symptom, the higher the number. This is how you measure the intensity.

What is the intensity rating on your problem or issue? Write down the number. Keep it handy because you'll want to refer back to it and compare it with the number you get at the end of the process. If you can't figure out the level of intensity, take a guess. What would it be if you knew?

Step 3: Choose a Set Up Phrase

The set up phrase is created by combining a statement of your problem along with an affirmation, such as "I deeply and completely love and accept myself." You will repeat this set up phrase in combination with using one of the tapping methods below.

To do the tapping, use one of these methods:

1. Using one of your hands, tap gently with your fingertips on the side of the opposite hand. The area where you will tap is known

as the karate chop point. This is where a martial artist would break a block of wood. See diagram below.

2. Bringing together both hands, with your palms facing up and your thumbs pointing away from your body, tap both hands together with pinkies touching. By stimulating both karate chop points at the same time, a powerful energetic clearing pulse is created that races through your system and cleans up the energy blocks.

3. With an open hand or gently closed fist, rub, hold or tap softly in a circular motion on your sore spot. See diagram below. Your sore spot is located on the sides of your upper chest area, about 1 ½" beneath your collar bone. To find it, palpate the area around your collar bone and move towards your underarm area. The spot that is most sensitive to your touch will be the sore spot. (This area is tender because this spot is a site of lymph congestion.)

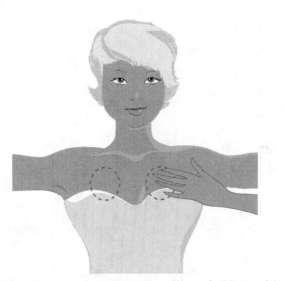

Any of the above tapping processes will work. Now, with your chosen method, tap the karate chop(s) or rub the sore spot continuously as you repeat the following Set Up Statement three times:

"Even though I have this_____(fill in the blank with your specific issue, pain, conflict, frustration, anger, sadness, craving, symptom, condition, etc.) I deeply and completely love and accept myself."

Examples of Set Up Phrases

In a situation such as our example, I would repeat a Set Up Phrase something like the following:

Even though I can't (stand my body) I deeply and completely love and accept myself.

For the sake of simplicity, you can repeat this same statement three times.

Your energy system is now poised and has a clear indication of what's bugging you based on what you've chosen to tap on. You've made a statement to your unconscious mind that you want to focus on this issue. Now you just have to hammer it home.

You will tap on the acupressure points at the same time that you verbalize what you're feeling so that you can neutralize your emotions.

Juicy Woman Note:

Please remember this is a very forgiving process and nothing is written in stone. You don't have to say the affirmation specifically as written, especially if you are uncomfortable saying, "I deeply and completely love and accept myself." For any number of reasons, many times people feel uncomfortable saying this.

If you notice that you feel twingy when you repeat the love and accept myself phrase, consider that you may need to work on improving a negative self-image. This is a good example of a psychological reversal caused by a disruption in the system. It could be chronic or it could be fleeting.

Your feelings are your best gauge of what's right for you. If it doesn't feel right to say the statement, your emotions are letting you know that work is needed to tease out the reasons why you may not love and accept yourself. Don't worry. You're not alone.

In my experience, I've found that there have been times when I've been perfectly fine with saying it, and other times when I just couldn't conceive of the possibility of loving or accepting myself, opting instead to say, "I wish I could love and accept myself."

Other times, if things are really down in the dumps, I'll say exactly what I'm feeling. By tapping or holding the points, I'll open up my ability to be more compassionate with myself and recognize that what I'm saying is no longer true, such as in the following example:

"Even though I don't love and accept myself, in fact I hate and can't stand myself, I would like to love and accept myself…"

Overall, I've found that your willingness and comfort in being able to say it depends largely upon what issues are standing in your way.

Here are several other variations on the love and accept myself portion of the affirmation:

I want to love and accept myself even though

_____

I might be willing to love and accept myself even though

_____

I am willing to consider the possibility of loving and accepting myself even though _____

I accept that I'm a child of God and worthy of love and forgiveness, even though _____

Even though I have this problem, I'm open to the possibility that I can accept myself If only I didn't have this problem,

---

You can choose to work on this or any other issue immediately as I outline here, or over time using The Personal Peace Procedure (a method of using EFT to deal with a mixed bag of all types of upsets). For more information about this process and all things EFT, visit the new website: http://www.eftuniverse.com

After you've finished saying whatever setup phrase you've chosen three times, take a deep cleansing breath and release it by blowing out. This first step is all you need to do to override the powerful programming of your subconscious mind, your inner saboteur.

Step 4: Choosing the Perfect Reminder Phrase

After you've made the decision and know what issue you want to work on using *EFT*, you will need to choose a reminder phrase that keeps your issue fresh in your mind.

Think of this step as a mental form of shorthand. You will use just a few words to keep your problem at the top of your mind. You will repeat your reminder phrase as you go down each of the points on your body.

Juicy Woman Note:

One day while tapping on my fears about speaking at an upcoming National Speakers' Association meeting, the phrase, "Even though I'm a bad girl," popped into my head. My logical brain tried to stomp it down and reason it away but luckily my intuition told me to repeat it. As soon as I said, "Even though I'm a bad girl," there was a tremendous surge of energy that came in the form of tears. It felt as though they had been built up forever.

Along with those tears, I was moved by my intuition to tap on many things that I would have considered unrelated. Within a few minutes of tapping I was back in the game, ready, willing, and able to take on this new challenge and head off to speak in Mexico. Set aside your judgments and listen to your intuition. Allow your inner wisdom to guide you to know what to say.

The more specific you can be in creating your set up and reminder phrases, the better will be your results. My recommendation is to really let yourself feel whatever you're feeling, because by connecting with the emotion behind the situation you associate fully into the problem and that stirs the pot and gets things moving.

 ## Juicy Woman Note:

Consider this your cursing coupon.

For me, having been so obsessed for such a long time with always having to act like a lady, it never felt comfortable to curse. Living with a father who used swearing to intimidate, I grew up feeling nervous and uneasy around people who cursed. So, for me, there's a lot of energetic traction that feels freeing when I curse. I don't do it often, but when I do it's like opening up the release valve on a pressure cooker—such a relief.

When I tap, I love to let out my inner drama queen and I always, always, always curse and rant and rave, scream and shout and stomp and bang and do whatever I can to vent when I'm using EFT on myself in private. That usually moves my energy and often gets the tears rolling. Many times you'll realize the absolute insanity of things that come flying out of your mouth. By being able to see the contrast and look at all your exaggerated thinking in a new light, you'll see how much easier it will be for laughter to follow. Pretty soon you'll be tapping and laughing hysterically wondering how on earth you could have ever thought the things you did.

When I'm working with a client, I ask them what they want. It's up to them. Curse, no curse. You decide. But if you're worried about being a lady consider this your cursing coupon.

Here's another example of a time when you might want to use *EFT*:

Let's say you're hit with a craving for a Snickers® bar but you know you just ate a really satisfying lunch. Your body is definitely not hungry, so you want to get to the bottom of what's driving the urge to eat. (I call this exploring your phantom hunger.) Your set up statement might go like this:

Even though I have this desperate urge for this Snickers® bar, I deeply and completely love and accept myself.

The most important part of the set up statement or affirmation is what you are working on, "this desperate urge for a Snickers® bar." You can use this phrase or you could shorten it even more "Snickers® bar," "want a Snickers® bar," "this urge." Any statement that reminds you of the problem will do nicely. But remember if you want some really powerful and quick relief, keep on getting more specific.

Remember that it's always beneficial to state specifically what is going on in your body or how it feels to you. For example, this burning anger searing through my gut like a red hot poker, these bitter feelings of hatred spinning 'round in my stomach, this spiky brown ball of gutless fear stuck in my throat, this fuzziness and confusion in my head, this piercing pain in my left shoulder, etc.

Juicy Woman Note:

At the risk of repeating this ad nauseum, it's so important to remember that in every relationship we have we teach people how to treat us. If someone is treating you poorly and not giving you the respect you deserve, i.e., cursing or putting you down, in addition to making it clear to them that this is not okay take note of what you've been telling yourself lately. There's a good chance they are just picking up on your negative mental attitude and treating you as you are treating yourself.

I've learned that every time I find myself in a negative situation and being put on the defensive, if I change my action and thoughts, the people around me change. This influences the entire relationship, creating more balance and harmony.

Change yourself, change your world: We're all reflections of one another. Each person is a mirror showing you how much you value yourself.

Juicy Woman Note:

My experience shows that sometimes you'll want the reminder phrase, other times you just won't need it. Since you are becoming more aware of your body's needs, you'll become much more sensitive to what's bugging you and you may not feel the need to repeat it. Your subconscious mind has it all locked in, but a bit of repetition especially at the beginner level never hurts. Trust that you'll know by listening to your heart what is best for you. Use the reminder statement or don't. It's all up to you.

EFT Tapping Sequence

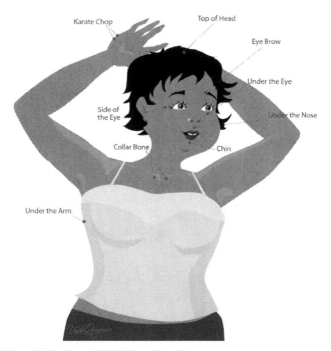

<u>Step 5: Perform EFT Tapping Sequence</u>

To start the *EFT* sequence, tap 7-10 times on each of the following acupoints (refer to the above illustration): Top of Head, Eye Brow, the Side eye, Under the Eye, Under the Nose, the Chin, the Collarbone, and Under the Arm. On points which lie on both sides of the body, it doesn't matter if you start with your right or left. However stick with one side for the first round of tapping and switch to the other side for your next round of tapping. You may also choose to tap on both sides at the same time.

In order to most effectively address the various aspects of your problem while tapping on each individual point, repeat one of the reminder phrases you chose. On the following page is an example of a round of *EFT* using phrases that might typically pop up for you when considering the possibility of eating at a buffet:

1. (EB) Eye Brow - Tapping the inner eye (where your eye brow starts at the bridge of nose) 7-10 times, saying, "Yum! Just smelling all this wonderful food is driving me crazy."

2. (SE) Side of Eye - Tapping the Side of eye where your eyebrows end, on the bone bordering the outside corner of the eye, saying, "I don't give a damn if I'm not physically hungry, I refuse to be deprived, so I'm going to eat anyway."

3. (UE) Tapping the Under Eye, on the "eye bag" area, or the bone under your eye about one inch below your pupil, saying, "I'm so afraid I'll lose control."

4. (UN) Tapping the Under Nose area between your nose and upper lip, saying, "I can't stand to have people watch me eat."

5. (Ch)Tapping the Chin area, between the middle of your chin and the bottom of your lower lip saying, "I'll never be able to stop myself."

6. (CB) Tapping on the collarbone located on the upper right and upper left portion of your chest. The collarbone is really any-where on the collar where you feel bone. "Oh God, I'm probably going to gain five extra pounds after I eat all this food right now."

7. (UA) Tapping the Under Arm point, about 3-4 inches below the arm pit, saying, "But I just have to get my money's worth."

8. (TOH) Tapping the Top of Head point, where a marionette's string would be attached, saying, "I feel so ashamed. I know I'm going to lose all control."

As you can see, the above phrases are several examples of individual isolated images or situations within the larger experience of going to eat at a buffet. Next you need to take a break to reassess how your tapping is progressing.

Step 6: Re-evaluate the Problem

After completing a round of tapping, breathe in deeply and fully, then exhale completely getting rid of any stale, residual negative energy. Next, go and measure the intensity again and see where you are presently. It's very possible that what was bugging you before is no longer a problem.

Many times huge and painful issues that have haunted you forever will disappear in the blink of an eye, such as was my case the first time I was introduced to *EFT*. These are called One Minute Wonders in *EFT* speak. This is an example of getting complete relief when you think about your problem.

Partial Relief

Other times you'll only get a little relief. This means that your problem or issue is more complex, and I recommend you either revise your set up statement as follows: "Even though I still have this _____, I deeply and completely love and accept myself." Say this several times while tapping on the Karate chop point.

While tapping on each location, repeat reminder phrase, "this remaining _____" For example:

(EB) this remaining buffet challenge

(SE) this remaining feeling like a pig

(UE) this remaining anger towards myself

(UN) this remaining guilt, etc.

Two of these quick-fire sets are equivalent to a full round of *EFT*. Measure the intensity after each completed set and note any progress or changes you might want to make for future rounds.

Watch Out For Tail-enders

If you still don't get any relief, then try looking out for those dreaded tail-enders. These are the "Yes, but" phrases that pop up in your head in response to the flurry of thoughts, memories, and scenes that you're likely to encounter while tapping. These may appear unrelated to what you're tapping on, like my experience with the tail-ender "I'm a bad girl." You will get amazing traction by handling those tail-ender statements.

Here's an example of a possible tail-ender using the above buffet example:

While tapping on the Side of the Eye point as shown above and saying, "this remaining feeling like a pig" you may get an instant memory of being called a pig by your father one day while eating out at a buffet. This is very likely another aspect of the same problem. Write it down and finish tapping on whatever you're already working on first before getting sidetracked in an attempt to resolve any tail-enders. Then, once you've cleared the current issue, tap on those tail-enders until they're gone.

If you're still not seeing any relief after about twenty minutes, record your results and take a break, returning back to your issue after a couple of days. You may just need to distance yourself and see a new perspective.

Getting enough rest and drinking plenty of water is essential whenever you do any energy process. If you still are unable to handle your issue with tapping, you may want to try addressing the issue with one of the other energy coaching tools in this chapter.

Hitting the Nail On the Head: Getting Even More Specific

I can't stress enough the importance of specificity! *EFT* newbies have a tendency to over-generalize and use broad statements to describe the problem. This can make you end up running around in circles chasing your tail. There's power in being specific.

For example, using the tail-ender in the example above, compare what I mean by nonspecific vs. specific:

Nonspecific: "Even though I remember being called a pig by my father ..."

Specific: "Even though I remember being called a fat, ugly pig by my father while standing on the buffet line at Aunt Jessie's wedding and feeling like I wanted to fall through the floor..."

As you can see, by getting as specific as you can with your choice of wording, you bring up more emotion and this brings up all the aspects contributing to the issue. Just like chopping down a tree, it takes many whacks of the axe. You've got to keep on tapping and eliminating the various bits and pieces of your problem one by one until the entire foundation supporting the issue collapses.

Hammering it Home

After you've drilled down, gotten specific, and hit the nail on the head, you'll find there will be times when you're tapping and you notice that a word or phrase has a particularly powerful energetic charge—a real ouch that hurts! Now you're in the perfect position to hammer it home so that this incident will never bother you again. To do that, I recommend you take the word or phrase that evokes those strong emotions and repeat it continuously as you move down each of the sequential tapping points. Do this until there is no feeling when you think about it.

I'll use the specific example from above to demonstrate this:

"Even though I remember being called a fat, ugly pig by my father while standing on the buffet line at Aunt Jessie's wedding and feeling like I wanted to fall through the floor..."

Let's say that when you repeat the words, "I wanted to fall through the floor" you experience a flood of emotion. That means there is some powerful energy there and in order to get it unstuck you have to neutralize its charge. So you take the phrase, "I wanted to fall through the floor," and repeat it as you tap 7-10 times on every point. Remember to keep on clearing and repeating until all points are clear.

> ## Juicy Woman Note:
>
> Why are you so hungry? I've learned that a case of the blues can twist you up in knots and make your internal hunger scale go from completely satisfied to ravenous in the blink of an eye. Since natural hunger creeps up on you slowly, that quick flash desire, desperate urge to eat is your first hint that something other than hunger is rattling your cage. This is a good time to explore your phantom hunger.

Hunger Pangs Alleviated With Simple "Imagine Tapping" Process

Hunger Pangs! We all get them. Typically, they occur when the body has gone without food for a number of hours. One day a few years ago when I was just getting started learning how to become an intuitive eater, I was walking my daughter and her friend, Malik, to school. I noticed that as I was walking I was feeling hungry so much earlier than usual and I wanted to explore the reasons why.

I decided to try a process I had learned from watching Gary Craig's *EFT* videos called Imagine Tapping.

I had tried it once before, but my mind had wandered and I fell off track. This time I committed to doing it for the length of the short walk home alone. I began by rating the hunger pain in my stomach at a 10 on a scale of 1-10. As I imagined tapping on my karate chop point, I said the following set up statements in my head:

"Even though I'm so hungry that my stomach hurts, I still deeply and completely love and accept myself."

"Even though I'm so hungry and would love to eat a huge breakfast and I'm afraid that I would lose control and fall back on my tendency to overeat because I am so hungry, I still deeply and completely love and accept myself."

"Even though I'm so hungry that I could eat a horse, I still deeply and completely love and accept myself."

Then I imagined tapping on each of the points while I repeated the following:

Eyebrow: Feeling so hungry

Side of eye: Don't want to overeat

Under Eye: Feeling so hungry

Under Nose: I don't want to overeat and feel like a fat pig

Under chin: I used to do that

Under Arm: Sometimes I still do, especially if I don't tap

Top of head: Tapping works when you work it. I know that now.

This completes one round of tapping.

Top of head: I'm hungry and want to eat

Eyebrow: But I don't want to overdo it and eat like a fat pig

Under Arm: I've been told things like that before

Top of head: That really hurt

Eyebrow: That reminds me of the time when my father used to say, "You're going to get so f***** fat, I'll be able to roll you down the hill like a f***** meatball."

Side of eye: Funny, that's what I chose to share in my email announcement for the next Juicy Call.

Under Eye: Thought I was over that one

Under Nose: I guess it still hurts

Under Chin: Not as much as before... but still a little

Collarbone: I used to believe that kind of stuff

Under Arm: I don't anymore

Top of head: I know that's nonsense and now I'm in control of my thoughts

Top of head: Meatball, hah, that's kind of funny. This is so ridiculous

Top of head: It feels good to be such a resourceful, strong woman

Top of head: I'm a grownup now, and I can take care of myself. Meatball! What kind of dummy would compare a child to a meatball? That's freaky. Guess he blew it on that one! I'd never say that to Cara.

After the last sentence I took a deep breath and checked in with my body to find that I was no longer hungry.

Then I remembered that walking with the kids to school, I had been explaining to them what anchors are. Anchors are thoughts that occur which stir our brain to remember. I gave an example of my grandmother's apple pie reminding me of feeling very loved. I explained to them that whenever I think about Nana's apple pie and remember walking into her apartment, I can almost smell the familiar aromas of cinnamon and vanilla which always make me feel all warm and peaceful inside.

The reminder of those memories must have put my brain on a search which reminded me that I really missed my Nana. That's probably what triggered those intense hunger pains!

Review of Tapping Points

With the exception of the karate chop point which most people prefer to tap on while saying their set up phrase, these tapping points are placed in such a way that they progressively move down the body, making them a snap to memorize.

Here's a quick summary of the abbreviations for each of the tapping points:

1. EB – Inner corner of the eye, beginning of the Eye Brow
2. SE – Side of Eye
3. UE – Under Eye
4. UN – Under the Nose
5. Ch – Chin
6. CB – Collarbone point
7. UA – Under the Arm
8. TOH – Top of Head
9. KC – Karate Chop

The Juicy Woman's Tips For Tapping

1. Keep it gentle, use light yet firm pressure.
2. Tap with either hand.
3. Many people prefer to use their dominant hand to tap.
4. Use your index and middle fingers to tap on each point to ensure covering all the meridian points possible.
5. Tap approximately 7 – 10 times on each point. This is the amount of repetition needed to iron out the kinks in your energy system. Don't worry about counting.
6. Feel free to switch hands or sides if you get tired.
    You can tap on one or both sides of your body at the same time or skip around. Do what's most comfortable for you. Alternate sides, be creative. This is a most forgiving process that relies heavily on the power of your intent. You can't get it wrong.
7. In my experience, crying comes with the territory of doing *EFT*, especially if you're doing it in a safe space or feel safe and comfortable addressing deeper issues with the support and assistance of a trained *EFT* practitioner. Keep in mind that crying is good. This is for several reasons. By crying, you are releasing toxins from your body. This activates a relaxation response and you'll feel so much better afterwards. Next, since tapping is one of the methods of moving energy in your body, tears or crying demonstrates energetic movement. Other signs to look for are yawning, sighing, laughter, any show of emotion, flushing, or blushing, skin color changes, breathing or vocal changes, a release of tension in the body, and much more. These are all examples of energy moving in the body.
8. Be appropriate. If you are in a public place, keep your emotion under wraps and say what you want to in your mind. You can mutter it under your breath or stay silent and just think about what you want to say. This is the process I described called Imagine Tapping.
9. After you've had an emotional release from using *EFT*, make sure you take the time to be gentle with yourself and your body.

In the process of resetting your brain's neural connections, much work and energy is being used by your body. Make certain that during this window of 24-48 hours following your *EFT* release, you rest as much as possible and take it easy. It's similar to feeling as though a weight has been lifted off your chest.

Juicy Woman Note:

I've learned that during the times when you are tapping on big, emotional issues, you may get a tremendous sense of relief and you'll feel entirely complete. But if after several hours or days you notice a pervasive feeling of being extremely vulnerable, as in weepy, sad, or withdrawn, then that means you must do more tapping to get to the core of the feeling.

I recall in the past having worked with my tapping buddy and we broke through a tremendous issue that had been plaguing me for a long time. The next day I left with my family for a vacation in Puerto Rico. For the several days that followed, I felt as though I had huge, open emotional wounds all over me. If someone looked at me crooked, I wound up crying. I was in a pitiful state for a while. After I realized that being there was setting off some old triggers from my childhood, I was able to go back and tap on the memories from my past that were coming up and neutralize those vulnerable emotions that were associated with them. Once I did that, I was back on an even keel, able to enjoy a wonderful vacation.

If EFT Doesn't Work

1. Hydrate - You may be dehydrated. Since our bodies are a low level electrically charged magnetic system, if we are dehydrated there is not enough juice to activate the flow of sludge backed up in our energy system. You need water to grease the mechanisms by which your tissues do their various jobs, including carrying away waste products in your body. Keep some water nearby and take sips often.

2. Energy toxins – There may be a problem with the energy in the room. Try going outside or leaving the room.

3. Dig deeper – If your set up phrase is too broad and general, get more specific.

4. Don't know where to begin – Begin wherever you are. I have often said, "Even though I don't know what to tap on,…" Or just start tapping and whatever you are feeling or thinking will come to the surface.

5. Limited progress – Do more repetition.

6. Tap often – Gary Craig recommends tapping several times a day: in the morning upon awakening, each time you go to the bathroom, before each meal, and in the evening—on average about five times daily.

7. Feeling disconnected from yourself — Tap in front of a mirror, looking directly into your eyes.

8. Blah set up statement — Energize and bring some power to your set ups by really feeling the truth of what you're saying. Yell, scream, curse, do whatever is necessary to connect with the rawness of the emotion you're experiencing. This is the key to releasing it so it won't remain stuck, welling up inside of you.

Try It! – Memorize a Useful Set Up Template

I suggest that you write down a very useful set up phrase and memorize it. Here's one that has absolute magic in it:

Even though _____,
I fully and completely accept myself, I love and forgive myself, I forgive everyone who has anything to do with this situation, and I choose to be pleasantly surprised by how easy it is to _____
_____.

Why Is My Sore Spot Sensitive and Will This Tenderness Go Away?

If you notice tenderness when you rub the area called your sore spot, this is due to a lymphatic congestion caused by a build-up of toxins in that area. This spot is a lymph drainage location that is usually tender to the touch. It's not a piercing pain, rather it is a dull pain and very manageable. By rubbing it, you are breaking up the source of that congestion. If rubbing it hurts, maybe you're being too forceful. Lighten up and be gentle using a lighter touch. For the most part, the more you rub or massage that spot, the less sensitive you will be to the soreness.

As always, keep in mind that you must take care of yourself. If rubbing the sore spot or any other point causes you intense pain, or if there is a medical, ethical, or physical reason that you choose not to use this point, switch to the karate chop. And always, when in doubt, consult your doctor or physician.

EFT Goes to the Movies

Most of us have some variation of the belief "I'm not good enough" floating around in our heads. This probably came out of a specific time in the past, and if left to rot will end up stinking up your life. By applying *EFT*, you'll be able to focus on these older, musty, crusty, dusty incidents, release the pain and feelings of limitation around them, neutralize their emotional charge, and whoosh them away like they never happened.

Juicy Woman Note:

In the hypothetical example below, I use a brother/sister relationship but this may not fit for you. I recommend you read through the example, substituting a relationship of your own that feels like a thorn in your side. Everybody's got one. What's yours?

Example:

Let's say you have a miserable relationship with your older brother, Jeffrey. To this day it seems like everything the guy says and does gets under your skin. Despite being a totally insensitive jerk when he was a kid, he's grown up to be a successful doctor and is now the golden child of the family. You're so jealous of him you could spit, but you'll never admit it to anyone.

When you were a kid he used to tease you mercilessly about being chubby, making you feel big, fat, and ugly. But now as an adult, your grown up logic tells you that you should forgive and forget but you just can't stand the guy. Everybody loves him, but you hate his freakin' guts.

Somewhere buried deep down you wish you had a better connection with him but you don't. You still hate him for always making fun of you and making you feel so uncomfortable about your body. It feels like a part of you is stuck in time and you can't move forward. To this day, you still cannot look at yourself in a full length mirror without hearing his voice chanting, "Fatty, Patty 2x4, can't get through the kitchen door." Thinking of yourself as Fatty Patty drives you crazy and makes you want to run and eat every time.

Now after reading and understanding about energy and how it works, you've discovered that the problem with your brother is causing you pain right now, today in this moment. Whether or not he feels the brunt of your anger, your body has soaked it up like a sponge, saturating every cell with the angry memories and resentment you're holding toward him—and it's affecting you.

Unconsciously you've been feeling this anger and acting upon it. Each time his name comes up in a conversation or you're reminded of him, you feel like you have to make a beeline for the nearest piece of chocolate to soothe your tattered nerves.

Knowing that your relationship has become a sore spot in your life and has been triggering you to eat out of control, you've decided to work on those unresolved feelings.

Juicy Woman Note:

It's important to realize that when you resolve old relationship issues, it won't necessarily play out in bringing you and the other person closer. It could, but you may not want that or be ready to take that step. Tapping helps you to see things more clearly and to remove the old filters.

The goal in doing the tapping is to give you a choice so that you can respond to the old stress triggers in a new way, moving beyond your knee jerk reactions.

This movie technique is exactly what you need to give you the resolution you seek. It will give you the framework necessary to be able to tease apart the tangled ball of your emotions so that you can focus on specific aspects of a certain incident in your past and release the pain and negative emotions surrounding it.

Let's say you've chosen to focus on a specific, isolated incident in your past—one of those times when your brother made you feel like garbage.

His annoying gestures and chants of "Fatty, Patty 2x4, can't fit through the kitchen door" may not have been the only part of the incident that laid down a negative emotional charge within you. By reviewing the situation as a movie, you can experience the scene from different angles, separate them out, deal with each one individually, and thus eliminate all the negative emotions connected to the entire incident.

First, give the movie of your problem a name and write it down in your *Try It!* journal. Let's call this movie, "Fatty, Patty 2x4." Next, close your eyes and imagine the scene unfolding in front of you. In your mind's eye watch as your mother fills your plate with a carefully measured portion of mashed potatoes, peas, and chicken fingers. You remember looking at the other plates on the table and thinking, "Ohhhhhhhhhhh Man! Wow! Only five chicken fingers. That's not fair. Why do I have to go on a diet? Everyone else gets to eat more than me."

Feeling like you're about to burst out crying, your body begins to clench up and your endocrine glands start pumping out stress hormones like crazy. Count this as Tapping Incident #1 and give it a title. "It's not fair. Everyone else gets to eat more than me." Give this portion of the movie an intensity rating and use regular rounds of *EFT* to tap it down to zero.

Next, as Mom sets the plate down in front of you, you look at it hungrily because you're starving. You haven't eaten since lunch. But as she turns away to tie your baby sister's bib, your brother snatches three of your chicken fingers off your plate and tosses them down to Ralph, the family dog sitting under the table waiting for scraps. Now you only have two chicken fingers left. You feel the anger boiling up inside of you and the tears start rolling down your cheeks. See this happening and count this as Tapping Incident #2, naming it, "Mom, Jeffrey stole my food." Give it an intensity rating and tap it down to zero.

Next, when you told Mom that Jeffrey stole your food, she refused to believe you because the dog had already eaten the evidence. That's when Jeffrey called you a liar and started chanting, "Fatty, Patty 2x4 can't fit through the kitchen door." This is Tapping Incident #3 "Mom, I'm not lying! Jeffrey really did it!" You may also want to break this up into several more incidents dealing with 1) the specifics of his name calling, 2) how hurt you felt, 3) feeling betrayed by mom, and any other aspects. See each individual scene playing out just like a movie in front of you and tap it down to zero.

Then, after being yelled at for fighting at the dinner table with your brother, you get sent to bed without supper. Feeling the injustice of it all, you probably experienced a painful, negative reaction. No doubt you wanted to kill Jeffrey. You probably hated your mother, the dog, and even blamed your baby sister. With such a tangle of emotions you may have felt angry, sad, hurt, guilty, depressed, and more. Number each of these appropriately, give each an intensity rating and tap each one individually down to zero.

After you've done all that tapping, check in with yourself and see if there is any feeling when you think about the whole incident. For example: Does it still hurt when you think of being called, "Fatty, Patty?" It shouldn't, but if it does, tap more.

Juicy Woman Note:

Really try to push your buttons and see if the memory still bugs you. You must always test out your work by trying to get yourself back to feeling or thinking the way you did before you started tapping. Feeling neutral or better is the goal. You'll know that the tapping has done it's magic if you are able to remember the incident and feel nothing when you think about it. Tapping won't take away your memory, but it can completely eliminate the emotional charge connected to it. It will become so distant for you that it will be like remembering a scene from a movie. You won't feel anything. Best of all, you'll start to notice that calling yourself "Fatty, Patty" is no longer okay because it's a sign of disrespect and that doesn't feel good. You'll realize that you don't deserve to be mean to yourself anymore.

If additional memories or other emotions surface, listen to your intuition and allow it to guide you to where you need to go next. Then tap that down to zero.

Between each round and after each tapping incident, take a few deep breaths. This will flush away the negative emotions and iron out the kinks, balancing out your energy. I find a tremendous benefit in taking several deep breaths after each emotional incident is cleared. Then after each breath I blow out the stale air, exhaling loudly.

Tapping Variations
Touch and Breathe

This is another variation of tapping. The only difference is that instead of tapping, you will gently hold each of the points as you breathe slowly and deeply in and out. This is great for when you want to tap in public, but don't want to draw attention to yourself. I use this method when I want to tap in the car. While I'm sitting at a light I will place one hand over my chest, covering both sore spots, and breathe in deeply as I focus on whatever is bugging me. Often I'm able to deal with the source of the upset before the light goes green.

Freedom at Your Fingertips

Your fingers are filled with acupressure points. In Gary Craig's basic recipe he shows the many different locations on your fingers where you can tap. Rather than bogging you down with more points to think about, I'll just suggest that you touch, tap or rub your fingertips together lightly in a way that feels comfortable and natural to you. You can either do this using only one hand or by using both. Remember the most important thing that will determine your success is to focus on what is bugging you.

Alternating Positive and Negative

You may want to do alternating rounds of positive and negative statements to enable yourself to vocalize the truth of what you're experiencing. This is a great way to resolve internal conflicts. For example if your intention is to get yourself up and out of bed, you may do a round of tapping complaining about how tired you are, why you don't want to wake up or any other negative association with what you are experiencing. Then to lighten the load and prepare your body to get up, you may do a second round based on how good you feel or how good you will feel when you get up. The way this works is as you verbalize the negative as you tap along the meridians, your energy will balance and you won't feel as resistant as before.

Borrowing Benefits

When Gary Craig began doing seminars and teaching *EFT* to large auditoriums packed with people, he would work with one person on the stage. He began to notice that as the whole room tapped along with the volunteer up front while focusing on their own problem, everyone experienced a shift in their issues. He called this phenomenon "Borrowing Benefits."

He also found practitioners started reporting to him that when they spent all day tapping with their clients for their clients' problems, their own problems improved even though the practitioners had not been tapping for or even focusing on their personal problems. This led to naming the phenomenon (Borrowing Benefits), calling attention to it in workshops and eventually producing a DVD devoted to it.

This is a good reason for tapping with others, on behalf of others, or while watching an EFT seminar online or on DVD, while attending a live seminar, or even watching the news on TV. This is because without any effort at all your own challenges become less intense. That's "borrowing benefits" in action.

This works because we're all connected to one another by invisible threads of energy. As one of us is affected, each of us experiences a shift and change. This is the beauty of the power of this simple and elegant little process. I often use tapping in my group coaching on my Curvy and Confident calls each week.

Try It! – Water Play: Clearing and Cleaning

There's incredible energy in water. You'll notice that some of your best ideas pop up when you're under the shower or sitting near a body of water. Water is alive with creativity, wellness, and goodness. I've found there's something magical about the combination of clearing your limiting beliefs while you clean your body. Although I recommend trying this with tapping, any of the other energy coaching tools I've shared will work.

When I'm feeling especially blue and have a lot on my mind, I like to go into the shower and sit down, positioning myself so that the water runs over my back and on top of my head. As I sit thinking about what is bothering me, I'll tap on the side of my hand, releasing those negative feelings to the universe. I may or may not verbalize what I feel. I usually just tap and cry.

It's comforting to me because the running water feels as though the universe is crying right along with me, feeling my pain and empathizing with my situation. Then as my mood lifts and I feel better, I think about the water as a gift from the universe filling me up with stores of energy and light, giving me the strength to handle whatever I face.

You may prefer to do this in a gentler way, without the water running on top of you, but I feel that if you are bursting with emotion this is a fabulous way to release your burdens. You can also tap or use any of the other stress relief tools while sitting quietly in a bubble bath. It's such a treat to get that added boost of stress relief right along with a nice squeaky clean feeling.

Afformations: Empowering Questions to Kick Yourself into High Gear

Your thoughts are the result of the evaluations you make in your life based on the way you interpret your experiences. We evaluate things by questioning them. Most of us are running around each day mindlessly asking ourselves some really lousy questions.

Do any of these ring a bell?

What am I stupid or something?

What the hell is the matter with me?

Why can't I do anything right?

Why am I so dumb?

Why can't I stop eating?

Why am I so fat?

Why am I so ugly?

Why is this happening to me?

What's wrong with me?

Why me?

Notice how each statement above makes you feel. Does it inspire you? Uplift you? Motivate you? Excite you? Impassion you?

Probably not, which means if you want to get out of the rut you're in, you need to do something different. You've got to ask a more effective question to get a better response.

What's the Difference Between an Affirmation and an Afformation?

Noah St. John and Denise Berard are co-authors of, *The Great Little Book of Afformations*. They created this new technique called "afformations" which is a delightfully simple, incredibly powerful method of using "how" and "why" questions that literally reprogram your subconscious mind.

First, an *affirmation* is a positive statement of intent designed to inspire you to achieve a goal. But here is what happens. Let's say you create an affirmation: I am thin. You say it a thousand times a day, repeating it with as much passion as you can muster, but nothing is happening. Here's why:

When you make that statement your brain instantly goes searching through all your memory files looking for evidence of you being thin. The problem is if you've had nothing but frustration each time you tried to lose weight and have been an emotional eater, you have negative memories pushing to the forefront reminding you that you're still not thin. Maybe you've been feeling like an absolute, total, and complete failure. Perhaps you're wondering "Why do I even bother?" Now let's be honest, self-talk like that is not doing you a bit of good.

Instead of simply making a statement of intent that your brain isn't buying, put your affirmation in the form of a question and then turn it into an *afformation*, like this:

"Why is it so easy for me to be thin?" I bet you could come up with a million answers to that. Here are some that come off the top of my head:

"Because I feel like eating foods that make me feel good from the inside out; because it's becoming effortless and fun to go out walking again; because my clothes are getting looser; because it's easier for me to listen to my body and eat when I'm hungry and stop before I get too full; because I

241

trust my body to know what weight is ideal for me; because I'm so grateful that I've let go of all that silly diet-y thinking and I'm free to eat what I want every day; because I'm a happier person knowing that I'm in charge of my body; because I like and respect myself so much more for making the choice to listen to my body;…"

Now consider that this question may or may not be ideal for your use now, but keep in mind that when you want to generate a million possibilities, never make a statement—always ask a question. This is called an afformation.

Afformation Script for Weight Control

The following is a script I've adapted from one that my friend and *EFT* instructor, CJ Puotinen, shared with me. You can use it along with your new knowledge of the tapping points. Just tap on each successive point as indicated as you repeat the script. It's a good one and many of my clients love it. You'll notice that the forehead is also included. This is just another of the common tapping points many practitioners use. It's up to you, if you choose to use it.

Since this is a long script, you may choose to take a break from tapping. Remember you can also just hold the spots as you read and take a deep breath in between each point. Holding the points is another way of moving energy so the effect is the same.

For the "even though" statements tap on the side of your hand or use the sore spot.

Even though I struggle to find the hidden reasons why I can't:

 Get slimmer

 Eat less food

 Feel comfortable with my body right now

 Successfully enjoy the process of intuitive eating

 Do more fun things just for me

 Give myself a break

 Get myself to tap each day

 Rest when my body needs to take a break

Relax and take it easy on myself

 Expect the best

I would like to accept myself as I am. I fully and completely accept myself just as I am.

Even though I have tapped all over the place trying to feel confident, beautiful, deserving of the best, enjoying life, feeling comfortable and safe with loving myself, and am getting slimmer, I'm still afraid to let go and don't know what to do when I feel disempowered. I nevertheless fully and completely love and accept myself. I forgive myself. I'm doing the best I can. I know that my subconscious mind is only carrying out its old programming and following its instructions to keep me safe.

I also know that I can change those instructions so that my subconscious mind works with and on behalf of my new conscious goals.

Top of Head: What if the hidden reason for my weight anxiety is all the struggle?

Forehead: What if the more I struggle with my weight, the worse I feel and the worse everything gets?

Eyebrow: What if I am too focused on losing weight and not on the underlying issues that shaped my beliefs and my subconscious programming?

Side of Eye: What if the struggling is causing so much anxiety that I can't think straight about what I'm eating or what I'm feeling or anything else?

Under Eye: What if I could just not worry about losing weight?

Under Nose: What if I could just accept myself totally and completely?

Chin: What if I just tap on other things?

Collar Bone: What if I release the struggle and just enjoy my life?

Under Arm: What if I wake up one morning and feel relaxed about my body?

Top of Head: What if I just enjoy the times that I take care of myself, listen to my body, find yummy foods to satisfy my taste buds, find life enhancing ways to nourish my body and mind, maybe even look at my weight for what it is, a temporary manifestation that exists in my life for now that shows how I used to feel about myself and the relationship that I used to have with food, something that I don't have to take personally, something that I can enjoy noticing daily behavioral changes and feel lighter and more empowered with each passing moment of every day? What if I just focus on knowing that I attract my ideal body with the power of my thoughts? What if I collect more happy images daily and use more resources to find ways of feeling good and taking care of myself on a moment to moment consistent basis?

Forehead: What if I stop struggling with my body and just focus on the things I love?

Eyebrow: What if I stop struggling with my weight and focus on what food I most enjoy that makes me feel good from the inside out? What if I focus on feeling good and healthy? What if I begin to allow myself to feel deserving of being beautiful? What if beauty is an inside job and it's mine for the taking? What if this silly tapping stuff really creates a wave of change that runs through my whole life? What if it just keeps on raising the bar of what terrific feels like? What if I can keep on focusing on loving myself more, appreciating my talents and abilities, nurturing my relationships and doing wonderful things for my body to feel good now? What if I just relax and let this all unwind naturally and easily and effortlessly as nature intends?

Side of eye: What if this is the hidden reason?

Under Eye: What if I release the struggle and just enjoy being me?

Upper Nose: What if I focus less on feeling fat and more on thinking thin and doing the things that I feel good doing?

Chin: What if I start realizing useful things about my body, allowing myself to notice and pat myself on the back when I see that I am changing old habits and creating new empowering behaviors? What if I felt more at ease living in my body, lovin' the skin I'm in now? What if I concentrate my efforts on finding new ways to keep myself occupied when I'm bored, new ways to feel my feelings and be okay with them instead of stuffing them down with food? What if I really believed Dr. Nancy Bonios' phrase, "Say it or stuff it, express it or wear it?" What if that inspired me to ask consistently for what I need, say what's on my mind, take care of myself, and feel more comfortable saying "No" to others and "Yes" to myself? What if I find new ways to eat foods that I love and become attracted to more and more perfect foods that love me too?

Collar Bone: What if I am free to enjoy longer periods between meals, feeling satisfied and comfortable without the gnawing feelings of deprivation and guilt around food?

Under Arm: What if each day I feel more confident about my body, enjoy noticing things about myself that I like more each day, take time to do the things that nourish me all over, and even allow myself the gift of dressing my body in lovely clothes that make me feel and look great, wearing colors that flatter me, having accessories that make me feel gorgeous, buying special little things for myself that make me feel good, finding new ways of pampering myself like the Juicy Woman that I am?

Top of Head: What if I enjoy myself for giving myself the gift of this process of learning how to eat to satisfy my body's hunger and giving my body the gift of freedom from dieting forever? What if I fancy myself as a gorgeous woman for longer periods of time? What if I really am succeeding at this right now?

Forehead: What if my confident times become more frequent than my doubtful times?

Eyebrow: What if I relax and one day realize that I have forgotten how to feel helpless, scared, fat, out of control, sorry for myself, anxious about food or my body, impatient, self-loathing, ignorant, afraid, and hopeless about feeling that I'll never lose weight?

Side of Eye: What if I stop letting other people run my life and stop giving them the power to make me feel sad, angry, bad about myself and my eating habits? What if I take back control of my ability to express myself and I feel confident and worthy of sharing my needs with others, not from a position of weakness but from strength? What if I look for the good in people and realize that they are doing the best they can? What if I don't take things so personally? What if I make it okay not to be a superwoman or feel like I have to do it all and be perfect? What if I find it easier and easier to assert myself on behalf of my greater good? What if I find myself becoming more comfortable with my body and acting in my own best interests and becoming more and more gentle and loving with myself? What if I get into the habit of paying myself first? What if I really invest in the highest quality of self-care that I can? What if I find new ways of having more fun in life, taking advantage of the joy that is around me, the people who I adore, and the life that I love?

Under Eye: What if I just simply forget all the anxiety that I used to feel about my body and trying to get this whole eating thing right? What if I'm doing everything right already? What if I am exactly where I need to be right now?

Under Nose: What if I stop trying to analyze the whys and just get pleasure out of my life now?

Chin: What if I am totally free and acceptable to myself as I am now, at this very point in time?

Collar Bone: What if I completely forgive myself for feeling like I needed to carry around excess weight in order to protect myself or be strong and throw my weight around? What if I completely let go of all the old beliefs and the underlying causes of that programming that has up until now reinforced that old need? What if I just release that all and let go? What if I learn how to live in the present moment and begin recognizing all the opportunities that every day holds? What if I find new ways of celebrating my freedom from dieting forever in a way that honors me as a strong, independent woman able to listen to her body and pay attention to the emotions that I feel without running to food and stuffing those emotions down? What if I became really focused on all the wonderful things in my life and feel a new energy and excitement for living, building like a wave in my life each and every moment? What if I let my inner child out to play, and let her lead me to enjoy more of my life right now?

Under arm: What if I start taking an interest in the many helpful books, magazine articles, videos, DVDs, radio reports, courses, activities, conversations, support communities, programs, podcasts, blogs, and all other sources of information about getting thinner naturally without pain or effort, learning more about intuitive eating, feeling really good about my body, enjoying activities that connect my mind and my body, do more fun things each week to take care of myself, spend more time with people who I adore, pay exquisite attention to my feelings, recognizing and becoming more able to discriminate the different types of hunger that I have, eat when I am hungry and stop when I am satisfied, release the clutter in my life, and eliminate all of the old excess weight bearing burdens I used to carry around? What if I tap more each day and that leads me to discover more things I really like about myself? What if I just sit back and watch my body change and my metabolism speed up and the pounds slide off me like ice melting so that I can easily and effortlessly reach my perfect weight and enjoy the feeling of being comfortable and having a smaller body, living longer, and loving life more?

Top of Head: What if I relax and let my subconscious mind follow the new instructions I'm giving it to completely change my reactions to thoughts about my body, my weight, my eating, my size, my ability to run a business, take care of myself and others, my ability to make money, lots of it, my expertise to do what I love, my willingness to reach out and grab what's mine, my confidence to sell my products and services, my poise in speaking with other experts and people who will continue to move me toward my ultimate goals of being a totally Juicy Woman, and that includes talking to other women who can support me, leading those who appreciate my help, and following those who are my role models, and walking beside others who are my fellow travelers in this journey of life, listening to my heart speak, connecting with my spirit, making friends with people who love me for who I am, learning from experts, enjoying a life filled with prosperity, health, love, passion, and abundance? What if I just let go and let all of that happen right now?

Z Point Process™ Saves the Day

Several years ago my daughter Cara got a hamster, Cocoa. They did everything together. Cocoa was more like a lapdog than a hamster. I remember I would sit and watch Cara in amazement as she lovingly stroked the sleeping Cocoa curled up on her chest.

It was a match made in heaven until little Cocoa died, a mere two weeks after he made his home with us. My little girl was inconsolable. As soon as she realized he had died she ran to the bathroom and vomited. Upon seeing this, I suggested we tap together.

After sitting, tapping, and snuggling together for a bit, she calmed down and soon fell asleep. Several hours later I woke to the sounds of her vomiting again. I knew that the anxiety and fear was still bubbling up inside her body.

Earlier that week in Maryam Webster's Certified Energy Coach Program, I had learned another wonderful stress relief technique called, *Z Point Process*™. I knew I could use this to help calm Cara's anxiety. I asked her permission to try this with her and she consented. She lay down on the sofa in her room and I read the statements as she responded by repeating her cue word. Within moments, she had drifted off into a peaceful sleep.

That night I learned that *Z Point Process*™ is an incredibly powerful and effective process that can be used successfully on a wide variety of issues. After experiencing how easily, effectively, and gently the process calmed my daughter, I explored *Z Point* Process™ further. I have since used it on clients with sexual issues, procrastinating, emotional eating, and various other anxiety related issues.

Z Point Process™
How-to Basics

Z Point Process™ is a simple and easy energy coaching tool you can use on yourself to manage your state or achieve a specific goal. It was developed by Canadian hypnotherapist, Grant Connolly.

As a completely hands-free intentional process, it's the method of choice for gals who just "can't find the time" because they're always on the go. It's great for a quickie energy boost, 60 second self-image makeover, or an instant attitude lift. It works on the basis of shifting your energy and concentrating your thoughts by guiding you to redirect your focus. It's all done in your head so you don't even have to worry about meridians, acupoints, or knowing where to tap. The beauty of *Z Point Process*™ is that it can be invisibly practiced anywhere; from the bedroom to the boardroom and everywhere in between.

It's the best belief bustin' tool I know that can be done in the heat of the moment. Whether standing in line, sitting in traffic, dealing with parenting frustrations, or in the midst of an argument, it's awesome for taking off the edge and putting you back in control.

Juicy Woman Note:

There's a strong possibility that you haven't been aware of how faithful your subconscious friend really is. It listens carefully to everything you say to yourself. And it's been keeping all of your old programming running at status quo. The subconscious mind loves to help you out. After all, it's in charge of taking care of you from tying your shoe laces to ensuring your heart keeps beating, to making sure your cells regenerate and your food gets digested every day.

To transform it from the old nasty critic it may have become to a kind and compassionate friend, all you have to do is give it some new instructions. Dr. Larry Nims has been known to refer to the subconscious mind as your faithful servant. It takes everything you say literally. Now that you know it doesn't have a sense of humor, you can use Z Point Process™ to reprogram your subconscious mind to get more of what you want and less of what you don't.

How Z Point Process™ Works

Z Point Process™ is based on a Healing Program that you read once and then it is activated by a cue word that you choose. Your cue word functions like a broom in your subconscious mind sweeping out the old programming and making way for the new.

Think of your cue word as a flashlight aiming your focus on what you want to change. Once you've chosen it, you will repeat it several times after saying clearing statements intended to keep you focused on "the problem."

Consider that every thought you have is connected to an emotion that lives in your body. You can use *Z Point Process*™ to let go of your attachment to whatever is bugging you. This will instantly create a shift in the way you feel. This mental down shift will then cause many of your old limiting beliefs supporting your "problem" to collapse, leaving you with lots more Ahhhhhhhhhhhhhhs in your life.

After using *Z Point Process*™ for a while, many people report feeling so much more calm and relaxed, enjoying more harmony and happiness in their lives. Many notice improvements in their relationships with their families, bosses, co-workers, friends, and even strangers. That's because *Z Point Process*™ gives you access to a much more Zen state of mind.

Many people love it because it creates an almost instant delightful feeling of wellbeing in minutes without having to meditate, focus or chant for hours.

249

I have found it to be incredibly effective and very pleasant in its peaceful approach. One client said, "It's so comforting, it's better than a warm shower and a teddy bear." As with all of the energy coaching techniques, after a good session, you'll feel so relaxed, you may just feel the need to settle down and take a nap after the process.

Juicy Woman Note:

Recently I was fostering a feral kitten in my home that had been abandoned on my back porch. When I took Peepers to the vet for the first time, she was skittish and upset as I placed her in the cat carrier. As we drove to the vet, I placed my hand over her tiny white fur covered body to calm her. It didn't work. She was becoming even more agitated and with my hand placed in the carrier, she bit me gently. I had a passing thought wondering if her saliva would cause an allergic reaction in me. Once I created that image in my mind, I began to develop a case of hives along my forearm that was causing me a great deal of distress.

Putting my coach cap on, I realized that Peeps was picking up on my fear and anxiety, so I had to first calm myself and then she would relax. I began to repeat several clearing statements to create a sense of calm for both of us. First, I worked on releasing my allergic reactions. (I clear all the ways I hold this allergy to cats in my body. I clear all the fears that I'm holding about driving and getting into an accident because my attention is being compromised. I clear all the ways I'm scared that these hives will get worse, etc.) Then, following each clearing statement, I repeated my cue word, "Juicy," several times after that. Within a minute or two, the hives reduced in size and stopped itching.

Next, I focused my statements on clearing any fear that she or I may be feeling. Throughout the entire fifteen minute drive I kept repeating different clearing statements that had to do with her specifically and others that were completely unrelated. Then after each statement I repeated my cue word, "Juicy," about fifteen times before each new clearing statement. No matter what image or fear I had in mind, I voiced it in each of my clearing statements.

By the time we reached the vet she had gotten so peaceful inside the carrier that she had fallen fast asleep. I actually had to wake her so that the vet could examine her. Throughout the entire examination and the ride home she was drowsy and peaceful. Z Point Process™ works to create a powerful energy field of peace for yourself and others, with fur and without.

The Cue Word

To get started, you have to choose a cue word. I recommend choosing a word that already has a positive feeling or image associated with it—one syllable is best. You can choose anything you like, but keep in mind that you'll be repeating this word many times. I suggest that you choose one that rolls off your tongue quickly and easily so that you can repeat it without stumbling. My word is Juicy. My Mom's chosen cue word is Love. Cara's word is Cocoa. You decide what's best for you. Make certain that you avoid choosing words that have strong emotional attachments such as "money" or "sex." Grant suggests starting with the cue word, "Yes."

Now that you've got your cue word, you will insert it in the blanks when reading the healing program below. Reading it aloud is best.

The Healing Program

The following Healing program provides the necessary instructions to your subconscious mind. It only needs to be read one time. If you ever decide to change your cue word, just repeat the program with the new word inserted.

Repeat the following:

"I hereby set a powerful intention within you, my subconscious mind, to effect the best of all possible outcomes by

251

this and every clearing, and that each time I notice a pattern or patterns I wish to eliminate as I say or think my cue word, you will eliminate all such patterns and components of patterns completely and safely, and each time I repeat my cue word in sequence like a mantra, you will eliminate and completely resolve and release whatever pattern or patterns I put my attention on, releasing everything about it, everything that relates to it, and everything that has resulted from it, and you will do so gently and easily always ensuring that the pattern or patterns being released never return."

Juicy Woman Note:

Z Point Process™ is one of the best attitude shifting tools I know that you can do with no hands. If you don't like the way you're feeling about something, you can change it. After you've read the healing program to yourself, all you need to do to achieve peace and relaxation is to repeat your cue word. Grant says, "When you change the feeling that you have toward a particular circumstance, situation, or relationship, you change your life."

The Z Point Process™

As you've already done with *EFT*, think about an area in your life where you are experiencing difficulty. Then repeat the following three statements to yourself or have someone repeat them for you. (I recommend recording what you want to say so that you can replay it anytime you like.) After you've repeated one of the following statements you'll repeat your cue word over and over for about 15 seconds. That could mean that you'll say it as many as 10-15 times before proceeding to the next statement. Keep on repeating the cue word until you feel a noticeable shift. This could be a muscle release, your body feeling more relaxed, or having a general calm feeling envelop you.

Using *Z Point* Process™ you can clear negative feelings, emotions, and unconscious patterns, cutting through them like butter.

Juicy Woman Note:

It may seem a bit complicated so to simplify things, I'll share with you that many times I've used Z Point Process™ in the midst of having a conversation with an annoying person and by just using the statement, "I clear all the ways..." Using this I can get the relief I'm seeking.

One day I was driving to confront someone because the consequence of something they did created so much stress I could barely think straight.

As I began to notice that I was so angry my body was shaking I realized that I was driving like a lunatic. I couldn't stop the car because I was heading down a hill with no shoulder with traffic behind me.

To instantly calm my nerves, I decided to use Z Point Process™ to take the edge off of my anger. I knew that I had to release the energy of my overwhelmed emotions and put myself back into a state of resourcefulness in order to handle the situation ahead of me with a cool head.

Frustrated out of my mind, I shouted clearing statements at the top of my lungs as I banged on the steering wheel, followed with my cue word. At one point, I remember saying "I clear all the ways I wish I could stick forks in her eyes, I hate her so much." As I repeated my cue word, I was struck by the horror of what I had just said.

I realized that I wasn't really that angry anymore and didn't want to do any harm to anyone. I just wanted what I wanted. I was basically having a temper tantrum. In an instant, just like a balloon had popped, my anger broke and I began laughing, realizing the insanity of what I had said. I continued to repeat clearing statements to relieve the feelings of guilt that I had about saying what I did. By the time, I arrived at my destination, I was as calm as a cucumber and the situation was resolved easily. From that day on, I have never doubted the effectiveness of Z Point Process™ for in-the-moment relief. My best advice to you is to say whatever is on your mind. Don't even think about cleaning it up and censoring yourself. Get down and dirty and feel the intensity of your feelings. Let it all go. That's what will really create the momentum necessary for it to work.

Basic Z Point Process™ Protocol:

Step 1. "I clear all the ways I feel _____." Just fill in the blank describing how you really feel, i.e., (depressed, angry, sad, hurt, intimidated, frustrated, cut off at the knees, resentful, jealous, etc.) Repeat cue word 10-15 times.

Step 2. "I clear all the patterns connected to these ways." Just repeat this statement and all the others that follow. Your brilliant subconscious mind knows exactly where to go to achieve what you want. Repeat cue word 10-15 times.

Step 3. "I clear all the reasons connected to all of these ways." Repeat cue word 10-15 times.

Step 4. "I clear all the ways these patterns and reasons are held in my body." Repeat cue word 10-15 times.

Step 5. "I clear all of the emotions connected to all of these patterns." Repeat your cue word 10-15 times.

Now, let's explore what goes on behind the scenes of each of the steps:

In Step 1, we affirm, "I clear all the ways..." When you make this statement to your subconscious mind, you are stating that you want to clear all of the possible ways you feel a single emotion or group of emotions linked to your stated problem.

Unlike *EFT*, with *Z Point Process*™ you don't have to have a very specific idea of what is bugging you. *Z Point* Process™ works just fine with making general statements because it instructs your subconscious mind to find all the specific areas in your life that need attention in order to achieve the clearing indicated.

However for the icing on the cake, I'll explain the other clearing statements:

In Step 2, we affirm, "I clear all the patterns..." This ensures that your subconscious mind will be guided to deactivate any silly, loopy, useless, victim oriented, knee jerk reactions that we act on in response to our circumstances. An example of this are the many mindless trancelike behaviors we do every day in response to dealing with stress in our life, like biting our nails, overeating, giving into road rage, etc. Your body has done these things so many times before you don't have to think about each individual movement, it's just a pattern that your mind follows by rote.

We are filled with patterns, some useful, others not. Showering, brushing your teeth, combing your hair, tying your shoelaces, and remembering your ABC's are all very useful, but nail biting, body hating, binging, panic attacks, and a variety of other compulsive addictions are not. This step will ensure that you clear all these types of patterns that are attached to "your problem."

In Step 3, we affirm, "I clear all the reasons connected to all of these ways." This is important because many times we have no idea why we do the things we do. By putting the burden of this responsibility on your subconscious mind to go in and sweep away all the underlying reasons that motivate your unconscious actions, you release the need to know what reasons hold "your problem" in place.

In Step 4, we affirm, "I clear all the ways these patterns and reasons are held in my body." This is useful because our bodies have become dumping grounds for the tension and trauma that has occurred in our lives. By repeating this clearing statement, you instruct your subconscious mind to clear all that old flotsam and jetsam still stuck in your body that comes as a bonus with your problem. This instruction allows physical symptoms, tendencies, and neuro-muscular tension to relax and release.

In Step 5, we affirm, "I clear all the emotions..." You've already learned how your emotions are the key to knowing what you are attracting. When you feel great, you're attracting more goodness into your life. When you're feeling miserable, you're attracting more misery into your life.

By instructing your subconscious mind to clear your emotions, you will clear all the mindless behavior connected to that pattern. Then your

255

pattern will no longer hold you hostage. Who'd a thunk it would be so easy to change the recipe?

Linking

When you've already got a good handle on what's bugging you and the emotions that are getting triggered, you can use *Z Point Process*™ to knock down more than one negative emotion at a time.

It's just like knocking over a set of standing dominos. You can combine several types of clearing statements to get great relief. Here's an example that I created:

Releasing Weight

After repeating each of the following statements, say your cue word 10-15 times before proceeding with the next statement.

> I clear all the ways that I'm stressed. (Repeat your cue word 10-15 times as usual.)
> I clear all the ways that I tend to eat when I'm stressed. (Cue)
> I clear all the ways I'm afraid of never trusting myself with foods I love. (Cue)
> I clear all the ways I'm afraid of not knowing when to stop eating. (Cue)
> I clear all the ways I'm afraid of feeling insatiable. (Cue)
> I clear all the ways I feel bottomless in my neediness. (Cue)
> I clear all the ways I feel the need to be mean to myself and criticize my body. (Cue)
> I clear all the ways I refuse to believe I'm lovable and acceptable as I am. (Cue)
> I clear all the ways that parts of me need to hold on to my weight. (Cue)
> I clear all the ways I doubt anything will work for me. (Cue)
> I clear all the ways that these issues have been held in my body. (Cue)
> I clear all the ways that these issues have been held in my energy field. (Cue)
> I clear all the patterns connected to all of these ways. (Cue)
> I clear all the emotions connected to all of these patterns. (Cue)

Fill In the Blank Technique

Just like a dog with a bone, all you have to do is point your subconscious mind in the right direction and it will dig up the problem and take care of the rest. You don't have to know the root causes of your problem in order to get to the bottom of it. Rather than doing all the hard work and trying to figure out all the ways, emotions, and patterns connected to things that make us feel bad in our lives, it's much more effective to send your subconscious mind on a treasure hunt by doing the fill-in-the-blank technique.

As you repeat your statements, you will purposely leave a portion blank so that your brilliant subconscious mind can go through all of its internal files and find the exact situations that fit your need. Here are a few more examples using the release weight script I created:

Grant suggests that you can also use modifying words like "if", "but," or "back then" in addition to the following types of examples:

I clear all the ways that parts of me feel that it's unsafe to lose weight because... (Cue)

I clear all the ways that parts of me need to seek out food for comfort whenever... (Cue)

I clear all the ways that I have any health problems, any pain or illness in my body... (Cue)

I clear all the ways that parts of me need to get something out of holding onto... (Cue)

I clear all the patterns... (Cue)

I clear all the ways that parts of me need to get something out of holding onto those pains because... (Cue)

I clear all the ways that parts of me benefit from beating up on myself whenever... (Cue)

I clear all the ways that parts of me feel safe when I put myself down because... (Cue)

I clear all the ways that I identify myself as lazy... (Cue)

I clear all the ways I feel entitled to give up on my weight because... (Cue)

I clear all the ways I'm hard on myself for doing this because... (Cue)

I clear all the ways I see myself as doomed to fail because... (Cue)

Juicy Woman Note:

It's extremely important to clear what is bugging you, but it's also essential to indicate what you choose. After I do all my clearing statements, I like to make several statements to my subconscious mind that leave me feeling absolutely, completely, and totally in charge. Here are a few examples I've used in closing my personal Z Point Process™ sessions:

"I claim my right to ask for what I need from myself and others."

"I choose to feel safe and loved in my body now."

"I claim my right as an eagle claims its wings to be proud of each of my achievements as I proceed along with this program because ..."

"I instruct you, my brilliant subconscious mind to guide me to take whatever action I need in order to be more gentle with myself every day..."

Have fun. You're only limited by your own level of creativity and art of delivery. Play with your words; use them to trigger yourself to feel wonderful and to love your body more each day.

After an emotional climax, it's no doubt that you will feel the weight of the world lifting off of your shoulders. With Z Point Process™ as with all the other energy coaching processes, you'll notice that your body will go through several changes. If you notice yourself yawning, stretching, or feeling like taking a nap, that's wonderful. It's a powerful indicator of the magic that is occurring in your body as your subconscious mind instructs your body to release the hold on what's bugging you.

Wrapping Up
Chapter 7: Coping with Stress: Your Anxiety Relief Tool Kit

Here are the juiciest bits covered in this section. Savor them mindfully.

- The real cause of your overeating is an imbalance in your body's energy system. Your wayward emotions are what keep you in patterns of feeling miserable and that leads to overeating. When you smooth out those hurt, angry, sad, and overwhelmed feelings, the distortions in your body's energy system will disappear, taking with it your desire to eat when you're not hungry.

- The basic premise behind *EFT* is that the cause of all negative emotions is a disruption in the body's energy system. To correct the imbalance, all you have to do is tap on your body's natural comfort spots (acupoints) as you focus on the problem.

- Remember that in order to release any emotion, you have to first allow yourself to feel it.

- I've learned that every time I find myself in a negative situation and being put on the defensive, if I change my action and thoughts, the people around me change. This influences the entire relationship, creating more balance and harmony.

- Change yourself, change your world: We're all reflections of one another. Each person is a mirror showing you how much you value yourself.

- Since natural hunger creeps up on you slowly, that quick flash desire, desperate urge to eat is your first hint that something other than hunger is rattling your cage. This is a good time to explore your phantom hunger.

- After you've had an emotional release from using *EFT*, make sure you take the time to gentle yourself and your body. In the process of resetting your brain's neural connections, much work and energy is being used by your body. Make certain that during this window of 24-48 hours following your *EFT* release, you rest as much as possible and take it easy.

If after several hours or days of doing tapping, you notice a pervasive feeling of being extremely vulnerable, as in weepy, sad, or withdrawn, then that means you must do more tapping to get to the core of the feeling.

 The goal in doing the tapping is to give you a choice so that you can respond to the old stress triggers in a new way, moving beyond your knee jerk reactions.

 What if I stop struggling with my weight and focus on what food I most enjoy that makes me feel good from the inside out? What if I focus on feeling good and healthy? What if I begin to allow myself to feel deserving of being beautiful? What if beauty is an inside job and it's mine for the taking?

 The beauty of *Z Point Process*™ is that it can be invisibly practiced anywhere; from the bedroom to the boardroom and everywhere in between. It's the best belief bustin' tool I know that can be done in the heat of the moment. Whether standing in line, sitting in traffic, dealing with parenting frustrations, or in the midst of an argument, it's awesome for taking off the edge and putting you back in control.

 Love Your Body

Chapter 8
Love Your Body -
Respect Your Boundaries:
Care Enough to Set
the Very Best

"We're always teaching people how we want to be treated. If you don't like the
way someone is treating you, don't blame them, change how you treat yourself."
– Andrea Amador

In our lives we separate ourselves from others by creating boundaries. Yet in a society where women are conditioned to think of their role in
life as limited to being pretty and pleasing, we grow up thinking of ourselves in a distorted way.

Raised as little girls to think of ourselves as cinnamon and spice and
everything nice, as good girls we've become the nurturers, caregivers, and
lovers, perpetually placing everyone else's needs ahead of our own. It's no
wonder that most women have limiting beliefs that make it nearly impossible to set healthy boundaries. Your boundaries or lack of them are the
result of the unconscious beliefs you hold.

Most of us gals have been raised to think of ourselves as second class citizens. After all, how many of the following bits of boundary busting advice can you recall hearing as a child?

- "A woman's place is in the home."
- "Be a good girl."
- "Keep quiet."
- "Look and act pretty."
- "Speak only when spoken to."
- "Keep a low profile."
- "Don't ask questions."
- "Don't complain."
- "Don't be too demanding."
- "You're so selfish."
- "Nice girls don't…"
- "Be a lady."
- "Know your place."

Like me, you've probably heard many of the above sayings, which is more than your fair share of other people's ideas of good advice. Although a part of you knows these are just antiquated and old fashioned beliefs, you still find yourself buying into them every now and again.

The truth is we have beliefs about things we don't even know we have beliefs about. These are the assumptions and interpretations we make based on living our lives and watching others. If you are overweight and unhappy with your body, it's most likely evidence of the fact that many of the beliefs you have today are preventing you from getting thinner and being happier.

Every Thought That Feels Bad Is Bad

Think about your beliefs like a setting on a thermostat. Unless you turn the dial, you will remain stuck in the same setting. According to the teachings of Abraham as delivered (channeled) through Esther Hicks, your beliefs are chronic vibrations. They keep you caught in a pattern of thinking that keeps you stuck in certain feelings.

Every thought you choose that is a vibrational match to putting yourself down, beating yourself up, fearing food, and hating your body, feels bad when you think it. It feels like anger, frustration, jealousy, envy, resentment, blame, guilt, sadness, or fear. Those thoughts are not good for you and you know that's true by how they make you feel.

If you think negatively you will end up feeling bad. This is because your body and mind are one. They are not separate—what you think, you will feel, and what you feel, you will think.

Has this ever happened to you? You could be feeling great one minute and then decide to try on a pair of your judgment jeans to check and see if you've been losing weight and making progress getting thinner. Then, after not being able to get them up past your thighs, all of a sudden you feel fat as a house. That awareness can make you go from feeling great to gloomy in the blink of an eye.

Since you are always attracting things to you by virtue of your thoughts, when you think negatively you will attract negative things. When you are negative, your point of attraction will be negative. You will be in resonance with a negative or low vibration.

In the same way that when you touch a hot stove it hurts, when you think a negative thought it hurts.

As you learned when we discussed the psychological reversal point in the previous section entitled, *Cope with Your Stress*, a part of you is in conflict with another part. This is why you may find yourself at odds with yourself, sabotaging your best efforts. In order to resolve the conflict and set new boundaries to empower yourself, you have to first uncover your values and beliefs which collectively make up the emotional foundation of your life.

In this chapter, first we'll go behind the scenes, dig into your head and uncover some of the values and beliefs which give your life shape and meaning. You'll decide which ones work for you and which don't. Then you'll learn how to set new boundaries.

Beliefs and Values: The Emotional Foundation of Your Life

In your brain you are always creating meaning. As a living, breathing being you are a meaning maker. A belief is a feeling of certainty about the meaning of something in your life. Everyone has a set of personal values. Beliefs rise up from what we value. Our values are emotional states that we have learned to think of as important. Because we give them significance, we want them in our life.

In the chapter entitled *Embrace Your Emotions*, we discussed the fact that in your pursuit of happiness, you're not really after the things or the action, like getting a new car, making boatloads of money, or even being thin, but what we all really want is to change the way we feel. More specifically you want to change the meaning of a circumstance and by doing that, you change the way you feel. The things and actions you may be wishing for are merely a means to an end. You really just want to feel better.

Let's take a look at a chart listing several different values:

Accomplishment	Efficiency	Integrity
Achievement	Equality	Intimacy
Accountability	Excellence	Joy
Beauty	Faith	Justice
Challenge	Faithfulness	Knowledge
Cleanliness	Family	Leadership
Collaboration	Freedom	Love, Romance
Commitment	Friendship	Merit
Communication	Fun	Patriotism
Competence	Goodness	Peace
Competition	Gratitude	Perfection
Concern For Others	Hard Work	Pleasure
Connection	Health	Prosperity, Wealth
Contribution	Harmony	Punctuality
Cooperation	Honesty	Reliability
Creativity	Honor	Resourcefulness
Decisiveness	Improvement	Respect For Others
Democracy	Independence	
Discipline	Individuality	Responsiveness
Discovery	Inner Peace, Calm	Results-Oriented
Diversity	Innovation	Rule Of Law
		Safety

Safety	Status	Tranquility
Satisfying Others	Strength	Trust
Security	Success	Truth
Self-Reliance	Teamwork	Unity
Self-Thinking	Timeliness	Variety
Simplicity	Tolerance	Wisdom
Stability	Tradition	

The list below is an example of what is known as a hierarchy of values—placing one's values in order of importance:

 Love

 Health

 Freedom

 Security

 Success

 Adventure

 Power

Intimacy

Comfort

Juicy Woman Note:

Here's a quick tip on how to analyze your values. By looking at the values hierarchy example above, you can tell at a glance that the person who made this list cherishes love most of all. This means that when push comes to shove they will always choose love. Success is fifth on the list and that means love is valued more than being successful. This person would most likely invest more time building a relationship as opposed to increasing their business.

Love also beats health, freedom, security, adventure, power, intimacy, and comfort. However, you'll notice that intimacy, a big part of love in a relationship, is close to the bottom of the list, which means the love they are valuing might not necessarily be manifesting as sexual or physical. This could indicate an internal conflict within them surrounding intimacy and love.

A conflict demonstrates that a person has mixed associations which are causing them to feel both pain and pleasure towards the same outcome, in this case love in all its manifestations. Although they may want love, they fear intimacy. Some people have been in intimate relationships and experienced a great deal of pain. Yet because they have a desire to have intimacy, love, and connection, when things get too difficult they tend to pull back and withhold themselves for fear of being rejected.

Doing your values chart and putting it in the order of your importance will be very useful to you. It will give you a sense of where in your life you have conflicts. You can deal with these conflicts by using any of the techniques in the previous chapter.

This hierarchal framework of understanding gives you an example of how you can define your values and determine the order in which they are most important to your life. It's fun to play with this. Go ahead and enjoy it. Also keep in mind that as you change, your values change.

Moving Toward Values vs. Moving Away From Values

The values you hold most dear to you are considered "moving toward values." This represents the good things you want more of in your life: love, success, freedom, passion, health, comfort. (See the extended boxed list above.)

The values you are eager to avoid are called "moving away from values." These are the emotional states that you don't want to experience, i.e., anger, sadness, pain, self pity, rejection, insecurity.

The Two Kinds of Beliefs: Global and Rule Based

There are two basic kinds of beliefs: global and rules based.

Global beliefs are generalizations that we make based on our life's experiences. These are represented by sweeping statements like:

"Life is..................."

"People are............."

"Men always............"

"Beauty is..............."

"I am...................."

Belief "Rules" are conditional ideas that are based on a cause and effect principle, "If this.....then that."

"If I'm fat, then I'm unlovable."

"If I'm short, then I'm inadequate."

"If I have cancer, then I'll die."

"If I'm thin, then I'll be happy."

"If I get my degree, then I'll be successful."

Beliefs have no power unless you accept them as true. This is because you give meaning to what you believe. You can either choose to believe something as true or not. If you've been struggling with your weight and hating or resenting your body, then it's important for you to take a look behind the scenes and uncover what you believe about yourself, your body, your relationship to food, your sense of worth, and what makes you happy.

I strongly suggest that before you continue reading into the next chapter, you take some time over the course of a few days and sit down with my next several Try *It!* Exercises! The benefits to you will be immeasurable. If you haven't been aware of the significance of your beliefs, doing these *Try It*! exercises may be as illuminating as turning on a light and breaking through the darkness. Awareness is the first step to change. Best of all—by sitting down and becoming more aware of what you believe, you will have a foundation upon which to mount your new arsenal of belief busting that I've shared with you in the previous chapter.

How I Began to Question My Beliefs

When I first began to learn how to listen to my body, all I wanted to do was eat. I felt like a tiger that had finally been let out of its cage. After being deprived and fearing food for so many years, a part of me went wild at the prospect of saying goodbye to dieting. It was horrifying and wonderful at the same time. I didn't know what to expect. I was so scared.

After my colleague, Doc Frost, told me a bit about intuitive eating, I devoured every book I could find on the subject and filled my bookcases with resource material. I was committed to finally solving the mystery once and for all—could I really trust myself around food? I had to know.

All those years that I was a dieter, depriving myself on and off, struggling with the constant temptation to sneak food to get my fix, I had always believed that I couldn't ever feel safe around the foods I loved.

When I was "in the zone" and working out all the time and eating light, my way of dealing with my fear was to keep tempting foods out of my home. Yet those were always the ones I craved. I couldn't imagine resigning myself to live this way forever.

I played the games that all women learn to play with food; eating like a saint during the week and a sinner on the weekends, slurping down buckets of free veggie soups or devouring huge naked salads with no dressing, eating no points, low points, fat free, low Cal, I did it all. But no matter what, by all that was holy I believed that I had to keep fattening foods out of my house when I was dieting because I would surely lose my mind and never stop eating. To my way of thinking, I was a fat pig who had no self-control.

My actual experience with learning to listen to my body taught me that I can be trusted around food. Once I got that understanding that I could be discriminating and not feel compelled to eat everything in my path, it initiated a ripple effect that created a wonderful upheaval in my life.

Try It! – The Limit of Lies

In the middle of a sheet of paper write a simple statement that you often tell yourself that describes your relationship to food. This is a belief you've come to accept as true. Now, draw a series of lines from different parts of that statement and write the following words, mother, father, siblings, mate/lover, children, work, associates, clients, co-workers, spirituality, and health.

Draw a line from your statement to each of those words and write a sentence that pops up for you that is a consequence of feeling that what you believe about food is unequivocally true.

For example, my belief "I can't be trusted" affected my relationship with my father/boss whereby I avoided making business decisions, became resentful, passive aggressive, and procrastinated. The consequence was that people lost respect for me, and I lost a ton of money.

Juicy Woman Note:

After I had my first mindful eating potato chip epiphany, I realized...

"If I can trust myself with food, then what other lies and criticisms have I bought into that have been limiting me?"

You'll notice this "if, then" statement is an example of what I described as a Belief Rule which works on the basis of cause and effect. This limiting belief of mine affected every area of my life; from the bedroom to the boardroom. Because I didn't think I could trust myself around food, and I thought of myself as a bad person by extension, I justified why I didn't deserve happiness and why I would never be able to feel safe enough to trust anybody, including myself. What a tangled mess!

Who'd think that with that one single stupid rancid potato chip, years of distorted beliefs would fold like a house of cards?

For me, that was the start of a new beginning. From that point forward, with the very consistent and dedicated use of my energy coaching tools, I began to question all the nasty things that anyone had ever said to me. Making peace with that part of my past helped me to lay to rest all the old criticisms and snide remarks that for years had made such powerful impressions on me. It felt so good to finally take out that garbage.

Isn't it time you started clearing out your emotional clutter? That's exactly what I'm giving you the chance to do in the next two Try Its! After you complete them, take a look at what your belief rules are and notice if you're still buying into those screaming meanie buggers. If you are, then run, don't walk, and go right back to the stress relief section. Run 'em through any of the processes there to give them a much needed attitude lift.

Now that you have a sense of which relationships have been affected by your limiting beliefs, let's dig a little deeper and get to the bottom of all this beliefs business.

Try It! – Exploring Your Beliefs

Since your beliefs and values guide your decision-making, you must become familiar with them so you can get back in the drivers' seat and understand what drives your actions. With that information you're in a position to choose what you want. You can change what doesn't work for you. This Try It! is one I adapted from Tony Robbins Personal Power II® Driving Force Success Journal.

I suggest that you do the following Try It! in manageable chunks over several days. You'll stack the odds in your favor by taking baby steps to avoid overwhelm. Let's begin:

 To uncover your values ask yourself this simple question: What's most important in my life? Write down the feelings you want. Then list the states of being you value most (love, passion, integrity, intimacy, excitement, contribution, etc.) Remember money, success, and losing weight are all examples of means, not values. You can differentiate between the two by asking yourself the following questions:

> If I had more money, success, or were thinner, what would that give me?
>
> What would I get from having, being, or doing that?
>
> How would it make me feel?
>
> After you've determined what's important to you mark this list as your "moving towards values."

- Put these "moving toward values" in a hierarchy and order their importance in your life. For example: contribution, love, intimacy, etc.

- Make a list of all the negative emotions or states of being you would do anything to avoid. By having a bead on what you feel compelled to avoid, you will be better equipped to know more about what motivates you. These are called "moving away from values" and they represent your greatest pain. Some examples of these are overwhelm, loneliness, rejection, frustration, anxiety, etc.

- Put these "moving away from values" in a hierarchy indicating their order of importance in your life. The one at the top of the list is the one you will do the most to avoid.

- On a separate piece of paper for each of the two different types of values, "moving toward" and "moving away from," write the following question:

- What has to happen for me to feel these emotions?

Consider the question and close your eyes as you paint a picture in your mind's eye of what would need to happen for you to feel these emotions in your life. Then write down your discoveries on paper.

Begin with your "moving toward values." If love was one of your values, what has to happen for you to feel loved? (For some people, they need to live with their mate, bound by the commitment of marriage. For others, just a promise is more than enough.)

Repeat the above instructions addressing each of your "moving away from values" describing what needs to happen in order for you to feel them. For example, to some people being rejected by someone might be the most horrible consequence imaginable. To others, rejection is just one more step bringing them closer to acceptance. Their rule is that it's all a numbers game and each "No" gets them closer to a "Yes." It's so important to understand the rules you have for feeling the way you do, because all too often we make it really easy to make ourselves feel bad and next to impossible to feel good.

Write down what your rules are for feeling good and feeling bad. I've learned that you can keep resistance at bay by lowering your expectations. This makes it easier to achieve your goals. Remember you can always raise the bar.

Examples of Rules for "Moving Toward" Values

 I nurture myself whenever I take ten minutes out of my day to sit quietly and listen to my inner wisdom.

 I feel healthy when I take a short walk around the block.

 Whenever I eat mindfully, I feel connected to my body.

Examples of Rules for "Moving Away From" Values

 I feel rejected when someone says, "no."

 I feel lonely when nobody has time for me.

 I feel depressed when I eat more than I wanted.

Review the values that you've uncovered with this *Try It!* Have you discovered any rules like the ones below which have been restricting your happiness and sucking up your joy? If so, which ones are you willing to change now?

Examples of Bad, Horrible, Terrible Rules That Will Only Set You Up to Fail

1. In order to be more <u>mindful</u>, I have to eat really slowly all the time.
2. I know I'm <u>healthy</u> if I choose to eat only light or fat free foods.
3. I can only make <u>progress</u>, if I get on the scale every day.
4. I can't feel <u>loveable</u>, unless I lose weight.
5. I'll never be <u>happy</u>, unless I do everything perfectly.
6. I'd be <u>disciplined</u>, if I never ate another piece of chocolate again.

Write any disempowering rules down in a list. Take your list of rules and flip back to the *Cope with Your Stress* section. Deal with those bugaboos using one of the methods I've shared like *EFT* or *Z Point Process*™ before they continue to suck the life and joy out of you.

Juicy Woman Note:

Feeling beautiful is very important to me and as long as I hated my thighs, it didn't matter what size I was, a part of me wasn't willing to consider myself as beautiful. That was my rule and I assumed it was universally true. The truth was I never knew anyone who was overweight and okay with their body as it was.

I didn't realize it, but now I know that I was caught in a losing game. You've got to focus on what you can change and the rest will take care of itself. In order for me to achieve the love and peace I value so dearly, I had to change the way I responded to my thighs. I did this by linking two of my highest values, love and peace to my thighs. That made self-acceptance for me a no brainer. If you ever want to change something quickly find a way of associating it to your highest values.

From my years of NLP training, I knew that being exposed to role models of women loving and accepting their larger bodies could put me on the fast track to success. After an enlightening conversation I had with Kevin Creedon, one of my NLP coaches, I was inspired to seek out movies and find examples of women comfortable with their bodies. As I started watching films showing beauty in different forms, I began to feel more comfortable with my own larger, curvier shaped body.

Movies like Hairspray, The Perfect Holiday, Phat Girlz, Beauty Shop, Disfigured, Queen-sized, and Real Women Have Curves showed me that I could love my body no matter what my size. I saw beauty in those women, so I wondered, "Why couldn't I generalize it and see beauty in myself?" It may have taken a bit of tapping before, during, or after watching some of the movies to install the new program but it's in good and tight now.

Before I had a handle on my newfound curvy confidence, I was faced with the doubt that said, "These women aren't real. They're only actresses playing a part. You need to find examples of real women who love their bodies."

Then just around the same time, in early 2009, I stumbled upon the Plus Model magazine site. That was when I realized that there was a whole goldmine of resources for plus sized women that very few women were privy to. I was dumbfounded as I leafed through the online magazine and read article after article about fashion, movies, events, and so many other wonderful things that opened up my world, expanded my vision, increased my appreciation for my body, and made me feel beautiful inside and out, surrounded by sisterly support. That completely changed my ideas of beauty and made it clear to me that with or without thighs, I'm a very beautiful woman at any size and in my eyes you are too!

Now it's lovely to finally believe that my husband loves my body as it is, because I can accept myself. His appreciation of it or anyone else's acceptance for that matter, is just icing on the cake. Remember the quote from the movie, Penelope. "It's not the power of the curse. It's the power you give it."

Free yourself from the curse. Do a quick internet search and find movies and real life role models that will empower you.

Now that you're getting a handle on what beliefs are driving you, you're ready to start re-examining this thing called boundaries. In the following section I'm going to weave many personal stories with practical information to give you the best of what I've learned about the importance of setting boundaries.

Boundaries: What the Heck Are They?

In their book, *The Power of Focus for Women: How to Live the Life You Really Want*, authors Fran and Les Hewitt say, "The single best way to improve your life is to learn how to set boundaries. Boundaries create healthy relationships."

By looking closely at your values and beliefs, you will clearly see what boundaries you want to define. If getting other people's approval is very important to you, as it was for me, then you'll have a challenging time setting boundaries. This whole book is intended to gear you toward listening to your own inner wisdom and recognizing that you have all the answers you need. Your answers are not outside of you, they are inside. In order to create a safe space to divine your own wisdom, you'll have to work on renegotiating or redefining your boundaries.

When you start shifting your boundaries your whole life will change. Not only will you like and respect yourself a heck of a lot more, but your relationships with others will be better than ever because you'll be more honest. By taking the steps to improve your communication skills and say what you really mean, you'll feel less resentful. Setting boundaries is a kind and loving thing to do.

Your ability to set boundaries tells the world how you think about the person you are. It makes a statement about how much you respect yourself,

275

your time, your values and your body. By making it clear to others that your feelings and needs are important, people will learn to respect you.

"Are you holding your happiness hostage by giving yourself
away to accommodate everyone else's whims?"
– Andrea Amador

Having boundaries stops you from over-committing and falling headfirst into situations where you get completely overwhelmed and end up feeling undervalued. By learning to be more assertive and stating what you will and won't do, you free yourself of the guilt of making empty promises and looking like a scatter brain when you don't do what you said you would do.

As you gain strength in becoming a more assertive and confident woman, you will be free to focus more time on doing what you love, those things that have real value for you, that make your heart sing.

Opportunities to set boundaries are everywhere: at work, in the home, with friends, relatives, acquaintances, even those annoying telemarketers who call when you're just about ready to sit down and eat dinner.

I've learned from personal experience that my relationship with food has reflected the way I've felt about myself over the years. The fact that I've subconsciously had the need to create a fleshy boundary to insulate and protect myself from others was evidence of my own low self-esteem. Because I felt so desperately afraid and out of control in my life for such a long time, it showed up in my eating. I didn't realize this until the day I learned that I had been too busy playing by everyone else's rules. That was when I knew I had been too deeply entrenched in my people pleasing world to understand that I was worthy of taking care of myself.

Now I realize that the ability to self-nurture and love yourself is the hallmark of a woman with a strong sense of self-esteem. It has nothing to do with what my Nana used to call being selfish. Think of taking care of yourself as being "self-full," filling yourself from the inside out. It is a way of fulfilling your needs without always having to resort to food.

My path to that awareness of self-respect started with a single potato chip that I chose not to eat because it was too stale. As a landmark moment in my life, it was the first time I was ever able to feel in control around food. From that point on, I began to question everything I'd been told about who I was and what I was capable of.

As you make strides toward legalizing all foods, you will also have the opportunity to step more fully and consciously into your power which will lead you to taking a bigger bite out of life. By doing that, you will regain your self-respect and reclaim parts of you that have been clouded over by fear, food, and weight obsession.

As you do that, more and more, you will increase your feelings of love and self-compassion for your body. As a side benefit, you'll notice that the duration, intensity, and frequency of your binges will naturally and effortlessly subside.

Let's discuss how changing the way you relate to your body affects your relationship with food.

Decoding Your Binges: Comforting Your Inner Crying Child

Gloria Arenson is a California based psychotherapist. As a writer and speaker, she is a powerful voice of empowerment and a credible authority on eating disorders.

After dealing with her own eating issues, Gloria went on to chronicle her learning and share it with her clients. In her book, *Binge Eating: How to Stop It Forever*, Dr. Arenson explains that binging is equivalent to having a temper tantrum. She says, "A binge always has to do with feelings, usually resentment, frustration, and rage. There are two kinds of temper tantrum binges: food anger and emotional anger."

Food anger is the sense of frustration and desperation that comes with long term or constant dieting. After weeks and months of carefully counting calories or eating "healthy" the dieter reaches a saturation point where she feels like she is about to explode if the deprivation persists a moment longer. This is when you start with one cookie and end up eating the whole box.

The second type of temper tantrum binge is all about dealing with your emotions, especially anger or frustration. Binge eaters are usually nice people, nonassertive, and accommodating. A binge is a great way to "swallow" anger.

Many people are able to stuff the anger so far down that they don't feel anything on a conscious level and just keep smiling. But their body knows that they're really feeling anger and resentment, and those emotions get translated into stress which, for the emotional eater, triggers a desperate desire to eat.

If you really stop and think about it—your binges are urgent messages to you. This is your body's way of screaming for help, alerting you to the fact that something is not right. It is as if the binge has a life of its own.

Wouldn't you like to stop beating up on yourself and start to love your body more? To do that you have to fulfill your most basic needs.

According to Dr. Arenson, human beings have three basic needs:

Identity... Who am I?

Relationship... Am I lovable?

Power... Am I in charge of my life?

In the next several pages you'll read case histories of my clients and see how their lives changed as a result of making peace with food and becoming friends with their bodies. I'll separate each case history according to the question or basic need addressed.

Identity...Who Am I?

"Who am I?" is a very scary question for bingers. It challenges them to become aware of the fact that their life revolves around serving others. This question of "Who Am I?" challenges them to face the truth that they don't really know, feel entitled to, or capable of being able to pursue what is important to them.

Many people who abuse food have become so accustomed to knuckling under to the wishes and demands of others that they don't feel safe asserting themselves for fear of not being loved.

When one of my clients, Shoshana, first came to me, she was struggling with her weight and unable to recognize when she no longer felt hungry. Here is an excerpt from her first Losing Weight without Dieting forum post:

"I have been trying to pay attention to my hunger, today especially. It is HARD! I find that most of my hunger is phantom hunger and that makes me feel angry and sad because I want to eat but I'm not biologically hungry. I never realized how many times a day I want to eat for reasons other than biological hunger! It is countless times a day. And when I look at it, I see that I want to eat when I am happy, when I am sad, when I am stressed, when I am bored, when I am tired, when I am lonely, when I have fear and anxiety, and when I have feelings of loss. Sometimes I just have random foods pop into my head for no apparent reason.

Food is the enemy, food is dangerous, food is my best friend and my passion, I love food, I hate food, I think about food all the time, what I want to eat, when, how, how much. Food is powerful, food is sneaky, food is fun, food is playful, food consoles me, food hurts me, food infuriates and irritates me, food celebrates me, food calls to me...this psychotic relationship with food makes me feel crazy!

I feel like I have so many aspects to my relationship with food, I don't even know where to begin with *EFT*. I am starting to realize the huge role food and all the messages around eating etc. have played throughout most of my life. It's no wonder diets don't work, it's about so much more than that. What a complex relationship!"

As you can see, food and weight obsession can be a twenty-four hour preoccupation. In Shoshana's case, her challenge was that she was not working in a career field that she loved. She didn't feel comfortable confronting her parents with certain truths and she was tired of living to please other people. As a consequence, she ate to soothe her emotional discomfort. In her words, "food was her best friend and her enemy."

She had spent many years educating herself to enter a profession that gave her no joy. And for far too long she lived in fear of telling her parents that she was gay. Once she finally understood that her heart was leading her to live and speak her truth, she followed through and took actionable steps to start her own business and make her voice heard. It was then her weight worries diminished.

Shoshana also struggled with a physical challenge. She said:

"I've had Chronic Fatigue Syndrome for over ten years now. Even though the symptoms have caused a lot of misery and seemed to have taken over my life, they've also been serving me in a way. Being worn out and in pain all the time has given me a great excuse to hole up inside my house and avoid getting back out there and fully participating in life again. The symptoms are VERY real and DO make it extremely difficult to do much outside of work, including spend time with negative family members I want to avoid...

"I used to be SO bad at setting my boundaries and the CFS was perfect for setting my boundaries for me!"

As Shoshana began to disentangle herself from her family's image of who she thought she should have been, she became free to be who she was. When she realized that she was wonderful exactly as she was and didn't need to focus on losing weight, then she started to treat herself differently and assert her needs, and made living juicy a priority. That's when her weight issues began to take care of themselves. When she changed the way that she saw herself, she was able to make peace with her family and that made it easier for them to accept her choices.

Her challenge was carving out her identity and risking disapproval of those whom she loved. When she started to approve of herself, then other people related to her differently. That's when she was no longer plagued with constant obsessive thoughts of food.

Relationship... Am I Lovable?

Many women have wonderful lives and people surrounding them, but because they are fraught with fear and negative memories from the past, they are unable to accept and appreciate their good fortune. Such was the case with my client, Ayla.

By all accounts, Ayla experienced a horrific childhood where she was beaten daily by her mother and sexually abused by her father from the ages of two to sixteen. She fluctuated between being bulimic and anorexic. At sixteen she ran away from home to live on the streets. Soon after, she met and married a man and they had a child. He was abusive and began beating her. One day he went too far and threatened her life. Acting on sheer courage, she took her baby, fled the country, and began a new life.

When she came to me there were so many parts of her life that she had already healed. She had a career she adored, a wonderful husband, and a beautiful relationship with her daughter. Yet she still struggled desperately with bulimia, purging meals soon after eating, fearing that she would gain weight.

In her words, "I was a lonely little girl and found comfort in food, however being an overweight ten year old is no fun so not being the pretty one at school made me a target. I was often picked on, bullied. This compounded the problem; now not only did I feel isolated in a very dysfunctional home but facing the additional stress at school I ate more. Back then a bag of chips cost around two cents so it wasn't too hard to eat junk food for a great price. My only lifeline was my grandmother who lived with us. While she didn't have a voice in the home and couldn't align herself in any direction with regards to me openly, I knew she loved me.

"Today it's clear to me she knew I was being targeted and would often slip me pocket change as I left for school—which I would promptly spend on candy. I'd eat half and try and use the rest to bribe those I was most afraid of. I guess in the hope that they would see that I was an okay type of person and hope that one day they would leave me alone. They took the candy and still beat the hell out of me on a regular basis.

"It was only in the past year that I made the connection that the reason I couldn't break the relationship I had with food was because it was the only security blanket I felt I had. It was the best friend who was there to comfort me at all hours of the night, the cheerleader to reward me when I did something good, and the substitute, via those beautiful homemade starchy goods, of a family support network which was loving.

"When I was angry at the world, instead of speaking out and addressing the issue with those who hurt me, I turned the pain inwards and somehow felt release via the bulimia. I never ate the six pounds of sausages the way many bulimics describe it. For me, it could be a slice of toast or two donuts. But there was something almost seductive and releasing in the process. I could comfort myself and at the same time punish myself for the particular stressful situation I found myself in at the time.

"The bottom line was that the connection I had made was that food really was the only thing that has always been there for me. No family member, friend, or relationship had shown me the total consistency of always being there for me if I needed them. I trusted food to be there and the years proved that it really was the only thing I could be certain would never let me down or hurt me.

"Today I have chosen to remove the power I gave to food. It's simply food. A beautiful part of living and necessary for life but it's only food. Today I have chosen to make myself my own best friend. It has taken me over thirty years to make this connection but I think I finally have. I know the story that was running around my head isn't true. Almost, but not quite. The reality is that I do have friends who care and love me and there are many other ways to celebrate situations or handle them more effectively than turning to something that can't communicate back.

"I take it day by day – but with each day I feel more empowered and less attached to needing my 'hit' of whatever food the situation used to call for."

When Ayla made peace with food and realized that she was in control and not the food, her life changed. After using *EFT* just one time, she had the insight and awareness to realize that she was indeed loved dearly by her family. She now finally recognized that she had the family that she desperately yearned for. It was her fear that kept her living in the past and that prevented her from being able to see the gifts and blessings she had in her life. When she became consciously aware of how much she was loved, her voracious appetite disappeared, her desire to purge was gone, and within less than six months she lost over sixty pounds.

Yet you may also recall that when she faced a crisis and feared her husband's infidelity, much of the weight that she had lost returned. This is why it is essential to be consistent in dealing with your stress and not let your fears and feelings build up to the point of creating sabotage or resistance. Always ask yourself, "How am I feeling?" If you're not feeling as good as you can, then deal with those negative emotions before you fall back on old habits of trying to stuff them down.

Power...Am I in Charge of My Life?

In many cases, women live their lives to serve others. My client, Elaine, had been married for twenty-nine years when her husband was diagnosed with cancer. After nursing him up to the point of his death two years later, Elaine was lost. She had no idea how to live in the real world on her own. Everything she had in her life was as a result of having a wealthy husband.

Elaine said:

"Food, especially baked goods, has played a very active role in my emotional life - soother, comforter, pick-me-up, anger venter, nurturer, and always-there best friend. As a child, trips to the bakery around the corner (and indulging on the way home), packages with cookies from my grand-mothers who lived in Illinois, learning to bake with my mom and sister, were great times.

"As an adult, marriage to a wonderful guy who loved my cooking, and then being fortunate to have a B&B for about twelve years where I enjoyed doing A LOT of baking, added to my exposure to rich carb meals which could put me into a stupor. Normal growing up was 'table groaning with food, groaning when getting up from the table.'

"My life has taken some unexpected twists and turns. My dear husband had a two and a half year experience with cancer prior to his death sixteen months ago. I became a widow after twenty-nine years of marriage. I've gained thirty-five pounds. About ten days ago, I was diagnosed with long term carbon monoxide exposure/ poisoning. The chronic fatigue, fibromyalgia, the anemia, the mental fog, all further contributed to my out of balance relationship with food.

"When I discovered Andrea, I realized that I had an anorexic kitchen, translation, almost no food in the house. I had closed into a pretty (not so pretty) narrow world and was giving myself very few choices, and the choices I had were not the highest quality."

Prior to being married, Elaine shared with me that she had a fulfilling life. She was an outstanding student and passionate about many things. During the course of her marriage she set much of her identity aside so that she could be a devoted wife.

When I began working with hypnosis to guide Elaine to re-access many of her former resources and positive memories, she tapped into one of her greatest joys: music. This memory of how much she loved playing the piano reignited her connection to herself.

Try It! – Treasure Hunting

An important building block to setting boundaries is to increase your sense of self appreciation. Keep your eyes peeled and watch for great things to happen today. As great things happen, put them on your list. What deserves your attention? What do you want to remember? Focus on good things. Here's an example of what your list may look like:

1. enjoyed a wonderful conversation with my friend
2. spoke my peace at the board meeting
3. watched a beautiful sunset

After making that initial association and remembering who she was before she was married, she regained the strength to handle many of the challenges that lay before her. She used *EFT* to deal with her fear of confronting people, voicing her opinions, expressing her discontent, asking for what she needed, and getting what she deserved.

After she stocked her "anorexic" kitchen with foods she loved and began eating them whenever she felt hungry, she started to feel better. Then she made a point of dealing with her stress each time it popped up. By doing this, she noticed that it became easier for her to speak to people and get out into the world and represent herself as a woman in charge. When we last spoke, Elaine proudly mentioned that her pants were too big on her and she was planning a shopping trip to buy some new outfits. As her self-esteem increased, her clothing sizes decreased.

As Elaine discovered, when you have something wonderful to focus on or look forward to, you become a happier person and your life becomes richer. When you focus on appreciating what you already have, it puts you in a state of higher vibration. You'll notice that you'll feel better. When you continue to practice appreciating things about yourself and your life that make you feel yummy, you'll recognize that you will have more to appreciate. When you begin your day looking for wonderful things, expecting great things to happen to you, you'll find them. No matter how you choose to do it, count your blessings.

As women, we are taught to focus so much on what is wrong with us and how we can improve ourselves that we rarely just stop and take the time to appreciate what we already have and what we've already accomplished. When you begin to change your point of focus, everything changes.

Now let's take a quick peek and see how healthy your boundaries are:

1. **Do you feel compelled to say "Yes" when you want to say "No?"**
    You are in a group of people and asked to volunteer your time. You know your schedule is stretched as far as it can go and you haven't a moment to spare. What will you do?
2. **Do you have a hard time being assertive"**
    You're standing in line at the grocery when someone shoves past you with only a few items and proceeds to put their items on the belt. What will you do?
3. **Do you give in to avoid conflict?**
    Your friend has borrowed a book from you. You need it back. You ask her for it and she tells you she doesn't have it. What will you do?
4. **Are you a people pleaser?**
    You're running late for an appointment. A friend calls on the phone and asks for help. After you tell her where you're going, she explains that she has no car and needs a ride. Since you're going her way she asks you to drop her off. What will you do?

Answers: In an ideal world, these are the correct answers: 1. Say "No." 2. Say "Excuse me. I was here first." 3. I'll need you to replace that book for me. It cost... 4. I'm sorry. I have an appointment and I must leave now.

Personal Boundaries: Creating Your Space

Boundaries come in several shapes and sizes: physical, mental, emotional, spiritual. Fences are great for keeping in your dog, but they don't work very well with a telemarketer or someone who wants to take up your time and suck up your energy.

Personal boundaries define limits and make it clear to you and others that you are an individual worthy of consideration and respect. These are the boundaries of your body, your personal space, and your sexuality.

Juicy Woman Note:

As a woman with a history of being sexually and emotionally abused, I had very few if any personal boundaries. As a consequence, I always felt vulnerable, frightened, overwhelmed, shocked, and completely bombarded by life until I first became familiar with NLP by way of listening to Tony Robbins Personal Power II® tapes. He teaches what he calls the science of neuro-associative conditioning, which is closely aligned with NLP. As a student of Neuro Linguistic Programming, Tony eventually parlayed his fascination with it into becoming a trainer.

I can't say enough about the power of Neuro Linguistic Programming and what it has taught me as a person. If I could, I would make a blanket recommendation to everyone who has ever experienced abuse of any kind to take the Practitioner and Master Practitioner training in NLP.

I can honestly say that nothing has been as practical and effective as actually being able to learn new ways of communicating with myself and other people. In the training, you'll learn how to set boundaries, feel more confident expressing what's on your mind, be more playful and wise, inquisitive and powerful, sensitive, and any other character quality you want to acquire. It's all yours for the taking.

It is the best thing hands down to give you the sense of being empowered that you need. It gives you the power of choice, and as I've said so many times before: Who doesn't love more choices?

Fences, property lines, and walls are all physical boundaries that are unmistakably clear. Yet other physical boundaries aren't always quite so obvious. These are the lines in the sand that you have to draw to define your relationship with money, your home, your possessions, and your time.

Mental and emotional boundaries involve our feelings, thoughts, relationships, choices, and responsibilities. Spiritual boundaries relate to religion, spiritual beliefs, your relationship to God, and your sense of purpose.

Having healthy boundaries means you'll have a happy, healthy life, because they give you balance, a sense of priority, self-protection, and inner harmony. Your boundaries are responsible for building and maintaining healthy relationships and for raising responsible kids. In the next several pages, I'd like to share with you some examples of the consequences of having either too few or too many boundaries.

Are You Putting Up Walls Or A Wide Open Field?

It's just as dicey to put up a wall as it is to leave yourself wide open. It's best to avoid extremes when setting limits. You'll recall in the first chapter I asked you to think about what type of armor or insulation your body has been carrying around to protect you. This is because whether you know it or not, your excess weight has been protecting you. In order to release it, you have to get to the bottom of why you've needed that protection and fulfill those needs in other ways besides overeating. Unless you take those steps and find out what is driving your urge to eat, your wall or suit of armor will only continue to expand and grow. This is the power of the subconscious mind hurtling along carrying out its old programming. It's a blessing to know that now you have the ability to overturn the default program using the stress relief techniques I've taught you in the *Cope with Your Stress* section.

Here's a quick story of a guy who refuses to change his program:

The Consequence of Putting Up Too Many Walls

I know a fellow who is a very angry guy. He was beaten from the time he was a small child up until he turned sixteen when he finally felt safe asserting his independence. He lives on his own, has no job, and his biggest goal was to be eligible for welfare. The several relationships he's had with women ended in disaster. Today he lives the life of a recluse.

He put up brick walls so thick and high that nobody can scale those heights. Although he's been successful in keeping people out, he also keeps himself shut away from the rest of the world. He's missed opportunities to be happy, spend time with those who love him, and enjoy living a fulfilling life. Yet living behind the wall is so important to him that he isn't willing to chip any of it away. Nobody can ever have a close relationship with this person because his pain keeps him a prisoner, shutting out opportunity and life. His wall gives him a sense of false security. He is alone and unhappy.

Does that describe you or someone you know? If it does, you can start to chip away at the wall bit by bit. Think *EFT* or any of the other stress relief methods I've shown you in the previous section.

Now let's get more specific. Maybe your challenge is that you don't have any boundaries and people are using you as a doormat. Take it from me, having no boundaries causes as much pain as having too many.

I'm going to keep on beating on this point. We teach people how we want to be treated. If, like me, you learned to keep quiet and speak only when spoken to, you won't feel safe saying that you are being treated unfairly or spoken to disrespectfully. Here's a story of a time when I started to learn the importance of speaking up for myself:

Ay Caramba! Me Duele Mucho! Ouch! That Hurt!

In 1990, when I married my husband, Angel, I was intimidated by my new mother-in-law, Luz. She was such a stickler for perfection. I remember cringing every time she came to visit because I felt so guilty that I couldn't measure up in her eyes.

My insecurities really bit me in the butt after my son, Paul (Thomas), PT, was born. At the time, I was smack dab in the middle of the worst postpartum depression any gal could ever have. I was resentful of the fact that I had a baby and absolutely horrified to see what had happened to my body with the fifty-five pound weight gain.

I was wracked with fear and couldn't imagine how my husband could ever love me at that size. Angel and I had just gotten married a year before. In my eyes, I was still supposed to be on my honeymoon. As far as I was concerned the best part of my marriage came to a crashing halt.

The tension in my life at that time was so thick you could cut it with a knife. I was trying desperately to juggle running a business I hated, dealing with employees who intimidated me, angry tenants knocking on my door at all hours, hounding me and complaining, nightly phone calls with my father grilling me and criticizing every move I made, fending off my jealous and greedy cousins accusing me of taking advantage of my Nana, taking care of my ailing Nana, figuring out what it meant to be a wife and mother, trying to adhere to a schedule of nursing my son every hour and half so that he would finally figure out how to latch onto my breasts and begin to thrive, and putting salve on my cracked, bleeding, and leaking nipples because the constant nursing was ripping them to shreds. I was so tired I was walking into walls and ...Good Grief! Victim, thy name is Andrea.

Anyway, 'nuf said. Suffice it to say that housework was not top of mind and that was a very important thing to Luz. To her, cleanliness was next to Godliness and I must have been one hell of a sinner 'cause at that time I was a heck of a slob.

Since Luz only lived ten blocks away from us, she would stop by often. The house was a wreck and everything was in disarray. Diapers everywhere, bottles in the sink, and dirty and clean baby clothes all over the place. Angel was working during the day so when she came by it was just her and me. Unless she brought my sister in law, Lourdes, then it was like a bad reenactment of The Spanish Inquisition. I was so ashamed of myself and the condition of the house whenever I saw her, I wanted to crawl into a hole and die. Good thing Luz couldn't really speak to me because she only spoke Spanish.

Since my Spanish was pretty rusty at the time, I couldn't follow all that she said, so I relied on family members like Lourdes and my friend, Lucy, as interpreters. From the grapevine, I learned that Luz was making snide comments about what a bad housekeeper I was, how messy the apartment was, how PT didn't get fed on time, and many other silly little put downs that sent me running, crying to the bathroom, feeling totally defenseless.

Feeling so insecure about my extra pregnancy weight, one day I went to Luz's house for dinner. As we all sat around the table she made a comment to me that stung me like a bee. She said, "Gorda" which in Spanish means fat. At the time, I wasn't yet **The Juicy Woman**, so I sort of shrank and let that word define me. It hurt so much. From that point on, the internal battle with her had officially begun. It waged for years.

Little did I know that my inability to speak my mind and stand up for myself showed up in overeating as I demonstrate in the next story. Unfortunately, I didn't put two and two together until several years later.

Binging: A Sure Sign Your Boundaries Are Being Crossed

In 2002, I was a Girl Scout® leader for a Brownie troop of six year old girls. As the new addition, I was eager to please, wanting everyone to like me and be my friend. You could see that I was the perky push-over.

During a monthly team leader meeting the week before Christmas, my Division Leader, Laurie asked for volunteers to bake five dozen cookies for a holiday party a few days away. None of the team leaders raised their hand.

Laurie then proceeded to pick several women out of the group and ask them individually if they would be willing to help. They each declined. She paused a moment and looked around the room. Her piercing blue eyes locked on mine and she stared me down for what seemed like an eternity. Then, with a disapproving glare and a sarcastic tone, she asked if I could find the time to help out the girls.

Every muscle in my body clenched. I felt so intimidated. I wanted the floor to open up and swallow me. I just knew that I couldn't say "No" and disappoint everyone and I really wanted to be considered a team player. I could feel my body screaming "No" but the word "Yes" tumbled out of my mouth.

That evening while baking those holiday cookies, I fell headfirst into a binge. Now, a couple years after finally giving up dieting and seeing food for what it is, just food, I realize that I've spent years stuffing my face with food when what I really wanted to do was just say "No."

The Disease To Please: My Take On Being a Former Yes Gal...

If you want to be taken seriously you must say what you mean and mean what you say. In the past, I've gotten into the worst scraps because I've over-promised and under-delivered. In an attempt to please everyone, all the time, I used to run around ragged doling out "yes" responses to everybody.

Sadly, most of the time they didn't mean anything because I was so overwhelmed and time stretched that I couldn't possibly keep my promises. Because I wanted everyone to like and approve of me, it was next to impossible for me to utter the word "No" to a single soul. On more than one occasion it led to having my reputation questioned and feeling guilty. This next story tells of a time when my people pleasing ways reached a crisis point which forced me to finally take a stand.

In June 2003, I was very active in my local church. I was a Sunday School teacher, busy with many after church activities and very involved in truly enjoying my church. I felt at home there.

But since I still had no idea about the importance of boundaries, I bent over backwards trying to be helpful to everybody. I was running my father's business, taking care of the house, volunteering with the local schools, being a Girl Scout® leader, and running back and forth from church to home to school getting quickly burnt out.

Because I had made myself so busy outside the house, I wasn't available to enjoy my home, help the kids with homework, prepare dinner, or do anything in the house because I was always rushing around, feeling exhausted. Around the same time, I had begun to take the practitioner's training in NLP and was starting to learn the meaning of setting limits. I knew that I had some real issues with this thing called boundaries.

At the suggestion of an *NLP* colleague, I started to look at the places in my life where I was overcommitted and overextended. I knew that church and girl scouts were the two areas that were taking up a huge amount of my time and the commitments to both were draining me. That's when I began to realize that the tension at home was my own doing. I was so busy living and running around for everyone else, that even when I was home, I wasn't really home. I wasn't present for myself or my family at all.

Although there were less than two weeks left until the end of the school season, I couldn't continue this way. My life had reached a crisis point. It was time for me to step up and speak my piece.

I called Laurie my division leader and explained that I couldn't devote any more time to being a leader because my family and home life were suffering and I was getting burnt out. She shocked me by being so deeply empathetic and understanding. After our call, I breathed a huge sigh of relief and made plans to schedule my last meeting with the girls in my troop the following week.

I explained to them that as much as I wanted to, I would not be back again the next year as their troop leader. I told them that sometimes people bite off more than they can chew and despite wanting to do it all, it's not possible.

After getting some bittersweet closure, we ended our three years together with lots of hugs, kisses, and tears. We said our goodbyes and I wished them well. In the back of my mind, I knew that the tougher nut to crack was the church. I had to break ties and disengage myself from all excessive commitments that I overzealously agreed to take on because now they were making my life crazy.

I made an appointment with the Assistant Minister, Julie, who was in charge of the youth leadership council. I explained that I had made a decision that I would no longer continue to run the carpool and be responsible for getting all the kids to choir and dance practice. I told her I would not commit to being one of the teachers for Vacation Bible School that year because my family and home life was suffering. I apologized and told Julie that my decision was final and I asked her to make alternate arrangements for Vacation Bible School and to replace me for the next two weeks.

Unlike Laurie's empathetic response, Julie clearly did not understand where I was coming from nor did she give a flying fig about my needs. She pulled every punch and tried to guilt me into going back and reconsidering my decision. She even called me a bad Christian and told me that Jesus was probably very disappointed in me. After I gave her a chance to speak her mind, I told her that I had nothing more to say to her and it was time for me to leave. Certain that I was making the right decision, I stood up for myself and stuck to my guns.

After that bitter confrontation I felt hurt and upset. Uncomfortable with the idea of seeing her again, I avoided church the next week. I continued to play the avoidance game all summer long.

The first week in September when I returned to church, I thought I noticed that Julie was giving me the cold shoulder, pretending to ignore me. Not quite certain if my observations were correct, I stood in line to say my goodbyes to the minister, Reverend Jack, and Julie.

As I approached her and our eyes met, I noticed a coldness in her gaze. Then in a sarcastic tone she made an offhand comment that she didn't know me and I was a stranger to the church.

Since I didn't yet have the skills to say what I felt when I was overcome with hurt and surprise, I was taken aback by her comment, and I could feel the familiar grip of the lump in my throat that always preceded a flood of tears. I ran out of the church and didn't return until years later.

Every Sunday since that time in 2003, I experienced a silent longing to go back to church but I was too intimidated to deal with Julie's nastiness to actually go through with it. When I realized that I had broken ties with my father, I felt a real need to fill that empty space in my heart with faith. I knew that I was ready to return to church. I considered going to another but I knew that wouldn't satisfy me. So I decided to go back to my church and face the Julie music.

I was completely ready to stand up for myself and give Julie a piece of my mind, letting her know how unfair I think she was and extending an olive branch to make peace with her. I also knew that I was going to make it crystal clear to anyone who asked that I refused to make any commitments at this time. After all, I'm no longer the same people pleasing person I once was. It's nice to know that I can always use *EFT* to give me courage whenever I get weak in the knees.

Now, after having taken the leap and gone back, I feel so relieved and overjoyed to be back home where I belong in the church that I love. When I returned in August 2009, I found out that Julie had been gone for almost four years and I wasn't her only can't say "No" casualty. There were many other Sunday School teachers like me afflicted by the disease to please.

Juicy Woman Note:

Since I've returned to church I'm right back in the swing of things, fully enjoying the experience. I've made new friends and reconnected with many of the old ones. I'm not yet ready to take on being a Sunday School teacher again at this time,

> but I've spoken to the new minister, Reverend Rob, and told him all about my experience with Julie. I decided that since I was one of many teachers who were scared off and felt the need to leave the church, I would offer to start a new ministry outreach and call up and touch base with the others and listen to them and perhaps just share my story.
>
> During times like this, when people need a dose of faith most, it's so sad to feel out of place or unwanted. Maybe some of the people I call will feel safe enough to return. Only time will tell.

Let me ask you...how many times have you gotten side tracked in life because you were tongue tied and didn't know what to say? How many binges could you have avoided if you would have felt more comfortable just saying, "No?" If you don't feel good about yourself, and deep down you don't like or respect yourself, you'll let other people use you for a doormat.

Some may be outwardly malicious and make no bones about treating you like garbage, others may be less aggressive in their attacks, but their barbs and backhanded comments are just as painful.

As a self-confessed former doormat, I now realize that I used to attract people into my life who took advantage of my kindness and pushed me to my limits. The problem was that for years I didn't have any limits, so I took out my frustration on my body and the people who deserved it least, my family.

But gradually I learned how to stand up for myself and set new boundaries in my life. The transformation started with my mother-in-law and continued from there. Thanks to *NLP*, I found out how to set limits without being overly aggressive and nasty. Since I wanted to really communicate with her in a heartfelt way, and get my message across as honestly as possible, I knew that I had to first bone up on my Spanish.

One day in 2002, while sitting in her kitchen, I was passionately enjoying a meal she had prepared. Watching me eat with gusto, she called me "Gorda" again. This time I refused to shrink and let her words put me under a spell. I put down whatever I was chewing, paused, looked her straight in the eye and said, "No estoy gorda. Estas palabras me molestan." This means I'm not fat, and these words hurt me. I then went on to explain in my best Spanish that the word "Gorda" hurt me because it was an insult, and I wasn't okay with being called that name anymore.

Since then whenever she's done anything to offend me, I'm able to let her know in Spanish or English that it's not okay and to please stop. Today we are two strong women who get along quite nicely. Now I especially treasure the times when she comes over to spend the weekend and cooks her special Spanish dishes just for me. I'm sure by now she knows that I'd do cartwheels for her rice and beans with calabaza (pumpkin). It rocks!

Sure, you might say it's easy to set limits with people who are mean to you, but what about those you really want to help? How do you know when it's the right time to say...

You Can Do It Yourself

In 1995, my son, PT, was about four years old. He was diagnosed with a speech delay and classified as learning disabled. At the time a part of me shattered and broke into a million pieces because I feared that my son would never be like other kids.

Steeped in guilt and fear, I vowed to do whatever I could to "fix" him. I was determined to show my full support. Since his reading level was below par, I went out and got The Phonics Game™. He needed to practice speaking so I sat with him for hours and we read. Since I worked from home and was always available, I became PT's other half.

Every day he came home from school I would stop whatever I was doing to help him with his homework. Sometimes it was a real pleasure, other times it was a big pain. Yet because it had become an ingrained habit, I continued to do the same thing I'd done for nearly five years. At that point, he was about ten years old. One day he told me he had a report to do for school and it had to be done for tomorrow. Then I asked him, "When was this assignment given?"

When he told me it was due the previous week it hit me like a ton of bricks. I was disempowering my son and making him think that he couldn't do anything without me. That's when it dawned on me to break the ties and wean him of expecting my help.

When I changed my tune and stopped hindering his progress, he became an outstanding student. After I embraced the IALAC way (see **Juicy Woman** note below), his confidence blossomed and his grades skyrocketed.

I.A.L.A.C.

I am lovable and capable.

Setting boundaries is a two way street that enhances all relationships. I've learned from Jack Canfield that the core message of a person with high self-esteem is represented by the acronym, "I.A.L.A.C."

When we let others know that they can do something for themselves, we empower them to believe in their abilities. This enhances their feelings of self-worth and boosts their self-image, which leads to much greater confidence.

As well, when you start doing more things for yourself you will recognize your own natural talents and gifts. This will enhance your feeling of self-worth and boost your self-image which will lead to kick butt confidence.

In 2010, my son, PT (Paul Thomas) graduated from high school with honors. Today he attends college and is passionately pursuing a career in business. His leaps began to occur the day I told him, "Honey, you can do it yourself. I believe in you."

How many times do you feel like you are holding up the whole house and bearing all the burdens? Are you asking for help? Have you told your husband/mate what you want? Are you holding your happiness hostage by giving yourself away to accommodate everyone else's whims? Is it causing you to reach for food when you're not hungry? Are you making the mistake I was by being an emotional rescuer?

Changing Your Response: Ask Yourself, "Whose Responsibility Is It?"

You'll recall in the chapter on Taking 100% Responsibility how important it is to change the way you respond to others instead of trying to change them. Remember, when you change yourself, everything else changes.

For years I thought it was my job to fix everyone else's problems, so I stuck my nose in many situations where it didn't belong. That led to a life filled with chaos for me. I used to get in the middle of everything.

When my best friend, Lucy, got divorced, I felt so deeply for her that I began to cause a rift in my own marriage. When several of my family members made choices that put them in awkward and uncomfortable positions, I was always attempting to turn things around and make it better for them. Always looking to save everyone and cushion the blow, I became a miserable person forever seeking solace in food.

Then one day someone asked me, "Are You A Rescuer?" It hit me between the eyes and I realized that what I was doing was holding back my life and living the consequences of other people's actions. My do-gooder ways had caused enormous unnecessary tension for me and my family. I began to realize the importance of people taking individual responsibility for their choices. That's when everything began changing for me and I started to emerge as **The Juicy Woman**.

As I've taken an observer's point of view and looked at myself over the past couple of years, I've noticed that my food addiction covered up my incessant need to insert myself in other people's lives and busy myself by being their "fixer." It was the identity that I carved out for myself.

As I've become free of my food obsessions, I notice how much easier it is for me to see when I am falling into the pattern of trying to be a 'rescuer.' As a result of being more self-aware, it is much easier for me to see when I am making something personal when it's not.

Since those years when I was so busy rescuing everyone in a desperate attempt to avoid looking at my own life, I've learned much about the value of taking personal responsibility. I've learned that when I overeat it's a signal to me that my boundaries have been crossed.

Try It! – Questioning Your Binges

The next time you overeat ask yourself the following questions:

What's happening?

How am I feeling?

How have I overcommitted myself?

By asking the above questions, you will be able to guide yourself to change your perspective. You'll switch from blaming mode to being more compassionate. These questions will put you right back into the present moment so that you can see what is going on in your life that is causing you to reach for food when you're not hungry.

Notice that if you're feeling resentment, anger, or guilt, or have trouble saying "No," these are all indicators that some part of your life is out of balance. If this rings a bell for you, then read this chapter carefully and commit the strategies to memory.

I know at first it's going to feel uncomfortable doing things differently, but that is what is necessary in order for you to see yourself in a more empowered light. In the following section, you'll find several different ways I've come up with to say "No" to various people and situations in my life. Use my list as a springboard to come up with more ways that work for you.

How Many Ways Can You Think Of To Say "No"?

In living and working with my Nana for so many years, I was raised by example to believe that if you are blessed in life, it's your responsibility to give back and share your blessings with others. That is still very much a part of who I am, however, now I can see how I confused my desire to share with being a doormat. Ah balance. Gotta love it!

Thanks to my *NLP* training, I've learned to respect and love having boundaries. That experience helped me to value myself much more and to realize that by saying "No" to others, I get to say "Yes" to myself. This is surely something that my precious Nana would have loved to know since I'm afraid to say she was known to everyone in the family as the consummate martyr.

Today I'm getting really good at saying "No" and practice it often. I've learned that "No" can be said gracefully with love and respect, it can be said in jest and it can be said with sternness and authority.

NLP is all about exploring the many wonderful nuances of communication and discovering new and unique methods for doing things differently.

Here are some of the specific ways that I've learned how to say no and set better boundaries. I've learned that apart from my old way of thinking that there's only one right way to do something, there are as many ways to say no as there are people in the world. Here are some of mine:

No!

That doesn't work for me.

I'm not seeing it that way at all.

I can't quite get a handle on this.

I guess we're not cut out to get this going.

I'm not willing to commit to that.

That may not be the best use of my time.

This doesn't hum for me.

I'm not in tune with this.

I'm not in sync with you.

This doesn't feel right to me.

I'm not digging this.

I don't agree with you.

I can't get my arms around what you are saying.

Yuck!

That's a no go!

Whoa Nelly!

What else can you offer me?

Is that the best that you can do?

Oh come on!

Give me a break!

What's that about?

Who are you kidding?

I'm not feeling it.

You want me to do what?

Fuggedabout it.

Next!

Let's be real.

Evidently, we just don't see eye to eye.

Maybe next time!

You'll have to do better than that!

That's not even close.

Be for real.

You've got to be kidding me.

That's insulting to me.

That's unacceptable.

I'm not okay with that.

I feel that you are intruding upon me.

I can feel your feet all over me. Get off!

That's quite inappropriate.

Are we done?

I don't think so.

No way!

I'm sure that you can do better than that, can't you?

Oh come now...

All in all, I truly believe that if you want to be a happier person and learn how to lose weight without dieting, one of the most important skills you must learn is how to say "No" without resentment, hurt, or guilt.

Try It! – Who's Crossing Your Boundaries?

In your journal, make a list of people in your life who may be crossing your boundaries and walking all over you in an effort to get what they want.

Basics on Boundaries

Vent your feelings, then discuss – Depending upon the head of steam that's built up, you may need to cope with that stress first and release that upset before you say what's on your mind. EFT is a great bet in this case. Don't explode or you'll be sorry.

Get in touch with your feelings – Use that internal GPS for paying close attention to the way you feel. It is your key to knowing when your boundaries are being crossed. Pay attention to the knots in your stomach and those lumps in your throat. They'll tell you much better than anyone else what you really want/need.

Never discuss or renegotiate boundaries when you are angry – Keep a cool head when stating what you need/expect of the other person. It's easier to see things from a cooler perspective.

Choose a time to discuss your boundaries – Timing is everything. Choose your time wisely. Keep it private, with no interruptions. Everyone deserves the respect that comes with privacy. Don't try to weasel and con someone into having a conversation that they're not ready to have. Make a list of benefits both you and the other person will experience by the new arrangement. Then discuss it.

Recognize your deal breakers and "flexi-boundaries" – Make it clear what things are essential and which things are no big deal and flexible. My grandson, Aiden, for example, knows that bedtime is flexible but it's never okay to lie or hit someone in anger.

Keep it neutral – Don't make it personal or the other person will feel as though they are being attacked. Make it clear to them that they are important to you, and that in order to maintain your relationship this is what you need.

Revise and create new agreements – Stay in constant contact and be attentive to feedback. When you don't like the way something is going, take steps to change it by renegotiating the agreement. By keeping it fresh it leaves little room for misunderstanding.

Speaking About Your Needs

Talking about boundaries and expressing your needs can be a difficult thing if you're not used to doing it. Others will surely think that you're crazy and they'll do everything they can to test your limits. The robot rule applies. Repeat, repeat, repeat. Keep on repeating yourself until they get it. Change is hard and people will resist doing things that are not comfortable and familiar.

Sometime in 2006, when I was doing **The Juicy Woman** Fabulous, Fit and Free Call each week, everyone in the house seemed to come into my office and want something from me. Nice as it was to be wanted and needed, it was annoying to be continually disturbed.

My husband wanted to give me a kiss. My son wanted to ask me a question. My daughter needed help with her homework. This went on for several days. At first, I used hand gestures to let them know if it was okay to come in or not. Then they started to forget or ignore what my hand gestures meant.

I told everyone that I was going to leave the door open and if they saw me on the phone to not bother me—seemed simple enough. Then each of them decided that it was within boundaries to stand by my door and either wave, blow a kiss, or toss me a note. This was getting upsetting.

Then I decided to close the door and tell everyone that they had to knock if they wanted my attention. I didn't realize that the knocking would disturb me and take me off my game when I was coaching. Then I realized that wasn't working either. I was getting really ticked off.

I tried a lot of things including penalizing my son for disrespecting my boundaries. I charged him $20 because I knew that taking something away from him that was precious would leave a lasting impression. It worked.

Juicy Woman Note:

Remember what I told you about linking up your values if you want to create a lasting change? Well that's what I did with my son, PT. My young man loves money. He adores the sight, scent, and feel of it. He is a natural born visual kinesthetic, which means that he is very observant and feels things keenly. He takes in information from his environment by what he sees and how he feels and what he can touch.

Like his great-grandfather before him, he is a proud numismatist, an avid collector of coins and currency. On occasions, I've walked into his room and found him studying notes of various denominations under a magnifying glass attempting to read the microprinting and challenging himself to find all of the security features on the bills.

Being a detail oriented, precision minded kind of guy with a photographic memory, he can recognize so many nuances, patterns, and discriminations by just looking at things that most people, including me, just don't see. He has a real artistic appreciation for money and whenever he can he saves every penny he gets. I've no doubt that with his level of respect and sensitivity towards collecting cash, he's going to have a lot of it one day.

So when I charged him a $20 penalty for disrespecting my boundaries, all of a sudden he had a new understanding and acute awareness of why he had to give me the privacy that I was demanding. Before I came up with the idea to charge him, I must have explained to him ten times why he was in the wrong. Each time he promised not to do it, but went ahead and interrupted me anyway. I could feel that he was sincere, but I just wasn't getting through to him.

Once I realized that my words were floating right over his head and I had to make him feel the truth of my intent by being more flexible and changing my communication strategy, that's when I was made some real progress because I could finally reach him in a way that he would get it.

My decision to take the money away from him hit him where it hurt. This created a powerful kinesthetic anchor in his brain that caused him emotional pain and made him realize that mom wasn't playing games. I didn't do it to be mean. I just did it to get my point across.

No amount of talking would have accomplished this kind of change. This is because PT's strength is in his ability to see and do things. He's not the best listener. That's why I had to reach out of my own comfort zone of talking and think of another way of getting through to him.

> ## Juicy Woman Note:
>
> Because I touched on what was important to him, he was more receptive to respecting and understanding my needs. Sometimes as a parent you've just got to do what you've got to do, always taking into consideration the uniqueness of the individual. Be flexible and always look for ways of connecting your values with others. Whether you use this information for yourself, parenting, or dealing with any other type of relationship, just remember that associating values to something you want to change is fiercely powerful stuff.

Naturally, PT hasn't ever interrupted me again while I'm on the phone in my office. Now I can work undisturbed. The key is being consistent and keeping it neutral. Make your demands. State what you want and for Goodness sake, stick to your guns!

Getting Clear With Emotionally Honest Communication

While teaching parents new ways of communicating with their kids, I learned this simple formula at EPIC[3]. It's called the When-Feel-Want Technique. It's a great way of talking to people without falling into the trap of blaming and shaming. It gives you an opportunity to share your feelings and state what you need from the other person.

Here are several examples of how to use it:

When ... (describe the behavior)

I feel ... (describe your feelings)

I want ... (say what you want)

For example:

<u>When</u> you come home late for dinner and don't call to let me know,

<u>I feel</u> unappreciated, disrespected, and ignored.

<u>I want</u> you to call when you know you'll be late.

---

3   EPIC –Every Person Influences Children, Inc. For more information on training to run a workshop, visit http://www.epicforchildren.org

When I am working in my office with the door closed and the Do Not Disturb sign up and you barge in,

I feel taken for granted and devalued.

I want you to wait until the door is open and I'm ready to speak.

Try It! – Boundary Building

 Who do you know who consistently intrudes upon your boundaries? How does that make you feel?

 Who do you know who is good at setting boundaries?

 How do you feel about this person?

 What would they do in the case of someone intruding on them?

 What relationship do you have that warrants a re-negotiation of boundaries?

 What would that look like?

 What are the benefits of setting better boundaries?

 What is the first step in doing this?

Speaking Your Mind in a Bold Rebelicous Way with The Rebel Belle – Tuck Self

It's never too late to make a change in the way you see yourself. All that's needed are some new criteria for setting boundaries. Perhaps, like me, you have felt that your life has revolved around taking care of others. If you don't put that into perspective and find a way to also take care of yourself, you'll end up in a real pickle!

One of my dear friends and colleagues is a gal named Tuck Self. She's a master of personal transformation. As a professional coach, speaker, and Voice of America radio talk show host, Tuck is known to many as The Rebel Belle.

Born in the '50s, she was raised to be small, quiet, polite, and inauthentic, a perfect southern belle. Early on she got the message that she was to look and act pretty, speak only when spoken to, and keep a low profile, ESPECIALLY around men.

When a divorce from her husband threatened to rock her world, she found her way to what she calls the "Rebel Belle." Tuck says, "It was my soul and inner 'BellePower' screaming to break free. It was my inner voice of bold self-expression looking to be big, loud, outrageous, and authentic. So, the Rebel Belle was unleashed."

Today, as The Rebel Belle, Tuck is **a Southern Voice for Bold Self-Expression**...

Here are Tuck's 7 steps to being a rebel belle:

Step One: Be the center of your world.

Celebrate your uniqueness. Commit to your personal empowerment and spiritual evolution.

Step Two: Overcome fear.

Take responsibility for creating your reality. Observe your triggers and emotional responses and ask, "What is my issue?"

Step Three: Tap your inner "Belle Power."

Discover who you are. Find your passion, purpose, and follow your heart.

Step Four: Trust your intuition.

Feel your way into alignment with your soul. Feel it, feel it, feel it!

Step Five: Embrace uncertainty.

Dream, imagine, and affirm. Boldly express your voice to the world by doing what you love to do.

Step Six: When the student is ready...

Observe the Law of Attraction at work as you manifest masterful mentors into your life!

Step Seven: Lighten up.

Have fun. Enjoy the ride. Celebrate, laugh a lot, and remember to play.

Since I met Tuck in 2005 and became one of her belle-friends, I've learned a lot about setting boundaries and taking better care of myself.

Luckily I've never experienced a health crisis like the woman in the next story, but thanks to her wisdom now I know that...

The Word "No" Is A Full Sentence

In 2006, I did one of my **Juicy Woman** seminars for a local group of women. Mary is a mature woman with a family. She shared with our group that throughout her life she was taught to care for others, set aside her needs, and make certain that everyone around her was happy. She admitted that deep down, in her heart, she considered her needs as less important than anyone else's.

Her life centered on what other people thought about her. She did her best to get everybody to like her so she always went out of her way to please everyone. Mary never felt comfortable saying "No." She reasoned that she didn't want to let anyone down or hurt their feelings.

Sadly, she attracted people in her life who took advantage of her kindness and had little respect for her. Without consciously being aware of it, she had allowed herself to be treated like a doormat.

One day she went to the doctor for a routine exam and was told that she had cancer. The doctor explained to her the deleterious effects of stress on the body and told her that she had to make some choices. She had to change her lifestyle and make herself a priority.

That's when she realized that if she were to survive, she had to weed out the things in her life that were toxic. She started by saying "No." Some people just disappeared from her life and some learned to respect her more. With that small word, came great power for Mary.

Today Mary is a cancer survivor.

She says that along the road to remission she lost a few "friends" and acquaintances, and she regained her sense of self.

She told the group that it was a hard and painful lesson, but today she now knows that she is worth caring for and loving. Without fail, each week Mary sets aside time for herself to do things that make her feel good. She gets a massage, a pedicure and a manicure. She also takes classes and goes out to lunch with friends. Mary learned a very wise lesson. She stopped being an emotional rescuer.

The Art of Setting Boundaries

If you are an emotional rescuer then you too have to stop because you will never get a chance to live your life.

When you start saying "No" and setting boundaries with other people, you are able to pursue your own life. Many times we eat because we're frustrated thinking that we can't, won't, or don't have what it takes to do something that we love. Too many of us busy women think that life is too short and it's a waste of time to do something for ourselves.

My Nana felt that way. She was the most giving person you would ever want to meet, but deep down she was resentful of never having time to herself. When we would talk in the afternoon after we finished working, she would tell me about her dream of going to the New York Foundling Hospital in downtown Manhattan and being a baby holder. All she wanted was to have time to give her love to little babies who had nobody to hold and love them.

Yet as much as she wanted to do that, she died never having done it! Your dream may be to start your own business, take over the garage and make it your sewing space, paint a self-portrait, or run your own newspaper. No matter what your dream, you must live it!

The most loving thing you can ever do for yourself or anyone else is to be a happy person. In the words of one of my *NLP* colleagues, Dug, who is now a trainer for Tony Robbins, His favorite quote is one adapted from Dr. Seuss. Dug always says, "Be who you are and do what you do for those who mind do not matter and those who matter do not mind!"

Now it's time for a quick reassessment.

Try It! – Unearthing Your Treasures

On four separate pieces of paper answer the following questions:
Who am I?
What do I want?
What makes me loveable?
What must I do to be in charge of my life?

When you get clearer about who you are and what you want in life, you will want to do more things that value your new awareness. By making a habit of being happy in the moment more often, you guarantee yourself a smoother ride.

Overcoming Learned Helplessness:
How to Create Spectacular Confidence

If the women in this chapter had not decided to assert themselves and go after what they wanted, they would never have acquired the confidence and skills that they did.

We've all been cut down to size by people who want to tell it like it is, set you straight, and make you feel small. The sad truth is there will always be people to beat you up and make you feel terrible and who will try to walk all over you. It happened to me and it's probably happened to you. The point is if we continue to allow that to happen, we disempower ourselves and fall into the pattern of belief that we don't deserve anything better.

You do deserve better but in order for you to have more and feel better, you've got to believe that you have the power to change.

I'm sure that, like me, you've faced situations in your life where you've come to accept a position of some degree of learned helplessness. It is said that a dog who is repeatedly beaten in a closed room will eventually stand still and suffer a beating even in an open field. How incredibly tragic is that?

Is that you? Are you letting people beat you down with their words and deeds? If you are, then I want you to see and understand that although you may not be getting physically beaten, by allowing other people to talk to you with disregard and disrespect, you are standing still and letting them stomp all over your self-esteem. If you're struggling with wanting to eat when you're not hungry, it's no wonder that those are the times when food cries the loudest.

First things first—you must realize that self-acceptance is a gift you give yourself. In the next chapter, we'll discuss the many different strategies you can use to love the skin you're in right now.

Love Your Body: Self-Acceptance Is A Gift You Give Yourself

"A waist is a terrible thing to mind."
- *Evelyn Tribole, M.S., R.D., and Elyse Resch, M.S., R.D., F.A.D.A.,*
authors of Intuitive Eating: A Revolutionary Program That Works

Are you torturing yourself daily because you're overweight? Can't stop focusing on your flaws? Frozen, fixated, and feeling frustrated with your fault finding ways? Most women are. Without even realizing it, our scales, mirrors, words, and clothes have become weapons of mass destruction that we've learned to use on a daily basis to create unnecessary agony and suffering for ourselves. Having imperfections and flaws doesn't need to make you feel bad about yourself, yet most of us treat our bodies like garbage because we're not prettier or slimmer.

Now that the cat is out of the bag, you know that any negative feelings you have about your body represent a distortion in your energy system. This means you can give yourself an entire self-image makeover by dealing with your stress.

Body Love: An Inside Out Approach to Self Acceptance

Your self-image is that mental snapshot you're carrying around with you that unconsciously affects every aspect of your life.

The way you feel about your body is determined by the meaning you give to your experiences. I've made no bones about my years of struggles with my thighs, and shared with you many of the painful memories that caused me to feel instant shame and embarrassment whenever I thought about my legs.

Growing up in the late 60's and 70's I used to love to look at fashion, teen, and movie magazines. One of the women I admired was the famous supermodel, Lauren Hutton. Being a gal with a gap between her front teeth, Lauren made me feel good about the little space between mine.

Despite it being considered a flaw or imperfection in dentistry known as a diastema, I never grew up feeling self-conscious about the gap between my teeth. I discovered that many of my favorite singers and stars like Elton John and Madonna also have a space there. Thanks to their positive role model of self-acceptance, I grew up feeling pride and appreciation for that brand of my particular uniqueness.

You see, the way you feel about yourself is all a matter of perspective. It's not necessarily true, but it's true to you. You believe it without question because it's anchored as an experience of truth in your body. Anchors are the sometimes icky, always sticky, Velcro-like ways that these experiences or memories gum up and adhere to your cells. Here's how it works:

Anchors: How Your Brain Forms Associations

Whenever a sense memory is emotionally charged, it creates a strong imprint on the brain. This imprinting is called an anchor. There are positive and negative anchors. Positive anchors make you feel good and happy, and negative ones make you feel terrible. Here's an example of a positive anchor:

Did you ever come home from school and tell your mother or other caregiver about someone bullying you? She probably then said something like, "Eat a cookie, you'll feel better." You ate the cookie and magically you felt better. Why?

Probably because as you took the cookie she started asking you about your day. As you talked, you felt better. You were soothed by her voice and held in her comforting embrace as she made the bully disappear and helped you to feel safe.

Mom's comforting ways helped your subconscious mind reframe the situation and you felt better. All of a sudden you were distracted from your thoughts about the bully and your brain focused upon the good feelings you were enjoying.

Naturally your brain was searching for the reason you were feeling better. It sorted for details and searched for what was unique to the situation when it landed on the memory of the cookie.

In reality, it was the energy your mother brought to the situation that soothed you. She reminded you that you were loved and your body responded by releasing the anger or fear and anchored that *good* feeling. Mom helped you feel better, not the cookie. But your mind and body created the link that you felt better after you ate the cookie. Locked and loaded, that mental recording would play every time you felt threatened or bullied and you'd turn to a cookie for comfort. This might explain why you crave cookies under stress.

In *NLP*, this is called an **anchor**. An anchor is described as a stimulus that stirs the senses to remember a specific event or sensation and this is recreated in the body.

You may remember that we experience the world through our five senses:

visual (sight)
auditory (hearing)
kinesthetic (touch)
gustatory (taste)
olfactory (smell)

Anchors can exist in all senses. In the case of the child, the visual of the cookie reminds her of the feelings of comfort that she associated in her body on the day of the original memory. This was that first event, with Mom offering security.

Here are some examples of conscious anchors. These are connections you have consciously linked in your brain with certain memories and events.

 The scent of freshly baked goods.

 Your favorite song.

The puckery sensation in your mouth when you think of lemons.

Negative anchors work the same way as positive ones. Here's a hypothetical example of how a negative anchor could be installed:

Let's imagine a smart little girl about seven years old whose name is Anna. Anna is tall for her age and feels out of place with her playmates. She's bigger and chubbier than the rest of them. Let's imagine that one day Anna is playing a game with the other kids and they don't want to play. Having limited abilities to express themselves appropriately and being intimidated by her size and intelligence, the children aim to hurt her feelings to make her go away. So they call her names. "Get out of here, fatso, nobody wants your ugly face around here." Pretty typical kids' stuff, wouldn't you say?

These types of experiences leave marks on your body. Bodies are made up of communities of cells with memories, and those networks are the energy source that runs our lives. Since our bodies are a low level electrically charged system, this remark that the children made about Anna's weight, known nowadays as a body snark, caused a short circuit in our little Anna's brain.

At that moment she was hit with an influx of stress chemicals flooding her body that caused her to feel a rush of emotions: hurt, anger, sadness, pain, embarrassment. The jarring words hit her like a truck and left their mark on her body. At this time her brain was busy creating certain memory markers known as anchors. Those anchors would then be set off throughout her life, and reinforced each time she encountered a similar situation of being hurt and judged or any other feeling or association that got connected with this event.

These memories will trigger arbitrarily in her thoughts and body leaving her feeling frustrated, hurt, and upset with no real sense of why. Since she's already associated food with feeling comforted and being loved, she'll have a tendency to eat every time she encounters anything that triggers off a reminder of this association of feeling bad in her body.

Today we'll imagine that Anna is a grown woman, successfully running her own business. She has a history of emotional eating, often seeking out food for comfort and to relieve stress. She often feels left out and uncomfortable in social situations, yet at ease immersed in work.

When Anna was first anchored to the belief that being fat equals being unworthy or unloved, her brain began to look for other evidence of that truth, seeking more examples to support that experience.

Maybe later that day Anna's mother said, "Anna, don't eat that cookie, you're already too chubby and boys don't like chubby girls." Wham bam, Anna's locked and loaded. Her brain is well on its way to establishing a pattern, and is still seeking out more evidence so the reinforcement anchors continue to affect her. Today, Anna is probably left feeling helpless, wondering why she can't stay on a diet and why in the world she can't lose weight.

As far as she knows, her years of experience with dieting have proven to her time and time again that she has no willpower, no discipline, she's too lazy, too stupid, and all those other too's. Yet the simple fact is that her subconscious programming has been sabotaging her every step of the way.

Deep in Anna's neurology, her brain has accepted that she will never fit in and that she's always going to be the fat outsider. Her painful associations and memories push her to binge and diet because the twin forces of pain and pleasure are fighting within her to survive. Poor Anna, without knowing that she has the ability to change her thinking and create new empowering associations, she's stuck—no therapist, no hypnosis CDs, no diet, no personal trainer, no boot camp, no doctor will ever successfully overturn her powerful brain's ability to keep her in safety mode.

Can you relate to Anna's story? Have you, like Anna, had a broken record playing in your head telling you all the things that you can't and shouldn't do? Are you stuck between a rock and a hard place having to listen to your mudslinging inner critic dragging your self-esteem through the dirt each day, constantly reminding you that you're just not good enough?

The sad truth of the matter is there will always be people who don't like you and who will say insensitive things bound to hurt you. Whether their intention is good, bad, or indifferent, if you're wide open and vulnerable, you will fall victim to their nasty, hateful, hurtful, critical, body snarking comments.

No matter what your past experiences have been, you do have a choice. You can weather the storm. Remember it's not what people say about you that counts, it's what you say to yourself that really matters. You can either re-parent yourself and do things to make you feel special and loving toward yourself now, as you are, or you can remain miserable. The choice is up to you. Now, if you're ready, let me teach you how to be in control of your own anchors.

Here's how to create positive anchors:

 Whip yourself into a highly emotional positive state. If you want to anchor excitement, you have to get yourself excited. To do that you would breathe the way you do when you're excited and think about the things you do when you're in a state of excitement, stand the way you stand, smile that smile, gesture or say what you would say when you're really jazzed. Literally put yourself into that peak state by remembering everything you felt when you were last experiencing the emotion of being excited.

 Now, while you're in the peak of that state, say or do something unique over and over again to condition your brain to create this new anchor to get you excited. You might want to snap your fingers, or clap your hands, stomp your feet, jump up and down, or raise your hands—whatever you choose to do or say that is unique and memorable is perfect. This is your trigger. Repeat it several dozen times continuing to increase your emotional intensity.

 Then do something to interrupt the pattern. Stop whatever you are doing and be still. Relax. Switch your focus to something else for a moment.

 Test the trigger. For example, if you decided to anchor yourself by clapping your hands and shouting "Yes," then clap your hands and shout "Yes." As you do that, your body should snap right back into that peak state.

 Whenever you notice that your trigger or anchor is losing its touch, go back and redo all the steps to recondition it again.

Anchors really work. I highly encourage you to use them and often. I use them all the time in every situation. Just to get yourself started you can practice using them with any one of the following Try It's! in the next section. Enjoy!

Where There Is Hatred, Sow Love...

In one of my favorite movies, *Pretty Woman*, Julia Roberts plays the character Vivian Ward, a hooker with a heart of gold. She meets and falls in love with "billionaire corporate raider, Edward Lewis" played by Richard Gere. Over the course of a week, Vivian's inner caterpillar transforms into a beautiful butterfly.

In true Pygmalion fashion, Edward takes her off the streets, buys her beautiful clothes, treats her like a lady, and introduces her to people who appreciate and respect her. Being treated in this new way gives Vivian a chance to recognize that she deserves more self-respect than she was giving herself. Each of those positive experiences changed the way she felt about herself. By the end of the movie, Vivian gets an opportunity to see herself and her life from a new perspective, and that leads to her decision to get off the streets and return back to school.

During a poignant pillow talk scene in the film where it becomes clear to Edward that he is starting to fall in love with her, he asks her why she became a prostitute.

Edward: "And you chose this as your profession?"

Vivian: "I worked at a couple fast food places, parked cars at wrestling, but I couldn't make the rent. I was too ashamed to go home. That's when I met Kit. She was a hooker and made it sound so great, so one day I did it and I cried the whole time. Then I got some regulars and, you know, it's not like anybody plans this. It's not like your childhood dream."

Edward: "But you could be so much more."

Vivian: (looking deeply into his eyes) "People put you down enough you start to believe it."

Edward: "I think you are a very bright, very special woman."

Vivian: "The bad stuff is easier to believe. Do you ever notice that?"

As the movie reflects, until you have an experience that is emotionally charged and powerful enough to shake up your hard wired negative self-image, your old limiting beliefs about your self-worth, about who you are and what you're capable of, will stick to you like glue.

Those put downs and critical remarks you heard people say about you over the years will remain stuck, continuing to play out in your thoughts like a broken record because, as Vivian says, "The bad stuff is easier to believe."

Remember that your subconscious mind is neither for you nor against you, it is just doing its job to keep you true to yourself. In her book, *Attracting Abundance with EFT*, EFT Master, Carol Look, a licensed clinical social worker and hypnotherapist says, "The beliefs you hold consciously or in your subconscious mind are compulsive. What this means is that whatever you believe in your subconscious mind must come true, no matter what. If you believe you aren't good enough, or that you don't deserve financial success, you will move heaven and earth to achieve this outcome. For the most part, your beliefs keep you true to who you believe yourself to be."

This is why you'll remain an emotional eater until you can separate your truth from the lies that people have been telling you. Without being able to create a new image of treating yourself and food with greater respect, acting and living as a naturally slender woman, you will always fall back on what is most familiar—playing the food and body hating game every time someone or some situation reminds you of feeling inferior.

Doing An About Face: Changing Polarities

I want to draw your attention to the law of polarity that basically says, "If you don't like what you've got, you've got to change the energy in the situation."

If you're focused on being afraid, find ways of drawing closer to courage. If you feel angry or hateful, add love. Add happiness to end sadness. Where there is doubt, add faith.

It's a fair assumption that right now you may not yet feel very loving toward your body. In order to get to that place of greater self-love, you have to build a bridge and gradually take steps to move closer. For me, tapping has worked wonders. I use it all the time because now I choose to be happy. How about you?

Choose to Be Happy

In her book, *Happy for No Reason*, author Marci Shimoff shares her findings and research on happiness done over a twenty year period. Her collection of data from various scientists in the field of positive psychology indicates that each of us has a happiness set point indicating how happy or unhappy we are.

To determine what influences those levels that create that set point, Dr. David Lykken, a scientist at the University of Minnesota, wanted to know how much of a person's happiness comes from nature vs. nurture.

After studying thousands of sets of twins, including twins raised apart, he found that 50% of our happiness set point is genetic and the other 50% is learned. In a later study following up the work of Lykken, psychology researchers Sonja Lyubomirsky, Kennon Sheldon, and David Schaade confirmed Lykken's findings and uncovered new information discussing the specifics of the 50% of our happiness that can be learned.

Of that 50% it appears that only 10% of that happiness set point depends upon our life circumstances. That means that regardless of whether or not you are rich, successful, and involved in a relationship, you can still choose to be happy. The 40% is determined by our habitual feelings, words, and actions. This is what makes it possible to raise your happiness set point. If your life is down in the dumps you don't have to stay there.

In the same way you'd crank up the thermostat to get comfortable on a chilly day, you actually have the power to reprogram your happiness set point to a higher level of peace and well-being.

I've spoken previously about the warning bells that go off in our lives telling us there is something wrong. I've noticed in my own life, as I continually use my tapping and take action to move out of my old fat thinking box and embrace my imperfections right along with my curvy self, I can see the many ways that I've been so incredibly unkind to myself over the years. As a result, I've become more aware of the signs that point to the old habits that thrive on dysfunctional and disempowered thinking. I wonder how many of the following warning bell situations and habits you, too, have found yourself in:

1. Avoiding social activities
2. Attempting to hide by wearing clothes that are baggy and shapeless
3. Avoiding friends who are dieters
4. Avoiding shopping
5. Feeling repulsed by your body
6. Procrastinating
7. Avoiding certain food for vanity reasons – I'll get bloated!
8. Pushing your body beyond its limits
9. Using your scale to measure your progress
10. Trying on clothes that don't fit
11. Filling your closet with clothes that don't fit
12. Avoiding intimacy
13. Feeling ashamed or intimidated for being who you are — no matter what size
14. Letting others push you around
15. Feeling uncomfortable eating around people
16. Playing the body comparison game
17. Trying to lose weight for a big event
18. Body bashing
19. Avoiding activity
20. Over-scheduling
21. Giving up your "me" time
22. Twisting yourself into a pretzel trying to please everyone else

Just like you, I also have my insecurities, but now I no longer habitually let them get the best of me. I realize that I have a choice. Now I know that when they pop up, whenever I want to, I can do something about them and change the way I feel instantly. The following story is an example of a time when I was still stuck in the loop of seeking validation outside myself. In this case it was in a beautiful dress.

Is Saying Goodbye to Dieting An Admission of Defeat?

In 2008, I cleaned out my closet and was amazed to find I had clothes I hadn't worn for nearly twenty years. Now, wearing a size 18/20, I had to come to grips with the fact that the size 6 Betsey Johnson black and purple mesh slip dress I had loved passionately wasn't going to fit me anytime soon.

As I longingly stared at it, draped over the light blue satin padded hangar, my thoughts wandered and I remembered the last time I had worn it. Angel and I were invited to his best friend Ricky's wedding.

It was November 1992, almost a year and half after our son, PT, was born. I was still a few pounds away from my goal weight according to Weight Watchers®, but at 137 pounds I was feeling pretty confident that I looked great.

All day long I stressed about wearing that dress. Although I knew it would look wonderful, I couldn't do anything to risk having a tummy bulge so I ate like a bird.

On the day of the wedding I ate steamed vegetables and salad with diet dressing and sipped on endless amounts of water. The reception was in the evening around 7:30 p.m. As I stepped into the car I smiled as I thought about how stunning I looked and the price that I had paid to fit into this dress; all the personal training sessions, the buckets of sweat, the weigh-ins, the special light cooking, all the money spent on low Cal foods, workout clothes, gym equipment, membership, personal training, and even sneakers.

I ran through my mental files remembering all the walking and running, the stair climbing and dancing, the pushups, pull ups, curls, sit ups, lunges, squats and sprints, and all the temptation that I did my best to resist, culminating in this very moment. I felt so incredibly proud of my accomplishments and as I slid gently into my car seat, I silently patted myself on the back.

When we arrived at the reception, I felt like the belle of the ball. All of my husband's friends and brothers swarmed around me, paying me compliments and saying how wonderful I looked with my satin skin and creamy white shoulders. My husband beamed with pride. We danced a bit and all during our time together all I could think of was how I looked in that dress.

"Did I look fat? Did my belly pooch out from that last glass of water?" I made up an excuse and told Angel that I wanted to sit down, knowing full well that my motive was my fear that standing up made my tummy bulge more obvious.

When it came time to eat at the reception, I picked at my food. I had a few grains of rice and some chicken along with a couple sips of water. I just couldn't risk not fitting into that dress and having my tummy bulge out. It was all I could think about.

It was just before midnight as we were coming off the highway heading home, and I was starving. I was so hungry I could have eaten a cow! I asked Angel to stop and pick up some Chinese food before the take out place closed. Ah! That marked the end of my obsession of fitting into that dress that night.

It was all over and now I could celebrate by eating.

That was the legacy that being food and weight obsessed for years taught me. I learned how to play the game and fool myself and others into believing I had control over food. It was all an illusion and in reality food had me in its thrall.

Today I thank the Lord that I don't obsess over food anymore and that I no longer fear my imperfections. Alert the media. The secret's out. I'm not perfect. That dress? Mmmm. First I passed it on to my daughter, Cara. For Halloween 2008 she was the most fashionably dressed witch on the planet. Then one day I found it tossed in her closet off the hanger. I realized she didn't understand what that dress really meant to me so I took it back.

For Christmas that year I gave it to Janelle. She beamed with joy when she opened the box. I just knew that she would love it as much as I did. When she asked me, "Andrea, why don't you want to keep this for when you can fit into it?" I told her, "No thank you, sweetie. It really was time to let go of that dress. That was the old Andrea, this is the new and that dress just doesn't fit in with who I am anymore. Wear it well, honey and take lots of pictures. I want that dress to go out dancing a lot. Okay?"

Today, when I think back to the days of craziness and insanity that dress represents, I realize that my decision to stop obsessing about food and my body was not giving up. In fact, it was taking a bold stand for myself and honoring the woman I've become.

When I gave up allowing a diet or a program to tell me what I could and could not eat, I took back control over the rest of my life. I've decided that like that dress, body obsession and dieting just don't fit anymore. I've simply outgrown them. There may have been some good memories from diets in the past, but for the most part, it was a lot of pain. Now I say, "Goodbye to Dieting" and "Hello Life."

How about you? Are you still consumed by hating yourself for not being perfect? Are you embarrassed because you sneak food and eat when people's backs are turned? There is hope and the way out is through. As you begin to release your food fears and recognize that you can take care of yourself, you will begin to enjoy life more and live in the present. I'll never get back those moments or years that I wasted obsessing about what I ate, how much, and when, but I can move forward with a greater degree of love and self-compassion so that I'll never waste my time like that again. And you can too.

Try It! – Noticing Distinctions

How are your desires for certain foods changing?

What are some of the food preferences you're noticing that are different? For example, rather than eating all the fries on my plate, I now prefer to eat only specific ones, only those of a certain size, shape, color, and texture.

What other non-food related things have you noticed in your life that no longer feel good to you?

Listen to Your Body

It was my very first, incredibly powerful, experience with *EFT* and tapping that taught me the unmistakable value of forgiveness. After years of building up resentment and sitting on my anger, living, breathing, and playing the role of victim, I realized for the first time that by refusing to forgive others I was only hurting myself.

All of us are in the process of healing something in our lives and that is often the thing that we let define us, our weakness. With the help of tapping and the other techniques I've shared with you, I hope that you'll take the opportunity to revisit those musty dusty corners of your mind and broken places in your heart and open yourself up to healing them. It is by doing this that you will discover your greatest sense of peace. It is these places that have set down the biggest and strongest anchors of truth in your body that determine how you think about yourself.

At one point I was having chest pains which I had never experienced before. Prior to making the decision to go to the doctor, I became aware of an incredible heavy feeling of sadness. One day, while tapping on it sitting in the shower with the water beating down on my head, I had an insight that connected my sadness with my chest pains. I realized that the pains had popped up out of nowhere immediately after I made a last ditch attempt to contact my father earlier that week.

After receiving no response to either my email or phone calls, I knew then that our relationship was over.

For months prior to that, I had been saying how heartbroken I felt. After having had several episodes of these fleeting chest pains, I realized after tapping that I had been sending the message to my body that I was "heartbroken."

One day I went for a walk to explore those feelings. Along the way I remembered the work of Louise Hay. I wondered what a problem with the heart meant. After I got back home, I ran to my bookshelf and opened my copy of *You Can Heal Your Life*. It was no surprise to me to discover that a dysfunction of the heart indicated a lack of joy.

After realizing that for the past eighteen months I'd been living under incredible stress, feeling as though I'd been stuck inside a pressure cooker, I knew without a doubt that I'd contributed to overtaxing my system. I wondered if it was possible that the heart murmur I was diagnosed with as a child had become more serious.

In an effort to participate in my future wellness, I decided to take measures to take care of myself and that included going to my doctor. I also gave myself full permission to feel whatever sadness and mixed emotions I felt toward the loss of my still much beloved father.

Until the day I went to the doctor, those pains persisted. Once there, all my fears were allayed. He explained to me that our bodies often react to our thoughts and my chest pains were a direct result of what I was thinking. Duh! He really hammered the point home. I had to change the meaning of what I was feeling. I had to change the way I felt about my father.

In their book, *Getting Well Again*, Dr. O. Carl Simonton and his wife, Stephanie Simonton, and Dr. James L. Creighton, discuss the importance of forgiving past resentments in order to heal the body. They discovered that in most chronic cases where patients died, resentments were at the core of the issue.

In describing their program and protocol for healing cancer, they use a phrase, "participating in your health." I love that image of being able to cooperate actively in my own healing through my relationship with food and my body.

As a key component of being able to do that, I now understand the importance of forgiveness and releasing the feelings of anger, resentment, and hurt directed toward others for having hurt me.

According to the Simontons and Creighton, you must take steps to recognize how you have participated in your own illness in order to be able to move toward a path of healing.

They say, "The first step is to assist patients in identifying how they participated in the onset of their disease. This process consists first of asking them to identify the major stresses occurring in their lives six to eighteen months prior to their diagnosis. Some individuals may have participated by creating or allowing undue stresses in their lives or by refusing to recognize that they have emotional limits. Others may have subordinated their own needs to everybody else's until they had no strength left to devote to themselves. Still others may have participated by reacting to stresses with feelings of helplessness or hopelessness."

Please understand this is not an exercise in finding fault or blaming. There's absolutely no sense in doing that. By being able to pinpoint what behaviors have led up to your current physical circumstance, whatever it may be, you'll put yourself in a position of power, aware of what's not working and able to make the decision to change.

Now you may not be facing any illness, and like me you may think of yourself as being healthy as a horse. But if you expect to maintain that current state of health, and resolve your dysfunctional relationship with food and find the balance you seek, you'll need to actively take steps to participate in your own wellness. And that means dropping the victim label and learning how to forgive.

Ho'oponopono: An Ancient Hawaiian Forgiveness Technique

I've learned that forgiveness is essential in learning how to love yourself because without it, you'll continue to remain a victim of the voices. You'll never really be in control of your life because your resentment will always get in your way, keeping you living in a box.

In the past I have used tapping to release my feelings of hurt and bring me to the point of realizing that forgiveness is a gift I give myself. I have also used another process called Ho'oponopono, an ancient Hawaiian forgiveness technique.

> **Juicy Woman Note:**
>
> Please realize that there is much more to Ho'oponopono than what I present here. I will also give you a website to access in the resource section so you can learn elements of it in a way that suits you best.

In ho'oponopono, you assume responsibility for things that you would tend to avoid or ignore, things that you would not actually consider yourself as being responsible for in the natural order of traditional thinking. This means that you open yourself up to being willing to accept responsibility for things beyond your control: global events that are occurring, war, famine, slaughter — all those things.

The reason behind this is as energy they are all stuck in your body, living and breathing anger and hurt and fear inside of you, waiting to pop out in the form of illness and pain. Whether or not you realize it, they are affecting you and by affecting you, they continue to manifest in what is known as physical reality.

One caveat I would like to offer is that as you use this technique more and more, you will see definite changes in yourself and your relationship to others. However, there will also be many times when you won't see any evidence of change. Don't despair. You have done what you could. As Mahatma Gandhi said, "Be the change you wish to see."

As with anything, let your heart be your guide. The most important part of this is the intention with which you approach it. If your intention is good and your heart is loving and pure, it will work, whether you see evidence of it or not.

This can be done in minutes or seconds or hours, whatever you feel is necessary and whatever works for you. The version I describe here goes from start to finish in about a minute. The whole idea behind doing this is to change your energetic vibration and to lift your emotions so that you are back in a state of joy and gratitude.

I've found this technique has worked for me. Here's how I do it:

1. Think about a situation or person who has caused you pain.
2. Find a comfortable position, close your eyes and imagine seeing the vision of that person's face or the situation that you were in that hurt you. See that playing out on a stage in front of you.
3. While thinking about the situation that is causing you pain, holding that vision of either an individual, God, or the universe, repeat each of these four statements:

   "I'm sorry."

   "Please forgive me."

   "Thank You."

   "I love you."

Here is a quick story to show how this actually works. A couple of months ago, I was taking out my frustrations on several poor little innocent Dove® dark chocolates. After I did this technique, I realized that I was upset with someone.

As I got clearer and realized what was bothering me and pushing me to overeat the chocolates, I saw an image of that person. Then holding their image in my mind, I said to them, "I'm sorry." I said this in recognition that we are all connected and that there may have been something that I said or did to have created feelings of hurt or anger that caused them to hurt me with their anger, rejection, or judgment.

After saying this in my imagination, the next thing I said while thinking of them was, "Please forgive me." This is a statement to the universe and to the individual in question. By asking for forgiveness, you open your energy up to attract grace and love, connecting you with your source of power—love.

Next in the process is the expression of gratitude by saying the words, "Thank You." As you acknowledge the feelings of release and relief that come with asking for forgiveness and clearing the negative energy between yourself and anyone or anything else, you feel at peace again.

In the final step, you imagine saying the words, "I love you." This is because by cleansing the energetic field around you that creates hurt and pain, you reconnect back to your source of love and spirit. In a state of gratitude, you recognize the many joys and wonders in your life. By saying, "I love you" to the universe or your higher self or God or any name that you so choose to represent a higher intelligence, you create a clearing energy that restores your connection to the loving and divine.

As I said, there are many wonderful variations of how to do this process online. Check it out and see. No matter how you slice it, forgiveness is truly divine.

The Wound is the Door

In her CD set entitled, *Food is Food & Love is Love: A Step by Step Program to Break Free of Emotional Eating*, author Geneen Roth says, "The wound is the door, the thing that you consider to be the worst mistake of your life, the thing you think you just want to get rid of, you want to fix, you want to make go away, you want to cut out of yourself, the thing that you believe if only you could wake up in the morning and have it be gone with—that's the very door. That's actually where the healing is."

"There's a crack in everything, that's how the light gets in."
– Leonard Cohen

Through this very relationship with food, through the thing that you believe is the worst mistake, your worst pain, that's how the light gets in. That's how the healing gets in, when you start looking at it, when you start being curious about it, when you start exploring it, because we eat the way we live. Zen teacher Sheri Huber says that the way we do anything, is the way we do everything. My version of that is what you do with food, you do in the entire rest of your life.

As you start a new way of being around food, all your beliefs will come into question; what you deserve, abundance, joy, sex, solitude, pleasure, taking time for yourself, responsibility, forgiveness, all these things in your life will become new questions as you take the time to listen to the wisdom of your body.

Now get ready for a fabulous strategy specifically designed to teach you how to listen to your body.

Connirae Andreas' Naturally Slender Eating Strategy

If you were raised to be a professional dieter like I was, then it's very likely that you've been brainwashed into believing that your power and virtue lies in being able to stick to the diet and follow it to a "T." The message I got was that my desire to eat when I wasn't hungry came from having no will power or self-control. Like that little elephant we discussed in an earlier chapter who grows up thinking that he can't do it, diets have pushed us as a society into thinking we can't trust ourselves around food.

Is There An Alternative to Dieting?

From the age of eleven onward, I was on a diet. I just came to accept it as a necessary evil, thinking that everyone who needed/wanted to lose weight had to do it through dieting. I couldn't imagine there was any other way to control one's desire to eat.

I've always been fascinated by people who appeared to be naturally slim. It seemed like they never had to work at it. In second grade I used to go to my friend Claudia's house for lunch. Her mother would prepare big bowls of spaghetti covered in mayonnaise. Although I've never had it since, it was delicious. Claudia and I ate it with great relish. She and her mother were both thin as rails.

My stepmother, Rosie, had a perfect figure that never seemed to change. She never lost or gained weight. Although our house was always stocked with goodies, she would just take one or two cookies or a piece of chocolate or a few chips. I couldn't imagine how she was able to stop eating such yummy foods so quickly.

Throughout my teens I babysat and raided the cabinets of people's homes like ours, where chocolate, chips, and cookies flooded the pantry. Yet many of those who lived there were small and slender.

I grew up equally fascinated and frustrated, enviously watching these slim people, and wondering how in the world they could eat real food and

327

I couldn't. I wondered what their secret was. Now I know and I'm going to tell you.

In this chapter, I'm going to share with you the value of what I learned about living and eating as a naturally slender woman as taught to me by one of my most beloved mentors, Connirae Andreas. Connirae is one of the co-developers of *Neuro Linguistic Programming* and the creator of the *Naturally Slender Eating Strategy*. For years, she's been an enormous inspiration to me and I've admired her work immensely. I'm tickled pink to have the opportunity to teach you her life changing technique.

The difference between Connirae's strategy and dieting is that, unlike diets, where the focus is solely on calorie restriction and eating lower fat foods, the *Naturally Slender Eating Strategy* focuses on tuning into what foods you want. You will learn to pay attention to which of them will make your body feel the very best over an extended period of time. There are no restrictions. You eat what your body wants and stop when you don't want any more. Stopping is not a matter of force and control—you discover how to stop eating when eating one more bite would actually make you feel worse. It's all about becoming more satisfied. The key is in learning to be more discriminating and discovering what foods actually feel good to you and which make you feel icky.

Remember this is not a diet. If you are a woman who has lived the majority of your life yo-yoing between diets and being enslaved by food, take heart. There is hope. By following Connirae's strategy you can learn to eat like a naturally slender woman and lose weight without ever dieting again.

Asking Connirae for Help: Desperate to Stop My Hunger

In pursuit of completing a final assignment to get my *NLP* Master Certification, I wanted to interview Connirae Andreas. She had been an iconic inspiration to me throughout my entire *NLP* training. I had read her books and amassed a library of her videos demonstrating her work with students and clients.

When I learned she was the creator of a process called *The Naturally Slender Eating Strategy,* I knew that I had to speak with her. I asked my *NLP* instructor, Rachel Hott Ph.D, to introduce me to Connirae. She shared Connirae's email address with me, and I wrote and told Connirae how much I appreciated her and what a role model she had been for me. Within a few days, I was shocked and surprised when Connirae graciously replied to my email and agreed to speak with me and teach me her *Naturally Slender Eating Strategy.*

At the time, I was running a series of Losing Weight without Dieting teleseminars. In that program, I was teaching women to use *EFT* along with the principles of intuitive eating. All the women who were using *EFT* and combining it with the principles were doing very well. They were not hungry between meals, they went for long periods of time without thinking of food, they stopped eating soon after they had the first sensation of feeling satisfied, they were more relaxed, and they were losing weight.

However, those who were not using *EFT* were unable to control their eating, were frustrated by constant cravings, they couldn't stop thinking about food, gave into constant binging, beat up on themselves, and were struggling with gaining weight.

I was among them since I doggedly refused to rely on any crutches. I was dead set on making intuitive eating work for me. In my heart I questioned whether *EFT* was necessary to control my ravenous hunger.

I shared with Connirae my theory of why we non-*EFT*ers were facing this food crisis. I suggested to her that those of us who were not using *EFT*, despite knowing its effectiveness, might have some kind of inner conflict. I assumed it was this conflict, or as Dr. Maxwell Maltz called it, a "fat self-image," that caused us to overeat and give into binges and self-destructive impulses.

Connirae said that sometimes there is an inner conflict, but sometimes the person just doesn't have a strategy for dealing with food that works. She said that a good place to start is to learn the *Naturally Slender Eating Strategy.*

She said, "If you know how to choose food and eat the same way naturally slender people do, you have an important foundation. In order for food to become a 'non-issue,' we need to know this strategy. Sometimes this is all we need. If we learn this strategy and *still* have difficulty with eating, that tells us there's more to do. Maybe there are other inner parts to work with or other inner beliefs or something else. If you take the *Naturally Slender Eating Strategy* and you teach that for starters, it gives you a reference point, and if something still isn't working about eating, then it's easier to be clear on exactly what that is. If something comes up, you can say, 'oh good, this is exactly bringing me to what I need to work on.'"

She went on to explain that "With this strategy, it's never a failure or a mistake to find yourself going off track. If you go off track, you can just think, 'good this puts me exactly where I need to be.' This experience is exactly what I need to make better choices over time." As I took in the full meaning of what she told me, I felt the perpetually hungry part of me breathe a huge sigh of relief.

From our conversation, I knew that I didn't have to fight with myself any longer--this was a complete and total reframe of what was traditionally believed about overeating.

By viewing a binge in this way, it gives you more choice, flexibility, compassion, and space to love that part of you and find out what you need. As you learn this strategy, you're going to discover how binging actually gives you good information.

I've noticed that many of the women who come to me with eating challenges don't have much self-love, so I asked Connirae about that. She said, "This is the same thing, really. If we find the places where we don't have self-love, then we can say, "Good, this is just what we need to be attending to, because any lack of self-love is something that got installed in our being's best effort to cope with something, and it just needs some healing. It's good if we are able to come to the place where we can welcome it, receive it, and begin to notice what healing it needs."

Juicy Woman Note:

If you're struggling with not knowing when to stop eating, and find that the loose guidelines of intuitive eating are not enough to give you the structure you crave, then I suggest that you try Connirae's strategy. If you find that after learning this strategy you are still inclined to binge, there is no judgment.

My suggestion is to deal with those inner conflicted parts of you that yearn for the love and attention that became connected with food. Connirae's strategy will re-teach your body how to make choices that feel physically good and keep you in a lasting state of well-being. With this process, most people end up actually choosing foods that are healthier—but without effort or force. We are simply choosing what will give us more pleasure over time. And when it comes down to it, most junk food doesn't make our bodies feel that great.

It will most likely take you several tries to get the experience "in your bones." You'll be paying attention to what different foods actually feel like in your body. It is natural to expect that you will do some overeating in learning this process. This is not a mistake, this is a way for your body to relearn what it feels like to feel good.

If you experience overeating and binging as you practice this strategy, this is not a problem. This is quite normal and will give you what Connirae calls, "a compelling learning experience." As mentioned before, there is absolutely no value in judging whether this is good or bad. It is all valuable learning that is creating new associations in your brain, resetting the default switch in your body to seek out more experiences of pleasure vs. pain.

If in the past you felt reluctant to allow yourself to have good feelings, I encourage you to try this strategy anyway. Actually do the steps and you may be surprised to discover that it's completely OK for you to feel good in this specific way. As you are doing it, know that at the end of the chapter I'll be offering you some suggestions for how to work with any unresolved emotional issues. For best results you may want to find a buddy, join a support group, hire a certified coach, or work with a professionally trained therapist. It's up to you to decide what degree of healing you seek.

The History Behind the Creation of
The Naturally Slender Eating Strategy

Connirae has always been slender and realized back in 1979 that this was no genetic accident. She recognized that she actually had acquired a strategy, or "thought sequence," that enabled her to maintain her natural slender body/mind connection.

One day she was leading an *NLP* Practitioner seminar with her husband, Steve Andreas. They were teaching their students how good strategies or "thought sequences" help us be more successful in all areas of life. A strategy is the way we think—the exact sequence of thoughts, images, feelings, and things we say to ourselves.

A woman named Clara raised her hand to volunteer to learn more about her strategy for deciding what to eat. This is the strategy she was taught. Here you'll be learning the specific thought sequence or strategy that naturally slender people use--most often without even realizing it. Clara was an overweight woman by 100-200 pounds. She brought up the issue of wanting to know more about what made her want to eat the foods she did.

After asking Clara a few questions, Connirae recognized that Clara's approach to eating was a simple two-step method that was basic and fundamental. Like many other people, Clara's eating strategy was simply this:

See food –>Eat food.

Whenever Clara saw food, she automatically wanted to eat it, whether or not she felt physically hungry. After she understood that, Clara was able to connect why she was heavier than she wanted to be. Connirae asked Clara if she would like to explore another option for making food selections. Clara eagerly nodded her head in agreement. This marked the moment that Connirae's Naturally Slender Eating Strategy was conceived.

Try It! – What's Your Eating Strategy?

Take a moment and think about what makes you know that you want to eat. What images do you see in your mind's eye? If there's any internal dialog, what do you hear? What feelings are you aware of in your body? Write down a few sentences describing what inner thoughts and feelings occur before you choose to eat. For now, think about what you do. What strategy do you think you have around food? Is it, See food −> Eat food?

Connirae intuitively knew what would work for Clara and immediately mapped out a new eating strategy for her. Later, Connirae realized that this was actually her own strategy—it was the thought sequence she had been using naturally for years that enabled her to make healthy choices in food.

After learning this strategy, for the first time Clara no longer felt compelled to eat anything and everything that came into her view. Now, Clara had a method for choosing food that worked and that she felt good about—and you can have this method too.

Alternate Sources for Learning the Strategy

Connirae has gone on to share her Naturally Slender Eating Strategy with many of her clients and students. It was also published in the book she co-authored with her husband, *Heart of the Mind: Engaging Your Inner Power To Change With Neuro-Linguistic-Programming.*

By using the strategy as I've outlined it here in this chapter, you will be able to recreate this method for yourself. However, to get the full benefit, you may choose to get a copy of her book and read the strategy directly.

You can also get another variation of Connirae's strategy by listening to a podcast of a colleague of mine named Reneé Stephens. Renee is a Certified Hypnotherapist, Master Practitioner of *Neuro Linguistic Programming*, and a Certified Life Coach, MBA. She's a student of Connirae's and, like me, was taught the strategy so that she could share it with others. Renee has two podcasts specifically devoted to teaching and explaining Connirae's strategy. Since she has struggled personally with overeating, she has refined her work to an art form. I highly recommend her resources.

You can also do an internet search on Google under, *Naturally Slender Eating Strategy*. There you'll find an assortment of people who comment on and teach the strategy.

When I asked Connirae about how to best teach her strategy, she suggested that I pretend to be one of my clients and just go through it "live." I could do that easily based on my work with other women struggling to come to a better relationship with food, and also based on my own experiences. The following several pages are excerpts from our conversations:

Connirae Andreas's Naturally Slender Eating Strategy

Connirae: You definitely want to have more choices around eating. Is that correct?

Client: Yes.

Connirae: What gets you to think about eating in the first place? (The first step is to find out, "What are your cues for eating?")

Client: I think about eating all the time.

Connirae: Great! That makes it easy. We won't have any trouble finding the cue. Can you give me some examples of times when you know that you want to eat?

Client: Whenever I walk into the kitchen and I see food I want to eat it. If I'm with friends and they're eating, I want to eat something too. If I feel lonely, I want to eat. If it's noon I want to eat, because that's when I usually have lunch. Whenever I drive back home from shopping with bags of groceries in the car.

Connirae: Now take one of those situations and let's find out what happens in detail. Imagine you're at home. What tells you that it's time to eat?

Client: When I walk into the kitchen and see food. I usually have something to eat on the counter.

Connirae: Great. Now imagine walking into the kitchen and noticing the counter with the food on it. As you see the food on the counter, the very next thing you can *do now* is to *tune into your body* and *notice how your body is feeling*. Notice the quality of feeling in your stomach and notice the quality of feeling throughout your body. Pay particular attention to how your stomach area feels.

Client: I feel tension in my stomach because I'm angry about something that someone said.

Connirae: Okay. That feeling of tension sounds like it isn't related to how hungry you are—it's not actually related to eating, but it could lead to an *emotional* desire to eat. Right now we just want to teach the basic strategy that works. So turn inward and welcome the feeling of tension in your stomach, and ask the feeling if it's OK to set it aside for a moment so that you can learn a simple strategy for eating food so that you naturally feel good and are well-nourished.

Client: Yes, that's OK. (Note: If this is not OK, we deal with that emotional upset directly so that the feeling is honored and cleared before we learn the strategy. You may want to use a method like Connirae's Core Transformation for this or any of the stress relief techniques in this book.)

Connirae: Great. So you can just notice how your stomach feels. How does your stomach feel now? I'm asking about the sensation itself--not any kind of evaluation or meaning we might put on the feeling.

Client: Okay. I don't really know how to describe how I'm feeling.

Connirae: That's okay. You don't need to put it into words. Just notice the sensation that's there and that's better than having words. Notice the quality of the sensation. Sometimes if we put it into words we lose the true *experience* of how we feel.

Client: I'm feeling hungry.

Connirae: Okay. So notice the quality and how strong this feeling is. In relation to how hungry you've felt before, how would you rate your hunger? How much would you say that your body desires food at this moment?

Client: Well, I'm not that hungry. I just ate a little while ago so I'm kind of full, but I'm still a little hungry.

Connirae: Great. Wonderful. Now make an image of one possible food that you can eat.

Client: Yes. I see chips.

Connirae: That's wonderful. Now notice the quantity of chips that you're seeing in your mind.

Client: I see a whole bag. They're up close, almost in my face, like I'm sitting in them. (Client sounds *extremely* enthusiastic. She is clearly very enticed by the *image* of chips!)

Connirae: Wow! That sounds like a pleasurable image all by itself so take your time and enjoy it... When you're done with that, imagine yourself eating a particular amount. Now this is going to be different than you've done before. Imagine actually eating the chips... Because you can enjoy the pleasure of the fantasy of the chips as long as you like. But if you're really going to eat them, you want to know if your body will feel better or worse when you're done. You want to know if you're going to feel great over time.

Client: Yum. Okay I'll do that.

Connirae: Okay. Now imagine or sense eating a certain amount of them.

Client: I'm having a hard time doing this. I can't taste them in my imagination.

Connirae: OK. That's just fine. You don't actually have to have a sense of exactly how they taste. Sometimes when we eat food we're not fully aware of the taste, especially at the conscious level. What's important now is that you are *intending* to experience what it would be like to actually eat a certain amount of this food—these chips. You have eaten this food many times in the past so at some level your body already has the information about how this food tastes, and then how it feels in your body over time.

Even though you don't consciously have the data available, your body was there and it knows. Keeping that in mind, you can just relax and have fun with this process. You can let your unconscious mind be the guide now and trust in its wisdom.

Client: Can I remember a time when I've eaten chips before?

Connirae: If you want to, you can go back to a specific time when you ate chips. This can help you remember what it's like. Or you can just go with whatever comes to you as you imagine having chips right now. When you do this, you will be drawing on your memories of eating chips, and you'll also use information from this moment—such as whether these chips look fresh or if you've just eaten a bunch of greasy food.

Now imagine and feel that sensation of the chips on your tongue and in your mouth. What is it like? Are you enjoying these chips? Do they taste good to you? Hold an image of that particular amount of chips that you've chosen and imagine eating all of them. Notice the quality of the chip. Notice if it is salty or sweet. Notice if it tastes fresh or stale. Is it crunchy and crisp or soft and chewy? Notice how the chips feel/taste to you.

Now we're going to check how eating these chips would make you feel over time. Because with this strategy you are learning to have more pleasure overall—not just in the few seconds you're actually eating, but more pleasure through time. So with the help and guidance of your sub-conscious mind, allow yourself to go forward in time through the next several hours, so that you can sense how eating these chips will change your experience.

Client: So is this like time-travel?

Connirae: Yes, you can think of it that way. You have eaten this amount of these chips (in your imagination), and you are feeling forward in time to experience how this food sits in your system. You might notice the feeling in your stomach, your whole torso. Do you feel satisfied and settled? Heavy? Light? Uncomfortable or queasy? And how about your mental state? Is your mind clear and alert, or a bit groggy, for example? Sense how you would feel over the next few hours if you ate these chips, in this quantity.

Client: It kind of feels a bit clogged and uncomfortable. It's like a heavy kind of feeling.

Connirae: Wonderful! It doesn't matter what the feeling is that you have. What's wonderful is that we can *notice* the feeling. It doesn't matter if your feeling is pleasant or unpleasant. It doesn't even matter if your guess about how you would feel if you ate the chips is right or wrong, because there is no right or wrong or good or bad in this. They're all just feelings. What's important is to practice making the guess. You are using all of the information you have to make the best guess you are able to make at this moment in time.

Whatever feeling you got, just notice and store it as information. You felt "slightly clogged." Now ask yourself this question:

"Is this feeling better or worse than the feeling I had when I first thought of eating?"

Client: No. I hate to say it, but it's actually a little worse (she says *very* reluctantly). Oh no, I just don't want to give up my chips!

Connirae: Don't worry. You don't have to. This strategy is completely about you doing what you want to do. It's good that you notice how your body would feel. And it's important to keep in mind that you don't have to give anything up. It's just a matter of what you decide at this moment will give you the most pleasure and satisfaction. Most of us want to have more pleasure, so it's completely up to you what you think will give you more pleasure. And if you think there may be something about the chips that would make you feel good, you might want to really investigate what this is.

It can help to make a distinction between the "pleasure" fantasy of eating the chips, which was really enjoyable for you, and the experience of actually eating the chips, which you found would actually make you feel "clogged." You can decide—if something about the fantasy of eating those chips was really pleasurable, you can go back to that anytime you want and really enjoy it. And if actually eating the chips makes your body feel better or more satisfied you can do that too. You're just noticing where the pleasure and satisfaction really is. You can either choose to enjoy the fantasy or have the reality of actually choosing the chips.

Client: Yeah. As much as I hate to admit it, those chips didn't make my body feel good.

Connirae: Okay, so let's go on to the next thing. Imagine one other possibility of food you could eat.

Client: Okay. I have some M&Ms® I like.

Connirae: Is that something that you would consider eating?

Client: Yes. Absolutely.

Connirae: Great. Okay. Now imagine eating a particular amount of those M&Ms®. Sense what that feeling is like in your mouth, taste it, notice the feeling or sensation of it sliding down your throat and the feeling of it being in your stomach. Notice the quality of those M&Ms® in your body and then project yourself forward in time again and notice how your body feels after having eaten those M&Ms®. How's that actually making your body feel?

Client: Wow! This one really makes me feel bad having all those M&Ms® in my stomach. I'm actually feeling pretty queasy.

Connirae: Okay, now just notice this feeling that you're calling "pretty queasy" and ask yourself, "Is that better or worse than the feeling you started with—the way you felt before you imagined eating anything?"

Client: Well, worse definitely. I feel worse after eating the M&Ms®.

Connirae: Okay. Fine. Now you're clear that both of these two choices would actually make your body feel worse if you were to actually eat them in the amounts you imagined. Is there anything else you would like to visualize? Let your mind come up with something that you guess might actually make you feel a little better. Don't limit yourself by only considering things that you already have on hand. You can trust that you will be resourceful and you'll know how to get whatever it is that you want.

Client: Ok. I know. It popped into my head right away. I'm thinking of a sandwich with a big piece of lettuce and some tomato, with some kind of meat in it, like turkey or roast beef or something like that and it's on whole wheat bread.

Connirae: Okay great. Now imagine eating that, even if you don't have it available. I just want to teach you how to use the strategy. We're doing this so that your unconscious mind can get really clear about what kinds of foods you want and when you want to eat them.

Now imagine eating a certain amount of the sandwich. What kind of meat is it?

Client: Turkey.

Connirae: Okay, imagine eating a certain amount of the turkey sandwich with the lettuce and tomato on whole wheat bread. Let yourself taste it, feel it in your mouth, feel the sensation of taking a bite and continuing to chew it until it goes down your throat... Notice how that feels in your stomach. Notice the sensation in your stomach and in your body over time... Imagine what it would be like over the next several hours in your body... How does this leave you feeling?

Client: I don't know how to describe this. It feels like a pretty good feeling. I feel just kind of fine.

Connirae: Okay, great. And now let's check. This sensation that you're calling "fine," is this better or worse than the feeling you had before eating the turkey sandwich?

Client: It feels better.

Connirae: Now we can add one small refinement to fine-tune your food choice:

With your subconscious mind guiding you, get a sense of how you will feel over time if you don't eat anything. If you don't eat anything, how will you feel over the next few hours? …Now compare the feeling you get in your stomach and in your body if you imagine going forward in time without eating anything, to the feeling you get going forward in time if you do eat the turkey sandwich.

Which feels better to you?

Client: After eating the turkey sandwich, I feel a little more solid. I feel more clear in my thinking and the feeling in my stomach is just fine. It's kind of neutral. That's better than the feeling that I would get if I ate nothing. But I'm also feeling like I want to top off my meal with some M&Ms®. I really do deserve to have them. I've made such a great choice with the sandwich.

Connirae: Great! So let's continue and run this idea through the strategy. We'll find out if adding the M&Ms® makes you feel better or worse. We can get a little confused by telling ourselves that we "deserve" something if we don't actually check to see if it makes our lives and our experience better or worse.

Do you really "deserve" it if it makes you feel worse? What we really deserve is to have a good experience. We deserve to feel the best and to have the most pleasure. You'll find that as you practice this strategy in your daily life, the more you use it the less you will be thinking in terms of what food you "deserve" or judging your eating as "I did good—I chose the 'right' food." You'll just be tuning in to what makes your body feel better.

So imagine having eaten the turkey sandwich in the amount that you chose, and now imagine seeing yourself reaching for a certain amount of those M&Ms® and eating them. You can notice the taste of the M&Ms®, notice how they feel in your mouth. Feel them going down your throat and get a sense of how they would feel in your stomach if you ate them.

Now, as before, imagine that you are moving forward in time and no-ticing what it would feel like if you ate both the sandwich and the amount of M&Ms® that you chose. What would that feel like after one hour? And then imagine what it would feel like after several hours… Is this feeling bet-ter or worse than the feeling you had from just having the sandwich? What we are going for here is the maximum pleasure and satisfaction for you.

Rather than doing what you think you "should" do, or even what we think we "should" enjoy because we've told ourselves it's a treat, we are going for "What actually makes me feel the very best—What makes me feel over time the most nourished, satisfied, etc." So which sensation feels better to you? Is it more pleasurable to have the M&Ms® after the sandwich or not? Using your best guess, notice how your body would feel. If you're looking for more pleasure, which choice gives it to you?

Client: I know that the M&Ms® don't feel very good in my stomach, but I feel so sad that the meal is over. I just want to eat more. I don't feel full enough in a way that I feel good. My body's full, but something else is missing.

Comforting Your Inner Crying Child

In the role-played example above, like so many of us can understand, the woman learning the process finds it painful to conceive of a meal as ending. She wants to keep eating despite having an image in her mind's eye of not feeling better after eating the food.

This is very common—many of my clients say this, and it was something that I struggled with before I spoke with Connirae. My thoughts were that following this strategy was too much like dieting. Also, in my scenario I wanted to eat a side of chips with my sandwich and top it off with some M&Ms®.

Connirae assured me that you can eat what you want following this strategy. It may seem like dieting, but it's not because the choice is always yours. The difference that discriminates between satisfying your body and overeating is when you eat past the point of fullness. For me that was a huge challenge since I had never been able to listen to my body's subtle signals of satisfaction.

In times like this, Connirae encourages us to turn inward to discover what we are really craving. If we recognize that eating would make us feel worse, yet we still want to eat, what are we really craving? When you turn inward and welcome that feeling, just notice what is there. When I did this, I found an inner crying child—a little girl who feels sad that the meal is over. And I found that many of my clients have a crying inner child also.

In Connirae's experience, most of us have younger "selves" or "parts" that want to be satisfied. This is natural because for most of us the world doesn't happen to satisfy all our wants. Çonnirae shared that when she was born the doctor told her mother that she shouldn't try to breast feed because she wouldn't be able to supply enough milk for her baby. Connirae said, "It always takes a few days after giving birth for a mother's milk to come in. This is natural, and I think it is Mother Nature's way of giving the infant several days to get accustomed to being born before also adjusting to eating. A newborn baby is already learning to breathe air and use their lungs, and a lot of other changes happen at birth. So a little time before also learning to use the digestive system makes some sense.

"But given the doctor's warning, my Mom thought, 'The doctor must be right—I'm not making any milk. I don't want my baby to starve.' So I was bottle fed. And you can guess the results of this for me, and probably for a lot of babies who were born in that era. We got bottle milk instead of breast milk, but also the experience of feeding is a lot different. With nursing there is a feeling of intimate connection and closeness that is just not the same when you feed with a bottle. I breastfed my own children and experienced it from the other side. So sometimes when I've turned inward, I've found a 'crying child'—an infant who was craving not just the milk, but that feeling of connection and affection that comes with nursing.

"If *you* experience wanting food when you know you aren't hungry, you may find something similar or it may be quite different. Be open to discovering what is really there for you. Often we find a younger 'us' who wants some kind of nurturing. There are many ways to work with this. One of the simplest is finding a way to meet that need or want. The little 'me' may just want to be held and loved, and we can provide that in our imagination now. As the grown-up me, I can go back and sit with the child, hold her, love her, listen, or just be present with her. By doing this I meet the real need. More food will never do it. The craving for love or closeness or connection will still be there until we meet *that*."

Similar to Connirae, I have found that in the case of having feelings of wanting more, you can imagine going back and nurturing yourself, providing what may have been missing in your life. I've learned that this is also a good opportunity for tapping since that neutralizes the sad feeling of a meal coming to a close.

As I mentioned before, even if we binge or overeat, this is what Connirae calls having a compelling learning experience—it becomes a useful part of learning the new eating strategy.

When I shared with Connirae my challenge around beating up on my-self for overeating, she shared that she has also gone through experiences of overeating and binging. She recalled that when she and her husband were first together, he always brought ice cream home and ate it every night. She would have a taste and think it was pretty good! So then she would eat more of it. She would eat a regular serving of it, but still want more, so she just kept on eating. She said,

"I kind of knew that I was eating too much ice cream, and I probably wouldn't feel so good later on, but that experience wasn't very 'real' for me. So I just went ahead and overate the ice cream in order to really get the experience of what a lot of ice cream felt like in my body over time. The next day, sure enough, I felt groggy and not very good. I really noticed this and after doing it several times ice cream just didn't have much appeal. I sometimes ate a small amount, but it was 'real' for me that if I ate more I would be getting less pleasure, not more."

Juicy Woman Note:

In the quote above, Connirae describes what she calls a compelling learning experience. Your body will automatically recognize how it feels after one or several of these episodes. You'll notice that after you get that in your bones, you won't be as likely to choose the same food in the same amount again.

If you do, and it feels awful, it's a signal that for whatever reason you are not connecting with your body and are ignoring the pain sensations. This is a great opportunity to seek out the awareness that tapping can provide.

Stumbling Blocks and Obstacles
Preventing You From Tuning Into Your Body

As mentioned before throughout this book, if you're struggling with knowing when to stop eating, it is because a part of you has shut down so that you no longer naturally do what feels the kindest to your body. This is often the result of some type of traumatic pain from the past that keeps you feeling unsafe and disconnected from your body.

In Connirae's book, *Heart of the Mind: Engaging Your Inner Power to Change with Neuro Linguistic Programming*, she says, "People sometimes overeat when they are unhappy or stressed, because it's a simple way to have some dependable pleasure in life. Dealing with the unhappiness or reducing stress will often remove the need to overeat, and many of the methods described in this book can be utilized for this.

"Some people don't have a good way to respond to sexual advances; being unattractively overweight can be an effective way to avoid such situations. When such a person learns how to respond comfortably to flirting, and how to say "No" firmly when necessary, the need to be overweight vanishes."

The example above only represents one possibility or aspect explaining why a woman may feel the need to remain overweight. You'll most likely know what your reasons are. At the core, Connirae is reinforcing the importance of dealing with your stress no matter what the source and taking back control of your life. Remember: Dealing with your stress must be the first priority if you want to make peace with food and love your body.

Choose Foods To Nourish Yourself and
Show Kindness To Your Body

Throughout our discussion, Connirae stressed the importance of choosing foods that "kiss your being." I encourage you to visualize your food choice as a loving mother and you as the infant child seeking nourishment.

Connirae said that the thing she considers most important when she is eating as a slender woman, is to seek nourishment from her food and to be kind to herself.

This means making choices and wanting to eat foods that make your body feel satisfied and happy. These are typically foods that create a good feeling in your body. She encourages her clients to choose food holding an image of tucking a child in at night and sending them off to sleep with a loving kiss. These are the foods that give her a nice light hum. As a personal preference, she enjoys eating foods that are organic and high quality.

Here are some examples of favorite ways that she considers being good to herself. Living in Colorado, it is often cold. When she's cold she feels it is especially nurturing to enjoy a big bowl of chicken soup chock full of vegetables. In the summer, she prefers to eat foods that would naturally cool her body such as salads and cooler treats like fruit and yogurt.

Choose Foods That "Kiss Your Being"

According to Connirae, foods that kiss your being are those that will be gentle and assimilate into your system effortlessly with no irritation or pain. They glide down your throat and settle in your body and warm your insides and fuel you throughout the day.

For her, this means choosing foods that feel good in her body, not only for the moment but as they settle over time. For example, when she considers what she wants to eat, she takes a number of factors into account. She monitors her hunger level, what type of texture or taste would be pleasing to her and what food would give her the energy that she desires for the tasks ahead in the coming hours.

What would that feel like to you? Can you visualize making a choice of what you want to eat using the criteria of looking for food that kisses your being? What kinds of foods feel good in your body in the moment you eat them and over time?

My Experience Using the Strategy

I've been using Connirae's strategy for several years now. It has truly enhanced my appreciation of the food that I eat. Using her guidelines for choosing foods that kiss my being, I continually see myself as a woman deserving of being more gentle, loving, respectful, and compassionate with myself. This enhances my continuously growing confident self-image. I also reinforce this positive image in my daily visualizations.

When I was learning how to eat intuitively, I didn't realize that my inclination and desire to eat foods that ended up making my body feel terrible was actually being unkind to me. It was downright abusive. I hadn't considered the implications of that before.

Since I've been using EFT to deal with my own screaming meanie negative self-talk, I've successfully been able to remove and neutralize the many negative influences that pushed me to eat foods that made my body feel bad. Now that I know that I can have potato chips and nobody is going to walk in and threaten me or put me down, I usually choose not to have them because they are often too salty for my taste even if they are the low salt variety.

In keeping with the foundation of Connirae's process, I've become a relentless pleasure seeker. This no longer means eating food that makes me sick. Now I often choose to do my own baking and cooking, because the foods I make are those that give me the greatest pleasure. I can also control the flavors and textures and get the recipe exactly the way I want it.

On occasion I'll still overeat and indulge in foods that are not entirely "kissing my being," but I do so with a much greater awareness of the consequences that will ensue from making those renegade choices. For the most part, it's become extremely distasteful to me to have a full, overstuffed feeling in my stomach. Now I notice that I have to be pretty careful about what I choose to eat, because my stomach gets full so quickly.

The other night my daughter made some sugar cookies. At the time they did not really capture my attention. However, in the morning when I woke up, they were the first thing I saw on the counter. From doing the strategy before I walked downstairs to the kitchen, my body was really looking forward to eating a couple of lightly scrambled eggs and a buttered English muffin, but I was feeling lazy. I saw the cookies on the counter and my plan went out the window. I lifted the lid and removed one of them from the cookie plate and took a bite. I decided that I didn't want to cook and that I wanted the cookies.

After taking a moment to do the strategy with this new image of the cookies to determine how many of them I wanted and how they would feel in my body, I made the choice to eat them. After having three of them with some soy milk, I felt unfulfilled and went to the fridge looking for something else.

My daughter, Cara, was eating pasta. It looked so good. By this time, since I was already aware of being pretty full from the cookies, I knew that if I also ate the pasta I would be doing emotional eating. I said to Cara, "Wow, it looks like I'm wanting to do some emotional eating now." She asked me, what's the emotion? I realized what it was and said, "It's uncertainty. I am doubting a choice that I have made." Just recognizing my emotion and what it was, I found that the emotion no longer had an unconscious hold on me. Now I wanted to eat what was right for my body.

Considering the new information I had at my fingertips, I went to the fridge and portioned out the amount of pasta I thought I wanted and put it on the stove to heat up. Then I looked at the huge pile of pasta and noticed feeling a little queasy. I decided to take a very small taste and see if I even liked it.

That first bite told me without question that I definitely didn't want it. It was over-salted and tasted terrible. That put the brakes on that meal. I realized that I didn't want to endure eating that pasta and feeling sick later.

Using Connirae's example of having a food fantasy has become pleasurable to me. By applying her guidelines for taking care of my body, I have little tolerance for doing things that don't make me feel good and happy over the long haul.

As I mentioned before, I've found it very effective to simply state out loud the fact that I am choosing to overeat and recognizing when I am wanting to eat for emotional reasons. I find that within a few minutes of making that statement the food no longer holds the same appeal as it did when I was eating in a state of oblivion. Eating it suddenly becomes a choice rather than an obsession.

The only tweak I would add to Connirae's strategy is to imagine how something smells before you eat it. I've become very sensitized to getting pleasure from food based on its aroma. Oftentimes if I imagine something to smell a certain way, and when I eat it and it doesn't smell appealing, I won't eat it.

My Favorite Fun Food Fantasy

One of my favorite ways of applying Connirae's Naturally Slender Eating Strategy is to have what I like to call a fun food fantasy. This is pleasurable to me because many of the foods I used to love I no longer enjoy the same way. My tastes have changed and since those foods are no longer forbidden, they have lost much of their allure. But they still have wonderful memories connected to them. Mostly many of the sweet junk foods that I used to crave remind me of the wonderful homemade favorites that my Nana and I used to whip up together.

For example I used to love the goodies at Dunkin' Donuts®. But now they're way too sweet. I still love their texture but not usually the taste. So now when my husband and daughter go to Dunkin' Donuts® to buy donuts for the family, my real pleasure comes from asking Cara to tell me over the phone the types of donuts they have in the store. As she mentions each flavor, in a split second I am able to imagine the taste and scent of it, exactly the way I want it or the way Nana would have made it. By doing that, I can revel in the fantasy of eating something that I truly enjoy.

On the rare occasion when one or a couple of those flavors entices my taste buds, I'll ask Cara to get it for me. I'll then take a bite and decide if I want to have more. If I like it and I'm hungry, I'll sit down, pour myself a glass of soy milk, and enjoy it. But if I'm not hungry I'll usually just stick the donut in the freezer for another time when I really want that kind of sweet taste.

Unfortunately, it's rare that the actual taste of the donut will match up with my food fantasy memory so I usually don't venture further than that first bite because it's just not that great!

I haven't yet figured out how to deal with the frustration of not getting to eat donuts exactly the way I want them, but I will. My thought is that I might one day make homemade donuts or apple fritters like my Nana and I used to make. We'll see.

I'd like to share a quick story so that you can get an idea of how different a positive, nourishing food fantasy is vs. a destructive food fantasy of wanting something and not being able to eat it.

My "Oh I Wish I Could Eat It!" Food Fantasy

One year for Christmas, I bought my friend, Lucy, and I tickets to see a Broadway show. Elton John's *Aida*. We had it all planned out. This was going to be our special girl's day out, no kids, and no husbands, just us gals.

As we left Lucy's house, laughing and talking, we scuttled down the street making our way toward the subway. We stopped dead in our tracks when we reached a local bakery shop window. At the time both of us were on a low carb diet, so eating baked goods was out of the question, a real no-no.

But we came prepared. To satisfy our cravings for something sweet, we had a bunch of sugar free chocolate peanut butter bars that we had bought earlier that week in preparation to eat at the theatre. That night we planned on eating dinner out and enjoying some fabulous prime rib.

But once we stood at that bakery window, looking at all those goodies, we were like a pair of giddy school girls. You should have seen it. The display was to die for; positively magnificent. The case was filled with wonderful rich, fruity, nutty, and cheese filled pastries, strawberry shortcakes, petit fours, custard tarts, fruit pies and cream pies, and mounds of fresh cookies. Everything in sight was all so beautifully arranged with the intention of pulling people just like us into the store.

There we stood, side by side with our mouths salivating and our eyes glued to the window, lusting hungrily after all the goodies we saw. I turned to Lucy and she turned to me and we squealed with nervous laughter.

We knew that we couldn't eat anything there and still stay on our diets, but we decided to go in any way. When the woman at the counter asked us what we wanted, we both laughed and said in unison, "No thanks, we're just looking." We left laughing hysterically because it all sounded so silly and dramatic. But deep down we felt a bit deprived, wishing that we could have felt free enough to have eaten what we wanted. Instead, we settled for those nasty sugar free chocolate bars that made us both sick to our stomachs which ultimately ruined the enjoyment of our dinner.

Looking back on it now, I know the experience that I had with Lucy was a fantasy based on feeling deprived, rather than wanting to extract maximum pleasure from imagining enjoying the taste of a food you may not want to actually eat. The fantasy experience that Connirae encourages is strictly based on seeking pleasure, rather than feeling deprived.

The core difference is that while on diets, Lucy and I knew that we couldn't or shouldn't eat what we wished we could. Connirae's strategy gives you all the information your body needs to decide if you really want to eat the foods you think you do.

I have become a freshness freak, always tossing out or refusing to eat anything that tastes the least bit stale. That's why I don't like packaged foods anymore. My ability to taste is so heightened from using this strategy that I rarely eat food that I don't make myself. It's a good thing I love to cook.

My tastes are simple. I love to create or choose foods based on how my Nana and I used to eat when we were together.

Try It! – Fantasy Eating

Go into a grocery store, bakery, or restaurant and choose a food that looks good to you. Imagine what it would taste like and how it would feel in your mouth. Imagine what texture it would have. Would it be soft and chewy or hard and crisp? Take the Mindful and Gentle Eating exercise on page 80, and apply that to your imaginary food. Notice the quality of your experience. Then you may either choose to actually eat the food or not, comparing the differences between what you expected/imagined and the reality of the taste sensation.

Similar to Connirae's preferences, I've returned back to my food roots. I love making my own food. I especially enjoy chicken noodle soup, either Spanish style or like Rosie used to make, Jewish style with matzo balls and noodles.

I'm nuts about my husband's rice and beans and barbecued chicken with a side of avocado. I love pan sautéed fish, especially turbot, tilapia, flounder, and catfish. I also enjoy roasting salmon in the oven along with a side of roasted onions, garlic, and tomatoes.

I like salads with croutons, and sandwiches are a huge favorite with me since I never felt that I could eat them while dieting. I also enjoy pasta, baked potatoes, and sautéed veggies in real olive oil. Nuts or pretzels are favorite on-the-run foods for me. For a special sweet treat, I'll often make fresh muffins or quick breads, choosing them over brownies or cakes.

When I do the strategy and notice there is nothing that I really want to eat, I'll choose nothing and have no problem with feeling hungry. I like knowing that I can play with my hunger and don't necessarily have to eat at the first sign of it. As I become involved in doing something I love, I often forget all about wanting to eat.

Another thing I've discovered is that I derive much more pleasure out of the act of preparing or imagining preparing some foods versus actually eating them. I guess that explains why I've been such a diehard fan of Food Network® TV since it first began. For me, food has been and perhaps always will be a source of enormous pleasure. Time in the kitchen really gives me a wonderful sense of belonging and being loved, remembering my time with Nana.

I revel in the experience of finely mincing a clove of garlic, watching the knife as it mills across bits of onions, and smelling the wonderful aromas of good food cooking. Unlike my old way of thinking about food, eating is a much smaller part of the overall enjoyment of my relationship with food.

Now I suppose you could say that although I eat much less than I ever did, I enjoy my food with the same quality of a Sony Imax theatre. It's larger than life. I never knew that food could taste so good and I could be so picky. I can't wait for you to try Connirae's strategy and experience this pleasure seeking adventure of total unrestricted food freedom yourself.

Try It! – One More Bite: Name That Feeling

When you are feeling as though your body has taken over and you're eating on auto pilot, take a moment and notice how your body responds differently to each next bite of food.

Using Connirae's strategy as your guideline, imagine choosing a certain amount of a food. Now imagine seeing the amount of food that you want to eat. Then eat that amount. As you approach the portion that you originally intended to eat, notice how your desire for the food changes. With each subsequent bite of the food, ask yourself these questions:

How does this taste?

What am I feeling?

Check in with your taste sensors, your body, and your emotions to find the answers to these questions. Notice how with your new awareness, your tastes begin to change. If you feel inclined to journal, then write down your findings and feelings.

Summary of The Naturally Slender Eating Strategy

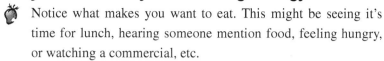 Notice what makes you want to eat. This might be seeing it's time for lunch, hearing someone mention food, feeling hungry, or watching a commercial, etc.

Check in with your stomach and notice how it feels now.

Ask yourself, "What would feel good in my stomach?"

Visualize a portion of a certain food: a sandwich, burrito, bowl of soup, piece of cake, etc.

Imagine eating that portion of food. Think of the taste and get a sense of how it would feel slipping down your throat and into your stomach. Get a feeling of how this amount of food would feel in your stomach over time if you ate it now.

Compare how you feel now with your stomach versus how you would feel if you ate the food you are considering. Decide which feels better to you. If it feels better to eat that food, consider it as a possibility and continue to sort for more options if desired. If not, discard the possibility.

Next, visualize another food in a certain amount that you may want to eat.

Imagine tasting this second item, and notice how it feels as it goes down into your stomach and remains there in your system for several hours to come.

Compare and notice how you like that feeling. Ask yourself, "Do I like it more than my best choice so far?" If you do, keep it. If not, move on, searching for another option.

Repeat steps 7, 8, and 9 as often as you choose, until you find a food or combination of foods that suit your needs. Keep in mind the kind of food you imagine and how it makes your body feel over time. Compare each new possibility to that imagined feeling.

When you're satisfied that you have exhausted your options and chosen what you want—the food that will make you feel best over time—enjoy eating it!

Wrapping Up
Chapter 8: Love Your Body – Respect Your Boundaries:
Care Enough to Set the Very Best

Here are the juiciest bits covered in this section. Savor them mindfully.

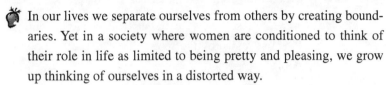 In our lives we separate ourselves from others by creating boundaries. Yet in a society where women are conditioned to think of their role in life as limited to being pretty and pleasing, we grow up thinking of ourselves in a distorted way.

A belief is a feeling of certainty about the meaning of something in your life. Everyone has a set of personal values. Beliefs rise up from what we value. Our values are emotional states that we have learned to think of as important.

Beliefs have no power unless you accept them as true. This is because you give meaning to what you believe. You can either choose to believe something as true or not.

If getting other people's approval is very important to you, then you'll have a challenging time setting boundaries. This whole book is intended to gear you toward listening to your own inner wisdom and recognizing that you have all the answers you need. Your answers are not outside of you, they are inside.

Your ability to set boundaries tells the world how you think about the person you are. It makes a statement about how much you respect yourself, your time, your values and your body. By making it clear to others that your feelings and needs are important, people will learn to respect you.

Many people who abuse food have become so accustomed to knuckling under to the wishes and demands of others that they don't feel safe asserting themselves for fear of not being loved.

Many women have wonderful lives and people surrounding them, but because they are fraught with fear and negative memories from the past, they are unable to accept and appreciate their good fortune.

353

- When you have something wonderful to focus on or look forward to, you become a happier person and your life becomes richer.

- It's just as dicey to put up a wall as it is to leave yourself wide open. It's best to avoid extremes when setting limits.

- Jack Canfield says, "The core message of a person with high self-esteem is represented by the acronym, "I.A.L.A.C." I am lovable and capable."

- The next time you overeat ask yourself the following questions: What's happening? How am I feeling? How have I overcommitted myself? You'll switch from blaming mode to being more compassionate. When you are feeling as though your body has taken over and you're eating on auto pilot, take a moment and notice how your body responds differently to each next bite of food.

- Remember it's not what people say about you that counts, it's what you say to yourself that really matters. You can either re-parent yourself and do things to make you feel special and loving toward yourself now, as you are, or you can remain miserable. The choice is up to you.

Chapter 9
Act to Attract: Be SMART, Mind Your Mouth, Watch Your Tongue, and Get it Done

"Make it so today is not like yesterday and
tomorrow will be different forever."
– *Anthony Robbins*

Up until now, you've been overeating because there are parts of your life that are not working; the gears are not turning and things are not going smoothly. You could be tootling along in every other area in your life, but in at least one nook or cranny you're stalled, hopelessly deadlocked, completely uncertain, and frustrated, not knowing what to do. What is required is action, not another Twinkie® and definitely not pointing a finger of blame at you or anyone else. That will only strip you of your power and put it in the hands of someone else.

As you practice eating mindfully and become more comfortable with food, you'll notice that you won't always default back to using food for comfort. But you may still find other ways of putting off doing what you want to do.

This is because changing your relationship with food is only the first frontier that you will need to conquer. In order to become curvy and confident at any size, you must change the way you think. Your words are the building blocks of your actions. Without first changing your internal self-talk, every step you take in an effort to change old habits will be like trudging through a mound of quicksand.

Self-sabotage is the resistance that hits all of us when we face our fears. If you've ever wanted something so much but couldn't find yourself making headway to get it, or couldn't make yourself do whatever was necessary to follow through, you were facing a fear. This is when it seems like you are going one step forward and three steps back. Are any of these situations familiar to you?

 From out of the blue you're hit by a wave of exhaustion and it becomes impossible to keep your eyes open. Although you felt wide awake a moment ago, all of a sudden you feel totally wiped out.

 All of a sudden you're starving. It seems like you have to stop whatever you're doing right now and get something to eat immediately because you feel so famished.

 You've drawn a blank. Despite the fact that you had a ton of fabulous ideas a moment ago, now you can't think of anything.

 You feel an overwhelming desire to procrastinate. Feeling certain that you have plenty of time, you decide to put off 'til tomorrow what you were planning to do today.

 You experience a sudden sense of being overwhelmed. All of a sudden you feel like there are so many things that you must have or do right now before you can complete the task at hand.

 You feel a compelling urge to give it all up. All of a sudden you've completely lost interest in your goal, and you just don't give a damn.

 A huge case of self-doubt hits you right between the eyes. You're left asking, "What was I thinking? I can't do this. Everybody else is better than me. Who do I think I am anyway? Why bother?"

When fear strikes you, either hitting you square in the face or masquerading as any of the above clever disguises, it's understandable that you would want to give up and take the path of least resistance which might mean running to food to soothe your frustrations.

But the truth is unless you deal with those fears and achieve what your heart dreams of doing, you won't ever be able to get out of the loop of using food to comfort you. In order to change the current state of your body, you have to get used to doing things differently. If, like me, you've decided that diets and deprivation aren't the way to go, that you want more food, freedom, and greater self-acceptance, then the path to change your relationship with food is to go back to the root of the problem: your thoughts. You must change your thinking.

As I've mentioned before, it's not the fat on your body that's the problem, it's the fat in your head. Bearing in mind that your main goal is to change the way you think, that will have a ripple effect on your decision making process and you'll find yourself doing things differently naturally. Ah, effortless weight control, what could be better than that?

Remember there are only three things over which you have direct control in your life:

1. You can change your thoughts
2. You can change the pictures in your head
3. You can change your actions

When you change your breathing, your body language, and the way you speak, you will change the way you think. This will change the pictures in your head and that will change your actions. This is because emotion is created by motion. Everything you feel is a result of what is happening in your body. When you don't like the way you're feeling, change what your body is doing. This is called changing your physiology.

The reason I am devoting this chapter to teaching you how and why you will benefit by changing your language patterns, is so you will create new associations in your body and therefore feel good more often. Certain words just make you feel weak and sad and strip you of all your power. To reclaim what is rightfully yours, I want to guide you to using your body and your words in a way that will make you feel good and radiate confidence.

In this section I'm going to give you a great deal of information including rules and suggestions for ways of speaking and expressing yourself going forward. They may not all agree with you. That's why I want you to have the final say, because you know what's best for you. Awareness is key.

Read through my suggestions and models, and then run them by the wisdom of your heart and body. If you cringe or feel uncomfortable in any way, then your body is telling you that something is not right. Pay attention and listen to that wisdom. Now let's begin with an explanation of how your language affects your body.

Know that the antidote to fear is taking action. You put yourself into the right frame of mind for taking action and stepping out into the world by the words you use to talk to yourself. To create effortless change, you've got to start by changing your negative limiting self-talk to positive possibility-oriented self-talk.

"Cancel, Cancel" Your Activation Key to Change Your Thoughts and Shift Your Behaviors

Research shows that we have over 50,000 thoughts a day. That comes down to about one thought for every second of every day. Many of these thoughts are beliefs and false assumptions. They are the diet and fat myths and negative self-limiting thoughts that are keeping you caught up in an endless loop of food and weight obsession. To interrupt the pattern and break the cycle, you have to first become aware that there is a tendency to think negatively.

Unless you have a system to become aware of and control your negative and disempowering self-talk, the inner critic drill sergeant in your brain will stomp all over your self-confidence, making you feel miserable, frustrated, good for nothing, out of control, dragging your self-esteem and body image through the mud.

Some people wear a rubber band around their wrist and pull it just enough to make it snap back and cause a bit of pain each time they become aware of a negative thought. This is what they need to remind themselves to pay attention. This is called negative reinforcement.

Since I'm not wild about pain, I'd like to share something else that has worked for me many times in the past to become aware of my own negative patterns.

I recommend that you use an activating word to make you aware of what's going on that will tell your brain to take a pause and review your thoughts. It's similar to what you learned in a previous chapter called the Z Point Process™.

Consider using one of the old standby phrases: "cancel, cancel." You can choose something else, just make sure it is a word that will remind you to stop and think. I'm going to follow through with my example by using "cancel, cancel." It's the phrase I learned when I was eleven years old and I did my first Silva Mind Control™ training. It's stuck with me.

From this point forward, I suggest that each time you notice that you've fallen into the rut of negative thinking, repeat the words, "cancel, cancel." This will give you a new opportunity to stop, take a breath, exhale, and then think about what you really mean. Then you can restate whatever it is you want to say. The words "cancel, cancel" will make you aware that whatever has been said before needs to be rephrased. It's like hitting the delete key on your computer. Since we can't actually delete what we're thinking, becoming aware and changing the pattern is the next best thing.

Let's take a closer look behind the source of some of the language that isn't serving you.

Stomp Those ANTS

Daniel G. Amen, MD, is a physician, child and adult psychiatrist, brain imaging specialist, bestselling author, Distinguished Fellow of the American Psychiatric Association, and the CEO and medical director of Amen Clinics, Inc. (ACI) in Newport Beach and Fairfield, California, Tacoma, Washington, and Reston, Virginia.

As an expert in all matters of the brain, he has named the limiting thoughts we hear in our head ANTS—short for Automatic Negative Thoughts. Dr. Amen says that just like real ants at a picnic, your ANTS can ruin your experience of life. To prevent that from happening you've got to stomp down those suckers and show them who's boss!

To get control of your ANTS, you first have to become aware of them. Then you are able to shake them off and stomp them by challenging them. Finally you have to replace them with positive and affirming thoughts.

> Don't believe everything you hear – even in your own mind.
> – *Daniel G. Amen, M.D.*

Quick Tips for Stomping out Your ANTS

Know that you're in charge – You decide what your thoughts mean and you determine what you want to do about them. Just because you're thinking or hearing something in your mind, doesn't mean that it's necessarily true. You can choose to listen to, agree to, or discard any of your thoughts.

Question your ANTS – Whenever you notice yourself thinking crazy thoughts, question them by talking back to them. Pay attention to whether your thoughts make you feel better about yourself or worse. Are they critical, angry, helpful or hurtful? Are they firing you up and moving you closer to what you want or further away? Are they lighting your fire or scaring the pants off of you?

Write them down: Keep a Journal– Doug Bench is the author of *The Mastery of Advanced Achievement Home Study Course*. He recommends becoming more aware of your negative self-talk by writing down what you're thinking over the course of three days. Make sure that two of those days are workdays and one is a weekend day.

Keep Yourself Accountable – Enlist your family's help and ask them to help you become more aware of your negative thoughts. Make it a game for everyone to fine you a dollar each time they catch you saying something nasty or sarcastic. Remember to include body bashing, name calling, and any victim-y, poor me statements that come out of your mouth.

Put Your Money Where Your ANTS Are – Ask your family, friends, children, and colleagues to help you become more aware of your negative thoughts. Each time they hear you say something negative or utter a pessimistic remark they get to fine you a dollar. Remember to include all body bashing, name calling, and any and all statements that are blaming, justifying, and self-negating.

I realize this may seem tough at first because of the size of this task, but break it down into manageable bits. Pretty soon you'll get good at catching those ANTS before they even get a chance to slip past your lips. In the following sections, I'll describe several other examples of ANTS that keep you playing the victim game, and I'll tell you how to stomp them.

Changing Your Victim Language

In her book, *How to Stop Playing the Weighting Game: A Step by Step Workbook to Help You Succeed in Losing and Maintaining Weight,* author Gloria Arenson talks about the importance of taking back your power by becoming aware of your victim language.

Whether you realize it or not, you're either playing the part of the victim or the rescuer. Victims fear change and in an attempt to maintain the status quo, they often fall into disempowering habits. You can recognize yourself as acting like a victim by the words you say and the tune you play. Most victims use the phrase, "If only..." See which of these *if only's* ring some bells for you. You can remove their curse and become aware of their ability to render you helpless by repeating your activating word or "cancel, cancel"

- If only my husband didn't bring home the cheesecake (cancel, cancel)
- If only I hadn't lost my job (cancel, cancel)
- If only the kids would leave me alone (cancel, cancel)
- If only I could pay my bills (cancel, cancel)

If only... strips you of the power to take responsibility and puts it out of your reach. This means that you are not really in control of your own actions and how scary is that? When you break it all down, you'll see that these are all sad excuses for making the choice to eat or overeat. Changing your language is the first step to believing that you can choose to change your actions. It's all in you!

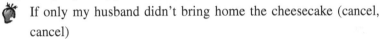

Juicy Woman Note:

For every victim, there must be a rescuer. For years, I made Weight Watchers® my big rescuer. I used those meetings like an addict would use a drug. During the weeks when I was having the toughest time, I would attend a meeting every day. It got to the point that I believed that I couldn't get thinner without the benefit of attending those meetings. Then when I decided I didn't want to continue to rely on going to those meetings, I transferred the responsibility for my weight loss onto my personal trainer.

The rescuer often takes the form of a doctor, a weight loss club, a medical clinic, or even a minister. Although these are professionals that may actually be able to help the person with their weight issues, the problem occurs when the individual loses sight of their own power and believes that the rescuer is the one responsible for making them thin. You are responsible for the condition of your body, nobody else!

Are you Catastrophizing?

Have you ever worried yourself into a frazzle? I sure have. All it takes is one small thought that gets fed and it grows bigger and bigger and bigger until you're ready to explode.

We tend to scare ourselves into believing things that aren't true and making ourselves out to be helpless when we're not. Catastrophizing is a natural tendency we all have to imagine the very worst happening in any situation.

We can diffuse the fear bomb by getting more specific and drilling down to focus on what really scares us.

Several years ago I attended Jack Canfield's *Living Your Highest Vision* seminar. One of the exercises we did as a group was to pick apart and explore our fears. For the first time ever, I realized that I was usually the one standing in my own way by spinning my catastrophic imagery.

Jack Canfield's Fear Busting Template

Here's an example inspired by the fill in the blank technique we used:

Rather than making a blanket statement saying "I hate my husband," get specific and dig another layer deeper to find out why. For example, "I hate it when my husband comes home late without calling to let me know."

Keep digging deeper.

In addition to understanding more about what scares you, expand your thinking even more to include an action step that you can take to overcome your fear. Jack provided this following template:

"I'd really like to _____, and I scare myself by imagining _____(what would happen) _____ if I did

Now your imagined fears get translated into action steps, things that you can do. For example, "I'm afraid to ask my husband to call me when he knows he'll be late," transforms into the following:

"I'd really like to <u>ask my husband to call me and reassure me of his love</u> and I scare myself by imagining <u>that if he is late, it means he's having an affair because he probably doesn't really love me after all, so he would automatically brush me off if I asked him to call me and tell me he loves me</u> if I did <u>ask him for the reassurance I seek.</u>

Here's another example. Rather than saying, "I'm afraid to sell my handmade lampshades," get more clear and define what specifically makes you fearful of selling your handmade lampshades. Here's a clarification that really changes the way things look.

"I'd really like <u>to sell my handmade lampshades</u>, and I scare myself by imagining <u>that nobody would recognize their value and be willing to pay for them</u> if I did <u>sell them.</u>

To paraphrase Eleanor Roosevelt "Nobody can make you feel bad without your consent."

When you get right down to the nitty gritty, we are the ones creating the illusions in our mind. We are the ones who frustrate ourselves, scare ourselves, depress ourselves, and confuse, trap, and overwhelm ourselves. Because you give meaning to everything you think, you have the power to change how you think and what you feel by the words you use to describe your thoughts. How many times have you used the following victim language?

- I'm scared
- I'm trapped
- I'm depressed
- I'm overwhelmed
- I'm confused
- I'm frustrated

Rather than saying the above sentences which make you feel awful, helpless, and hopeless, let's get clearer about what is really going on and further define the problem.

I'm scared really means – I am scaring myself by imagining.

I'm trapped really means – I am standing in my own way, trapping myself by believing things that are not true which keep me paralyzed with fear and terrified of taking action.

I'm depressed really means – I am depressing myself by holding my feelings in and refusing to express my anger or sadness about something in my life.

I'm overwhelmed really means – I am overwhelming myself by refusing to say "No," by not setting priorities, by not making decisions, and by refusing to take action in my life.

I'm confused really means – I am confusing myself because I have more than one belief about myself or someone or something in my life. One is how I, or things should be, another is how I really am, and the third is how I wish I, or things could be.

I'm frustrated really means – I am frustrated because I believe that people, things, or I should be different from what already is. I refuse to accept what is.

By learning how to change and flip around your language, you will reclaim much of the power you have let slip away. Remember, it's up to you to re-parent yourself and retrain your brain to think and believe in yourself, feeling safe and comfortable around food and at ease lovin' the skin you're in. Those big changes all begin with knowing what to say to yourself.

There are several soul crushing phrases we all learn as children. Below, I've taken each of them and decoded them by giving you a brief explanation of what they mean. Then I offer you an alternative phrase you can use that puts the power back in your corner.

I Can't – A great place to use your activating word or "Cancel, cancel

I can't is a phrase that screams, "I'm helpless." It implies that although you wish you could do something, you know you're not capable of accomplishing it. Think about that big elephant that you see at the circus who is trained as a baby calf to stay put by placing a thin chain attached to a stake in the ground around his ankle.

In reality this massive animal is being held captive by his own limiting belief that he is not strong enough to free himself. This is only a limiting belief because with one small tug on the chain he would instantly be freed.

Can't and won't have very different meanings. By using the word "can't," you're instructing your brain to think like that little elephant—cutting off and limiting your options. Without knowing it, you've cut off your right to choose and you've created a self-fulfilling prophecy believing that you are hopelessly and helplessly deadlocked, bound by your self-imposed limitations.

The word "can't" implies that you have no choice in the matter, and that something is stronger than you so you're not able to overcome the obstacle. Unless you're actually stuck because you're pinned under some heavy furniture and you physically *can't* move, the word "can't" will not serve you. The truth of the matter is, you know that you can do things, but you may not be willing to do them. The word "can't" will cut you off at the knees. Here are some examples of how it's often misused:

For the sake of simplicity, I'll give the examples only using the pronoun "I." Naturally they can also apply to "You" and any other pronoun, such as we, she, he, they, etc.

- I can't eat just a few potato chips
- I can't stop at having only one slice of pizza
- I can't seem to keep weight off
- I can't insult Nana by not eating the cake she made
- I can't charge for my services
- I can't ask my husband to help me with the dishes
- I can't say, "No"
- I can't do it

The next time you're tempted to use the dreaded "can't word, I challenge you to get to the bottom of your fears and break free of your resistance by digging around to find out how you really feel.

Ask yourself these questions:

"What's stopping me?" or "How do I stop myself? What makes me believe this? What's the real truth? What would happen if I felt more entitled or capable of being in charge? What would happen if I did..."

Now that you know that can't is victim-y language, the next time this nasty little creepy crawling ANT is about to crash the party, think for a moment and repeat the sentence by just substituting the word "won't." Notice how that changes the meaning of the sentence. It puts the responsibility right back on you. Now you are no longer a victim of anyone else's choices. Are you?

Observe how that makes you feel. I had a client who had this to say about tapping, "I can't even bring myself to tap on my resistance to change. Staying as I am feels so much safer." When I told her to change can't to won't, she realized that she actually did have a choice and that she was the only one who was standing in her way.

Don't – A great place to use your activating word or say, "Cancel, cancel."

If your language is filled with words like don't and can't, you're unknowingly setting yourself up to fail. This is because your brain works on the basis of making pictures and it is not capable of processing negative commands.

Let me give you an example that might hit home. While dieting or "watching your weight" in the past, you can probably put your finger on an incident when someone told you, "Don't eat those cookies." Because sweets may have been considered off limits before, they became that much more desirable. Then if you were told that you couldn't have something, you wanted it more. Didn't you? Here's why:

Automatically your brain made a picture of the thing you couldn't have and you found yourself craving it more than ever.

This is because in order to comprehend the meaning of the word "don't" in the sentence, your brain first had to make the picture of the cookies, which activated your desire for them.

Therefore, if you choose to avoid something and give yourself a new directive, rather than saying don't or can't, find a suitable alternative and state it in the positive. For example, let's say you want to eat fewer cookies because you notice that you've been binging on them each time you feel pressured.

The first thing you'll want to do is forgive yourself and move on. Next you'll deal with the source of the stress. Then once that is handled, your next response to addressing your negative self-talk and neutralizing your emotions around those cookies might be saying, "Cancel, cancel."

I can choose to eat fewer cookies…or I can choose to eat more cookies. It doesn't really matter.

Remember, it's the distortion in your energy system that causes you to think in wonky ways. The majority of your cravings will disappear when your stress is managed and you realize that you can eat what you want. From this point on, I want you to hold tight to your activating word and each time you become aware of a negative thought pattern repeat your activating word. At the risk of being a total pain, I'm going to keep on reminding you to do this each time I introduce another word or phrase that screams victim. Let's begin:

I Don't Know – A good place to pause and use your activating word or "Cancel, cancel"

This phrase, "I don't know" is actually top secret code for "I don't want to know and I don't really care."

Again, it's up to you to take back responsibility for your happiness and that means becoming much more aware of what's going on in your life. When you know what is happening around you, you are taking responsibility. Responsibility is having the ability to respond.

If you're stuck and can't get out of the mess you're in, it's natural that you'll be frustrated and unhappy. But as long as you say "I don't know," this absolves you of responsibility and you won't feel the need to change. When we say "I don't know" it means that we can continue to complain about the situations and people or things that we believe are preventing us from getting what we want, we feel completely justified thinking that the responsibility for our happiness is not even ours. Here are some common expressions:

 I don't know where to start.

 I don't know what happened to me.

 I don't know what to do.

In order to change, we have to be willing to find out what is needed to achieve our goals, otherwise we'll always remain in the same rut. First, you have to ask yourself the question, "Do I want to change?" If you decide that you do, then you have to be willing to do some digging and learn new things. You need to realize that if you want to be in charge of your life, then there are things you may not yet know how to do that you'll have to learn.

That means that you'll have to put yourself in a state of willingness to learn by telling yourself, "I want to know and I can find out." Remember, knowledge is only potential power. If/when you actually apply it, then it becomes real power.

Another example of when you might say, "I don't know" is when you don't want to hurt someone's feelings, or you fear their anger, rejection, or retaliation. "I don't know" is a great way of covering up, shirking responsibility, hiding your true feelings, and staying the nice guy. Saying "I don't know" in this situation is a dead giveaway telling you that you could use a little more confidence in saying "No" in your life. If that's the case, then Quick! turn to the section on Boundaries and Beliefs: When You Care Enough to Set the Very Best.

> ### Try It! – Stomping Down Your ANTS
> Pay attention to the words and language you're using this week. Are you catastrophizing and making mountains out of molehills? Are you exaggerating and creating a sense of overwhelm? Make note of how many times you say "I don't know" or "I can't" then decode what that means for you.

I'll Try – As soon as you hear yourself saying this, use your activating word or say, "Cancel, cancel"

Ah, this phrase is probably responsible for more broken commitments than anything else. This is what you say when you don't really intend on keeping a promise to yourself or someone else. To say "I'll try" doesn't mean that you will do it, it means that you're only willing to make an empty promise and fear backing it up with being more specific. It's kinda wimpy. Wouldn't you agree?

Know that when you say, "I'll try" it's code for I'm not willing to make any promises. If I succeed that's great, but if things go wrong don't blame me. "I never said I would do it." If you say, "I'll try" it screams that deep down you're planning to fail, and this is your escape hatch. Trying won't enable you to succeed, but you won't ever succeed unless you actually commit to doing whatever it is you plan to do.

Don't be afraid of making mistakes, that's all part of learning. It is okay to make mistakes. The important thing is to take responsibility for your decisions. Instead of saying "I'll try" say "I will!" or "I won't!" Both are powerful phrases that demonstrate it's you who's running the show.

SHOULD, HAVE TO, MUST, OUGHT, and more – all good opportunities to use your activating word or say, "Cancel, cancel"

OK, who's really in charge here? Is it you? Then why on earth would you ever want to use these dirty words? As long as you use these guilt tripping ANT phrases, you're deluding yourself into thinking that you're a puppet and somebody else is in charge of pulling your strings.

The words "should" and "have to" smack of gobs of guilt and shame. You can almost picture the fowl finger of fate going "Shame on you." As long as we're on the subject of what bubble bustin' joy suckers to avoid, you may as well lump "must," "have to," "better," and "ought" into the mix as well. All these words imply that somebody or something above you is dictating, in charge of, and judging your actions. Careful. Big Brother's watching.

In the example, "I should really stop eating now," what your words are actually saying is that despite having a desire to stop eating, you don't feel in control and therefore can't stop yourself from eating. You're saying, "I don't really want to eat out of control, but something outside of me is forcing my hand and making me want to eat more."

To get more clear about what is really going on when you find yourself saying "should" or "have to," ask yourself the following intervention question:

What would happen if I didn't?

In the case of "Have to," if you're like most people that phrase leaves a bad taste in your mouth. Who wants to "have to" do anything? For example, if you say, "I have to eat more healthy foods," you're saying that in order to be acceptable and considered good, you have to buckle under, respect, and comply with authority by changing what you're doing.

Who's in charge of making the rules for what you eat? Isn't it ultimately you? Maybe in the past you let others tell you what to eat, but not

now. The decision is now yours. Nobody else's. There are no more "have
to's," only "want to's."

To assert your newfound independence from now on, replace
"should" and "have to" with "want to" or "choose to." Ah! Doesn't that
feel so much better?

Try It! – Who's In Charge Around Here?

Think of a person or cartoon character with a whiny, annoying, sing-song, or monotonous voice that never fails to get under
your skin. You're searching for the voice of someone who embod-
ies your image of weakness and lack of certainty.

If nobody comes to mind, then think about times when you
felt pushed around, taken advantage of, and victimized. See if you
can remember what was going on inside your body. Did you feel
lethargic, exhausted, sapped of energy? Was your breathing shal-
low? Were your shoulders slumped, was your neck drooping and
your head hanging low? Or was your head so heavy that you needed to support it with one hand or both? Holding whatever pose you
remember, now imitate that tone and body language sounding as
victim-y and weak willed as possible. Now in that stance, repeat
all the sentences in my examples that follow:

I must ....always put other people first.

I can't ......eat just one.

I don't know ....what to do.

I have to ....do things her way.

I'll try ....and meditate each day.

I should ....really avoid all fats.

I better ....do everything perfectly.

I ought ....to be more assertive.

I want you to test it out by doing a comparison. Imagine that
you can just unzip yourself and step out of that victim-y persona
and instantly slip inside the shoes of someone who is supremely
confident, knows exactly what they want, and never hesitates to

ask for what they need. Someone whom you respect and admire. I'll choose my friend, Lucy.

Holding an image of that person in your mind, stand as they would stand, imagine breathing as they would breathe, and speak the way they would speak. Repeat each of the sample phrases above with the character quality of their voice filled with certainty, glowing confidence, and a sense of being in control. You're going to substitute each of the emboldened words with either one of the following: "I choose to..." or "I want to....."

Check and see how that makes you feel inside. Is there a difference? Do you feel more in charge? Do you feel better about yourself? If you do, isn't that lovely? Now each time you're tempted to use the old guilt tripping phrases and victim-y language, pause and breathe. After using your activating word or phrase like "cancel, cancel," restate your sentence using either the phrase, "I choose to..." or "I want to." Make a quick mental note of how this feels different in your body, and then unzip yourself from your confident self and slip back into the victim image that you created earlier and repeat the old guilt inducing phrases. Ask yourself, "Which feels better?"

I'll bet that it felt so much better knowing you can slip right into a confident self. The choice is yours. When you choose to do something because you want to and not because you feel pressured, you will be able to accept your actions without feeling guilty. Now you're in charge. Bingo! Keep on using the substitutions I've shared with you and watch your resistance melt away!

Always, Every, Never, Nobody, etc. (Generalizations) – Ding a ling a ling. These limiting patterns scream for the use of your activating word or mine "Cancel, cancel."

Using all-or-nothing thinking, you're probably used to making sweeping generalizations and thinking of things as either black or white, good or bad. In reality, there is very little in life that is either always or never. If you think something is always going to happen to you, or you'll never be able to get what you want, you may as well toss your hands up in despair and give up now.

If you use words like, always, never, everyone, no one, every time, and everything, you know you've fallen into the trap of all-or-nothing thinking. Since it's not useful or accurate to make these broad assumptions, you'll usually be wrong and it's not unusual to find yourself getting frustrated.

When you notice that you're slipping into bad habits using those slippery little suckers, replace them with what is really true. For example, rather than saying to your husband, "You never listen to me," replace that with "I get so angry when you don't listen to me, but I know you've been busy lately and you have a lot on your plate with all the stress that we've been under and whenever I really need you, you're there for me."

Note: For more examples of how to use this language pattern, go to the Boundaries section.

Here are several examples using each of the above generalizations, and questions that you can use to change your path from thinking about problems to possibilities.

"I <u>always</u> beat myself up after I've eaten too much."

Use these questions as an antidote to break the spell and get more clear:

 "Do you always beat yourself up when you eat too much?"

 "How has that been working out for you?"

 "Have you ever eaten too much and you didn't beat yourself up?"

 "What would happen if you stopped beating yourself up after each time you ate too much?"

"Men <u>always</u> lie."

 "Do men always lie?"

 "Does every man always lie?"

 "Have you ever met a man who was honest?"

 "What would happen if you were open to believing that men could be honest?"

"I <u>never</u> do anything right."

 "Have you ever done something right?"

"Unless you finish college, you'll <u>never</u> succeed."

🐦 "Succeed at what?"

"<u>Every</u> woman in the world is smarter, prettier, thinner than me."

🐦 "How true is it that every woman in the world is smarter, prettier, and thinner than you?"

"<u>Nobody</u> loves me."

🐦 "Nobody loves you?"

🐦 "Who specifically doesn't love you?"

Exaggerations – Another example of rampant thoughts gone wild. Use your activating word.

"I'll just die if I can't fit into that dress in time for the reunion."

🐦 "Will you really die if you can't fit into the dress in time for the reunion?"

"It just kills me when my husband criticizes me."

🐦 "Does it actually kill you when he does that?"

🐦 "What do you mean when you say, 'It just kills you?'"

Mind-reading – When you assume you know what someone else is thinking, it's time to get a quick reality check. Use your activation word to regroup and reground your thoughts.

You are mindreading when you presume to know what someone else is thinking even though they haven't told you. You'll know that you're mindreading when you think thoughts like, "My husband is ashamed of me because he thinks I'm too fat. He's going to hate me. She'll laugh at me if I tell her the truth about my fears." To sort out fantasy from reality, check out your assumptions and ask, ask, ask!

🐦 "How specifically do you know that?"

🐦 "How willing would you be to ask him if that's the truth?"

"He doesn't care about my feelings."

🐦 "How specifically do you know that he doesn't care about your feelings?"

"Everybody must be thinking I'm as fat as a house."

🐦 "How specifically do you know what everybody is thinking?"

🐦 (interjecting humor) "Wow! You can tell what everybody is thinking?"

🐦 "You must be a master at mindreading!"

Getting Specific (Deletions) – Ah, those words unspoken that could fill volumes of books. Tame those uncertainties and remind yourself to get clear by using your activation word.

By using the words, who, what, and how, you can get really specific and dig deeper to find the core of what's going on.

- I'm afraid. – What are you afraid of?
- This is painful. – What is painful?
- I am upset. - What is upsetting you?
- He's the best. - The best at what?
- She's the best writer. - She's the best writer among whom?

Note: We often are quick to make negative judgments about others without actually speaking about the people in question directly. Here are some examples:

"They are so stupid."
- "Who is stupid?"

"Women are smarter than men."
- "Which women are smarter than men?"

"That's not fair."
- "That's not fair to whom?"
- "That's not fair compared to what?"

Personalization – It's not personal, it just feels that way! – Say "Cancel, cancel" and pave your way to clarity.

This happens when you burden a neutral event with personal meaning. For example, he didn't call me because he doesn't like me, or she didn't return my email because she's ignoring me. The truth is there are plenty of reasons people do and don't do the things they do. For example, she may not have returned your email because she was out of town, or her computer may not have been online, or she was sick over the weekend. When in doubt, check it out!

Creating S.M.A.R.T. Goals

As tempting as it may be to believe that your overactive appetite is the result of lack of self-discipline around food, it's not. Your overeating is merely a distraction telling you there are aspects in your life that are keeping you unhappy. If you want to change the way you think and feel about yourself and effortlessly transform your relationship with food, the most effective method I've learned is to focus on doing more things for yourself that make you feel happy.

Most people gain an incredible amount of satisfaction by accomplishing goals. Once you find something that lights you up, your soul will continue to nudge you in the right direction. By creating goals that move you forward, you will maintain positive momentum that keeps your fire burning.

If you're a busy gal like me, you know how self-defeating to-do lists can be. Before you know it, you have a list of 100 things to do that keep you busy all day long and prevent you from getting anything really important done. By the end of the day you just feel drained and frustrated. This is because to-do lists are not goals that are stated in a workable, easily achievable way. What you need are SMART Goals.

The word "SMART" is an acronym for:

Specific – You've got to get specific and really clear about what you want. The more specifically you can state your goal, the better chance you have of achieving it. To firm up your goal and make it specific, answer the 6 "W" questions as follows:

 Who? – Who is involved?

 What? – What do I want to accomplish?

 Where? – Identify where you want to have your goal.

 When? – Establish a time frame.

 Which? – Identify requirements and restraints.

 Why? – Specific reasons, purposes, or benefits from achieving the goal.

For example, a general goal would be:

I want to start my own business.

A SMART version of that goal is:

Because I love doing crafts so much and I am very talented, I've decided to start my own crafts business. I will sell my crafts and handmade lampshades on eBay and to the local consignment shops. I will work from home, planning, designing, and creating my inventory. I will dedicate three days a week for four hours a day, on Mondays, Tuesdays, and Thursdays from 1:00 – 5:00 p.m.

Measurable - Establish specific mini goals or milestones for measuring your progress as you move toward the attainment of each goal you set. By consistently measuring your progress, you stay on track, reach your target dates, and maintain the momentum of excitement as you get closer and closer to your goal.

To determine if your goal is measurable, ask questions such as...... How much? How many? How will I know when it is accomplished?

For example, I will make two lampshades a day and plan to sell at least four each week.

Attainable – As you get clear and identify goals that really jazz you, you'll get carried forward by the positive momentum that comes with setting a powerful intention. We'll discuss that further in the next section. You'll notice that you begin to figure out ways you can make those goals become realities. You develop the attitudes, abilities, skills, and financial capacity to reach them. You begin seeing previously overlooked opportunities to bring yourself closer to the achievement of your goals.

By planning your steps carefully and wisely, and by setting clear time frames for when you will carry out each of your steps, you will accomplish your goals. As you notice yourself getting closer to your goals, you'll find that you are more willing to reach beyond your old fears and limitations. The excitement of attaining your goal is more important to you than staying afraid. You're more willing to take risks to achieve what you really want.

People who make a habit of listing and writing down their goals are more successful than people who don't. Writing down your goals and taking note of your achievements will build up your self-image. You see yourself as worthy of achieving these goals, and you become who you need to be in order to reach those dreams. You stretch and become a bigger person when you aim for a goal that is beyond your reach.

Realistic – Realistic goals represent objectives toward which you are both *willing* and *able* to work. Your goals can be high and still be realistic. It is up to you to decide what feels like the best fit for you. As long as each step of your goal represents a degree of progress, you're doing fine. Sometimes you can reach a higher goal more quickly because it spurs your motivation and pushes you toward it faster.

Believing that you can accomplish a goal is what determines if it can be accomplished. You also stack the odds in your favor if you've accomplished a similar goal before. Ask yourself what conditions would have to exist to accomplish this goal.

Timely - Your goal should be grounded within a time frame. With no time frame tied to it, there's no sense of urgency. If you want to write 100 articles in 100 days, decide how many articles you will write each day, or each week, what time you will devote toward writing, and then plan your day around that schedule. Saying "I'll do it someday" won't work. But if you anchor it within a timeframe, "By December 1st," then you've set your unconscious mind into motion to begin working on the goal.

T can also stand for Tangible - A goal is tangible when you can experience it with one of the senses, that is, taste, touch, smell, sight, or sound. When your goal is tangible you have a better chance of making it specific and measurable and thus attainable.

Now that you know how to create S.M.A. R. T. Goals, where do you want to set your sights and what do you want to achieve? I've learned through writing this book that the process of writing and expressing my thoughts and feelings is much richer and more fulfilling to me than eating. In fact, many times I choose to ignore the first few hints of my body's hunger just so I can keep writing and finish whatever it is I'm working on.

Having a compelling goal will definitely satisfy that need for fulfillment that you may have been filling up with food.

Gratitude: The Doorway to Fulfillment and Stress Release

Being grateful is an ability that few people have. I was taught the gratitude lesson by a dear friend named Sandra. She was grateful for everyone and everything in her life and, at the time, I couldn't understand why. Sandra was able to look at the events in her life and bring some sense of order and beauty into each and every one of them, no matter how challenging or painful.

By watching her gracefully reframe situations in her life, I was able to see how she could focus her attention on things that were useful to her and avoid wasting time on situations she could not change.

Sandra always used to say, "I'm so blessed to have you as a friend because…" and she would list a hundred different reasons why at that moment she felt blessed for having my friendship. I admired her ability to be so proactive and to choose to make a difference in the world. I noticed that she took time out of her busy day to devote much of her energy to caring for others through volunteering and guiding people to be more aware of their gifts.

I would often open up my email box and see a note from her just saying thank you for being such a wonderful friend. That used to light me up and brighten my day.

Unfortunately, we've since lost touch with one another since we've chosen to pursue different paths. I realize that I could be bitter by focusing on the loss, but I choose to remember all the wonderful times we shared and all the blessings that she brought into my life.

This is another example of changing the way you think about holding on and letting go. I can hold onto my happy memories of our friendship and let go of the resentment that I felt when she made the choice to fall out of touch. I prefer to remember the good things about our friendship. Her model of gratitude has given me the ability to reframe many events in my life that I once perceived as my cross to bear. For that alone, I am eternally grateful. Sandra was a very special friend and I was blessed to have her in my life for the time that I did.

I often hear people complaining about what's wrong in their lives, and yet they spend little time sharing what is wonderful. Since meeting Sandra, I have found that when I pay attention to the blessings in my life they seem to multiply. I've also realized that when I pay attention to things that remind me of being sad, I become more depressed. In tribute to my friendship with Sandra, now I am more grateful and often tell my family, friends, clients, and colleagues how lucky I am to be blessed by their presence in my life. Since doing that my life has become much richer with love and blessings.

My friend, I'd like to challenge you and encourage you to elevate your energy and look at how you can become more grateful. Like Sandra, that means taking a proactive role in your life and sharing and expressing gratitude with others. I encourage you to brainstorm ways that you can supply comfort or alleviate discomfort by sharing your gratitude. You'll notice that when you begin to do this, amazing changes will occur in your life.

My Experience of Learning About the Value of Friendship

There's an old saying that you can't choose your family but you can choose your friends. I believe that God has blessed me with an abundance of friends who have become much more to me like family than my blood relatives. My friends Carmen, Dawn, and Yvonne are all kindred spirits and dear friends, but it's my relationship with my husband's ex-wife, Lucy, which is extremely unique and special.

When I met Lucy, she and Angel had been divorced for over eleven years. She was a corrections officer and married to a policeman named Tony. Born and bred in the Bronx, Lucy was tough as nails on the outside. At first I was intimidated by her, but as I got to know her I grew to love and respect the woman behind the badge.

Every other weekend, Angel and I would pick up Janelle and she'd stay with us until Sunday evening. That always gave Lucy and I plenty of opportunities to talk. I learned that, like me, she also came from a dysfunctional family, enduring so many of the same challenges I did. Seeing her vulnerability, I recognized a softness and a grace in her that made me feel safe knowing we both understood each other's weaknesses and pain.

Ever since Lucy welcomed me into her heart and home, our lives have been woven together like a tapestry. Over the years we've been through thick and thin: weddings, funerals, biopsies, postpartum depression, a miscarriage, christenings, new babies, breast and bottle feeding, teething, solids, first steps, getting married, Janelle's first boyfriend, graduations, baby showers, muffins, garage sales, Sweet 16's, housewarmings, hiring's and firings, lawsuits, closings, becoming grandmothers, hospital scares, and all of the everyday living in between. The sad and the glad, the laughter and tears, we've shared it all.

When Angel and I had our first child, PT, Lucy became my go-to expert for baby advice, always there lending a helping hand or saying a kind word. A couple of years later, when I was told that PT would never speak properly and he would always remain a Special Ed student, it was her shoulder I cried on. After my mom had a nervous breakdown and was diagnosed with bipolar disorder and admitted for treatment, it was Lucy who kept me strong by letting me cry. When Nana's health began to fail, and Lucy saw me crumbling under the pressure, she was there for me. In good times and in bad, Lucy's been lighting the way as my emotional beacon.

Giving

For several years on end, Lucy faced crises, loss, and pain. And never once did I see her faith in God waiver. Through it all, I was there for her every step of the way, doing whatever I could to ease her suffering. When it came to lending her money, I had no qualms about it because I had plenty. Unlike my husband, Angel, I never feared not having enough.

In 2008, when everything hit the fan, I felt lost. Drowning in a sea of self-pity, anger, and fear, I was consumed with hatred for my father. The money, the joy and life that used to fill my happy home was gone. Fearing the possibility of foreclosure, smiles had turned to frowns. Debt collectors kept our phone ringing off the hook. Everything in the house seemed to be falling apart and with no money left for repairs, we were losing our sense of security. With tempers flaring my health was suffering, my marriage was in jeopardy, we were all angry and scared, and pain from lack was spreading all over our house like a cancer. My level of confidence was at an all-time low. Nothing but debt seemed real. With Angel's salary not nearly enough to pay the bills, we had to reach out and accept public assistance.

Because I felt so deeply ashamed of our predicament, I cut myself off from all my friends including Lucy. I justified my decision by thinking we were growing apart. Fearing her judgment, my pride kept me from reaching out to ask for help from the person who understood me the most.

Angry all the time, my petty jealousies were turning me into someone I despised—I was envious of people with money. One day, after months of ignoring her calls, Lucy came to the house and confronted me. I took a risk and shared my feelings, telling her how my father's rejection had destroyed me. In true Lucy-style, she told me to buck up and pull my sh** together and forget about him. She seemed tough and angry, and I didn't get a sense that she really cared. When she suggested I turn back to God and increase my faith, I felt that made a mockery of my suffering. After she left, I convinced myself that my friend was abandoning me.

And Learning to Receive

Lucy offered her help in so many ways, and rather than being grateful I sent her an email telling her I felt we had grown apart. Within a few hours, she left a tearful message on my voicemail, saying, "I don't care if you don't want to be my friend or see me ever again, I respect whatever decision you make, but I'll never stop loving you. I'll never forget that you were always there for me when everyone else left. Just know that I'll always be here for you."

As I listened to her message repeatedly, I could hear the sincerity in her voice. My heart cracked open and the dam of tears broke, but my pride kept me from admitting I was wrong. An insight from an email I received helped me understand that I had to push my ego aside and talk to my friend, telling her how I felt. I knew I had to tap to deal with the rawness I felt inside. Once I cleared those fears and hurts, I felt like myself again. Thanks to my time spent tapping, that day marked a new beginning for our friendship. I learned a lot from that experience.

> "A friend is one who walks in when others walk out."
> – *Walter Winchell*

Recently, looking back on my friendship with Lucy, I realize she taught me a great lesson about loving unconditionally. She helped me realize that it's equally important to know how to receive as it is to give. Throughout my life I've always been a giver. When Lucy reappeared in my life and took on the role of being my gracious giver, I tried to annihilate her because I couldn't accept being the one in need.

Lately, thanks to dealing with my issues around increasing my feelings of self-worth, I've gotten much better at receiving, and I have my friend Lucy to thank for holding me up all the times I was ready to fall. That's what a good relationship is: supportive.

Now I understand that the distance I created from my friends was actually due to my feeling of low self-worth. Once I started realizing that I was worthy and lovable, it became a no brainer for me to decide that I could stop feeling sorry for myself and avoid feeling miserable and misunderstood. I could seek out the women who have loved and accepted me as their friend. Back in January 2009, I realized that what I wanted most was to reconnect with my friends, so I started calling them again and emailing and touching base. One by one, I invited them all back into my life.

How 'bout you? Can you relate to pushing friends away when you need them most? We all lead such busy lives, and it's often something that just happens. But I've learned you can always choose to do something different. Have you been holding a friend at arm's length assuming something that may not be true? Are you letting your pride keep you from being with your friend? What could you do today to change that? How willing would you be to take that step?

As you move forward on your path to learning how to value yourself and your body differently, your relationships and your life will naturally go through changes. Divorce, death, loss, jealousy, disappointment, hurts, and resentments—these can all threaten the best of relationships, but they don't necessarily have to end them. My experience has taught me to never give up on the people I love without a fight. Many times we create our own misery by assuming the worst. It's those automatic negative thoughts that keep us stuck and afraid. They must be questioned in order for you to determine if the relationship is right for you. When you find yourself feeling distanced from someone you love, it's time to re-evaluate your connection. Here's what I suggest:

1. Make a list either in your head or on paper to clarify for yourself why you feel the way you do. It's my belief that as long as the person's good qualities and loving actions toward you outweigh the bad, it is in your best interest to remain in that relationship.

2. Find a private place where you can be alone and feel safe to vent your feelings. This could be the shower, in your car, at home, anywhere you like. As you uncover the causes of your pain, use any one of the tapping methods (as explained in the Cope with Your Stress chapter) to deal with unspoken resentments, angers, fears, or hurts. Expect that this will bring up a lot of emotion. Continue to tap until you feel ready to speak with the person.

3. If you can, contact them and arrange a face to face meeting. You can break the ice using email, texts, or leaving a phone message. But unless you are absolutely certain that you want to end the

relationship, don't rely on technology and run the risk of being misunderstood. Once you get their undivided attention, tell them honestly how you feel. Listen closely to what they say. If what they are saying, triggers more negative emotions for you, take a break, step away and tap. Take the time you need to regain your clarity.

4.   Now, listen to your heart. And do what feels right to you.

Try It! - Playing the Appreciation Game

Look for things to appreciate in every situation, good, bad, and ugly. Take 7 minutes each morning and evening and write down the things for which you are appreciative. The challenge is to avoid repeating any of them. If you write down that you're appreciative of your sister, and if you want to continue recognizing more things about her that you appreciate, then begin to explore her various qualities. Here are some examples, I appreciate my sister Susan's cheerful smile, I appreciate Susan's generosity, I appreciate Susan's wisdom, I appreciate Susan helping me to fix my computer, etc.

Now it's your turn, what do you appreciate? If you want to break free of your resistance and change your relationship with food, I've learned that you can learn to appreciate your body, even though you can't stand it, and doing that will lead you towards even greater self acceptance.

Dressing the Body You Have

Bodies. We all have them. They come in different shapes and assorted sizes, but what makes one shape or size better or more desirable than another? Who says only thin women can be beautiful and sexy? Who made these stupid rules? Who says if you're a big, plus size woman you can't wear sexy clothes? The truth is you can. But you probably don't because you don't think you should.

Maybe you're waiting to dress your best or invest money in clothes when your arms are perfectly toned or your tummy is flat or any and every other part of you is exactly the way you want it to be. But time's a wastin' and running 'round in ugly baggy clothes while you wait to become perfect isn't going to make you feel any better about yourself. There's no rule that says you can't rock the body you have.

Ready to get out from under a fat and ugly self-image, and stop thinking of yourself as a fashion disaster? Then here's some advice for you from a couple of well-seasoned style experts who have spent years devoting themselves to empowering women to love their bodies. Clinton Kelly and Stacy London are hosts of TLC's show, *What Not to Wear* and authors of the book, *Dress Your Best: The Complete Guide to Finding the Style That's Right for Your Body.* In discussing why it's important to dress the body you have, not the body you want, they say:

"What we've learned is that looking good now will help you feel better later. Walking around in oversized sweats makes you look like you've given up. And you may start to internalize that feeling. So this is one time in life when a quick fix can actually have long term effects. We've seen it hundreds of times. Don't wait for what may or may not change about you in the future. You are perfect now. So read this book and get shopping."

Clinton, Stacy, and I agree that what you wear has a profound influence on how you think and feel about yourself. If you want to accept the body you have today and pave the way for the slimmer you to come in the future, the trick is to dress the body you have, not the body you want.

This is a lesson I've really taken to heart. It's changed the way I think and feel about myself. Since I've realized that I'm worth it, I now spend more time putting myself together and looking great. That boosts my confidence like crazy and I feel fabulous having much greater respect for my body than I ever did before. I know that if I can make peace with my body as it is, then you can too.

The Avenue: My Peaceful Warrior Path to Helping Women Love Their Bodies

As a coach, my deepest passion is to reach out and touch women who struggle with negative body images, offering them the practical tools they need to change their lives in very real way. Yet during the course of editing this book, I went through a series of personal challenges that caused me to do a lot of growing up. Out of my tragedy came my triumph, bringing me an enormous amount of self-acceptance and compassion for my body.

Somewhere along the way I forgot what it was like to hate my body and to refuse to accept my imperfections.

During this time I began to notice that I was talking a different language and disconnecting from the women who I was meant to serve. After searching for a while, I found new inspiration that would soon take my coaching to a higher level.

In September 2010, I decided to combine my newfound appreciation of fashion and my curvy confidence creating know-how, with my coaching skills to teach women to love the skin they're in. I took a part time job working at Avenue®, the plus size women's retail clothing store and I loved it. I had a blast working with the gals there and I loved doing my thing – inspiring women to see and think of themselves as beautiful and loveable.

Except for the time I've spent coaching women and working with kids, I never felt so deeply loved and appreciated as I did working at Avenue®. It was truly one of the most profoundly satisfying experiences I've ever had working with a group. It gave me insights about women and their relationships with their bodies that I could never have gotten any other way. Thanks to my time at Avenue® I have the real inside scoop into what women want.

Sadly it was a common occurrence for me to have the experience of consoling a woman who was standing in the fitting room in her underwear, telling me all the reasons she had to hate her body. Sometimes they cried. Sometimes they just got angry, not with the clothes, but with themselves. How 'bout you? Can you relate to this fitting room frustration?...

I sure can and it makes me crazy because I can't stand seeing curvy women suffer a moment longer.

If you're ready to stop singing the body hating blues, then here are a ton of fashion secrets that will make you look and feel fabulous right now. Here are some tips to get you started:

Fabulous Fashion for the Curvy and Confident Woman

Be Daring - Try on everything. If you see something you like, take a chance and try it on. You'll never know what you're missing if you stay stuck in the same rut.

Educate Yourself - Look for clothes on women shaped like you whom you admire. Watch shows like *How to Look Good Naked* and *What Not to Wear* to get ideas for how to buy clothes to accent and highlight your body type. Read books, blogs, articles, newsletters, magazines, on and/or offline written by people you respect dedicated to teaching you how to dress to flatter your shape.

Accentuate the Positive – All great style gurus agree, "If you've got it, flaunt it." Show off your best features.

Know Your Body Type

Female bodies are categorized into four basic geometric shapes. Within each of these body types are several sub-types. The most common shapes are as follows:

- Apple – bigger on top –Apple-shaped women are generally bigger on top and have broader shoulders compared to their narrower hips. They tend to have slim legs and thighs and carry their weight in the stomach, chest, and face area.
- Pear – bigger on bottom –A woman with a pear-shaped body has narrow shoulders, slimmer arms, and smaller breasts. She has a bigger rear and larger, curvier hips and thighs.
- Banana or Straight (rectangular) – Commonly referred to as banana shapes, these women carry their weight predominantly in the abdomen, butt, chest, and face, giving them the appearance of a straight ruler.
- Hourglass – Women with hourglass figures have hip and bust measurements that are nearly the same, drawing attention to their small waists. They tend to gain weight in the arms, chest, hips, and rear, thus maintaining their hourglass shape.

Height: Getting it Right - In order to get the best fit for your clothes, it's wise to find pieces that not only fit your shape, but also suit your height. There are three height distinctions that designers often use to mark sizes; petite, average, and tall.

- Petite: 4'11" – 5'3 ½"
- Average: 5'4" – 5'7"
- Tall: 5'7 ½" – 5'11"+

Fashion Fixes for Common Body Types

The following are a few common body types that can often be a challenge to dress. Remember that with everything, a superb fit is what makes your clothes look great. You have to make sure that you fit the biggest part of you first, otherwise nothing will fit properly. Whenever you're shopping, always opt for a larger size and alter the rest of the garment to fit you. Make your tailor or seamstress your friend.

For hourglass figures – Keep it in proportion. Wear a wrap dress to accentuate your curves. Knee-high boots worn tucked into your jeans will give your body more length and balance curvy hips. To define a small waist, choose tailored shirts with V-necks or look for blouses with ruching (gathering). Choose jackets with waist seaming or pretty details that emphasize a tiny middle. This will create more visual balance. To balance both top and bottom, choose heavier weight, stiffer, structured jackets that fit well, sit snug on the shoulder, and cover the top of the hip. Leather can work magic on an hourglass shape.

 For plus size women, with a little extra tummy – Your challenge is to create a longer and leaner silhouette and de-emphasize your middle by adding more structure. Jackets work wonders. Choose jackets and blazers that will create the illusion of having an hourglass shape. They will nip you in at the waist, making you look thinner in your tummy.

If you're petite, use short-structured jackets to balance a wider torso. Look for structured tops or dresses with an empire waistline to deflect the eye upward toward your chest, de-emphasizing your tummy. Never wear low rise pants. They will put all the focus on your hips and give you love handles. Opt for dark wash jeans with a mid-width, mid-rise in a trouser style to make your legs look thinner. To get the sleekest look possible, go for a trouser with a permanent crease sewn down the front of the leg.

Bold prints balance a bigger frame. Play with accessories. As a larger woman, you can carry off bigger, bolder, and more statement pieces of jewelry. Here are Stacy and Clinton's top 5 picks for the latest what-to-wear must-have accessories:

 brooches

- bangle bracelets
- multiple chain necklaces
- cocktail rings
- chandelier earrings.

The Plus Size Figure - Since the plus size silhouette is considered to be proportionately larger than the average size woman, your goal is to make your shape appear slimmer overall. Choose monochromatic outfits to create a long, slenderizing line from top to bottom. Wear skirts that taper in, then flare at the hem to balance you. Draw attention to the center of your body by wearing bright tops under jackets. Try on clothes that are different shapes and colors. Pointy toe shoes of any height will always lengthen and slenderize a heavy bottom half.

For Busts with Bam! – Your goal is to complement your curves and show off The Girls without letting them steal the show. Buy the best bra you can afford and get it sized by a professional. Find a lingerie or clothing store that will do this for you. Create an overall streamlined look by balancing out your top and bottom. A-line skirts that fall below the knee are great for adding volume without bulk. To compliment your curves and create balance use scoop necks to draw focus away from the bust.

Look for high armholes on jackets. This will ensure a thinner sleeve. Choose either multi-button or single button jackets with high stances (button hits directly below bust line) to create a more balanced, slimmer silhouette which will support your bust line while cinching your waistline. For a hint of sexy, wear delicate necklaces that end just at the top of the cleavage.

For Big Arms - Your challenge is to hide your problem areas while drawing attention to your assets. Wear open-neck wrap tops to flatter the cleavage and waist area. Three-quarter-length sleeves show only the thinnest part of the arm. Look for jackets with puffed shoulders for a roomier fit. If you're feeling self conscious about baring your naked arms, then try a wrap or shrug.

For Petite, Full Fannied Gals Like Me – If you are petite, this means you are smaller in frame and that your arms and legs are a bit shorter than average. Create a sense of proportion on your bottom and top by choosing fitted jackets that end just above the widest part of your leg. To create an elongating slenderizing effect, think pinstripes. This optical illusion creates a sense of height by forcing the eye to move downwards and see vertically. Shop for petite clothing made with lightweight materials. Thicker fabrics tend to bunch and can make you look bigger than you are.

Choose smaller prints that suit the scale of your body. Wear tops in bright colors with pretty detailing to draw the eye upwards. Don't wear tops long enough to cover your butt. They will only make your legs look short and stubby. Also, avoid jeans with small back pockets. Choose a uniform dark wash. Avoid any and all bleaching, wash or whiskering on or near the hip/thigh area. These dye treatments will only highlight your hips and thighs and make your rear look bigger. Wear belts low to create an illusion of a smaller butt. Choose A-line skirts with natural waists to flatter your figure.

Note to curvy gals: Step away from the dreaded skinny legged tapered jean. To make the most of your assets, look for trousers or jeans with legs that fit the widest part of your calf with either straight, boot cut, or flared bottoms. Caution: Never miss out on a great fitting pair of flattering pants because they're too long. Have them hemmed professionally or if you have the know-how, invest some time in sewing them yourself.

Wrapping Up
Chapter 9: Act to Attract: Be SMART, Mind Your Mouth, Watch Your Tongue, and Get It Done

Here are the juiciest morsels covered in this section. Savor them mindfully.

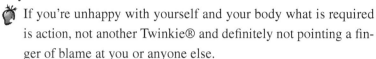

- If you're unhappy with yourself and your body what is required is action, not another Twinkie® and definitely not pointing a finger of blame at you or anyone else.

- In order to become curvy and confident at any size, you must change the way you think. Your words are the building blocks of your actions. Without first changing your internal self-talk, every step you take in an effort to change old habits will be like trudging through a mound of quicksand.

- Know that the antidote to fear is taking action. You put yourself in the right frame of mind for taking action and stepping out into the world by the words you use to talk to yourself.

- Use "cancel, cancel" or another activation key to change your thoughts and shift your behaviors.

- We tend to scare ourselves into believing things that aren't true and making ourselves out to be helpless when we're not. Catastrophizing is a natural tendency we all have when we imagine the very worst happening in any situation.

- If your language is filled with words like "don't" and "can't," you're unknowingly setting yourself up to fail.

- The only goals you'll ever need are SMART: Specific, Measurable, Attainable, Realistic, and Tangible.

- To be a good friend, it's equally important to know how to receive as it is to give.

- To find the self-acceptance you crave, learn how to dress the body you have, not the body you want.

- The only three things you can do to change your life are:
  - You can change your thoughts
  - You can change the pictures in your head
  - You can change your actions

OK, now that you've got a bead on how to look good and what mindset you need to make the changes you want, I want to teach you how you can transform your fat and ugly body image without spending a dime. In the next chapter, you'll learn about the power of setting a powerful intention. This is truly the secret to making the law of attraction work for you. Turn the page and let's get started.

Chapter 10
Intention – Set a Powerful Intention

"Our thoughts can penetrate through time and space and change things."
— *Lynne McTaggart, bestselling author and speaker*

If you're struggling with excess weight then your body has learned to remember and think of yourself as fat. No matter how you slice it, you can't be thin if you're thinking fat.

Intention Expert and bestselling author of several books including *The Intention Experiment*, Lynne McTaggart says, "Your self-talk has become equivalent to sending yourself a consistent stream of negative intention."

To neutralize that negativity, you have to learn how to set a powerful intention.

If your goal is to get thinner as you eat the foods you love, then you must learn how to use the power of your mind to create your ideal body from the inside out. The only thing holding us back from using the power of intention and focused meditation to shape our bodies is a limiting belief. We wonder, "Does it really work?"

In this section I'll discuss the power of intention and will share scientific evidence proving that our thoughts do in fact affect our bodies and the world around us. If facts and figures are not your thing and you'd like to zip along and blow past this section, skip ahead to page 397 that starts with the sentence, ***Basically all you need to know is that your thoughts count!!***

The Field: The Quest for the Secret Force of the Universe

Lynne McTaggart is a journalist and author of five books, including international bestsellers *The Field: The Quest for the Secret Force of the Universe* and *The Intention Experiment.*

In *The Field*, Lynne describes witnessing a series of miracles in her life. It was later proved through hard scientific evidence that it is possible to heal with the power of the mind.

Lynne witnessed studies and trials of patients being given nothing more than water and watching them miraculously get better. She also learned that acupuncture, poking the skin with fine needles at certain points of the body along so called energy meridians, worked for many conditions.

As a top notch reporter, she instinctively knew this was worth exploring further, so she put her heart, soul, and all her knowledge into writing the book *The Field*. Since, she's won praise from not only the scientific community but also the medical community.

Among those who endorse her work are Oprah, Wayne Dyer, Deepak Chopra, Dr. Bernie Siegel, Fritz Albert Popp, Gregg Braden, Bruce Lipton, Caroline Myss, John Assaraf, and many other highly respected and well known thought leaders.

Scientific Evidence Proving the Power of Intention

Let's take a peek at some of her most significant findings.

Ed Mitchell is an American pilot and astronaut. As the lunar module pilot of Apollo 14, he became the sixth man to walk on the moon. While staring out the window of the spacecraft, Ed could see the earth framed through the window, shaped like a tiny crescent engulfed by a sea of stars.

As he sat dumbfounded attempting to process all that he had learned and experienced on his mission, he noticed that the sky as he knew it did not actually exist. The image of an overhead sky had been replaced by an all-encompassing entity that cradled the earth on all sides. This was the first time that Ed experienced the strangest feeling he would ever have; a feeling of connectedness, as if all the planets and all the people of all time were attached by some invisible web.

There seemed to be an enormous force field here, connecting all people, their intentions and thoughts, and every animate and inanimate form of matter for all time. It was as though in a single instant Ed Mitchell had discovered and felt "The Force."

During that time, Ed, along with two of his colleagues who were doctors, had been studying the work of Dr. Joseph B. Rhine, a biologist who'd conducted many experiments on human consciousness and ESP or extra sensory perception. They recognized that Ed's journey to the moon presented a unique opportunity to prove the ability to communicate telepathically.

On the last day of the Apollo 14 mission, Ed conducted his experiment as his fellow astronauts slept peacefully. On a paper he copied down random sets of numbers, each of which represented one of Dr. Rhine's famous Zener symbols: square, circle, cross, star, and a pair of wavy lines.

The experiment called for him to concentrate intently on each of the symbols and to attempt to transmit his choices to his colleagues back home. After he returned safely to earth and compared his selections with those of his colleagues, the correspondence between them was shown to be significant, with a 1:3000 possibility that this could be due to chance.

In her report, "The Secret Science Behind the Secret," Lynne explains that what we think of as our reality is considered by the universe to be more like unset Jell-o. Our thoughts can penetrate through time and space and change things. Research shows that thoughts are capable of affecting everything from the simplest machines to the most complex living beings. This evidence suggests that human thoughts and intentions are an actual physical something with the astonishing power to change our world.

Cleve Backster's Primary Perception Experiments

Cleve Backster isn't a scientist. He's the country's leading lie detector expert.

Yet over the course of thirty years he's performed a series of experiments demonstrating the power of thought transference from one living object to another. Here's how it all started. One night he was sitting in his office, feeling bored. As he looked over at one of his plants, he wondered what would happen if he hooked it up to one of his polygraph machines.

At the time, polygraph equipment consisted of a set of electrodes attached to a read out mechanism like a pen describing a sideways S. If you're telling the truth, it will make a small S, if you're lying, it will make a great big S.

After he attached the plant to the polygraph, he thought to himself, "I wonder what would happen if I pour some water in." He poured in the water and the plant acted as though it were bored. Recognizing that he needed a more compelling thought to activate the needles on the polygraph, he wondered, "Maybe I'll burn its leaf."

At that same moment, the polygraph reading on the plant went wild. The readout mechanism described a giant "S" as though the plant were stressed. Still holding the thought in mind, he went and got a book of matches. As he lit the matches, the plant readout went crazy. He couldn't believe what he was witnessing. To test his theory that this plant could actually read his thoughts, he stopped thinking about burning the plant's leaf. Immediately the plant's reading showed a calming effect with a much smaller "S."

After settling his thoughts, he realized that this plant was able to read his mind. He called this testing process Primary perception. And for the next thirty years he did experiments with plants, eggs, yogurt, bacteria, blood, and even human sperm, seeking to prove that there was communication between all living things.

He had some amazing results. In one experiment, he developed an automated system whereby he had a little batch of brine shrimp attached to a mechanical arm. When he flipped a switch, the shrimp would fall into boiling water. At that exact moment the plants he had hooked up to his polygraphs all registered alarm.

The plants in Backster's studies demonstrated a connection to each other in addition to him. Whenever he left they reacted in real time to his absence. They even appeared to respond when Backster made the initial decision to return home.

The plants also demonstrated an ability to learn by showing that they were able to discern whether or not he was serious in his intent to harm them.

In later years, Backster collaborated with a young parapsychology researcher named Ingo Swann in an attempt to duplicate Backster's original experiments with the plants. After an immediate and sudden surge of activity when Swann imagined burning the plant with a match, the polygraph needle connected to the plant suddenly stopped. Again, the plant had demonstrated an ability to learn and decipher what was true.

Next, Swann thought about putting acid in the plant's pot. At first the needle on the polygraph went crazy, zigzagging wildly. Eventually the plant appeared to understand that Swann was not serious and the polygraph tracing flat lined.

Unfortunately, Backster was not a scientist so nobody took his findings seriously. But he was technically the first person to prove that all living things are in constant communication with each another.

In later years, scientists like German physicist, Fritz Albert Popp, discovered that this communication is actually the result of light emissions. These emissions are picked up by other living things. Eventually, it was determined that this was the actual source of the communication that Backster had attempted to prove.

So you may ask, what does loving your body have to do with things like crying plants?

Basically all you need to know is that your thoughts count!!!

The Power of Focused Thought on a Specific Area

In the movie, "What the Bleep Do We Know!?" one of the featured segments of the film focused on an experiment conducted by a well-known Unified Quantum Field theorist from Harvard, Dr. John Hagelin, who has published over 100 scientific papers in his field.

In the segment, Dr. Hagelin discusses a social experiment that was conducted in Washington, D.C., the so called murder capital of the world. In the summer of 1993, 4000 volunteers came together from a hundred different countries to collectively meditate for long periods of time over a two month period (June 7th to July 30th, 1993).

The purpose of the experiment was to create a collective intent to increase peace and lower the crime rate in the area. It was predicted in advance that with such a large group there could be up to a 25% decrease in violent crime as defined by the FBI.

Statistically, crime rates rise during the summer months due to the intense heat. Wanting to voice his skepticism, the chief of the Washington D.C. police, Emmanuel Ross went on television prior to the experiment and said that it would take "twenty inches of snow to lower crime by 25% that summer."

By the end of the study the police department actually became a collaborator because the results showed a 25% drop in crime that summer. This decrease had been predicted by scientists based on forty-eight similar studies previously conducted on a smaller scale.

The meditators had a peaceful ripple effect on the entire surrounding area.

Juicy Woman Note:

Dr. Hagelin and his research associates theorize that it would take a very small percentage of people meditating to affect the world the way they affected D.C. that summer. In fact, the exact ratio Hagelin estimated to reduce war, deaths, crime, and accidents on a global scale is the square root of 1% of the world's population, which is only about 8000 meditators. That means it is estimated that it would take only 8000 people holding a common intention to change our world. This is the foundation of the work that Lynne McTaggart teaches through her various intention experiments.

The intention study of Hagelin's and others leads us to wonder, "Do people actually have the power to affect the reality we see?"

Hidden Messages in Water

In 2004, a Japanese scientific researcher and doctor of alternative medicine named Masuro Emoto became interested in the molecular structure of water and what external forces affected it.

He chose this experiment because water is the most receptive of the four elements. Anticipating that water would respond to a series of nonphysical events, he set up a series of studies and applied various forms of mental stimuli to the water and photographed it with a dark field microscope.

To begin the experiment, Dr. Emoto drew several water samples from Japan's polluted Fujiwara dam. One of the samples was blessed by a Buddhist monk before it was frozen, another was left as is and labeled as such.

After viewing both samples underneath the high-powered microscope, it was obvious that the crystalline structure of the water that had been blessed had undergone a transformation. As opposed to the amorphous misshapen image of the water crystals that had not been blessed, the samples that had been blessed by the Zen Buddhist monk resembled a clear, bright snowflake image, showing great symmetry and beauty.

In his next series of experiments, Dr. Emoto printed out labels with different key words typed on them, and he taped them onto regular bottles of distilled water. After leaving the water out overnight, he viewed the samples through the microscope. His findings showed that each sample from a different bottle took on a different crystalline structure.

It was found that the water samples with labels that had positive and loving words and messages like the "Chi of Love," "I love you," and "Thank you," all had formed beautiful crystalline structures that were clearly defined and shaped.

The bottles that had negative words and messages like "You fool," "I hate you," "You make me sick," and "I will kill you," had formed completely different crystalline structures. When these images were viewed under the dark field microscope, they were distorted, dark, and misshapen.

Now consider this. If our bodies are made up almost entirely of water, what is the potential impact that our thoughts and the thoughts of others have on us?

How are we being affected by our body hating thoughts? After all, what are you believing about your body? What do you think of aging? What's your position on pain? Is being in pain natural and expected as you grow older? Or...Not?

Take a moment and ask yourself, "What are you saying to yourself about your body?" Are you saying, "I hate you?" I hope not, because your body's listening. Dr. Emoto's experiments showed that water is vulnerable to thoughts and images directed toward it.

In his book, *The Hidden Messages of Water*, Dr. Emoto compared examples of the different water sources and concluded that water is affected by various external stimuli. He theorized that it is connected to our consciousness in that the photos showed that water has an ability to absorb, hold, and retransmit human feelings and emotions. Dr. Emoto believes that since people are 70% water, and the earth is 70% water, we can heal our planet and our bodies by consciously expressing love and goodwill.

Remember, those thighs that you look down on with disgust, or any other part of your body that you may despise, are merely what Lynne calls, "Packets of moving energy whipping and flipping around, passing energy back and forth as if participating in an endless game of basketball."

The question begs to be asked, how can you stop playing the body hating game, undo your body bashing thoughts, and create a new loving intention toward yourself and your body? Let's take a look and understand how you can become a powerful intender so that you deliberately manifest more of what you want and less of what you don't.

What Makes a Good Intender?

After completing *The Field*, Lynne began doing her own experiments on the power of intention. She learned there are certain techniques that make someone a good intender which are shared by all masters of intention.

To set your own intention to change an aspect of your life, Lynne recommends the following:

1. *Choose a situation in your life that never happens.* This will prove to you that it will more than likely be your intention that created the change, rather than chance. For example, a woman whose husband never brought her flowers, would choose to set an intention for him to buy her flowers. This was the case in one of Lynne's workshops. A woman approached her and said, "My husband never brings me flowers." Lynne suggested that she set an intention that week for her husband to bring her flowers. Within that week the woman wrote saying, "When I got home and opened the door, there he was holding a bouquet of roses for me."

2. *Clean or clear up one little space in your home.* This can become your intention space. Always use this place to send your intention. In your mind's eye, it will become a sacred space. If

you're traveling, you can still imagine being in your space and send an intention from there.

3. ***Create a connection*** - Zone in and focus on the object of your intention. In the case of having the benefit of physical contact, you can hold the person's hand for a few minutes. In remote circumstances, use a picture to keep your intentions focused and clear.

4. ***Timing is important*** – Lynne found a lot of evidence showing that we are very much affected by solar activity with intention. The sun is a powerful influence on our bodies. It hurls vast amounts of gases toward the earth at huge speeds called solar flares. They hit the earth's geomagnetic shield and have a profound effect on two of the human body's major engines: the heart and the brain.

The sun affects all living creatures, but for humans it can cause heart attacks and strokes, People have epileptic fits and the sun affects our psychic ability influencing whether or not we can easily tap into The Field. If you have a personal intention, Lynne suggests keeping tabs on what is going on with the sun by going to the NASA site. It has consistent updates on the status of the sun.

There's so much more information about Lynne's wonderful experiments and her findings on how to be a great intender. If you're not an experienced meditator, then you can learn how to meditate like the masters by reading Lynne's book, *The Intention Experiment.*

Now let's jump into an explanation of how to make visualization work for you.

Using Your Thoughts to Create Your Ideal Body From the Inside Out

"At every moment, your body is in the best
condition that your mindset allows."
– *Lisa Bonnice,* author of *Shape Shifting:*
Reclaiming Your Perfect Body

Years ago when I was a kid, there used to be a TV variety program called, *The Flip Wilson Show*. Flip Wilson was a comedian that created characters. One of his characters was Geraldine. Geraldine's famous words were, *"What you see is what you get!"* Boy was she right!

Everything we are and are not in this life is the result of our thinking. So now it's really time to clear out whatever's not working for you, and open yourself up to an image of the wonderful new you.

I've already discussed how modern science has proven that our brains cannot tell the difference between an "actual" experience and an experience imagined vividly and in great detail. By imagining what you want for yourself, your body, and your life, you create artificial memories in your brain that lead you to attract the real thing. This is known as visualization.

You have to tell yourself a different story to make the impossible seem possible. When world famous runner, Roger Bannister, was preparing to break the world record by running the first four minute mile in history, in addition to practicing on the field he had to make a mental shift in his head to believe that it was possible.

As far as he knew it wasn't possible to achieve, because for centuries nobody had been able to do it. Since he didn't know what it would be like physically, he created an image of what it would be like in his head and he visualized that constantly. Once the new image was in place, and he was certain that he could achieve the goal, his body pushed him the rest of the way and he became the first person to ever run a four minute mile.

Within two years of Bannister's record breaking accomplishment, twenty-seven other people had been able to run the four minute mile.

Jim Carrey: From Comedy Bust to Blockbuster Success

Many years ago, before he made it big and became a huge box office success commanding upwards of $20M per movie, Jim Carrey was a struggling improvisation actor saddled with a painful past.

As a kid he lived with his mother and father and three other siblings. His mom, Kathleen, suffered depression along with many real and imagined illnesses which often confined her to bed for long periods of time. His dad, Percy, was a struggling sax player who was sharp witted and fun loving, but when hard times hit he decided to sell his sax along with his dreams and took a job as an accountant.

After witnessing his alcoholic grandfather's constant put-downs of his dad, Jim took on the role of family comedian in order to take the heat off his father and in hopes of making his mother laugh. When Jim was in ninth grade, his dad lost his job and the family had to sell the house and move to a sad and lonely industrial town. The whole family took jobs as security guards or janitors. Jim Carrey scrubbed toilets for eight hours after school every day.

At sixteen, he went out on his own to pursue an acting career. He began as an improv actor. His father believed in him and was his greatest fan. He showed his support by writing several of Jim's first comedy sketches. One night, after being booed off a comedy stage in California, Jim reached his lowest point. But instead of accepting failure, he chose to move forward and strive for success. He reached into his pocket and took out an index card. He made it into a blank check and wrote it out for $10M. As a notation he wrote, "For acting services rendered."

Several years later, he was paid $10M to act in the film *Ace Ventura Pet Detective*. As a well-known and outspoken advocate about the process of visualization and his good fortune using it, he talks about the power of affirmations and visualization sharing his story:

"I've always believed in magic. When I wasn't doing anything in this town, I'd go up at night, sit on Mulholland Drive, look out at the city, stretch out my arms, and say, 'Everyone wants to work with me. I'm a really good actor. I have all kinds of great movie offers.'

"I'd just repeat these things over and over, literally convincing myself that I had a couple of movies lined up. I'd drive down that hill, ready to take the world on, going, 'Movie offers are out there for me, I just don't hear them yet.'

> "It was like total affirmations, antidotes to the
> stuff that stems from my family background."
> – Jim Carrey, Actor/Comedian

Jim's story is a great example of the power of setting a positive intention to create a desired outcome. Rather than continually telling himself the same story, harping on his problems and blaming his misery on others, he found a way to overcome his frustration by creating a new reality that began in his mind's eye.

403

When you look in the mirror, do you love what you see? Are you tired of focusing on all your flaws? Are you obsessed with hating your thighs like I was? You may wonder how in the world you can love your body if you don't even like it, or perhaps you even hate it!

Heaven knows! It's soooo easy to get stuck complaining about and hating your body, comparing yourself to others and always coming up short, running the same negative story. How many times have you said, "I'm too fat. I've got my mother's thighs, I'll never lose weight, I can't stop eating, blah, blah, blah." It's the same old broken record which when push comes to shove only makes you feel awful and powerless to change anything. When you're down and out, that's just about the time your next binge waits right around the corner.

In order for excess weight to come off your body, you have to get the fat out of your head! That's why you must change your story and create a different internal image of yourself. You need to create a slimmer, more confident version of yourself in order to take the baby steps necessary to release your excess weight and reshape your body.

The daily practice of visualizing your dreams as already accomplished can rapidly accelerate your achievement of those dreams, goals, and ambitions.

In this chapter, I'll teach you how to create a slender image for yourself right now no matter what you weigh. I'll show you how to marry a powerful intention with visualization and affirmations to create the body of your dreams. Before we get down to the nuts and bolts of using visualization and affirmation, let's begin with an interview and a story of two people who have both successfully used their mental abilities to change their physical bodies.

Dr. Joe Dispenza: Recreating Your Body from the Inside Out

Dr. Joe Dispenza is one of my biggest role models. Dr. Joe was one of the featured experts in the movie, *What the Bleep Do We Know?* As a neuro physicist and quantum physics expert, he is one of the most credible authorities on how your thoughts truly create your reality.

In a recent interview with Angela Treat Lyon, EFT Master, on her *I Dare You* radio show, she spoke with Dr. Joe. This is his story:

"In 1986 I got run over by a truck in a triathlon. I wound up breaking six bones in my back and was diagnosed to never walk again. The radical surgery they were prescribing for my injuries was called a Harrington Rod surgery. That's when they put long stainless steel rods in your spine. Because I broke six vertebrae, they wanted to basically fuse my entire spine from the base of my neck to the base of my spine. Anyway, after four opinions from four of the leading surgeons in Southern California, I chose to not have the surgery. That was pretty daring."

Before the accident occurred, Dr. Joe was at the top of his game. As a twenty-seven year old successful chiropractor, he was enjoying the high life. He was used to fast cars and having fun, doing martial arts and yoga training every day. He was a busy person enjoying a great life. But one day he went from being very active and busy to being flat on his back in a matter of moments. He was paralyzed.

With his background in neuroscience, he believed the power that created his body would also heal his body. Joe said, "If I could just connect with this power, this intelligence and begin to give it some orders, some directions, and begin to interact with it, maybe it would begin to do the healing for me."

That decision changed his life. This is what he did:

1. *No doubts* - The first thing he decided was, "I'm not going to let any thought go by unchecked. I'm not going to let any thought go by that is derived from fear or doubt or any of those thoughts that kind of slip by our analytical mind on a daily basis."

2. *Faith* – Recognizing that faith was at the core of his future success, he knew that if he believed in a power greater than himself, he would overcome any adversity. He reasoned "that the intelligence that keeps our heart beating, digesting our food, filtering our blood and organizing our DNA, processing 100,000 chemical reactions in every cell in our body in one second—If I could just interact with that, just because I couldn't see it, or smell it, or taste it, or feel it, or hear it—If I could just begin to understand that there was a subconscious mind that was organizing all these things."

3. *Create a mental picture* – "I was going to give it a picture, a very clear picture of exactly what I wanted as an outcome."

4. *Wandering Mind Means Rewind* – "So when I started creating that picture and my mind wandered to something else, I would start all over again." After getting into the habit of returning back to the beginning after each interruption, he said, "I was able to go through the whole picture, without my mind wandering to anything else, and what I did felt like hitting a tennis ball in the sweet spot. I felt like I connected and that's when I started to notice measurable changes in my body. The moment I started noticing changes in my body, I knew that this mind was real."

Making a Pact: Setting Your Intention

The following set of statements are what Dr. Joe uses to set his intention each day. He recommends saying this following your visualization work. I'm going to encourage you to either follow his intention or create one of your own that feels right to you. I recommend that you write it down someplace where you will see it several times a day. This will make it clear to your subconscious mind that you are seeking signs from the universe confirming that your visualizations are working. Here is Dr. Joe's pact:

"I'm taking this time to create my day. And I'm infecting the quantum field. Now if in fact the observer is watching me the whole time that I am doing this, and there is a spiritual aspect to myself, then show me a sign today that you paid attention to any one of these things that I created and bring them in a way that I will inspect so I am as surprised at my ability to be able to experience these things and make it so that I have no doubt that it has come from you."

According to Dr. Joe, the quantum law says, "Can you believe in a future that you can't experience with your senses? You've thought about it enough times in your mind that your brain has changed as a result of it. If you can do that, then your brain is no longer a record of the past, now it's a map to the future." Such as the case with author, Lisa Bonnice, when she visualized herself into creating a thinner body.

Shape Shifting: Reclaiming Your Perfect Body
with Lisa Bonnice

Lisa Bonnice is the author of *Shape Shifting: Reclaiming Your Perfect Body*. She's an example of a woman who has been successful in using the principles of the law of attraction to shift her shape and become thinner without dieting.

In a recent interview I had with Lisa she said, "I was never really skinny, but for most of my life I was just okay with my size. But as I got older, it was just one of those things that gradually built up over the years when suddenly I realized, 'Oh my God, I'm fat.'"

During the time she was gaining weight, she kept asking herself, "Why can't I lose weight?" For God Sakes, I'm doing everything I'm supposed to be doing. I'm starving myself. I'm exercising. I'm punishing myself. I'm doing all the stuff they tell us to do. I'm hating my body. I'm being good.

"And the more I did those things, those horrible, mean cruel things to myself, the more my body reflected in being something that I really hated. So once I realized that, I kept asking this question and the more I keep punishing myself, the worse my body looked and the worse my health became. And that's when I started figuring out that there was more to this than just the body. Maybe there was something to do with the way I was treating myself. And maybe this had something to do with my own self-image, spirituality, and the law of attraction. Nobody had yet coined that phrase so I wasn't able to turn to Abraham or whoever talks about that kind of stuff. I just realized that the more I hated myself, the more I was giving myself reasons to hate myself."

Seeking Answers Outside the Box

Lisa realized that the more she tried to lose weight, the more she would gain. "Since I was already dabbling in the world of alternative medicine and just starting to learn about the body/mind connection, I began looking for books or something in that realm, hoping that somebody could help me out. Nobody had written anything like this, so I finally realized that I'm gonna have to write this book myself."

After this insight she realized that she could use metaphysical/spiritual principles to start improving her life in general, and she decided that she would also apply those same principles to her weight. During the course of her writing and researching, she wound up losing over fifty pounds.

Lisa describes herself as a work in progress and acknowledges that she still has issues to work out. But her journey taught her that the most important thing is to be okay exactly how you are. She says, "If I still am at my original weight, I'm still okay, I'm still a being of light and all that good stuff. And I am a powerful creator. I created my life. I created this body and I am a piece of God. If I am over 200 pounds at 5'2", then that's fine."

Lisa says, "There's this new epidemic of obesity and this incredible ability to lose weight and to be healthy. I think it's got a lot to do with the fact that the media message is 'You are too fat.' No matter how big or small you are, you are told 'You are too fat.' Those of us who know that we create our own reality, that we are energy beings who create our lives and therefore our bodies, if you're told constantly, 'You are too fat,' finally you just begin to build that. I think that explains why everyone is having such a hard time losing weight these days. Everyone's looking for pills and gadgets and things, and it turns out that you just have to stop listening to people who tell you you're not good enough."

Lisa says that, "Your body right now is a reflection of how close to fine you really are. Once you recapture that sense of 'God, life is so good,' your energy just raises and your metabolism naturally goes up and life just falls into place. Your body turns into what your DNA holds in its memory for your healthiest form.

"Your DNA is your energetic skeleton. When you are born it has encoded on your cells your ideal form. By changing your thoughts and becoming accepting of your body in the present, you allow that form to take shape. It begins with your thoughts and the last place it shows up is in the physical, your body."

Lisa explains that your ability to focus and continue to reset your focus is the secret of success in changing your thoughts in order to reshape your body. This is not obsession, because, as she explains, "Obsession doesn't feel good." You've got to pay attention to how you feel all the time.

Most people believe only what they see with their eyes. This is why it's so easy to get discouraged when you look in a mirror and see your fat thighs or flabby stomach. It just feels so permanent and mind numbingly real. Doesn't it?

But I've learned that you can create a new image of yourself starting with a single belief.

What Would I Do Today If I Were Brave?

At one point during the Jack Canfield seminar I attended, I was able to give a presentation to the group. I spoke about my intention to help other women. A professional speaker and singer named Jana Stanfield came up to me later and said, "Andrea, you are a powerful speaker and you'll help so many women."

I was amazed that this woman, who I considered such an eloquent speaker, could think of me as a powerful speaker. In my eyes, as a highly paid and much sought after professional speaker, she had instant credibility and knew what it took to be a powerful speaker. From her belief in me, I began to believe in myself. She lit a fire in me.

I took her words to heart and bought her CD, *If I Were Brave©*. Every day of that following year, I listened to that song imploring me to ask the question, "What would I do today if I were brave?" In my mind's eye, I replayed the scene of Jana telling me that I was a powerful speaker. I could feel her touch, see her tearful blue eyes, and hear her words, as she said, "Andrea, you are a powerful speaker."

Propelled by her faith in me, I knew that I could take whatever steps I needed to help the women who needed me. Now, whenever I get stuck in my fear, I tell myself "Andrea, you are a powerful speaker." Then I ask myself the question, "What would I do today if I were brave?"

So let me ask you, what would you do today if you were brave?

Using Maltz' Theater of the Mind
Techniques to Create Your Ideal Body

There's no arguing the fact that thought precedes every action. There cannot be an action without a thought. In order for you to be able to eat scrambled eggs for breakfast, you have to first think about it. You may picture the eggs in your mind or hear yourself say, "I want some eggs." Perhaps you feel the urge in your body to eat the eggs. However the message was interpreted, it began with a simple thought.

In order for you to leverage the law of attraction to lose weight without dieting, you have to focus on the outcome of what you want.

In Maltz' book, *Psycho Cybernetics: How to Use the Power of Self Image Psychology for Success,* he recommends the following:

"Set aside time to re-create your self-image. In a comfortable position, close your eyes daily for a period of 30 minutes for 21 days. Imagine seeing yourself as you will be when you lose the excess weight, wearing the clothes you love, feeling great, moving with ease, smiling and joyful. It's important to really feel this in your body and enjoy it as though it has already occurred. Be in a state of gratitude."

Dr. Maltz recommends imagining as many details as you can. In your mind's eye, visualize any habits that you want to acquire. Visualize yourself taking smaller bites, enjoying food more, chewing slowly and eating less, and being able to stop eating at the first sign of satisfaction. He suggests refining this over the period of the first eleven days, tweaking the images, and editing them as if you were a producer of a movie. Then for the next ten days, run that movie in your head consistently for the period of thirty minutes each day. He calls this the Theater of the Mind Technique. Notice how similar this is to Dr. Joe's method of creating his day.

By doing this visualizing, you will alter your subconscious programming causing your brain to send new signals to your body that it is no longer fat. Soon after, without trying, you will notice that you will actually begin to manifest the different specific elements of your visualization. Your weight loss will begin to go on autopilot. This visioning work takes effort and persistence.

How Visualization Works For Me

I use EFT combined with visualization to overcome fears that prevent me from doing what I need to spread my message of hope and healing with others. Recently, I've decided to pursue national media coverage and become one of the first plus sized women advocating that women say goodbye to dieting, make peace with food, and love the skin they're in.

Today I continue to use visualization and deliberately manifest opportunities, people, and things that assist me in the pursuit of my goal to empower women and children. As far as using visualization for weight loss, I know from past experience that if I do affirmations and visualizations seeing myself as thinner, it will happen faster. But to tell the truth I don't want to continue to use visualization to see myself as thinner. I use it all the time for other things, but to get thinner, that doesn't do it for me anymore.

I rather use the precious tool of visualization to see myself doing things that challenge me, gaining more confidence and doing more things that I enjoy with the people I love. Because then I know that I'll continue to balance and harmonize my relationship with food, and getting thinner will continue to be a positive benefit of that.

I've noticed that without doing daily visualizations and seeing myself as slimmer, my body is nonetheless slowly beginning to reshape itself back to the way it used to be. My waist is beginning to nip in a bit more and my thighs are getting a bit smaller. Unlike Lisa Bonnice's fast weight loss using visualization, I've chosen for my transformation to be a slow process and I refuse to push it.

After giving it a lot of thought, I realize that I want my outsides to catch up with my insides. I know the pain of experiencing weight gain after investing so much time and energy to lose weight, and I won't let that happen again. So, as I've said before, I'm in no rush to beat myself back down to a size 8. If/when I get back there, I'll be a very different person than I am now. I'm just going to focus on loving this body I have right now and continuously push myself to achieve more in my career, be more present with my family, spend more time with my friends, be more intimate with my husband, and just in general enjoy my life more.

As many of the experts suggest, I highly recommend you start a visualization/gratitude ritual if you want to autopilot your success and blast your goals through the stratosphere.

In my experience, I directly attribute this short morning ritual to many wonderful things that have been happening in my life and in my career over a short time. Before I actually interviewed many of the people in this book, I first imagined talking with them and asking them questions in my mind while sitting quietly in the mornings. Many times my visualizations led me to take certain actions that would bring me closer to my goal.

For example, recently it was recommended to me by my friend, Sally Shields, that I should have my own radio show. A day later, when I happened to mention it to Lisa Bonnice, she graciously offered help in getting me all set up. Many times I set an intention of wanting to choose foods that make me feel really good. On those days, I notice that I'm craving more water, fruit, and fresh vegetables.

In every possible way, visualization has helped me. I'll admit that many times it scares the Bejesus out of me how quickly and easily it works, and I'll find myself stopping and sabotaging myself for days. When I become aware of my old pattern of paralysis, I pull myself back up by the bootstraps and go back to using what I know works.

Here's what works for me:

1. Define a time and place when and where you will relax each day. I used to set a timer each morning for 21 minutes, but now I've learned that Abraham says 15 minutes is more than enough to overcome resistance and increase the flow of abundance. Rather than jar myself with the timer, I prefer to open my eyes and take a quick glance at the time before I resettle myself again. It's much less intrusive.

2. I sit on my office sofa cross-legged or sometimes with my legs extended.

3. Get into an alpha state. I close my eyes, face forward, and tilt my eyes upward as though I am looking at the hands of a clock pointing to 12. Doing this naturally causes a bit of eye strain so don't do it for long, just for a moment until your body feels more connected and relaxed. It automatically puts you into an alpha state, which slows down your breathing and heart rate, making creativity and connection with your source of inspiration flow more easily.

4. Visualize who and what you are grateful for. With my eyes closed, I start off my visualization by generating images of those people and situations in my life for which I am already grateful. This changes my vibration and puts me in a receptive state of

gratitude, making it easier to attract to me more people and situations for which I will be grateful.

5. Make a movie in your mind. With only a few seconds of focusing your attention on what you want, you will activate the vibration of the subject of your attention within you. This means that you will elevate the vibration you are sending out and raise your vibration in order to resonate on the same level as that which you desire. Remember, it only takes 17 seconds of focused thought to change your vibration. I imagine seeing myself through my own eyes, standing on a big stage in front of hundreds of women sharing my juicy message, jumping up and down excitedly.

Sometimes I picture myself as I look now wearing a rich red suit and leopard pumps. I am gracefully floating across the stage, interacting, laughing, and talking into a lapel mike, sharing stories and creating connections with a large group of women, feeling wonderful and confident in my body. In this movie, I also have images of me doing live talk shows with Rachael Ray, Oprah, and Tyra, having a ball chatting with the women and talking passionately about my work. I call this my red suited gal. This is the visualization I use to expand **The Juicy Woman** brand.

I have another version of the red suited gal specific to being more present with my family. In that version I am dressed more casually, in jeans or khakis. I am spending time with the family cooking, baking, watching movies, RVing, camping, and doing all the fun things I love. I also have another version of the movie with just my husband and I in it. Ah! That's the one I use to do my visualization when I want to spice up our sex life. You get the idea. Choose a movie of what you want to be, do, or have in your life.

6. Using your movie, imagine yourself in situations that are a bit challenging. By doing this, you program your subconscious mind to see and think of you as already having achieved what you visualize. Since the brain cannot tell the difference between an imagined thought and reality, your brain sends signals to your body that you have already taken these steps and achieved the outcome you envision. This increases a flood of feel good chemicals from the brain that put you in a state of feeling good. This

413

new state raises your vibration and sets the internal tuning mechanism of your brain, called your Reticular Activating System or RAS, to attract the situations and people necessary to achieve your desired outcome.

7. Refine your details. In order to increase your emotional investment in your visualization, imagine seeing as many details as possible. If you are a person who thinks they are unable to see while visualizing, then use tricks to elicit the same emotional response.

Find a picture of yourself or someone who personifies what you want to look like. Tear out pages from a magazine and use those images to create the focus for your details. For example, since I don't yet own a red suit or a pair of leopard pumps, I have decided to look in the fashion magazines to see what types of suits and shoes I like. When I find something that pleases me I cut out the picture and look at it, creating a new memory in my brain of that red suit and those pumps. This way when I return to my visualization, it will be easier to imagine the specific details of how I will look on the stage at that presentation.

8. Share your visualization. Support is key to achieving any goal. When you take the time to think about, focus, and actively share your visualization with people who support and care about you, you carve that intention out and breathe life into it, enabling its manifestation. Get excited, share your dreams, and make it happen!

In Richard Webster's book, *Creative Visualization for Beginners*, he shares details of Arnold Schwarzenegger's creation process. Long before he became a movie star or the governor of California, Arnold Schwarzenegger was a weight lifter. One day he decided that he wanted to compete for the title of Mr. America.

He says, "I visualized myself being and having what it was I wanted. Mentally I never had any doubts about it. The mind is really so incredible. Before I won my first Mr. Universe title, I walked around the tournament like I owned it. The title was already mine. I had won it so many times in my mind that there was no doubt that I would win it. Then when I moved on to the movies, the same thing, I visualized myself being a famous actor and earning big money. I could feel and taste success. I just knew it would all happen."

Step Up Your Progress with A Vision Board

Years ago I attended a teacher training program at the Waldorf Institute. One of our assignments was to create something called a dream mat. We were instructed to cut out pictures, words, and articles from magazines and other periodicals that reflected what we wanted in our lives. We then pasted them to a sheet of poster board.

One of my goals during that time was to own a home. I was highly skeptical that this would happen anytime soon. At the time I was running the family real estate business. I lived in one of the three buildings that my family owned and managed. I felt certain that I would never be free of the irritation of living in the same building as my tenants, many of whom felt that it was perfectly okay to knock on my door at three o'clock in the morning if there was a problem. Although I had a superintendent on the premises to address their needs, they still came knocking on my door. It made my life a living hell. Now I know that it was my inability to set boundaries that created that misery, but at one time I believed that their constant intrusion on my privacy was governed by the fact that I lived in the same building.

Nonetheless, moving seemed like an absolutely impossible dream. I didn't seriously consider it until nine years later when my Nana had a heart attack. My husband and I decided that we could no longer have her live on her own. She was ninety-four at that time.

To make a long story short, we now live just about a mile away from where I had decided that I wanted to live over twenty-two years ago. We've been here for nearly thirteen years.

It's important to keep in mind that the more clearly you set your intention, and the more you reinforce that message, the quicker you will manifest what you want. Also know that when you set an intention, you release control of the "how" part of getting what you want. By focusing on what you envision and desire, you open yourself up to the universal law of attraction.

Soon after we moved, my husband Angel unearthed that first dream mat I made and I realized to my shock and amazement that I had manifested each image that was represented in that collage with the exception of one, a daughter. Cara was born a few months later that same year.

Bear in mind that this manifestation was generated with almost no effort on my part, other than pulling together the pictures and images for my collage and wanting to live in that particular area of New York. Since then, I have gotten so excited about the process of setting an intention that I have learned many ways of making it a part of my daily life by putting it in front of me and simplifying it even more.

I use a transparent blotter on my desk, and under it I have a dream mat that reflects images of me or representations of me doing yoga, speaking in front of a group, Cross Country skiing, running, singing, and all the things I love to do. I have cut and pasted combinations of words out of magazines to help me generate feelings of excitement toward the things that I want in my life. The words are also reminders of ideas and images that are important to me.

Here are some of the words or phrases that are on my current dream mat. Laughter is the best medicine, Entrepreneur, A Circle of Friends, Dream Big, HOT STUFF, LEARNING ANNEX, HOME IS WHERE THE HEART IS, Don't Postpone Joy!

I even have a powerful affirmation that I learned years ago in a Tony Robbins, *Unleash the Power Within* seminar. It says,

 Now I am the voice

 I will lead, not follow

 I will believe, not doubt

 I will create, not destroy

 I am a force for good

 I am a leader

 Defy the odds!

 Set a new standard!

 Step up!

I also have a quote from Eleanor Roosevelt that continues to inspire me which is as follows:

"You gain strength, courage and confidence, by every experience in which you really stop to look fear in the face. You must do the thing you think you cannot do."

These are just a few examples of how you can create a more compelling future by setting a clear intention of what you want.

Keep in mind that you can mix up images and ideas on your mat so you can generate multiple levels of sensory acuity or awareness for your brain to seek out what you need in order to achieve your goals and fulfill your intention.

On a smaller scale, I use visual imagery to remind myself of what is important to me. Years before, I experienced the healing benefits of Emotional Freedom Techniques®. I considered myself a person unable to express myself. I used to get easily overwhelmed under stress, causing my throat to close and making it hard to breathe or speak. I used to cry at the drop of a hat because I had no other way of expressing my feelings. Today, I make self-expression a high priority in my life.

I've made the decision that, for me, it is most important to be self-expressed. Therefore, I concentrate on finding many ways to be able to say what I really mean in my life.

Let's suppose that you feel tongue-tied whenever you are on the phone with an acquaintance, family member, or client. You can change that limitation by changing the belief that you are not self-expressive. You do this by using imagery to set the intention to become more expressive.

Have a picture near the phone that reminds you to express yourself. Perhaps you could cut out a picture of a beautiful mouth. That is a visual anchor to remind you to express yourself whenever you see it. Use visual anchors to your greatest advantage.

Recently I purchased a book entitled, *Water with Lemon*. It has a wonderful and compelling image on the cover. The design is a simple combination of shades of yellows and white. The photo leads the viewer to imagine the experience of drinking from a clear glass of cold water with slices of lemon floating in it. It is positively mouthwatering.

Since then, I've been craving water with lemon. I don't tend to think of myself as a water drinker. I guess years of dieting and having drilled into me the message of the importance of drinking water, created a certain amount of resistance to the idea of being more hydrated.

However, this idea of using a picture to seduce my taste buds in a specific direction really flips my skirt and jazzes me no end. This is an outstanding example of how you can create new habits by using pictures to motivate you and generate new behaviors that don't come naturally.

If you want to eat more fruit, get pictures of fruit. If you want to smile more, paste a big old smile in front of you. All these visual anchors stimulate the brain to remember experiences you have had. These stir your brain to remember positive feelings, and they create subconscious desires to renew and refresh those experiences. This is the secret to creating new habits and making them stick effortlessly. Keep those pictures in front of you and look at them often to continue to reinforce the new image of the new you.

This is truly powerful stuff. Use this tool and enjoy it!

Having a dream mat is a great example of creating a passive stream of joy in your life.

Here's how:

Create Your Own Dream Mat

1. *Make it big.* Choose a large background upon which to build your map. It could be a poster board, a large piece of flip chart paper (see my example on Page 415), foam core, a tri-fold foam core display, even several pieces of paper taped together to make it big. One of my friends has dedicated two walls of her home to her treasure mapping.

2. *Collect magazines.* Gather your favorite inspirational magazines from all subjects. Some of my favorites are O, The Oprah Magazine, Success, Woman's World, business magazines, fashion, wine, and food magazines, etc. Have some real fun and get together with friends and have a gluing party.

3. *Dedicate time to looking for the right pictures.* No scissors needed for this part. Just flip and feel your way through, letting your eyes fall where they may. Notice what photos, words, and headlines grab your attention.

4. *Rip, tear, or cut the page out.* It's yours. Claim it!

5. *No second guessing.* Avoid justifying why you can't have, be, or do something. Shoot for the stars!

6. *Time for precision.* It's scissors time. Revel in your choices and

have fun trimming and cutting your pictures to the perfect size and shape. Once done, just stick it all in one big pile.

7. *Making the puzzle.* Now it's time for putting all the pieces of the puzzle together. With plenty of time to spare and a large work surface, begin laying out each piece. Don't worry about it being perfect. Just make it feel good to you. Play with each piece and position it and reposition it until it feels right and has a sense of harmony. Some pieces will hang off the page and you'll end up tucking others and moving them back and forth until you find the perfect shape and style for you.

8. *Use your printer.* I like using words on my dream mat so if I can't find a specific word in a magazine printed in the way I want it, I'll print it myself. Play with your words, center them or place them under your pictures as captions, or use meaningful acronyms.

9. *Random or themed?* You can either choose a hodgepodge of images or a specific theme. You might have one vision board representing your career and another for your love life. Be creative.

10. *Get gluing*. When you feel ready to commit, get gluing. You may want to first get your page laid out and then proceed to gluing. If that's the case, I recommend taking a picture of the page layout and working from that as a template. I've used Elmer's® glue and I've used glue stick. The first vision board I did over twenty-four years ago was done with Elmer's® glue, although it was a real mess at the time, it's still in great condition. The other later versions I've done have been made using glue stick or craft spray adhesive and I find that they are always peeling. To make it a more permanent bond, Mod Podge® works great.

11. *Display it.* Place in a spot where you can see it often. I used to have mine under my desk blotter. Since it became too much of a visual distraction, I moved it to hang over my desk. Place it wherever you like, in your office, in your bedroom, on your closet door, in the bathroom!

12. *Inspire yourself.* Make a habit of looking at it often. And do so with the belief that this is already yours. Imagine the feeling of having it now.

13. ***Get the kids involved.*** This is such a great activity to do with kids. I made a board with my daughter, Cara, several years ago and it was a wonderful and unique bonding experience. Talking about your dreams together is powerful.

14. ***Expect good things.*** Sit back and wait for wonderful things to come your way. In making the choice to create your vision board, you set a powerful intention within your subconscious mind that you are open to receiving what you have chosen. Before you know it, you will start attracting those conversations, resources, and people who hold a piece of your vision.

Affirmations: Recipes to Success

At the Jack Canfield training I attended, I learned all about how to use affirmations. This is a wonderful technique for setting powerful and clear intentions which you can do using nothing more than a set of 3x5 index cards, a recipe box, or a photo album.

On each separate index card, compose an affirmation which is a positive statement intended to help you take action toward your goals. According to Jack, there are eight rules or guidelines for creating great affirmations. They are as follows:

1. Affirmations start with the words, "I am…" Think of being in the present. Use words to describe something that you want to be, do, or have now. For example, "I am enjoying drinking my glass of water with ice now."

2. Affirmations are positive. Remember all those words that you want to avoid. Refrain from using negative language such as the words not, never, can't, won't, shouldn't. (You can always refer back to the section on Mind Your Mouth, Watch Your Tongue.)

Wrong: I won't drink any Hawaiian Punch today with my lunch.

Right: I am drinking water with lemon and ice with my lunch today. An image of this is a great idea to add to your vision board. You'll be amazed at how often you'll crave water.

3. State the affirmation as if it is happening now.
4. Affirmations are short.
5. Affirmations are specific.

Wrong: I am driving a new car.

Right: I am driving a new red 2008 Jeep Liberty.

6. Affirmations require the use of an action verb in the present tense, ending in -ing.

I am *enjoying* a relaxation vacation with my husband

7. Affirmations express your feelings. Interject a feeling word in them.

 I am happily driving a new red 2008 Jeep Liberty

 I am *passionately* and *animatedly* presenting my Mindful Munchins seminar to a group of women in a restaurant in Bergen, New Jersey.

8. Affirmations are all about you. They are intended to help you change your own behavior, up-level your thinking, and feel great as you accomplish mini challenges and move toward your intended goals.

Wrong: My son, PT, is keeping his room clean.

Right: I am calmly and joyfully expressing my pride and gratitude to PT for keeping his room clean.

Those are the eight guidelines for creating powerful and compelling affirmations that direct your internal goal-seeking mechanism to hit the target of what you want.

Vision boards, affirmations, and visualization are all important tools on the road to making peace with food and loving your body. They are cheap and easy to make and their value is priceless. Figure out what you want in your life, and then commit yourself 100% toward making that first step by creating your vision board and activating the law of attraction to pull your dreams into reality.

Wrapping Up
Chapter 10: How to Set a Powerful Intention

Here are the juiciest morsels covered in this section. Savor them mindfully.

 What we think of as our reality is considered by the universe to be more like unset Jell-O®. Our thoughts can penetrate through time and space and change things. Research shows that thoughts are capable of affecting everything from the simplest machines to the most complex living beings.

 Cleve Backster's Primary Perception experiments proved there is communication between all living things. Basically all you need to know is that your thoughts count!!!

 You can make a difference. It would only take 8000 people holding a common intention to change our world.

 In 2004, Japanese scientist Dr. Masaru Emoto, proved that water is vulnerable to thoughts and images directed toward it. Now consider this: If our bodies are made up almost entirely of water, what is the potential impact that our thoughts and the thoughts of others have on our bodies?

 "The more you focus on hating yourself, the more you'll find reasons to hate yourself." "At every moment, your body is in the best condition that your mindset allows."
  • Lisa Bonnice, author of *Shape Shifting: Reclaiming Your Perfect Body*

 It's important to keep in mind that the more clearly you set your intention, and the more you reinforce that message, the quicker you will manifest what you want. Also, understand that when you set an intention, you release control of the "how" part of getting what you want.

 Having a dream mat is a great example of creating a passive stream of joy in your life.

In the next chapter, I'll go into more detail and explain the benefits of creating and participating in success teams.

Chapter 11
Mastermind: Don't Hang with Turkeys When You Can Soar with the Eagles

"Isolation is the dreamkiller."
– *Barbara Sher,* author of *Wishcraft*

How many times have you caught yourself eating when you really weren't hungry? I'll bet, like me, those are the times when you felt the least supported, unappreciated, and completely and hopelessly alone and unhappy. I'm sure you'd agree that as emotional eaters, we've used food to fight boredom, depression, anxiety, anger, to ease stress, reward ourselves, and mask emotional emptiness—all of which have absolutely nothing to do with eating for hunger.

In American society most of us women have been conditioned from the time we were little girls to accept the belief that we are not equal to boys. We've been taught to take on the role of the caregivers, nurturers, and fixer uppers.

Learning to be people pleasers at an early age meant many of us have felt compelled to bear everyone else's burdens. We eagerly do it all for everyone else and never quite feel comfortable asking for what we need ourselves. When it comes to asking for help most of us just can't do it.

The Secret to Success: Ask for Help

Like many women, I was taught "If you want something done right, do it yourself." Only years later, after I learned the values of having a support team, asking for help, and delegating responsibilities, did I understand that this foolish, self-limiting thinking was the cause of so much of my emotional overeating.

I'd like to share with you the story of a colleague of mine, Robin Hardy. With the help of having what she calls, "A great sphere of influence of wonderful people in her life," she overcame her painful history of years of being abused by an emotionally disturbed mother. She has since emerged as a powerful public speaker dedicated to empowering women. If Robin can come through her experience with the power and passion to live her dreams and love her body as it is, then you can too.

But before I launch into the how-to's of creating your support network and sharing Robin's story, I'd like to tell you how I learned about the importance of having a success team behind you.

My Experience with Success Teams

Since 2000, I have participated in many of these types of Mastermind groups. Once I understood their power I decided that I wanted to lead them. Today, I work with groups of women from coaching corporate employees in well-known companies like Avon® and Lane Bryant®, to hosting live meet up groups and teleclasses each week on my Curvy and Confident Coaching Club calls.

Back in October 2003, my life was at a crossroads. I knew that I would have to find a new livelihood and I was overwhelmed by the prospect of starting over at forty-two years old.

My friend, Dawn, and I attended a Learning Annex® event for women in transition. One of the speakers was a woman named Barbara Sher. I was impressed with her from the moment she stepped on the stage. She was so real and authentic and just spoke from her heart.

When Barbara spoke of women's tendencies to ignore their dreams and goals and instead to sacrifice themselves for their family, I felt like she was talking to me.

She led the group in an exercise called The Lying Game. The object of the exercise was for everyone to partner up with their seatmates and share a story about themselves of something they wished they had but that they didn't.

Some people told stories saying they were famous photographers, others said that they owned a villa in France. There were stories of Nobel Prize winners and famous actors, bungee jumpers and athletes.

When it came time for me to introduce myself, I turned to my partner and said, "Hi I'm Andrea Amador. I'm a bestselling author and world famous speaker. I've just begun a nonprofit organization to benefit abused women and kids named Nana Cares, and lately I've been traveling the world in search of creating a network of sponsors." I explained to her that I was about to close a deal on some prime oceanfront real estate along the Florida coast, and I was excited to own my first vacation home where I could spend the summers with my husband and two kids.

I don't know about everyone else's story, but I knew for sure mine wasn't true. It was what I wished for but didn't yet have. After everyone had taken a turn, Barbara explained that inside of us we all have unfulfilled dreams and desires. Most of us have spent much of our life trying to ignore them or make them go away because people have discouraged us and told us to be realistic.

Barbara said that many of our dreams may not seem realistic at face value, like wanting to be a Playboy bunny or jumping out of an airplane naked, or being the next Donald Trump. But when we dig beneath them, we can find what she calls touchstones to lead us toward being able to manifest our dreams.

She explained that within each of our "lies" were goals and dreams in hiding. Just like unpolished gems they were waiting to manifest into reality, but in order to make them shine, we needed to get some help.

Then she launched into another exercise and told everyone in the room to use the paper we had by our seats and write down and complete the following two phrases:

My wish

My obstacle

The idea was to get the group members circulating and for them to share a quick sentence about what they wished for and state the nature of the obstacles that prevented them from getting it. After we all settled down, Barbara asked anyone who didn't get much satisfaction from the previous activity to volunteer and share their wish and obstacle.

One woman raised her hand and said that she had always dreamed of opening a spa business in Greece, yet had no clue or any connections to anything to do with spas or Greece. Barbara asked for people to raise their hands and say what they could do to help out this woman. Within a few minutes, this woman had met several people who could all provide resources or support to help her reach her goal of actually owning a spa in Greece.

I was astonished as I watched this woman's vague dream begin to become a reality with one person after another sharing their ideas, services, or suggestions. It all started with one person saying, "I have a piece of property in Greece that I'm not using that I'd be willing to discuss renting to you." Just like a snowball rolling downhill, her wish started becoming a reality, getting bigger and bigger and gaining more momentum.

Stanley Milgram and Six Degrees of Separation

You're probably familiar with the saying, "It's a small world." Well, there's actually a lot of truth to that statement. Stanley Milgram is a psychologist who conducted what has been known as The Small World Experiment.

He gathered twenty strangers in a room with a wall filled with phone books. The purpose of the experiment was to prove that there are only six degrees of separation between any two people in the world. This means that you are only six contacts away from being able to connect with someone who can help you do whatever your heart desires.

Let's say you wanted to meet Brad Pitt. According to Milgram's theory, you would already know him through six different people. For example, you tell your friend Suzie you want to meet Brad Pitt. She knows Bob, who knows Jane, who knows Heather, who knows Steve, who knows Bill, who knows Brad Pitt..

The object of the Small World Experiment was to get a note hand delivered anywhere in the United States within just three days by using only the resources available in the room. One of the participants was blindfolded and opened a random phone book and put his finger on a name and address of a woman in North Dakota.

Every one of the twenty people in the room began brainstorming and thinking of ways they could get that note to the woman. One person in the room had a friend whose cousin was a trucker who could get there the next day. In addition to that idea, there were eleven other suggestions and strategies that the group came up with that day to get the note to the woman within only three days.

Now consider that this was only the collective brainstorming ability of twenty people. Imagine what kind of oomph you get when you have a room of 100 or 200 or 1000 or more. This is why in the group of several hundred at the Learning Annex presentation it was possible to generate solutions for the woman who wanted to own a spa in Greece.

How about you? What would you like to do, be, or have that requires help?

Accountability: The Difference that Makes the Difference

The first time I leveraged the power of accountability was when I listened to and followed a series of Tony Robbins tapes with my friend, Sandra. As a small group of two, we were committed to ensuring each other's success. When one of us made a promise to take action, we held each other to it.

If I promised Sandra that I was going to make three phone calls to several interested buyers, then that's what I had to do. This is called Accountability.

Joining Jodie's Success Team

My second experience with accountability came from being a member of a larger success team. This group really packed a punch and gave my goals legs. Each week we would get together and share what we had completed during the previous week. The difference was that now I was accountable to a group of people instead of just one. I realized this had some real power. It was less feasible to try to weasel out of the commitment by begging off and making an excuse, such as was possible with a friend.

Jodie was our leader and she led us through the next eight weeks with passion and poise. To this day, she still remains a dear friend of mine and we often get together for lunch, enjoy catch up time, and brainstorm solutions to each other's challenges. I believe it has been largely due to Jodie's faith in me that I have taken many of the leaps that I have. Without her encouragement and that of my success team, I wouldn't have believed in myself enough to have pursued coaching. On more than one occasion, my teammates Jodie, Anisa, and Shirley have been the wind beneath my wings!

I can honestly say that on the first day I arrived I had a whole armload of fantasies of what I wanted for my life. And thanks goes to my buddies because they helped me put those pipe dreams into plans and realities. Without them, I would still be spinning like a top, unable to fix on any one thing and wishing, hoping, and dreaming that my life was different.

Sadly, over the years a few of us have gotten separated, but I still know that I can count on Jodie and my buddy, Anisa, to help me find a fresh perspective to any challenge I face. To beat all, it turned out that Anisa lived only about two miles away from me. How's that for six degrees of separation? She's become such a dear friend.

Online Accountability

Until I had my first experience with Barbara Sher's *Success Step by Step* bulletin board, I had no clue of the value of online accountability.

One day, I faced a monumental task. None of my team members were available and I needed help because I didn't have a clue how to begin the huge task that lay before me.

In preparation to sell the buildings, I had to clean out a huge area that I had made into my personal storage space where I had been stockpiling my junk for more than fifteen years.

Facing the pressure of the deadline, I thought I would go out of my mind. It was eight rooms filled with stuff floor to ceiling. Old craft projects, clothing, furniture, papers, boxes, photos, pictures, china, bric-a-brac, all the things I didn't want yet couldn't find it in my heart to release. These were the things that kept me holding onto the past.

One day there was a steam leak in the building and a radiator pipe burst flooding the area. When I surveyed the damage, I was broken hearted to see the destruction that had occurred.

Seeking instant support, I decided to take a chance and post my request on Barbara's Sher's message board. After I wrote down my request, I broke it down into several goals and further subdivided that into baby steps as follows:

Goal #1 Clean and clear storage area

Baby steps:

1. dispose of 10 large 3 mil garbage bags full of junk

2. separate clothes for donations

3. get assistance with removing heavy items

4. get assistance with upgrading all lighting

As soon as I wrote my request to the group I left the house to begin the task. As if by magic, people popped up all day long willing to help. One of my superintendents, Andres, and his wife, Juana, offered their help moving furniture and taking out garbage. Other people filled bags and helped clear the area. I was able to fill up ten bags in no time at all. Within less than a week the task was done. But the toughest part was getting started. I couldn't have done it without the benefit of feeling the pressure of being accountable to somebody else.

After that, I was a believer and I fully understood the value of online accountability. For the next several years, I used Barbara's online message board as my means of support when my team was not available.

Thanks to accountability and success teams, I feel as though I am never alone, and I know exactly where I can go for instant support, 24/7.

Choosing Your Success Team:
Don't Throw Pearls Before Swine

My Nana used to say, "Don't throw pearls before swine." After learning the value of having a success team, I've taken that to mean that my dreams and goals are precious, and to share them with people who will not appreciate them or those who will stomp all over them can do so much more harm than good. I've learned to keep certain aspects of my life compartmentalized, and that it's not realistic to expect support from everyone.

You may recall in an earlier section in this book I asked you to write down the names of the people in your life. For those who are generally good, strong, positive influences, mark their names with a plus sign. For those who are negative Nancy's and grouchy Gus's mark them with a negative sign.

Many times we have friends and family members who are so deeply entrenched in their own stuff that they are unable to take the time to listen and support us. They may just be stuck in the muck. These can be wonderful people who you adore, but they are unable to give you the time and attention you want from them. Don't make the mistake of showering them with your hopes and dreams, because in their frustration and perhaps jealousy, they might end up pissing all over you.

When I first decided that I wanted to be a coach, and for the first year of my *NLP* Practitioner training, all I wanted was to practice the skills and techniques I was learning. I decided that I would try them out on my family. They didn't realize it, but they were my guinea pigs.

Every chance I got I shared my thoughts and ideas with them. I tried to engage them in discussions and even attempted to coach them without their knowing it. But they were clueless and had no idea what I was talking about. They were completely out of the loop and not able to help me at all. I ended up getting myself and them very frustrated.

Maybe you can relate to trying to gather a flock of people together as a support team, and realizing that not only are they unwilling but also incapable of helping you achieve what you want.

Many times clients have told me that they love their husband and have a great relationship, but they get so upset when they notice hubby's eyes glaze over whenever they talk about work or some other area of interest their significant other does not share.

If you're trying to fit a square peg into a round hole like I was, it's understandable that this is something that would make you want to run to the fridge to soothe your hurt feelings. My suggestion is to find a group of like minded people who can offer you the support and guidance that you seek, rather than trying to get it all in one person or a few disinterested suspects. Join a success team.

Tips to Join a Success Team

"You can't soar like an eagle when you're surrounded by turkeys!" That saying has stuck with me for a long time. I don't know to whom I can attribute it, but I do know that I love it and it has helped me realize that some people are natural born optimists and others tend to see the glass as half empty.

You are the company you keep. If you're noticing that you are struggling with motivation and feeling positive, it's time to look at who makes up your support team. You can find great support teams either on the internet or in your local region. Here are a few tips to help you choose the right support network:

Birds of a Feather – Choose people with whom you have something in common. You may prefer just women or a combination of men and women. Whomever you choose, base your decision on people who will support you. In one product creation mastermind group I participated in, I became buddies with a gentlemen in Chicago named Cordell. Cordell and I were the only two people on the team who took accountability seriously.

We had certain days when we would check in with each other every hour. These were called Accountability Days. Everyone else laughed at us and thought we were being ridiculous. Nonetheless, that kind of nose to the grindstone accountability worked for both of us. Knowing that we were both committed to getting our products done, we decided to check in with one another every hour on the hour to stay accountable. The result was that we accomplished more in less time and had the benefit of brainstorming with each other whenever we came upon an obstacle. In my opinion, Accountability rocks.

Types of Success Teams

Choose Your Support Style – Barbara Sher has divided support types into three basic categories: informal, structured, and a combination of both.

Informal – Best for people seeking solutions to problems. An informal group can help you by generating lots of ideas. This can be as simple as having coffee with a friend, talking one on one, or meeting a group of mothers at the playground and having a chat about child safety.

Structured – A structured group gathers together for the sole purpose of furthering each other's goals. This can be done in someone's home or in a large institutional setting like a school or hotel. Let your imagination go wild. The sky's the limit.

Combination – You can switch between an informal type of group and a more formal group by dividing your time between locations. For example, when I was on Jodie's success team we met each Wednesday morning in her home.

Juicy Woman Note:

Most people rarely share their personal business with others, especially those with whom they are unfamiliar. In, The Aladdin Factor, co-authors Jack Canfield and Mark Victor Hansen explain the value of asking for what you want. Here are things you can start asking for when addressing your success teams:

companionship	a sale
volunteers to assist you	forgiveness
an extension	caring
discounts	the universe for help
a hug	pray
a mentor	on behalf of a charity
directions	money to start a business
to make a trade	qualified investors

You can ask for respect, love, nurturing, more time, a massage, healing, an explanation, a commitment, a favor, secrets, homework, clothes, ask for a joint venture partnership, a better table at a restaurant, airline tickets, hotel upgrades, more money, a loan, better terms, lower interest rates, support, help, teaching, coaching, instruction, etc.

Since learning about the power of asking for help from others, I like to return favors and kindness by asking, "How can I support you?

For the last session in Barbara Sher's program, we had what she calls an "Idea Party." An "Idea Party" is a brainstorming get-together where people share food and ideas. In order to get the most benefit, Jodie arranged to combine our success team's group with two others, and we met in a larger venue.

Now if you're just looking to get started. Here are a few guidelines for Brainstorming One-on-One:

Brainstorm One-on-One

1. Sit down together in a quiet place where you can be undisturbed for about an hour.
2. If both of you want to solve a problem, divide your time in half.
3. Have your pen and paper ready to capture great ideas. I recommend bringing a tape recorder.
4. Tell your partner what you want and what the problem or obstacle is you're facing.
5. Before beginning, phrase your challenge in a positive light. For example, how can I develop a support program without being computer savvy?
6. Accept all suggestions and ideas offered by your partner—no editing.
7. Write everything down.
8. After time is up, review all the possibilities and find something useful for each.
9. Beef up those parts that aren't useful.

Shout it from the Rooftops- Small Groups and Personal Networks are great ways of planting your little seed in a much more fertile field and crossing beyond the coffee clutch consciousness.

You can either do this informally, by telling everyone you come in contact with what you're seeking, or you can leverage the power of a group and get them all together in one room, either in a physical space or a virtual room, as in an online community or even a teleclass setting. Examples of local or physical groups are church groups, book clubs, girl and boy scouts, community centers, PTA meetings, etc.

Having this opportunity to brainstorm in a large group setting is another example of what Barbara typically calls an idea party, which was the example I witnessed when I went to her Learning Annex® workshop

The Secrets of A Master Asker

1. <u>Know what you really want</u> – Get clear and be specific. Write down 10 benefits you get by asking for what you want.

2. <u>Be confident</u> – Believe in your heart that you are worthy of receiving whatever you're requesting.

3. <u>Creative phrasing</u> - You will do that, can't you, don't you, won't you, couldn't you? Aren't you? I can't imagine this project without you, etc.

4. <u>Be passionate</u> – Put your heart into it, and take a risk.

5. <u>Be persistent</u> – Don't give up. "Success is failure turned inside out."

6. <u>Visualize your ideal outcome</u> – Imagine what it would look like if your request was granted. Spend time focusing on that image.

7. <u>Gratitude</u> – After taking the two steps of asking and believing, focus on what it will be like to receive your request as granted. Send thanks to the universe for having made that so.

Say what you are thinking and ask for what you want, no suffering in silence. Realize that asking improves your chances of receiving by 200 percent. Remember: Anything is possible ... if you dare to ask!

The Power of Role Models

As an *NLP*er, I've learned the incomparable value of finding role models to move you closer to your specific goals. I credit three women as being my greatest role models in creating my business who have taught me and inspired me to believe in myself and to spread my message:

Jessica Weiner's work as the Global Ambassador for Dove's® Self Esteem Fund helped me to set my intention. Getting to know Robin Hardy made me believe that, exactly as I am, I could follow my dreams and speak from my heart. And Sally Shields, my media buddy, taught me the specific steps necessary to become an Amazon.com bestseller, a well-respected radio and TV guest, and a much-sought-after speaker.

Prior to meeting Robin Hardy, I had mistakenly decided, "I'm too overweight, and I'd be laughed off the stage," and then I saw Robin, a beautiful, curvy, plus-sized woman, and I realized, "My God, if this woman can do it, then so can I."

In the following story, you'll meet Empowerment coach, radio host, and speaker, Robin Hardy. She learned the hard way that you can't always depend on family in order to be happy and successful. In fact, sometimes you just have to reinvent yourself with a little bit of help from your friends.

Robin Hardy: Empowering You

Robin Hardy is a powerhouse woman. Her methods empower people to stretch beyond their limitations, re-invent themselves through a solid sense of self-esteem, and to deepen their levels of confidence for unstoppable success. Robin speaks nationally, teaches on college campuses, and coaches individuals, small business owners, and entrepreneurs.

On a personal level, beyond all her professional expertise, Robin is an inspiration to any woman who has ever been overwhelmed with having a dysfunctional family member who feels the need to criticize and beat down others in an attempt to remain in control.

Life with an Abusive Mother

Robin was raised by a severely mentally ill mother whose schizophrenia made her "a miserable, hateful person." She created a lifetime of painful and harmful memories for Robin, including lies, stealing, and even threatening to kill her own daughter. For many years, due to her mother's dysfunctional influence, Robin's life was filled with drama and trauma.

Despite living in the belly of the beast, Robin survived. When she was young, she intuitively knew to ignore the rantings of her rageful and hateful mother constantly telling her that she was stupid, fat, and ugly.

It was thanks to Jay, the man who raised her as his own daughter, that Robin had a sense of being loved. Although she knew that Jay was not her actual father, both of them were as close as they could be.

She said, "I always knew I was daddy's girl, and there wasn't anything that I couldn't ask for that he wouldn't give me. He never hit me or anything. Mom was the one who beat the crap out of me. She hit me with whatever she had in hand. I remember one time we had an Electolux® vacuum, and she took the hose off and swung it at me. It was Jay, my dad, who raised me and protected me by telling her to back off."

At fifteen years old, Robin eagerly accepted his help to secure her first job working at a local mall. Even at that young age, something inside her understood the path to change and healing lay in taking action. From the time she was a young girl she understood the value of working. Self-described as a doer, Robin says, "Just say you need to get this done and get out of my way."

Because of her many painful life experiences with her mother's damaging and hurtful influence, Robin struggled for a long time with a very low self-worth. Her growth has been an evolutionary development, spurred by wanting to help other women

At twenty-one, Robin's world was shattered when her dad died of a sudden heart attack on the evening before Thanksgiving. Devastated by the loss of him, she found herself drawing closer to her faith and her church family.

It became clear to the people around her that Robin was a very special person with many gifts, but for many years she didn't see it. Supported and appreciated by her friends, she's gotten many compliments from people telling her, "You're a really good listener, you're a really good encourager, you're a really good edifier, but you don't believe in yourself."

Because she didn't believe in herself, she automatically discounted all the wonderful things people said about her.

Gradually, as she began to feel loved and accepted in the safe space that was her church, she started to find her own footing and expand her thinking about what could be possible. Robin says, "Through everything it became natural to encourage women, to build them up, and then I started realizing how much power I did have to help people and to actually put it into play."

Robin realized that as she became more aware of women needing support and encouragement, she felt called to offer her services and that was what she needed to push beyond her own fears and insecurities.

Over the past couple of years since she's been in the media, she's gotten a great deal of feedback from others telling her what a wonderful source of inspiration she is to women.

After hearing about all the pain she endured, one would naturally wonder how she has been able to keep it all together. Robin credits her ability to overcome the many painful storms in her life to several important lessons she's learned over the years.

Connection to God – Robin found great healing and love through her church. She says, "If I didn't have that nucleus there, I don't know what would have happened. I could have been a totally jacked up person. I believe that we have to have faith in a power greater than us."

Make a list – Write down a list of all the good qualities people have with whom you want to be associated. What kinds of personality characteristics do you seek in peers, mentors, or friends? What qualities do you want to find in your clients? After getting clear in that way, you will find that the right people will start coming to you.

Sphere of influence – For maximum support, choose wonderful friends and create a powerful network of loving and supportive people. When Robin finally found her birth father, who she adores, she realized that "Your sphere of influence can heal you and redirect you."

She says, "I was tight with my friends, more so than with my family. Unfortunately oftentimes the people who have hurt us most in our life are our family. That's why it's good to know that you can always surround yourself with people who love, appreciate, and support you."

It's important to keep in mind that the people who are positive influences in your life won't always tell you "Yes." Robin says, "There are people in my life who correct me, they'll question me and say, 'Are you sure that's the right option?'" These are the people who push Robin to think on her feet and to stand her ground. This is what she calls her sphere of influence.

Desire to change — We have to have a desire inside that says, "I want more of something. I don't want to be here anymore." You can always find something better if you believe it's there. When you're tired of where you're at and you want to do something with your life, it's that passion and desire that lets you change.

Believe – When you believe in yourself, you become unstoppable. When I didn't believe in myself, others did. Robin believes that by embodying the characteristics of the person she wanted to attract, they would find their way to her. "If I dealt with my fear and spoke from my heart, I would attract those who I am meant to attract."

Take action – What good is passion if you're too afraid to do anything with it? You've got to take action. Robin shared a story about a friend of hers who said, "I believe that God is going to bring me the right job." Robin agreed that she believed that too, but realized that the woman never went out and interviewed or never went to apply for jobs. She said, "What do you think? Do you have it in your head that people are just going to call you and ask, 'Do you want a job?' Nowhere in the bible does it say, 'Just sit down and wait and I'll provide.' Action. If we step forward and choose to pursue something with passion, vigor and life, there's almost nothing that we can't do. Nothing can stop us."

Ask – You have to ask. Nobody's going to know what's going on in your brain unless you say what's on your mind.

Juicy Woman Note:

Success Step by Step

I'm sure you're wondering what's up with all this talk about goals and dreams. Believe me, I understand your desire to address the need at hand: reshaping your body without dieting. Naturally, like most women who are unhappy with their body, you'd love to find a fast way to progress. I've found that scales and other measuring tools don't work, because they only leave you feeling worse, not better.

When your days are stress-filled and life gets crazy, it's all too easy to fall back on the old catastrophic way of thinking, "I'll never lose this weight." That's when your thoughts go to your thighs or any other part of your life that is not changing as fast as you'd like.

Remember, this is a journey and that means it takes time. In order to enjoy the trip, change the focus. Instead of paying attention to the outward signs of weight loss which everyone looks for, seek out the inward changes you're making.

438

> Notice when your behavior takes a turn evidencing a new way of honoring your internal wisdom, that quiet intuitive or naturally slender eater within you. Think about the things you do each day and notice that as you make peace with food, your life changes!

To address the need to chart your progress without having to deal with the messiness that comes with getting on a scale or trying to squeeze into a pair of tight jeans, I use another benchmark. It's a simple exercise I created called, "Pennies From Heaven."

Pennies From Heaven: A Fun Way To Track Your Progress

Before we start the exercise, I want to remind you that Intuitive Eating is made up of many different incremental changes that take place in your behavior as you begin to welcome back all foods and learn to love yourself more. Here is a short list of things to note as you travel along the road to making peace with food and friends with your body:

Listening to your body, paying attention to your hunger, eating what you want, refusing to eat what you don't want, taking care of yourself, saying "No" to others establishing personal boundaries, taking "me" time for you, expressing yourself more, asking for help, being gentle with yourself, forgiving yourself, accepting your body, stepping out of old comfort zones.

For example:

 Did you speak up today in a way that you wouldn't have before?

Did you decide to set aside some time to play today?

Did you call a friend and ask for help?

Did you jump in and take a risk instead of playing it safe?

Did you get and eat exactly what you wanted at your last meal?

Are you feeling comfortable around fattening food?

 Have you cleaned your refrigerator and cabinets and tossed out stale and rotten food?

Each time you do something that is remotely connected to changing your relationship with food or learning to be more gentle and loving with your body, reward yourself.

I use the following exercise to challenge my clients to think bigger about themselves.

Try It! Pennies From Heaven

Choose a small glass or jar that you like.

Place it near you so that you can have easy access to it.

Each time you notice a small internal change that you have made due to becoming an Intuitive Eater, put a penny or other coin or even a token in the jar.

Decide on something you would like to have when the jar gets full. My clients have used this to earn new clothes, shoes, books bubble baths, a trip to the movies, lipsticks, even vacations. The possibilities are endless. You go as big or small as you like with the goals that you set. Whatever you choose, take a few moments each time you add to the jar and visualize yourself achieving the goal, feel the feelings attached to it, and see yourself as you will be when you earn your special prize. You may also like to keep a log of the individual changes either written or recorded.

When the jar is full, empty it and redeem your prize. Then choose something new and begin all over again.

This exercise is an example of the power of anchoring. You'll recall that an anchor is a stimulus that stirs your brain to remember something. In this case, you'll remember that you are succeeding in your goals. By putting a coin in the jar each time you notice an action or internal change that supports your new self image, you are creating a new memory for the subconscious mind to prove that you are progressing on the road to becoming an Intuitive Eater.

Wrapping Up
Chapter 11: Mastermind: Don't Hang with Turkeys
When You Can Soar with the Eagles

Here are the juiciest morsels covered in this section. Savor them mindfully.

 "Isolation is the dream killer." – Barbara Sher, author of Wishcraft

 Get in touch with how much you want to change. You can always find something better if you believe it's there. When you're tired of where you're at and you want to do something with your life, it's your discomfort that pushes you to change.

 We eagerly do it all for everyone else and never quite feel comfortable asking for what we need ourselves. When it comes to asking for help most of us just can't do it.

 In Stanley Milgram's Small World Experiment, he set out to prove that there are only six degrees of separation between any two people in the world. This means that you are only six contacts away from being able to connect with someone who can help you do whatever your heart desires.

 Your dreams and goals are precious, and to share them with people who will not appreciate them or those who will stomp all over them can do so much more harm than good.

 Don't make the mistake of showering everybody with your hopes and dreams, because in their frustration and perhaps jealousy, they might end up pissing all over you.

 Don't take it personally if the people you love are not capable of helping you. They've got their own problems. Adding yours would be too much to ask them to bear.

 You are the company you keep. If you're noticing that you are struggling with motivation and feeling positive, it's time to look at who makes up your support team.

 To get the support and guidance you seek, choose people with whom you have something in common. You may prefer just

women or a combination of men and women. Whomever you choose, base your decision on people who will support you.

- When you have a big project or challenge to handle, maximize your productivity for your home and business, by finding a buddy and doing hour by hour accountability check-ins. You can get so much done in such a short amount of time when you know that you have to answer to someone.

- The secret to losing weight without dieting is getting the other stuff in your life done so that you won't feel the need to stuff down your frustrations. Take action. Use a team of people to support you in doing whatever you need to get done.

- An "Idea Party" is a brainstorming get-together where like-minded people share food and ideas.

- Don't reinvent the wheel. Use role models to teach you how to get to where you want to be. Learning from others to expand your perspective is the short cut to success.

- You have to ask. Nobody's going to know what's going on in your brain unless you say what's on your mind.

Conclusion

"It's not the power of the curse. It's the power you give it."
— From the movie, *Penelope*

Above all, remember that you are a Goddess and nothing is too good for you. So move forward with your day, hold your head high, and know that you are fabulous just as you are right now.

You, my dear friend, can do anything. Although you may not believe it, it is true, and I know this from the bottom of my heart. I and the other women represented in this book are living proof of that truth.

You may have been pounded and pressured all your life by people telling you that you weren't good enough, smart enough, pretty enough, or thin enough to go out in the world and accomplish your dreams. They may have tried their best, pulled every punch, staged every drama, toyed with your emotions, intruded upon your body, and trampled all over your heart.

They may have been masters at using guilt, fear, and intimidation in an attempt to get you to buckle under, settle for less, downsize yourself, and stuff your dreams in a box and forget them.

You may have been convinced that you're small and insignificant and have nothing of value to offer. But that's not true. It was their dysfunction and their pain that prevented them from loving you and giving you the support you needed, because they didn't know how to love themselves.

Because of their weaknesses, they weren't willing to let you shine for fear that you would one day outshine them.

Your dysfunctional relationship with food and your body was never your fault, it was merely an outcropping of the hurts that you've endured, the pounds of pain that have emotionally burdened your heart, a desperate cry asking for love, looking for love, trying to find it in the hearts of those who were incapable of giving it.

Emotional eating is the curse that pushes us to eat when we're not hungry. But as in the movie, *Penelope*, it is not the power of the curse, but the power you give it. We've all been hurt by life and knocked down by circumstances beyond our control. But, as Sylvester Stallone says in *Rocky VI*, "It's not how many times you've been hit, it's about how hard you can get hit and keep moving forward, how much you can take and keep moving forward. That's how winning is done."

Now, after reading this book, I hope you understand that the voices in your head that hold you back from fully embracing your heart, mind, and soul and from lovin' the skin you're in, are just old tapes from the past that have gotten stuck in your brain because they came packaged with painful emotions.

You may not have had the power to do anything about them at the time, but you have the power now. You have a choice. The future of your emotional freedom is literally at your fingertips. Go forth and conquer. The world's anxiously waiting for you. Shine on, my Juicy Woman. Shine on.

Juicy Woman Checklist

The following questions are intended to give you a tool to evaluate your progress on a daily basis:

❑ Am I taking extremely good care of myself? Do I take time out of my schedule each day just for me?

❑ Am I tuning in and paying attention to my inner wisdom?

❑ Am I aware of what's on my Bug List?

❑ Am I tolerating any person, place or thing that is sapping my energy?

❑ Am I enjoying the foods I love?

❑ Am I eating more mindfully?

❑ Am I taking responsibility for whatever I can in my life?

❑ Am I avoiding the scale?

❑ Am I handling my stress consistently?

❑ Am I wearing and buying clothes that make me feel great now?

❑ Have I created or joined a group of like-minded women who are invested in supporting me on my journey to making peace with food and friends with my body?

❑ Am I fueling my body, mind and spirit with premium sources of fuel?

❑ Am I taking action toward my goals?

❑ Am I strengthening my loving relationships with the important people in my life?

❑ Am I spending time appreciating all that I have?

❑ Am I being gentle with myself?

- ❏ Am I talking to myself with a new loving gentle tone?
- ❏ Am I setting better boundaries?
- ❏ Am I able to forgive more easily?
- ❏ Am I feeling better about myself, my body and my life?
- ❏ Am I expressing myself more honestly?
- ❏ Am I more confident?
- ❏ Am I more sensitive to my needs?
- ❏ Am I feeling more confident asking for what I want?
- ❏ Am I in tune with what I'm really hungry for?
- ❏ Am I more okay with feeling my feelings?
- ❏ Am I being true to myself?
- ❏ Am I questioning my limiting beliefs?
- ❏ Am I clearing out my mental and emotional clutter?
- ❏ Am I empowering myself by giving new meaning to my past experiences?
- ❏ Am I clear about what my values are?
- ❏ Am I linking things I want to change to my highest values?
- ❏ Am I recognizing that I am lovable and capable? (IALAC)
- ❏ Am I avoiding the temptation of being an emotional rescuer?
- ❏ Am I asking the question, "Whose responsibility is it?"
- ❏ Am I questioning my phantom hunger?
- ❏ Am I forgiving myself for overeating?
- ❏ Am I exploring what's behind the cause of my overeating?
- ❏ Am I over committing?
- ❏ Am I getting more comfortable saying, "No" to others and "Yes" to myself?
- ❏ Am I clear about who tends to want to cross my boundaries?
- ❏ Am I ready with an action plan to prevent them from crossing my boundaries?
- ❏ Am I using more emotionally honest communication?
- ❏ Am I avoiding the temptation to blame and shame myself and others?

- ❏ Am I avoiding language that disempowers myself and others?
- ❏ Am I moving toward greater self-acceptance?
- ❏ Am I anchoring more positive associations for myself to gain greater confidence, motivate me, excite me, juice me?
- ❏ Am I taking full advantage of the movies, websites, support groups and books that are available to empower me?
- ❏ Am I seeking out positive role models?
- ❏ Am I choosing to be more happy more often?
- ❏ Am I moving out of my old comfort zones?
- ❏ Am I being more self-compassionate?
- ❏ Am I listening to the wisdom of my body?
- ❏ Am I taking steps to release my resentments?
- ❏ Am I more accepting and compassionate with my resistance?
- ❏ Am I actively taking steps to change my "victim" language?
- ❏ Am I avoiding the tendency to catastrophize?
- ❏ Am I avoiding the tendency to "make it personal?"
- ❏ Am I finding more of my passions?
- ❏ Am I creating SMART goals?
- ❏ Am I paying more attention to my general state of wellness?
- ❏ Am I comfortable and feeling in tune with my doctor?
- ❏ Am I setting a powerful intention each day?
- ❏ Am I enjoying a piece of quiet each day?
- ❏ Am I visualizing what I want to achieve?
- ❏ Am I creating my day?
- ❏ Am I using a vision board to further my goals?
- ❏ Am I using affirmations to manifest my desires?
- ❏ Am I using afformations or empowering questions to reprogram my subconscious mind?
- ❏ Am I making myself accountable to others in order to achieve my goals?
- ❏ Am I taking steps each day to make peace with food and friends with my body?

Acknowledgments

There's a saying that it takes a village to raise a child. I've said many times that this book is my baby. Here I do honor to all the helping hands who have come together in my life to help me directly and indirectly to bring this book baby to life. Thank you to you all.

Thank you, God for giving me a rich life filled with blessings and the strength and love to deal with all the challenges.

Thank you, Nana – There isn't a day that goes by when I don't feel you near me and know that I'm so deeply loved. I've been so incredibly blessed to have known you and loved you for a lifetime. I could never repay all the kindness and gifts you've given me. My only hope is to pay it forward. This book is the beginning of that lifelong endeavor. Thank you for endowing me with the will and the passion to serve and always cradling me in your heart guiding me to live and love by the golden rule. You are truly the original Juicy Woman. Thank you Nana for teaching me by example to always keep an open heart to let love in and to remember that true beauty never fades and love never dies.

A special thanks to my precious husband, Angel and my beloved son, PT (Paul) and my wise beyond her years, wonderful daughter, Cara who put up with me through the toughest of times. Thank you to all of you for showing me the meaning of love and acceptance in countless ways.

Honey, my precious Angel, thank you for giving me the constant message with your words, hugs, kisses and caresses telling me that I am always lovable and desirable and guiding me to love the skin I'm in.

PT, my Buttercup, my young man-- thank you for pushing me to always dig deeper inside myself and to reach for the stars and to always remember not to take things so personally. I am so incredibly proud of the young man you've become.

Cara, my love, thank you for all the love, grace and enduring support you've given me, not to mention all the wonderful shared foot rubs we've enjoyed sitting together on the green room sofa watching DVDs, *The Nanny* or Food Network. I'm so incredibly proud of the graceful and beautiful, wise young lady you've become.

I am deeply grateful to my parents, Frank and Doris for bringing me into this world and giving me the many opportunities and experiences that have molded me into the person I've become. Thank you, Mommy for loving me enough to let me go. Now having a daughter of my own, I understand the soul wrenching sacrifice you made when I was 11 and you let me go live with dad. And thank you, dad for being a great friend and mentor for many years, leading me to believe in myself at a time when I was most broken. Now that I'm older and wiser and have learned how to heal my own hurts, I know that I can take the best of the both of you with me and release the rest. May God bless you both.

A special thanks to my step daughter, Janelle who one day decided to playfully dub me as "The Woman." You don't know it, but by doing that, you've given me an image of myself to aspire to. I am so incredibly proud of everything that you've done from the time that I first met you when you were 12 years old to now. But becoming a Master Sargeant in the United States Air Force truly beats all! What an awesome achievement. I'm so proud of you I could burst. You are my hero! Thank you Sweetheart, for always believing in me with unwavering faith even when I doubted myself. And Janelle, I'll never be able to thank you enough for giving me your shoulder to cry on when I needed it most. Thank you, Woman. From one to another, my heart is exploding with pride when I think of all you've accomplished. You've become an amazing woman and my life is deeply blessed by your presence.

To my little Aiden, thank you for being a wonderful grandson and a precious little boy. Thank you for always giving me the opportunity to keep on trying to be the same kind of special Nana I've had. You deserve the very best, my little angel and I'll keep working on it.

A loving hug and prayer of gratitude goes to my brother-in-law, Carlos and my sister-in-law, Jeannie for keeping the fires burning in me. You'll never know how much your gifts of love and support have meant to me and the family. And to the whole Amador clan for loving and welcoming me as their own. Thank you for teaching me the value of having a loving family who sticks together through thick and thin.

My deepest gratitude goes to my dear friends who are more to me like family, Lucy, Carmen, Barbara and Dawn. Thank you for holding a vision of me as a strong and competent woman and for constantly reminding me that I could have, be and do more. Watching the four of you navigate throughout the stormy seas in your lives, I've learned how to hold myself steady when the going gets rough.

"Sally Shields"– Thank you, my dear friend, colleague and media buddy, Sarah. Without that first inspiring meeting when we met last September 2008 at the Riverdale Diner, I would never have gotten up the courage to come out and share my story. Thank you for showing me and leading me to see what is possible by just sharing myself and my experience with others. I'm blessed to have you as my role model, and friend leading me and allowing me to learn from your example as an Amazon.com bestselling published author. Now that I've finally finished my own book, I can really and finally put to use all that brilliant wisdom you've so generously shared over the past year and follow your footprints in the sand to becoming my own bestselling author.

Wayne Kelly – Special love and blessings to you, Wayne for being an amazing media coach. Thank you for coaxing, cajoling and inspiring me to mold myself to become a person who can actually get excited about always expanding myself and moving out of my tiny comfort zone. Thank you for extending your love and patience, consistently believing in me and encouraging me to know that by coming out of my shell and being authentic by sharing myself and my story, I could help millions of women.

Keke Dillard, Editor-in-Chief of Curvy™ Magazine – My deepest thanks to you, Keke for having the passion, foresight and gumption to create a magazine that caters to the full-figured woman. And most of all, thank you for honoring me with the responsibility of being the Body and Soul Editor for Curvy™ Magazine. I'm tickled pink to be given this amazing platform to share my message with your millions of readers.

Jessica Weiner – Thank you for being a model of bravery and teaching me how I could share my unique message of empowerment with the women and girls of the world. By watching and learning from your example, I know that I can lead with power, panache, humility, grace and style. Thank you for giving me my first inkling to believe that as a plus size woman, I could be curvy and confident and lead others to love their body exactly as they are. Thank you for inspiring me to spread my message of self-acceptance throughout the media. From reading your books and watching you speak, I feel a great kinship with you, as though I've known you forever, but in reality, I look forward to finally meeting you and thanking you face to face.

Sanyika Calloway Boyce – Thank you for teaching me how to make my message sing on TV and for showing me that I really could make my mess into my message.

Milana Leshinsky – Thank you Milana for giving me a glimpse of the vision of all that I am capable of achieving. Milana, you are an amazing coach and I simply adore you!

Michael Port – Thank you, Michael for teaching me the importance of standing in service of those whom I'm meant to serve. Thank you also for showing me how to put the heart back in marketing.

Geneen Roth – Thank you for being a great inspiration and writing so many wonderful books sharing your journey to overcome emotional eating.

Robin Hardy – Thank you, Robin for helping me recognize that as a curvy woman, and competent coach, I am already fully baked and don't have to wait to share my gifts until I reach a size 6.

Tuck Self – Thank you for being such a wonderful love muffin yourself and for giving me such astounding support and encouragement all the way through. Thank you also for doing my human design chart and explaining to me the answers to so many questions I had about myself.

Jan Beasley and Deb – To two of the best and greatest Virtual Assistants anyone could ever have. Thank you for helping me to create a vision and image for my company, The Juicy Woman. Thank you for your tireless hours and passionate work and precision always superceding my every expectation and over delivering on every promise.

Maria Escobar – thank you from the bottom of my heart for breathing new life into The Juicy Woman and giving me the ability to do what I love by handling everything else. You are amazing and I love you.

Lia Allen – Bless you for finally giving me the know-how and the plan to make it all happen. I deeply appreciate your wisdom and I love working with you.

Penny Calcina – Thank you Penny for sharing your heart and your soul and for extending your faith and love to me and wanting to share my work by having me on your show. I am truly blessed and deeply appreciate your graciousness and generosity. You are the epitome of my image of abundant thinking.

Karenna Awtry – Thank you for editing this book and for taking on the enormous task of reducing a 597 page manuscript into this much more manageable version. Thank you for putting your signature stamp of love and care on each page with your comments and suggestions for improving and clarifying my message and for capturing and brilliantly encapsulating the true essence of what I always wanted to say.

Karen Lacey – Thank you for encouraging me to toss out all the talking head stuff and come out and be real and share my true voice. Thank you for telling me that what I had to offer is sorely needed. Working with you was such a treasure and I can't wait to do it again!

Bev, my fabulous formatting angel – thank you for giving my words and ideas form and structure and making them look great on the page with your fabulous formatting finesse. Thank you for being patient and helping to restore my sense of calm when it seemed like everything was unraveling before me.

Simone Reddick – Thank you for putting your heart and soul into this project and for offering to continue even when unforeseen crisis circumstances were tearing you away. I deeply appreciate all that you've done to polish this book.

Carolyn Sheltraw – Thank you so much for working your graphic magic and bringing my precious book baby to life, giving her a stunning new cover and a beautiful body.

Heather Goff – Oh Heather, you are truly my tech angel! Thank you so much to you and to everyone at Goff Grafix for creating such an amazing, stunning and easy to use website for me. And best of all thank you for teaching me how to be completely self-sufficient in making it my own. You rock!

Simone Kaplan – Thank you for appreciating me and seeing me as a leader and helping me to realize and see my own potential.

Beverly Nadler– thank you my dear friend and coach, Beverly for all the many hours you spent devoted to tapping with me and helping me to unearth and release my painful memories and emotions and guiding me to finally make the choice to let go of my identity of being a victim.

My tapping Angel, J. – for being such a willing and capable coach and friend, leading me by the hand and guiding me safely though my own depths.

To all my wonderful buddy coaches and friends at the Certified Energy Coach program, I love you and bless the ground you walk on. Thank you for giving me a safe place to practice and polish my skills.

Carol Look – Thank you for showing me the depth and breadth of how *EFT* can heal.

Carol Solomon, Ph.D – Thank you, Carol for giving me the safe space I needed to vent and express myself when my step father, Jorge passed away. Having the awareness that it was okay to feel anything and everything enabled me to gather the strength I needed to put my past behind me and to go back down to Florida and care for my mother when she needed me most.

To all my past, present and future clients, Juicy Woman forum members, *EFT* Forum and my *Lovin' 'the Skin You're In* Power Circle Meet up and Facebook gals – thank you dear hearts for being a very special part of my life and for being so ever present as the wind beneath my wings. You are the reason I wake up each morning with a smile on my face ready to serve.

Toastmasters – Thank you to all my colleagues and buddies in my Toastmasters' group. As professional speakers, you've inspired me to infuse passion and purpose in everything I say.

Rosie – My dearest Rosie. Thank you for taking me in and treating me like a daughter, making me feel so warm, loved and welcomed. You've given me so much to be grateful for, but most of all thank you for being my first role model of a powerful woman with a mind of her own, unafraid and unapologetic about expressing her needs.

Grammie – thank you, Grammie. I'll always love you for showing me how to be a woman who stands strong in her power.

To my dear grandpas, thank you for being such wonderful role models of kindness, warmth, support and love and for being the gentlemen and wonderful people you were.

Doc Frost – Thank you for showing me that there is indeed an alternative to dieting. I'm so grateful that you led me to an understanding of how important it is to listen to my body and for stepping aside to let me figure out how to do it.

Connirae Andreas – A special thanks to you, Connirae Andreas, the amazing creator of the Naturally Slender Eating Strategy. Thank you for taking me under your wing and teaching me how to fly. If it weren't for your explaining about the importance of paying attention to the messages behind our binges, I would never have stopped eating.

Kevin Creedon, Doug O'Brien, Rachel Hott, Ph.D, Steven Leeds, and David Gordon – all my NLP instructors for endowing me with a passion and love for curiosity, leading me on a journey to explore my senses and expanding my view of the world of possibilities

Tony Robbins – Thank you for first opening my eyes up to the road that lay ahead before me and for giving me the tools to discover my personal power.

Barbara Sher – A big hug and lots of love to you, Barbara for showing me that I could do anything I want and guiding me to find Jodie's support team so that I could figure out what that was and how to get it.

Peggy Ahn – Oh Peggy! What can I say? Thank you so much for being such an amazing friend and first ever buddy coach. Without your support and love and steadfast faith this book would probably still remain unwritten

Jack Canfield – Blesssings to you for teaching me the value and the how to's of building self-esteem in myself and others.

Jana Stanfield – Thank you for inspiring me with your beautiful song, "If I Were Brave" and believing in me. Thanks to that beautiful song you created a powerful anchor in me that keeps me asking every day, "What would I do today if I were brave?" As my friend and mentor, you keep me reaching higher. Thank you, Jana for lighting my spark the day you said, "Andrea, you are a powerful speaker."

Doug Stevenson – Thank you for coaching me and for guiding me to know that I have a gift to share that lives and breathes in my story. I'll be ever grateful for your guidance teaching me that I am the only one who can share my gifts by reaching out and touching the hearts of those women who I'm meant to serve in my very unique Andrea way.

Thank you to all the teachers, friends, mentors, principals and advisors in EPIC and throughout all of the East Ramapo school system. Bless you all for guiding me on a journey to begin expressing my gifts as a speaker. Without your love, encouragement and never ending faith and appreciation, I would never have taken that first step into coaching.

Thank you to all my friends, colleagues and troops at Girl Scouts. You lit the camp fire that burns in my heart.

Sandra Gabriel – Thank you, Sandra for endowing me with a deeper understanding of having an attitude of gratitude.

Thank you, Reverend Rob and my church at UCSV for welcoming me back with open arms and giving me a place to rest my faith. Reverend Rob, you make it almost impossible to not want to go to church every week. I love you and thank you from the bottom of my heart for your ability to continue feeding the fire of my passion to love God and for continually guiding me to build my faith.

Thank you, Rev. Julie for teaching me about the importance of setting boundaries and standing up for what you believe in.

Maryam Webster – Blessings to you, Maryam for being a great teacher and coach, and showing me how to seamlessly weave EFT and energy coaching into my life and how to share it with grace and skill with others

CJ Puotinin – Thank you, CJ for teaching me that it can always be easier than I think it can and for helping me overcome my stage fright by sharing Lucille Ball's inspiring quote, "Here I am, you lucky people." Thank you for guiding me to remember to be humble and to always bear in mind that my message is so much more important than me.

Gary Craig – a special thanks to EFT founder, Gary Craig, who had the vision and passion to create EFT. Thank you for your generosity in making it widely available to everyone.

Thank you to Gail Bayles for being the first tapping angel to rescue me from myself and share EFT and the world of tapping with me. You may not know it but I'll let you in on a little secret. From that single experience I had with EFT, you helped me to reframe a near lifetime of suffering and for the first time ever I was able to recognize that forgiveness is a gift we give ourselves. Thank you Gail, for showing me the direction out of the darkness and lighting the way to recognize the potential for healing that I could share with others.

Ruth Rosenbaum and Marie Margenau Spatz, Ph.D – Thank you for the many years you've provided a safe space in therapy to come each week and share my fears.

Jodie Anisa, Shirley, and all my success team buddies – thank you for being an incredible support team and helping me to realize that I can fulfill my dreams, because in reality, they're just goals with deadlines. Jodie, thank you for being the best success team leader ever. Thank you for the many times you've patted me on the back and encouraged me to 'go for it' making me believe in myself every step of the way. Anisa, you've been such a dear friend. Thank you for teaching me that the only person who was truly in my way was me. Thank you Shirley for really making me feel appreciated and ten feet tall.

Linda Storey– Lovely Linda, thank you for giving me the tools and support to appreciate and respect money, recognize my own worth, and fly like an eagle.

To all my soul sisters for prosperity, Donna Marie, Giselle and Linda – Blessings to you all for sharing your hearts and your souls with me and making it perfectly okay to be just me.

Thank you to Debbie, my amazing hair dresser and friend, who always keeps me styling. Your words of encouragement, praise, guidance and wisdom at the perfect time every time have continued to keep me coming back for more. And all this time you just thought it was for my hair! Wrongo!

Thank you to all my coaching colleagues, support buddies and friends who have not been named, your support, love, encouragement wisdom and guidance has meant the world to me and will never go unnoticed.

Yvonne – Thank you, Yvonne for the many wonderful heart to heart chats we've shared. As my friend, colleague and neighbor, you've been a wonderful role model showing the power of a woman's strength to carry on.

To all my managers and friends at Avenue – Mindy, India, Peggy, Patty, Tiffany, Gerrlynn, Beth, Words can never express the gratitude I feel for the love and wisdom you've shared.

C.A.T.S & cats – Thank you, Eileen from Care About the Strays for helping me to care for the precious cats that have found their way into my heart through my backyard. And thanks to you all my precious kitties, especially my Owie for reminding me that the real gift of love is having the ability to feel. May all you outdoor felines find wonderful and safe homes soon. Big warm hugs and oodles of love to you all.

Nancy Bonios, Ph.D – Thank you Dr. Nancy for guiding me and shining the light to recognize that permanent change requires a climate of love and understanding and not hate and contempt.

Lisa Cherney – And a huge thank you from the bottom of my heart goes out to Lisa Cherney of Conscious Marketing for creating her amazing Stand Out Be Juicy Program. Lisa, I feel like you've given me wings to fly because now I can finally put words to my passion and describe what I do. Thanks to your coaching, and the guidance and support of all my buddies in the SOBJ program, I finally know exactly what to say when people ask me, "So what do you do? Words will never express my gratitude for the gift you've given me to be able to touch the hearts of so many.

Wendy Y Bailey - Thank you so much, Wendy Y Bailey of Brilliance in Action and Group Coaching Mastery. I feel incredibly blessed to have learned so much from you about how to do group coaching right. Thank you for creating your Group Mastery program and teaching me how to enrich my group programs to give my clients the best, most exciting and valuable experience working with me. And an endless debt of gratitude goes to you and Denise Wakeman of The Blog Squad for creating the Fill Your Coaching Groups program. What can I say? It's the bomb! Thanks to FYCG, I have all the tools necessary to become a force to be reckoned with in social networking.

Marisa Balletti-Lavoie, Owner of Sassy Mouth Photo in Meriden, CT – Dearest Marisa, How could I ever have hoped to have had such amazing pictures taken of me without your brilliant eye and your masterful photography! You make me feel like a movie star! Thank you to you and to everyone on your team at Sassy Mouth Photo for an extraordinary shoot, but especially thank you for taking the photo that makes this book cover POP!!! Can't wait to reschedule another photo session.

A big debt of gratitude and thanks goes to all those who have challenged and tried me in the past and to the many waiting in line attempting to do the same and derail me in the future, thank you for leading me to recognize that which doesn't kill me can only make me stronger.

To all the brave, beautiful, sexy, wonderful and vivacious women whose stories light up this book and the many more to come, thank you for sharing your vulnerabilities and allowing your truths to touch the hearts of other women to guide and inspire them to love the skin they're in.

I want to thank you, my dear reader who is seeking to find the solution to this challenge of overeating. Thank you for taking the risk and picking up this book and believing in yourself enough to know that deep in your heart you have the answer to all of your questions.

And at the risk of being conceited, I'd like to give myself a standing ovation for finally getting the hell out of my own way.

About the Author

Andrea Denise Amador is **The Juicy Woman**. She is a professional certified empowerment coach, speaker, and body image/self-esteem expert and the author of *Lovin' the Skin You're In: The Juicy Woman's Guide to Making Peace with Food and Friends with Your Body*.

As a Master Practitioner of *Neuro Linguistic Programming* and *Ericksonian Hypnosis*, Andrea is dedicated to creating self-esteem building products and programs designed to empower women and kids. By sharing her expertise and experience she helps women who are emotional eaters make peace with food and friends with their body so they can yummy up their lives. As an abuse survivor, Andrea is a rare combination of raw experience and professional training which gives her the edge in helping women and girls who struggle with body image and/or abuse issues.

Andrea lives in upstate New York with her husband, Angel, and their two children, twenty year old PT (Paul) and fifteen year old Cara. She enjoys a close, loving relationship with her step daughter, Janelle, and loves to hang out, watch movies, and bake cookies with her step grandson, Aiden. Double blessed, Andrea has a great support network of dear friends, including Lucy, Carmen, Barbara and Dawn.

In 2004, after her heart was cracked open and taken hostage by a charcoal gray and white declawed stray cat who her family adopted and named Owie (short for Oreo), she is now passionately involved in cat rescue. When she's not reading, writing, or cooking, Andrea continues to fuel her passion for learning, serving others, and dedicates her life to doing her Nana proud.

And, yes, on most days Andrea really does love the skin she's in.

You can contact Andrea at
andrea@thejuicywoman.com
or at:
The Juicy Woman
http://www.thejuicywoman.com

Made in the USA
Charleston, SC
07 June 2012